NOBLE
ENDEAVOURS

ALSO BY MIRANDA SEYMOUR

Fiction
The Stones of Maggiare
Daughter of Darkness
Count Manfred
The Goddess
Medea
Madonna of the Island: Tales from Corfu
Carrying On
The Reluctant Devil: A Cautionary Tale
The Telling

Non-fiction
A Ring of Conspirators: Henry James and his Literary Circle
Ottoline Morrell: Life on the Grand Scale
Robert Graves: Life on the Edge
Mary Shelley
The Bugatti Queen: In Search of a Motor-Racing Legend
In My Father's House: Elegy for an Obsessive Love
Chaplin's Girl: The Life and Loves of Virginia Cherrill

Children's Books
Mumtaz the Magical Cat
The Vampire of Verdonia
Caspar and the Secret Kingdom
Pierre and the Pamplemousse

Miscellaneous
A Brief History of Thyme, and other Herbs

NOBLE ENDEAVOURS

The Life of Two Countries,
England and Germany,
in Many Stories

MIRANDA SEYMOUR

SIMON &
SCHUSTER

London · New York · Sydney · Toronto · New Delhi

A CBS COMPANY

First published in Great Britain by Simon & Schuster UK Ltd, 2013
A CBS COMPANY

Copyright © 2013 by Miranda Seymour

The right of Miranda Seymour to be identified as the author of this
work has been asserted by her in accordance with sections 77 and 78
of the Copyright, Designs and Patents Act, 1988.

1 3 5 7 9 10 8 6 4 2

Simon & Schuster UK Ltd
1st Floor
222 Gray's Inn Road
London WC1X 8HB

www.simonandschuster.co.uk

Simon & Schuster Australia, Sydney
Simon & Schuster India, New Delhi

A CIP catalogue record for this book is
available from the British Library

ISBN: 978-1-84737-825-5
eBook ISBN: 978-1-84737-826-2

Typeset in Bembo by M Rules
Printed and bound by CPI Group (UK) Ltd, Croydon, CR0 4YY

Dedicated to
Felix Gottlieb and Eva Tucker
and
in memory of
Herbert Sulzbach

... Long is the way
And hard, that out of Hell, leads into light

CONTENTS

PART ONE

*From a Protestant Alliance
to the Ending of an Empire
(1613–1919)*

1

NOBLE ENDEAVOURS

On 28 June 1914, the Austrian Archduke and his wife were murdered by two Serbs at Sarajevo. Herbert Sulzbach, the son of a wealthy banker from Frankfurt-am-Main, had just turned twenty. Recording the event and its likely consequences – 'dreadful things may be in store for Europe' – young Sulzbach, in the first of thirteen small notebooks, noted that twenty was 'a fine age for soldiering'. On 8 August, he signed up to fight. Four weeks later, he was on his way to the Western Front.

Sulzbach began the war as a German patriot. 'We certainly did not want this war!' he wrote on 21 October 1914, amid the smoking ruins of a French village and trenches filled with corpses. 'We are only defending ourselves and our Germany against a world of enemies who have banded against us.'[1] Marching home from the Western Front four years later, a lieutenant decorated with the Iron Cross and a Front Line Cross of Merit, Sulzbach remained convinced of the rightness of Germany's cause. 'It is really marvellous,' he wrote on 29 November 1918: 'this whole march is wonderful and our home country really seems to have understood that we are undefeated and unconquerable.'[2]

Sulzbach's family were Jewish, as was his second wife Beate (a member of the celebrated Klemperer family that included the conductor, Otto, and his cousin Victor, the diarist). In 1932, he wrote a letter to a leading Berlin newspaper, *Der Tag*, in which he criticised the Nazi party. His only response was an anonymous note, warning him that his name had been noted. In 1937, he was identified as of Jewish blood and put on the Black List. Following the confiscation of Herbert's Berlin paper factory by the Nazis, Sulzbach and his wife emigrated to Britain. Made stateless in their homeland, the outbreak of war classified the couple as 'enemy aliens'.

In May 1940, Beate and Herbert Sulzbach were arrested by the British authorities and separately interned. They were still imprisoned on the Isle of Man in the autumn of 1940, when their small London house was hit by a Luftwaffe bomb and flattened.

In November 1940, Sulzbach was due for release; he had just obtained permission to fight for Britain as a private in the home-based Pioneer Corps. But it was his subsequent work in two POW camps for captured Germans that enabled Herbert Sulzbach to begin his greater task: the reconciliation of his two beloved countries, England and Germany.

When Britain declared war on Germany in August 1914, Frank Foley, an engine-fitter's son from Somerset, was studying philosophy in Hamburg. Disguised as a Prussian officer, the thirty-year-old Englishman made his way west to the mouth of the River Ems, where some sympathetic shrimp-fishers agreed to ferry the small and earnest-faced fugitive across the lagoon to their base in neutral Holland.

Frank Foley's brief period of service as an acting British captain at the front ended when he was shot in the lung at Ecoust on 21 March 1918 and sent home to England on sick leave. Recruited by British Intelligence after his recovery (he was fluent in German and French), Foley was despatched, first to Cologne (where he met Kay, his future wife), and then to Berlin, where he was officially employed from 1921 as Head of British Passport Control. Unofficially (the Foreign Office provided no diplomatic status for Passport Control officers), Foley was employed by Mansfield Cumming, head of the British Secret Service in the city regarded, during Germany's chaotic post-war years, as the Service's leading overseas station.

Foley met Wilfrid Israel, the cultured heir to one of Berlin's leading department stores, shortly after his arrival in Berlin. Following the rise to power of the Nazis and their campaign to despoil and exile all German citizens designated as non-Aryan, Foley joined forces with Wilfrid Israel and their mutual friend Hubert Pollack, another British Secret Service agent. Pollack identified the families in need of visas; Wilfrid Israel provided the cash and vital contacts; Foley, at considerable risk (he regularly harboured Jews under his roof and also travelled to camps to rescue them), signed the visas. One of his last actions before leaving Berlin in August 1939 was to arrange eighty permits for young people hoping to reach Great Britain.

Foley's death in 1958 passed without notice in Britain; in the recently formed state of Israel, however, a grove of trees was planted in his honour. The idea had come from Hubert Pollack, who stated that the number of Jews rescued from death in Germany would have been tens of thousands less, 'yes, tens of thousands less, if an officious bureaucrat had sat in Foley's place. There is no word of Jewish gratitude towards this man that could be exaggerated.'[3] Benno Cohn, a former Jewish leader in Berlin who had worked with Foley and Mossad (an organisation originally dedicated to helping Jews to reach Palestine), added a tribute of his own during the 1961 trial of Adolf Eichmann. Foley, Cohn declared, had stood above all others of his time 'like a beacon. Captain Foley, Passport Control Officer in the British Consulate in the Tiergarten in Berlin [was] a man who in my opinion was one of the greatest among the nations of the world.'[4]

In July 2012, a plaque honouring Foley's achievement was

placed at the entrance to the Jewish cemetery at Golders Green where he, like Herbert Sulzbach, lies buried.

In 1948, speaking on the BBC, Herbert Sulzbach stated that the best envoys for future peace and understanding between Britain and Germany would be the German POWs who were finally being allowed to return to their homeland.

Sulzbach knew what he was talking about. In 1944, he had been transferred by the British from the Pioneer Corps to the 'Interpreters' Pool'. In January 1945, he was posted as a staff sergeant to Cultybraggan Camp, Comrie.

Built on the site of Agricola's old marching camp in Scotland, Comrie was already known for the hardened spirit of its Nazi inmates. On 22 December 1944, five young German POWs (the eldest was twenty-one) had beaten up a new arrival and hanged him backwards, over a water pipe.* Wolfgang Rosterg's unforgivable crime had been to dare to criticise the Reich in a camp where 'When Jewish Blood Spurts from the Knife' was still being sung with fervour. What would such brutal men make of a slightly built Jewish interpreter who had fought for Britain in the recent war?

Bernard Braine, a politician paying tribute to Sulzbach at the memorial service held at the German Embassy in July 1985, described the dapper, blue-eyed Herbert as 'that greatest of all charmers'. Charm alone cannot explain the measure of Sulzbach's achievement. By 11 November 1945, he had persuaded all but a handful of the Comrie prisoners to acknowledge that Germany had been wrong and that its arrogance had led to misery. To stand beside Sulzbach on Armistice Day required some 4000 German POWs to volunteer their solemn promise to return home as good Europeans, 'and to take part in the reconciliation of all people and the maintenance of peace'.[5]

Encouraged by the remarkable response at Comrie, the newly

---

* The five guilty youths were hanged at Pentonville on 6 October 1945.

promoted Captain put his project forward at another camp. A large number of high-ranking SS officers were imprisoned at Featherstone Park in Northumberland from 1945–48; Sulzbach's mission was to send them home with a clear understanding of the principles and values of a liberal democracy. One simple way in which he drove his message home was to abolish any form of censorship, a fact that was approvingly noted by the POWs who edited *Die Zeit am Tyne*, the camp's newspaper. Captain Sulzbach's success was apparent from the fact that some 3000 liberated prisoners (who had little by then to gain from the process) would later write to thank him; many went out of their way to maintain contact with the remarkable man who had striven to cure them of their preconceptions.[6]

Herbert Sulzbach never stopped working for reconciliation between England and Germany, the two countries that he loved. A European branch of Featherstone was established at Düsseldorf by twenty-five former German POWs in 1960; annual meetings were held there until Sulzbach's death in 1985. From 1955 until 1973, Sulzbach made use of his position as cultural affairs officer at the German Embassy in London to spread further his belief in the power of tolerance and international friendship. Speaking at the tribute that marked Sulzbach's eightieth birthday in 1974, Bernard Braine praised his old friend for having led the way forward in restoring Anglo-German relations. Six years later, a group of former German POWs laid a plaque at Featherstone camp. It honoured their former interpreter as the man 'who dedicated himself to making the camp a seedbed of British-German reconciliation'.

Speaking once again on television in 1984, a year before his death, a white-haired Sulzbach told Channel 4 viewers that he had been working for reconciliation between his two beloved countries for nearly forty years. Recalling the war in which he had fought for the Kaiser ('It was then *our* Kaiser'), he described it as 'nearly a miracle that today, nearly seventy years later, my two countries are allies and friends'. He spoke of his ardent conviction that the restored friendship between Britain and Germany would provide 'the foundation stone for a once to come United Europe'. 'But first,' he added, 'the old distrust must disappear.'[7]

Almost thirty years after Sulzbach made his final plea, the old distrust of which he spoke remains in place. The horrors inflicted by the Nazis cannot be forgotten and should never be forgiven. But it is time to remember that Britain's close-knit relationship with Germany predates the Third Reich by over 200 years. We abhor the idea of making comic stereotypes of any ethnic group; our justified attitude to the Nazis has made it unjustly acceptable to continue to treat Germans as an exception to that code of civilised behaviour. Herbert Sulzbach would be further saddened to note that Britain and Germany have failed to unite in providing today's Europe with a secure foundation. On the eve of marking the centenary of the opening of the hostilities that devastated the world and changed its history, old wounds gape rawly open.

The time has surely come to listen to Sulzbach's words. No two countries in Europe possess a stronger history of cultural and familial sympathy, trust and mutual respect than Britain and Germany. This book sets out the diverse stories of some of the people who contributed to the building of a house of shared dreams and aspirations, of mutual enlightenment and fruitful exchange. These are the stories of emperors, kings and queens (opening with the journey from Whitehall to Heidelberg of the future Winter Queen whose grandson became England's first Hanoverian monarch); of travellers, writers, artists, students and political exiles; of ambassadors, reformers and the families so closely woven into the fabric of both countries that, when war came, divided loyalties ripped them apart. 'I feel,' said a member of one such family, 'as if my mother and father have quarrelled.'

All these people have played their part. All, in their different ways, are remarkable; all deserve to be called noble for what they set out to achieve. All – glimpsed here only at the point where they contribute to the story of England and Germany – have earned their place in a history of the love and mutual admiration that two nations once shared – and that they deserve to share again.

2

EXILES AND TRAVELLERS

(1613–1782)

The marriage contract between two great Protestant powers had been signed in May 1612. In October, Prince Frederick, the sixteen-year-old Elector Palatine, arrived in London to meet his fresh-faced future bride, Elizabeth Stuart, daughter of King James I. A month later, King James's beloved eldest son, Prince Henry, died, plunging the court into mourning. It was decided, nevertheless, that the wedding celebrations should go forward, and – appropriately for a young couple so evidently in love – that the nuptials should take place on Valentine's Day. Celebrating what one masque named as *The Marriage of the Thames and the Rhine*, John Donne wrote in his 'Epithalamion' of the lovers as two phoenixes: 'Whose love and courage never shall decline / But make the whole year through, thy day, O Valentine.'

Elizabeth, having added seventeen pairs of silk stockings to her trousseau and received assurance that she could take along a cargo of favourite pets to her new home in Germany, gave orders for the performance of six Shakespeare plays at Whitehall. The decision to include among them *The Winter's Tale* would prove both apt and prescient.

In June 1613, Elizabeth arrived at her new home in what was then a Germany comprised of many small duchies and principalities. Seeking to make his bride at home in the great fortress of Heidelberg, set high above the River Neckar and looking out towards the distant Rhine, the young Elector ordered the creation of an English suite of rooms. Salomon de Caus, the great architect and hydraulic engineer who had laid out the gardens at Wilton in England, was summoned to create a Renaissance garden from a barren hillside. By 1620, when Heidelberg was sacked and the garden abandoned, de Caus had already created what was being described as the eighth Wonder of the World, an exercise in elegant playfulness that included a water organ, an animated statue, clockwork-driven singing birds, a 'Venus Fountain' and a magnificently dramatic double stairway.

Elizabeth loved the theatre. In England, she possessed her own troupe of actors. Today, plays are staged in the well of Heidelberg's grass moat; back then, actors surely made use of the wonderful new garden, strutting towards its highest terraced length through the new 'Elizabeth' arch (a nineteenth-birthday surprise from a loving husband, this ruddy, four-columned gateway featured ivy-entwined pillars thronged with little stone animals of the kinds Elizabeth loved best).

In 1613, the year of Elizabeth's marriage, London's famous Globe Theatre burnt down and was not rebuilt for a year. Possibly, the young Electress made use of London's loss that year to invite the actors out to Heidelberg. More probably still, a performance of *The Winter's Tale* was put on in Heidelberg in 1618, when talk of Bohemia was in the air. A Protestant ruler was being urgently sought for a country situated far away on the eastern borders of the German principalities, in what is now the Czech Republic. Bohemia was best known to Elizabeth from Shakespeare's play, written in 1610, as the birthplace of Prince Florizel and the haven of lost Perdita, the Sicilian Princess who, by marrying Florizel, will become Bohemia's happy queen.

Elizabeth and Frederick were themselves less fortunate. Offered the Bohemian throne, they were crowned in Prague on 7 November 1619. Losing both their Palatine lands and their new kingdom to the evidently superior Catholic forces of the Holy Roman Emperor within a single tragic year of their coronation, the defeated couple were forced to seek refuge at the Protestant court of The Hague. There, the formidable but desolate Elizabeth – best known today as the Winter Queen – lived out her lengthy widowhood in exile. Returning to England at last in 1661, when her nephew had been restored to the English throne as King Charles II, Elizabeth died the following year.

In England, Elizabeth's most loyal admirer, the Earl of Craven, had built a home in her honour: Ashdown House, an exquisite dolls' house of a Dutch mansion, fashioned from chalk and standing high on the windswept Berkshire Downs. Elizabeth never saw Lord Craven's shrine. Chalk, when wet, crumbles and dissolves; today, the windows of Ashdown are thinly veiled in white moisture, as if in mourning for the Queen who never took possession of this, the graceful tribute of a devoted cavalier.

Rupert of the Rhine, the dashing cavalry general who led the troops for his doomed uncle, Charles I, remains Elizabeth's best-known child. But it was Rupert's spirited sister Sophia, the Electress of Hanover, who provided England with its first German king.

The Royal Act of Succession of 1701 had granted England's throne to Sophia and her heirs in order to protect it from recapture by a deposed Catholic monarch (James II) at the time when William of Orange had no heirs and Anne, the queen-in-waiting, had lost her one surviving child. When the lively and intelligent Sophia died of a chill in 1714, just two months before the death of Queen Anne, the English throne was handed to the Electress's son, George, a German-speaking monarch who made no secret of his desire to remain comfortably ensconced at the Herrenhausen Palace, his family home in Hanover.

Visiting the Herrenhausen two years later, on her way to Constantinople, Lady Mary Wortley Montagu (who thought England's stout new king an amiable fool), was startled to find the town of Hanover thronging with English visitors. The rosy cheeks and jet-black brows of the local girls put Lady Mary in mind of a Fleet Street waxwork display, but she informed her sister, back in England, that the palace gardens were very fine, the opera house superb ('much finer than that of Vienna') and that words could not do justice to the glory of German stoves, a heating system that permitted the consumption of oranges and lemons in deepest winter, 'and even pineapples, like Brazil'.[1] A hit with the King, Lady Mary left Hanover with the sense of having regained the ground she had lost the previous year with *Roxana*, a rashly witty skit that made fun of a royal court filled with untrustworthy foreigners.

James Boswell, passing through Hanover fifty years later, admired the palace and a spectacular avenue of limes (but not, for once in his amorous career, the local beauties). Travelling east from Leipzig (where he enjoyed a dish of larks), Boswell praised the castles perched above the River Elbe for their Scottish appearance, and – on arriving at Dresden – voiced his disgust with Frederick the Great for shelling the Saxon city during the recent Seven Years War: 'It was from mere spite that he did it.'[2]

Dresden apart, Boswell was desperate to meet a monarch who was revered almost as a deity in eighteenth-century England. Newly arrived in Berlin, the young Scot caught a glimpse of Frederick strolling in the palace garden at Charlottenburg and restrained himself, with difficulty, from performing an act of complete prostration before this figure of 'iron confidence'. A month later, however, poor Boswell was still only known to his hero as the wearer of a peculiar 'little cap'. Boswell's bright blue Ayrshire bonnet had caught Frederick's attention – but not, alas, his fancy – as he surveyed the eager onlookers at a royal parade.

Visiting England from his small principality beside the Elbe in the same year that Boswell made his tour of German courts, a youthful German prince, travelling in the company of an architect friend, inspected the artfully naturalistic gardens of Stourhead, Stowe, Wilton and Kew. Back in Anhalt-Dessau, Prince Franz created the Wörlitzer Gartenreich, a kingdom in miniature that included – in the English style – temples, bridges and a pagoda. Offering a discreet home to the Prince's mistress, Luise Schock, Germany's first Gothic garden building had been copied from Stowe. Luise's father, taking advantage of his role as Prince Franz's resident landscape designer, added a sly touch of his own: a phallus-shaped flowerbed, thrusting forward from the nearby Temple of Venus at the chaste doorway of the Gothic House. Goethe, visiting the Garden Kingdom in 1778, when he was twenty-nine years old, informed a friend that he had walked into a perfect fairy tale, set in the Elysian Fields. More than this, the Wörlitzer Gartenreich represented Prince Franz's faith in England as the home of enlightenment and reform.

Visiting England in 1782, Karl Philipp Moritz, a teacher from Berlin, set off on a two-month walking tour in search of the England he had encountered from reading Milton, *The Vicar of Wakefield* and – inevitably – Shakespeare. 'Shakespeare, my friend, if you were among us, I could live only with you,' the 22-year-old Goethe had announced, to loud applause, at a 1771 German celebration of the playwright's birthday.[3] Moritz, arrived at Stratford and clasping the mandatory souvenir, a chip of wood allegedly hacked from the bard's own chair, thrilled to the thought that here, in the tranquil Warwickshire landscape, 'a soul like Shakespeare had been first awakened by the spirit of nature'.[4]

Moritz, sharing with Prince Franz of Anhalt-Dessau a keen admiration for England's political system, was entranced by the spectacle of democracy in action in a country where, so one mischievous innkeeper persuaded him, even a chimney sweep burdened his dining table with silver candelabra, and where the appearance of Charles Fox to give an impromptu speech to cheering crowds on election day surely had nothing to do with the wily politician's desire to assist the chances of a favoured crony. Disappointed, while in London, to find that no public street or park had been named in honour of his compatriot Handel, Moritz was doubtless comforted to find that a handsome new Lutheran church, St George-in-the-East, regally ornamented with the coat-of-arms of King George III himself, was serving the hard-pressed and underpaid German population who lived in the grim area known as 'Little Germany' that lay between Smithfield and the docks.*

Charmed by the spirit of patriotism that he encountered in even the smallest, navy-mad child and impressed to find that his London landlady, a tailor's widow, was sufficiently educated to quote Milton by the yard, Moritz's only real objection to the English was that they showed so little interest in his own country. Looking about him for any evidence of German literature, the only works he saw were the philosophical writings of Jacob Boehme, much admired in the circle of William Blake, and a sugary pastoral epic by one Salomon Gessner that he despised as thoroughly mediocre.

This was galling. The Sturm und Drang generation of Germans, to which Moritz himself belonged, were besotted by English writing. They revelled in the Gothic terrors of Edward Young's *Night Thoughts*; they quoted from Henry Fielding, Oliver Goldsmith, Samuel Richardson; they dreamed of travelling to the remote Scottish island on which the mysterious James Macpherson had discovered Ossian's Lays, read aloud to his beloved Charlotte by Goethe's tortured young Werther.

England, it was true, had already begun to respond with enthusiasm to Goethe's heart-rending novel, which ran into twenty-six English editions in the twenty years following its first appearance in translation, in 1779. But where, Moritz wondered, was the corresponding trumpet call in England for Herder, Lessing, Schiller

---

* Moritz did find a – rather horrid – marble statue of Handel, by Roubiliac, at Vauxhall; he was understandably disappointed to find no other tributes to the great court composer who had given England thirty-four operas and its first oratorio. Despite the absence of public memorials, Handel was buried in Westminster Abbey.

and Kant? And why was it not resounding, when the University of Göttingen, founded by George II and richly endowed by his successor, offered such a splendid opportunity for young Englishmen to gain an education in Germany, and to enrich their minds with German culture?

Studying an English newspaper one day, Moritz found his worst suspicions confirmed when, in an advertisement for foreign novels, he found, tersely appended, the words: 'even German'.

England, despite her conspicuous lack of interest in German literature, had not disappointed Moritz. Setting off home for Hamburg and bidding farewell to a kindly Lutheran pastor who had befriended him during his final days in London, the German visitor wrote that he had said farewell to an island that he still regarded as the home of true democracy 'with a very heavy heart'.

3

ROMANTIC EXCHANGES

(1790–1830)

Karl Philipp Moritz's wistful desire for a champion of German literature to emerge from England was granted in 1798. Funded by two brothers, Josiah and Thomas Wedgwood, and accompanied by William Wordsworth and his sister Dorothy, together with John Chester, a young farmer keen to study German agriculture, Samuel Taylor Coleridge left behind his wife and baby son to travel to Germany, where he planned to visit the University of Jena, meet up with Schiller, his hero, embark on a translation of the playwright's works, and wrestle with the metaphysics of Kant.

Rapidly jettisoning Jena in favour of Ratzeburg, an old-fashioned little town where a young man who enjoyed skating parties as much as dancing at the weekly balls soon became a favourite figure, Coleridge had spent four months in Germany before he decided to enrol at Göttingen to study under Dr Blumenbach, admired throughout Europe for his (uncontroversial) writings about racial types. The philanthropic Wedgwoods raised no objections; Coleridge's education was considered too important for him to be disturbed by the dreadful news (in February 1799) that his baby son had died.

Arrived at Göttingen among the young group of English dissidents whose religious views debarred them from an English university education, Coleridge felt instantly at home, and adored. Vainly, the Wordsworths appeared, to mention, with reproachful looks, that he had outstayed his three-month visit by almost half a year. In May, the following month, Coleridge led Göttingen's English students off on a fast-paced tour of the nearby Harz Mountains, climbing up to Goethe's famous witches' mound, the Brocken. Talking incessantly as he raced along, the visitor held his exhausted followers enthralled – as Coleridge always did once launched into monologue – both by the rich melody of his voice and by the ideas and images that sprang up, like airy castles, from a playful, endlessly creative mind. Years later, the ageing students were still reminiscing about their Harz pilgrimage as the experience of a lifetime.

A local artist painted Coleridge's portrait during his stay at Göttingen. The sitter's hair flows lightly over a high collar; a clean white cravat is knotted at his throat; his large, light eyes are fixed upon the painter. He looks exactly what he was: inquiring, religious and romantic – a combination perfectly attuned to the mood of Germany's universities in the 1790s. His reluctance to come home was selfish. It was not hard to understand.

Attending a party in his honour shortly before he finally left Göttingen in June 1799, Coleridge may have been both inspired and under the influence of the opium to which he was already enslaved as he began to extemporise upon the superiority of Kant to all other philosophers. Back in England, he began to ponder a metaphysical epic that would communicate Kant's system of knowledge and perception, time and space, all to be contained within a religious framework. Nineteen years later and still planning, Coleridge wrote with undimmed admiration of the great German thinker who first took possession of him at Göttingen, 'with a giant's hand'.[1]

More immediately, Coleridge began to translate Schiller's new three-part epic, *Wallenstein*, and then *Mary Stuart*, bringing, as he had hoped, a new English audience to the author whose dramatic genius he rated only marginally inferior to that of Shakespeare.

In 1798, the year in which Nelson defeated Napoleon at the Battle of the Nile, Coleridge's party had been rapturously received in a country from which, in 1803, when Napoleon occupied anglicised Hanover, 28,000 Hanoverian soldiers defected to England. Stationed on the south coast at Weymouth and Bexhill, the King's German Legion earned a reputation for courage, skill and discipline that was second to none.

Napoleon's subsequent blockading of Baltic ports was intended to sever communication between Germany and her staunchest ally. Banking families like the Schröders and the Rothschilds found a way around the difficulty by despatching their sons to start new branches of the family firms in England, strengthening the Anglo-German bond.

Individuals slipped through the French net. By 1810, Bohn's Reading Room was stocking 2500 German books for a new audience of educated exiles. One of them, Rudolph Ackermann, opened a fashionable print shop on the Strand and published the volumes that introduced delighted English readers to the fantastic artistry of Moritz Retzsch, one of the most influential illustrators of the nineteenth century.

In 1810, the exiled but indefatigable Madame Germaine de Staël was informed by letter that the first two volumes of her newly published *De l'Allemagne* had been pulped at Napoleon's command, and that proofs of the subsequent volumes had also been destroyed, together with their blocks of type.

There were several reasons for Napoleon to dislike de Staël's book about contemporary Germany. She had dared to rejoice at the German Duke of Brunswick's defeat of French forces; she had praised Schiller and Kant, the German writers who most strongly opposed tyranny. Worse still, she had presented England as a model democracy. Napoleon had already ordered de Staël to confine her skills to knitting; the suppression of her book was intended to draw the line under any further subversive activities by his most infuriating adversary.

The Emperor underrated his opponent. Arriving in England in June 1813, Madame de Staël had already chosen her course of action. Established with her current lover and attendant entourage at a house in what was then the fashionable area of Soho, de Staël graciously permitted London to call upon her. Awed by a woman who had dared to stand up to Napoleon, English society put away its usual prudishness about unmarried sex and queued at Madame's door for the honour of an interview.

It isn't known who provided the crucial introduction of Germaine de Staël to London's canniest publisher, John Murray, but a strong candidate for that important role is Henry Crabb Robinson.

Born into the dissenting stock that looked to Germany, where religion played no part in the university curriculum, for the education of its sons, Robinson matriculated from Jena and spoke German like a native. He was visiting friends at Weimar, back in January 1804, when Madame de Staël swept into town, gathering information for her book and demanding the introductions to Schiller and Goethe for which, since her German was poor, an interpreter was required.

Sitting up in bed in a nightcap, with her bright black eyes fixed upon his face, Madame de Staël did not immediately captivate her chosen recruit; nevertheless, once persuaded to act as joint literary advisor (his contacts were excellent) and part-time interpreter, Robinson fulfilled his role with a mixture of grace (he introduced Germaine to August Schlegel, the translator of Shakespeare who became de Staël's colleague and lover) and misgiving. She would never, Robinson once irritably informed her, be capable of comprehending Goethe; de Staël, unfazed, retorted that the point was irrelevant, since she already knew everything that was worth knowing. When Robinson later apologised, Madame informed him, with her usual briskness, that his rudeness was forgiven: 'it is all over now'.[2]

Robinson resumed his connection with de Staël in 1813, when she was seeking an English publisher. As a respected advisor to John Murray, he may have acted as the go-between who arranged for 1500 guineas to be paid when *De l'Allemagne* appeared, in simultaneous French and English editions, on 4 November, the very day that news reached England of Napoleon's defeat at Leipzig.

Murray must have rubbed his hands with glee. The French edition of *De l'Allemagne* sold out within three days; the English version (edited by a very young William Lamb, later Lord Melbourne) had sold 2250 copies by the end of the year. Its author found herself the toast of British society. Having already whiled away a pleasant summer at Bowood, the country estate of her admirer Lord Lansdowne, de Staël could now take her pick of where next to shine. Even Byron, grumbling about having to undertake a sixty-mile drive for the honour of lunching with an overweight and opinionated banker's daughter, did not dare to refuse.

The success of *De l'Allemagne* proved phenomenal. Four years after publication, Thomas Carlyle was still rapturously discussing the book with Jane Welsh, his future wife; in 1823, a *Blackwood's* essayist announced, with only a little exaggeration, that de Staël's volume was in every English hand.

How could the English not be gratified by a book in which England was praised for its perfect system of enlightened and tolerant government, a model to the world? Perched upon this agreeable pinnacle by an author who excelled in flattery, an English reader was in a fine position to take a benevolent interest in Germany, a country, according to the account provided by *De l'Allemagne*, that was gratefully indebted to their own.

De Staël helped to create a feeling of warmth, goodwill and a little bit of kindly condescension towards Germany. Napoleon's first defeat, in 1814, generated a further burst of fraternal enthusiasm towards the gallant German troops as comrades-at-arms and fellow opponents of the French tyrant. Young Leopold of Saxe-Coburg, arriving as part of the Emperor of Russia's train for the celebrations held in London that summer, was astonished by the cheers that greeted General Blücher, the Prussian military leader. No less than four portraits were painted of Blücher during his brief visit. At Oxford, he was honoured as a doctor-of-law; in London, he was all but carried through the streets. Blücher's refusal to pay a second visit to London in June 1815 says more about the Prussian General's hatred of Napoleon (Wellington had denied him the satisfaction of having their mutual enemy shot at Waterloo) than about his feelings for England.

The romance between the English and the Germans continued unabated. The wedding, in 1816, of the Prince Regent's strong-willed only daughter, Charlotte, to a German prince (the artistic and dashing Leopold of Saxe-Coburg), was a genuine love-match; Leopold's visible misery when his adored Charlotte died in childbirth a year later touched even the hearts of hardened anti-monarchists.

Charlotte's unexpected death opened up an alarming possibility: without an heir, the Hanoverians might lose their English throne. New royal links to Germany needed to be forged; Charlotte's uncles, the ageing Dukes of Clarence and of Kent, were ordered to put aside their mistresses and start breeding for the future. William (Clarence), a good-hearted roué, picked the girlish and innocent Adelaide of Saxe-Meiningen, but produced no surviving heirs. Edward (Kent) married Leopold's widowed and highly strung sister Victoire and did better; with the birth in 1819 of the Kents' daughter, Victoria, the future of the House of Hanover was once again secure.

Anglo-German culture flourished in the period following those twelve long years (1803–15) in which war with the French had held England and Europe apart. In London, Coleridge attended the dinner parties given (at a brand-new house in Euston Square) by the German-born Charles Aders and his pretty English wife

Eliza Smith, meeting – along with a steady supply of German engravers and illustrators – the lively little Henry Crabb Robinson, William Blake, James Flaxman, Charles Lamb, Samuel Rogers and (a new face in England) Washington Irving.

No diaries survive to tell us what brought an impoverished American author to a German art collector's table in 1817, but it isn't hard to guess. Irving's hero, Walter Scott, had been, by his own admission, 'German-mad' since the early 1790s, when he first read Schiller and began to translate Goethe's ballads; the Germans had returned the compliment with a vengeance. Scott's poetry had captured the imagination of the German people; from 1814, the year of *Waverley*, Germans devoured his stream of historical fictions with a passion (especially for *Ivanhoe* and *The Fair Maid of Perth*) that was only rivalled by their enthusiasm for Byron's glittering chorus of pirates and robber kings.

Washington Irving's meeting with Scott in 1817 earned him an invaluable tip. When the oddly titled *Sketch-Book of Geoffrey Crayon* was published two years later, winning an American author his country's first place in world literature, it was apparent that Irving had been following Scott's advice to saturate himself in German folktales and ballads. One tale, 'The Legend of Sleepy Hollow', told of a headless Hessian horseman, one of the 30,000 young German soldiers despatched to support England's war against its own colonies (the American War of Independence). Germany provided a precious source of inspiration, for the rest of his working life, to an author whose influence upon younger English novelists like Dickens, Thackeray and Wilkie Collins would prove profound.

It was Scott's love of Germany that provided the most immediate bond between himself and John Gibson Lockhart, the intelligent and industrious young man who married Sophia Scott in 1820, two years after falling almost as deeply in love with her celebrated father. In 1818, Lockhart had just returned from Weimar; Walter Scott, meanwhile, had become an enthusiastic supporter of *Blackwood's*, a new Edinburgh-based magazine for which Lockhart had just begun to write on German subjects.

Blackwood's has grown notorious for its dismissal of the London-based poets Leigh Hunt and John Keats as representatives of 'the Cockney School of Poetry'. (Lockhart, an admirer of Wordsworth, Coleridge and Shelley, was not the culprit.) Today, it is still often regarded as a promulgator of reactionary nonsense, fit only for country squires. Examination of the publication during the years when Lockhart was a major contributor (John Murray lured Lockhart south in 1835, to edit *Blackwood's* London rival, *The Quarterly*) reveals a different story.

From 1817 on, *Blackwood's* set out to make itself the hub and cornerstone of German culture in England. Subscribers could enjoy the lectures of Schlegel and the plays of Goethe, Grillparzer, Kotzebue and Schiller, while being encouraged to visit a country where they could admire spectacular castles and enjoy delicious wines (March, 1819). They could congratulate themselves on belonging to a country that one ardent German pilgrim, visiting Wordsworth to discuss the relative merits of Coleridge and Schlegel, had embraced as 'my birth-right – the mountains, the rocks, the lakes, the clouds, the very blue vault of heaven itself were felt to belong to me . . . a stranger – a foreigner – in this heavenly land' (January, 1819).

Gently and insidiously, Lockhart and his publisher promoted German culture at every opportunity. Reviewing a dismissive account of north Germany in 1820, *Blackwood's* pointed to the author's ignorance of Kant and Goethe, while urging the need for a more informed study of 'that highly interesting country'. An 1823 essayist (probably Lockhart himself) paid homage to Schiller and described Coleridge's *Wallenstein* as 'the best translation of a foreign tragic drama which our English literature possesses'.

'I take it for granted that every person of education will acknowledge some interest in the personal history of Immanuel Kant,' announced a *Blackwood's* contributor in February 1827, before passing on the curious and comforting information that the philosopher, while insisting that his rooms should be kept at sweating heat, 'never perspired'. Subsequent issues included a three-part series on Shakespeare's German critics (whom *Blackwood's* considered far superior to the dramatist's English ones) and a long essay (in 1835) devoted to Jean-Paul Richter, master of German irony, and already revered by no less a Germanophile than Thomas Carlyle.

One of the most striking facts to emerge from the British magazines of the 1820s is the immense volume of travel between England and Germany. Some pilgrimages were undertaken in the spirit of frank curiosity that had inspired young William Beckford, back in 1780, to set off in the company of his memorably named tutor, Dr John Lettice, to seek out horrid thrills, while heaping contempt upon a less successful German effort than the ravishing Wörlitzer Gartenreich to pay homage to England with 'a sunburnt, contemptible hillock ... decorated with the title Jardin Anglois'.[3] Mr Sherer of Claverton, touring Germany in 1826 and feeling unashamedly relieved to find that English newspapers and reviews were easily available, was unnerved by the martial spirit of Prussia and by the spectacle of marching boy-battalions ('far too young') whose immaculate discipline made him long for the sight of 'a saucy English light company ... true old English grenadiers who could all sing the same old song, with its noisy tow, row, rows, in harsh and happy chorus'.[4]

Mr Sherer, like William Beckford, was travelling in a spirit of general interest, but most of the English who visited Germany after the Napoleonic Wars were attracted by its culture. Coleridge and Wordsworth, visiting the Godesburg home of their London friend Charles Aders in 1828, had made the trip in order to meet August Schlegel, long admired by Coleridge for his magnificent lectures on (and translations of) Shakespeare. Thomas Arnold, the future headmaster of Rugby School, had his mind fixed on Tacitus's *Germania* and Scott's *Ivanhoe* as, visiting Germany in the same year, he rejoiced in his discovery of the Real Thing: a pure Germany where the newly published tales of the Nibelungen were being studied, according to one *Blackwood's* writer, with the reverence usually accorded only to Homer. Here, Arnold announced, was 'the land of our Saxon and Teutonic forefathers – the land uncorrupted by Roman or any other mixture . . . the Teutonic nation – the regenerating element in modern Europe . . .'[5]

Henry Crabb Robinson, travelling to and fro whenever an opportunity arose, remained one of the most ardent ambassadors for Anglo-German culture until the end of his life. Calling in at Weimar in the summer of 1829, Robinson was doing so largely for old times' sake. Twenty-four years after his first visit, he was welcomed into Goethe's study as a cherished friend and invited to admire one of the German author's treasures, a singularly unconvincing bust of Byron. Robinson was not an admirer of the poet. Trying to change the topic, he was instead requested to read 'The Vision of Judgment' to his host, and to agree that Byron's poem surpassed Milton in his entirety. Finally, Goethe handed his guest the first page of Byron's 1820 poem 'Sardanapalus', a work dedicated, as he pointed out with considerable pride, to himself. Prudishness, Goethe announced, had persuaded England to undervalue her greatest writer. He, deploring such narrow-mindedness, intended to play a part in his beloved Byron's redemption. Robinson was requested to convey the precious page home and present it to Thomas Moore as evidence, to be used in Moore's forthcoming life of Lord Byron, of the bond between the late poet and himself.

What was it that drew Goethe to Byron? The German master's admiration for the young English poet can be traced back to 1816, the year in which Goethe's wife, Christiane, died, leaving her faithless husband pierced with remorse and ready to empathise with the bad conscience and turbulent emotions of Byron's heroes. From that time on, Goethe embraced Byron as his alter ego, his prodigal son. In 1817, he read 'Manfred' (the poem which emerged from the stormy summer Byron had spent with the Shelleys by Lake Geneva) and detected the inspiration of his own *Faust* in a work that – as he told Byron – he considered masterly. For a man who had just left England for good in a flight from debts and scandal, to receive such written homage from the great German master was not displeasing. It is significant, however, that Byron never felt personally impelled to bend his knee at Weimar. The two men never met.

An admirer during Byron's lifetime, Goethe's interest in the Englishman was further quickened by the poignant news, in 1824, of the 36-year-old poet's death at Missolonghi. Talking about Byron in 1823 with Johann Eckermann, his own obsequious Boswell, Goethe remarked that 'a character of such eminence had never existed before, and probably would never come again'.[6] Grieving for Byron's loss, he informed his respectful companion that Germany had no poet to compare with the man who had written 'The Vision of Judgment'. Eckermann, sounding strangely like Uriah Heep, slipped in the observation that he himself never wearied of hearing his master speak upon the subject of Byron. This, given how frequently Goethe was moved to pay homage to the poet whose idealised countenance gazed down upon his writing desk, was probably just as well.

A postscript survives to Henry Crabb Robinson's final visit to his old friend at Weimar. The dedication page of 'Sardanapalus' was dutifully conveyed to Byron's biographer. No comment about it appeared, however, in Moore's book. The reason was embarrassingly simple: the dedication had been faked.

Byron was not to blame. He had indeed promised Goethe a dedication, but his publisher forgot to include it. No further thought was given to the matter until Goethe, accepting an invitation to join a London committee being set up to honour the late poet, requested a copy of 'Sardanapalus'.

Not even John Murray was willing to risk Goethe's anger if the oversight was discovered. On 26 March, a delighted Goethe received three handsomely printed dedication copies of 'Sardanapalus'. Fortunately for Murray and his fellow conspirator, Douglas Kinnaird, the gratified old gentleman never doubted that they were originals.

4

COUNT SMORLTORK'S PROGRESS

(1826–32)

Not all travellers between England and Germany were quite so high-minded as Samuel Taylor Coleridge and Henry Crabb Robinson.

The son of divorced parents whose marriage had brought together the neighbouring Saxon estates of Branitz and Bad Muskau, Prince Pückler was a good-hearted Lothario whose affectionate marriage in 1817 to Lucie von Pappenheim, a divorced woman nine years his senior, did not prevent the 32-year-old Prince from swiftly seducing his beloved 'Schnucke's' adopted daughter. Lucie – as she always would be throughout all the coming years of their long-lived partnership – proved remarkably forgiving. A word with her father, the Prussian State Chancellor, resulted in Pückler's rank being raised from a count to that of a prince; sadly, Chancellor Hardenberg had less luck in persuading the pious Crown Prince Friedrich Wilhelm to offer the dashing Pückler a lavish sinecure at the court of Berlin.

The princely title was welcome, but what Pückler needed was money. Funds were urgently required for the grandiose landscaping projects by which the Prince – ardently supported by Lucie –

had begun to transform the estate that he had inherited from his father in 1811 into one of the glories of Europe.

The inspiration for Muskau had originally come from England. Back in 1814, Pückler and his garden director had followed in the footsteps of Prince Franz of Anhalt-Dessau, undertaking a whirlwind investigative tour of the great English gardens created by Capability Brown and Humphry Repton. By 1822, when Repton's son arrived at Muskau to contribute a few such aristocratic touches as an enclosing fence, Pückler's park had acquired a distinctly English look, its streams and paths designed to lead the stroller's eye – as at Stourhead and Wilton – towards strategically placed statues or patches of colourful foliage. The addition of a thatched cottage (complete with resident hermit) paid playful homage to England's Picturesque style; Pückler's larger achievement was to create from dull terrain a lovely and varied landscape that betrayed no hint of a controlling eye.

Muskau's park was beautiful; maintaining it was ruinous. The worried Prince cut his retinue in half and sold off his beloved English horses; Lucie's failed attempt to create a fashionable spa (Muskau's remote position kept the fashionable world away) was followed by the voluntary sale of her jewellery, and then her silver plate. The bills continued to mount.

In 1823, Lucie came up with a more radical solution: divorce, to be followed by her spouse's speedy remarriage. True, her husband was now pushing thirty-nine and beginning to grey, but dye could be purchased. Pückler still possessed charm, height, elegance and a title: these attributes were surely enough – so Lucie schemed – for the Prince to ensnare a young woman who was both rich enough to pay their bills and tolerant enough to set up household with a new husband and his very tactful ex-wife.

The Prince, to his credit, was hesitant: he loved his ageing wife almost as much as his beloved park. In the end, however, he agreed that they had found no better alternative strategy. In January 1826, the Pücklers' legal divorce was finalised. Eight months later, leaving the estate in Lucie's capable hands, the Prince embarked upon his hunt for a golden bride.

With money as the prime objective, there was only one place to go. Twenty-two years of warfare had inflicted surprisingly little injury on England, an island with ready access to raw materials that could – with the help of a magnificent merchant navy – be imported from its colonies, processed (with the aid of sweated labour) at English-owned factories, refineries and mills, and exported at a handsome profit. English finance was booming, a fact that Prince Pückler's genial London banker, Nathan Mayer Rothschild, was happy to demonstrate at his own dinner table, where he loved to show off the astonishing range of dress-uniforms required for his professional visits to the courts of Europe's impoverished nobility.

As a venture into matrimonial enrichment, Pückler's two-year sojourn in England ended in abject failure. The Prince had no real heart for his dubious mission; he preferred flirting with pretty young milliners to proposing marriage to the daughters of a prosperous fleet of merchants and mayors. Few British daughters would, in any event, have gained permission from their parents for such an improper match; divorce was a subject that the English still found shocking, while the suggestion of a ménage à trois, even if established in faraway lands, was beyond their worst nightmares.

On the other hand, as an open-minded traveller's chance to experience and report back home (to the faithful Lucie) about the houses, monuments and strange habits of the English when at home, the Prince's journey proved – with a few reservations – a resounding success. Fortunately for the future finances of Muskau and Branitz, Pückler was an assiduous and witty correspondent; his pleasure in writing shines out of every page of the book that would later make his name.

One of the great joys of Pückler as an historian is his candour. Mr Thomas Cooke's celebrated (but entirely unnuanced) performance in the play adapted from Mary Shelley's *Frankenstein* left a cultured visitor as cold as the rowdiness of the English audiences. Shakespeare, performed in the age of Kean, Kemble and Macready, was another matter. Goethe was quite wrong, the Prince announced, to assert that Shakespeare was intended only to be read. His compatriot's misfortune (in Pückler's view) was never to have seen Shakespeare performed upon an English stage.

Off on tour, with Byron's works tucked under his arm for company, the energetic Prince paid his respects to the ruins of Newstead Abbey and travelled on to Wordsworth's Tintern. Henry VIII was praised, tongue-in-cheek, for adding such ravishing ruins to the landscape, while the great landowners of Wentworth Woodhouse and Petworth were scolded for swelling their funds by allowing cattle to graze right up to the windows of their elegant dining rooms. Such unimaginative use of private land, Pückler announced, was nearer to sacrilege than the destruction of monasteries by an angry Tudor king.

It was inspiring to stride through the chilly vacancies of a ruined abbey; Pückler, accustomed to the generous heat of German stoves, was less happy about the English habit of keeping their large homes at the same temperature as their drafty monuments. The coldness of country-house bedrooms was almost on a par, the Prince complained, with the peculiar behaviour of the English when at table. Why was it that he must always be placed so close to the sharp elbow of his hostess and so far from the soft bosoms of her pretty daughters? Why did an Englishman have to wait to catch another's eye and initiate a toast before being allowed a second glass of wine? And why, after leaving the dining table, was it considered acceptable for one rude English youth to bury his nose in Madame de Staël's book and speak to nobody, while he himself must work so hard to be unfalteringly amusing to society?

The Prince was a restive guest at the homes of England's aristocracy. His favourite hostess came from an entirely different milieu.

Harriet Mellon was a plump and chatty ex-actress whose first marriage, to an elderly and enormously rich banker, Thomas

Coutts, had been followed by a second, to the young and desperately poor Duke of St Albans. The widow (or her sacks of gold) had bewitched the youthful Duke while they were both staying with Sir Walter Scott at Abbotsford in 1825; Scott, in turn, had a very soft spot for the loquacious Harriet.

And so it was that on one of the many nights that Prince Pückler dined at jolly Harriet's Highgate home, he was thrilled to find that the Duchess (knowing how Scott loved all things Germanic) had placed Britain's most celebrated author next to him at the table. The meeting was a huge success. Pückler told ghostly stories of the sort that Lucie loved to hear; Scott, an eager collector of German folktales, listened enthralled. The gentlemen's conversation continued long enough after dinner for the Duchess to complete a sketch of Sir Walter's worn but animated face. She posted the result to Pückler, a literary trophy for the finest of the four elegant scrapbooks he had recently purchased (no expense spared) from his compatriot Rudolph Ackermann's smart new shop in the Strand.

Pückler failed to return home with the richly endowed wife who had been the object of his venture. An improvement in the Prince's fortunes – as it turned out – would owe more to his loyal Lucie than to the improbable Lady Bountiful of their shared dreams.

In the summer of 1828, when Pückler had been away in England for almost two years, Lucie received a visit from Karl August Varnhagen (a close friend of Goethe's), whose wife Rahel Levin (one of a new and sizeable group of Lutheran converts who had exchanged their Jewish faith for social acceptance) was among the most renowned literary hostesses in Berlin. The Varnhagens were enchanted, both by the glorious gardens and by Lucie's doting stories of an absent husband. When the Princess read aloud from some of Pückler's witty travel letters, Varnhagen insisted that they should be published. He even volunteered to act both as editor and publicist.

Letters from a Dead Man, as the German edition was cautiously presented, in order to protect the name of the garrulous – and still very much alive – Prince, came out in 1830. Garlanded with tributes from Varnhagen, Goethe and even the brilliant young Heinrich Heine, the book was an immediate success. In the words of Pückler's most recent biographer, Peter Bowman, *Letters from a Dead Man* became 'the publishing sensation of the decade'.[1]

A second and equally forceful boost to Pückler's career came to him from England. Hearing about the success of the *Letters* in Germany (and doubtless remembering how well he had done from de Staël's *De l'Allemagne*), John Murray was keen to publish an English translation. He was also anxious not to act without advice. When his chosen translator, Sarah Austin, disclosed that the Prince's book poked fun at the English nobility, Murray recoiled. Mrs Austin, charmed by the book, tracked down a braver publisher.

Mrs Austin had her own reservations about Pückler's letters. England, in 1831 (as the era of Romanticism ebbed), was growing primmer and the Prince's book was being targeted at a Christmas market composed principally of female readers. Saucy jokes and stories of sexual encounters would not improve its sales. To Pückler's disgust, Mrs Austin wrote to advise him that she had appointed herself as his sole censor.

Sarah Austin knew her audience. *Tour of a German Prince*, as it appeared in her judiciously amended four-volume translation, earned generous plaudits both for its author and for Austin herself. Objections to the Prince's lack of reverence for the English nobility who had so graciously entertained him were drowned in praises for – in the words of the *Westminster Review* – 'our friend, our warm-hearted, noble-minded, imaginative, though somewhat wayward, friend . . . we take as much pleasure in his letters, as if we had had the satisfaction of having them addressed solely to ourselves'.[2]

Translating Prince Pückler into English, Mrs Austin never suspected that the author she so admired had visited her homeland primarily to lay hands on a rich wife. Pückler, engaged in one of the epistolary flirtations at which he excelled, was not about to disillusion an adoring translator.

In 1831, Sarah Austin was a pretty, clever, lively woman in her late thirties. Her home life was not (she wished the Prince to know) satisfactory. (Mr Austin was a depressive hypochondriac, a quasi-Casaubon whose respected writings on legal philosophy were only to be published after his death.) When Pückler began to drop hints to Sarah that she had captured his heart, her response was prompt and ardent. She was not (so she told the Prince) strait-laced. Her energy was far beyond that of the average English woman; her figure – she was eager to assure him – was quite remarkable. Copious specifics followed on, almost in the form of a shopping list: broad shoulders; tiny waist; firm, round bosom; finely turned knees and ankles; a body (as Sarah enticingly stressed) of uncommon flexibility. Venturing further still, Mrs Austin informed the intrigued Prince that her hips 'and all below them' were handsome to the point of perfection. All of these delights, as she hinted with no delicacy at all, were currently in need of proper appreciation.[3]

Pückler's letters to Mrs Austin have not survived, but, even without them, it's clear that the Prince offered no discouragement to his bold translator. In the summer of 1832, Sarah blithely announced a new plan: she and her husband would move to Berlin. Here, she calculated, she would be close enough to pay regular visits to Muskau, where she would bear her splendid prince a child and live, embowered by roses, in his park's thatched cottage.

In the event, it may have come as some relief to the besieged Pückler that John Austin stepped in at this critical juncture, to place a flat embargo on all foreign trips. Sarah's hopes did not immediately diminish; time and an increasingly one-sided correspondence gradually whittled her last illusions away. When the longed-for first meeting with Pückler finally took place in Berlin in 1842, the occasion proved friendly rather than passionate.

*

Pückler's affections for Sarah Austin may have waned, but his attachment to her homeland remained undimmed. In Germany, he replicated the English style of country life. Travelling around Europe, he always took along a volume of Byron's poems, a bottle of Harvey's sauce and a tin of strong English mustard powder.

In 1851, Pückler finally made a return trip to London. This time, instead of courting rich girls, he came to inspect the Great Exhibition and the new Houses of Parliament. But it was a view of the gas–lit bridges arching above the bobbing lamps of shadowy river-craft along the Thames that reminded the nostalgic Prince of what it was that he had always found so charming about England, a country that had provided him with everything except a well-heeled second wife.

Lucie, greatly mourned by the husband whom she fondly addressed to the end as her dearest 'Lou', died in 1854. Her modest grave was marked by the Prince with the simple words: 'I think of you in love.' For himself, dying seventeen years later at the age of eighty-six, Pückler designed something entirely different.

The pyramid that marks the Prince's grave can still be seen today. It forms part of the gardens of the Branitz estate that Pückler, paying homage to the England he so loved, had playfully renamed Bransom Hall.

England has not as yet returned the compliment to a remarkable man. The *Tour* is often rifled for snippets of social comment, but Pückler himself remains a bit of a joke, known chiefly as the inspirer of a comic battalion of fictitious moustache-twirlers, among whom the charming Count Smorltork holds first place in Dickens's *The Pickwick Papers* (1836).

Elsewhere, the story is quite different. *Hints on Landscape Gardening*, published in 1834, together with fifty colour illustrations of Muskau, cemented Pückler's reputation at home as Germany's pre-eminent landscape architect. It also carried his name to the transcendalists in America. Respectfully visited during

Pückler's lifetime by Bronson Alcott and Margaret Fuller, Muskau later became a source of inspiration for Frederick Law Olmsted. In 1906, Samuel Parsons (the man whose shaping eye contributed so much to New York's Central Park), singled out Pückler's genius for painting with nature as being in advance of anything in the world of landscape design that was being achieved in Europe or America at the opening of the twentieth century.

The last word about the man sometimes described as the Goethe of the landscape garden should go to Sarah Austin, whose dedication and sensitive translating skills first won a readership for Pückler outside his native Germany. Publishing, in 1854, a book called *Germany from 1760–1814, or Sketches of German Life*, Austin remarked that the Germans stand next only to the English as the greatest of travellers: 'They have more knowledge, simpler habits, less arrogant nationality, and less intolerant prejudices, than any other people.'[4]

Mrs Austin's thoughts as she wrote those words, it's fair to guess, were not too far from her memories of the delightful Prince Hermann Pückler, lord of Muskau and Branitz.

5

THE AGE OF VIRTUE

(1830–60)

A German, however fickle, could do no wrong in the eyes of Sarah Austin, praising Germany to the skies in the short history she wrote in 1854 of a country that had become as admired for its tolerance as for its ardent engagement with culture and philanthropy. While the appointment of Baron Charles de Bunsen as Prussia's official representative in London in 1841 had already ensured that this brilliant and devout friend of Prince Albert and Baron Stockmar was in a position to import some of that enlightened spirit into England, George Eliot was eager to visit Germany, a country whose bold views on religion had earned the admiration of a non-believer.

George Eliot, in 1854, was thirty-five years old. Not yet known by her famous pseudonym, nor as the anonymous translator, aged twenty-seven, of David Strauss's 1500-page *The Life of Jesus* (a book that outraged orthodox Christian readers by suggesting that Christ was not divine and that his miracles were mythical), Eliot had just made use of her own name, Marian Evans, to translate an equally controversial work, Ludwig Feuerbach's *The Essence of Christianity*.

Having exploded these German fireworks in an England where Lord Shaftesbury described Strauss's work – which he read in her 1846 translation – as 'the most pestilential book ever vomited out of the jaws of hell', Eliot had settled into a blissful period of exile at Weimar, accompanied by her married lover, George Lewes.

In England, the religious-minded author Charles Kingsley was ready to dismiss the strong-featured, brilliant Miss Evans as Lewes's 'concubine'. In Germany, the unconventional couple suffered from no sense of ostracism, while winning appreciation for their open, intelligent minds.

An intellectually productive relationship (Lewes's influence upon Eliot's literary development was immense) added a glow of its own to the happiness of Weimar's English visitors. The place enchanted them. Lewes, like Eliot, was charmed by the little town's old-fashioned atmosphere: the pretty riverside walks, a park laid out upon the anglicised designs drawn up by Prince Pückler, the glimpses of ladies knitting on their doorsteps, a leafy chestnut avenue linking the town to the Belvedere, home to Weimar's benevolent rulers. Writing home to his young sons, Lewes told them that Weimar was 'the Athens of Germany', home of 'the greatest of them all ... I mean Goethe. I am writing his life.'[1]

Lewes's projected life of Goethe, the chief reason for the couple's journey to Weimar, was published the following year when, besides becoming the standard English biography, it won the rarer compliment of an admiring audience in Germany.

Lewes's only problem in 1854, as he researched the background for his book, was that Goethe had been dead for over twenty years, surviving only in an eclectic variety of monuments. (Eliot, while repelled by a statue at the Belvedere of Goethe naked and attended by a cringing Psyche, viewed the poet's unspoiled house with keen approval, favourably comparing his simple study with the baronial trappings of Walter Scott's home at Abbotsford.[2])

For a glimpse of Goethe in life, rather than in statuary and shrines, Lewes turned to his colleague, William Thackeray. *Vanity*

Fair, published with great success as a serial in the 1840s, had described the imaginary German duchy of Pumpernickel in a way that artfully combined references to a Rhenish spa with allusions to Weimar, where – as Lewes knew – Thackeray had stayed as a young man. Lewes's request must have reached the busy English author on a day of untypical serenity; his response was both tender and prompt.

Thackeray had been a boy of nineteen when he visited Germany in 1830; recollection had robbed the experience of none of its charm. Life for the twenty or so young Englishmen studying German culture in Weimar had been, as the author recalled in his letter to Lewes, both playful and ceremonious. Performances of Shakespeare and Schiller at the conscientiously high-minded town theatre were attended at least three nights in every week; invitations to visit Goethe were a rare and terrifying honour. Thackeray himself was granted just one interview, during which his ancient, grey-robed host impressed a future journalist both by evincing a keen interest in British affairs and by the number of English newspapers spread about his room. (Extracts of these were translated for Goethe's benefit by his English-speaking daughter-in-law.)

Invitations to the homely little ducal court of Weimar were apparently less intimidating, but the palace's relaxed atmosphere did not mean that a guest could show up for a reception without wearing some kind of uniform. Thackeray, having none of his own, resourcefully purchased an old dress sword belonging to Schiller and thrust it, with a swagger, across a tightly buckled waist. The sword, still hanging aslant his study wall, served as a pleasant reminder of those far-off days, the now-famous author added with a sigh for the happiness that his youthful self had experienced. 'I think', Thackeray concluded, 'I have never seen a society more simple, more charitable, courteous and gentlemanlike, than that of the dear little Saxon court where the good Schiller and the great Goethe lived and lie buried.'[3]

Lewes's delight at Thackeray's letter is not in doubt; he incor-porated it, entire, into a biography which paid handsome tribute to Goethe, while offering a portrait of Weimar that echoed Thackeray's own nostalgic tenderness.

Travelling on from Weimar to Berlin, Eliot found less to charm her. The beds, both here and elsewhere in Germany, were short, high and generally unsuited to the inclinations of an amorous couple. (Eliot's husband John Cross would later primly correct the observations made upon this indelicate subject in his late wife's journals.) Neither did Miss Evans care for the ubiquitous presence in Prussia's capital of officers in blue and scarlet broadcloth: the tall and strutting 'puppets in uniform' of whom all English visitors to Berlin complained.

Nevertheless, reviewing her experiences abroad from a Dover hotel on 27 March 1855, George Eliot decided that the warmth and lack of bigotry and prejudice among the Germans more than made up for their 'unreadable' books, 'un-sit-out-able' comic plays, and an obsession with military etiquette which did not extend to the dinner table. (She was aghast by the German habit of using knives like spoons.)

'Recollections of Weimar', an unpublished essay still preserved in a manuscript book at Yale, suggests that Eliot, like Thackeray, never forgot the happiness she and George Lewes had once expe-rienced at that little town whose innocence would later be so compromised and tainted.

Munich, Nuremberg, the Rhine and Dresden remained unvis-ited. 'May the time come soon!' Eliot noted with longing in 1855. In 1858, her wish was granted by a three-month journey with Lewes to Munich – a disappointment – and, more happily, to Nuremberg and Dresden. Here, in the paintings by Pieter de Hooch on display at Dresden's celebrated gallery, George Eliot found what she described as 'the precious quality of truthfulness'. The richly domestic interiors of *Adam Bede*, published the fol-lowing year, owe as much to recollections of the Dutch interiors

Eliot had admired at Dresden and Berlin as they do to memories of her English country childhood at Arbury Hall.[4]

Lewes and Eliot were visiting Germany during a period steeped in the consciousness that England and Germany shared far more than divided them, and that they could serve each other best by a system of mutual support. 'The combination in the Napoleonic Wars should never be forgotten,' a *Blackwood's* writer urged his readers in 1841. A 'warm-hearted sympathy' had come to prevail between the two countries, and this anonymous author believed that it should be cherished. 'An Anglo-German alliance is worth three times as much as a hollow friendship with France,' he admonished any Francophiles who happened to be perusing his lines.[5]

Victoria's marriage to Albert in 1840 would famously come to epitomise the flourishing relationship between two nations that shared literary, royal, philanthropic and mercantile interests. Evidence of a growing mutual attachment between England and Germany was, however, apparent for at least a decade before the royal wedding gave visible form to this international romance. United more strongly in their victory over Napoleon than by the continued presence of a Hanoverian monarchy in England, the countries had been further welded together by their shared respect for the benefits of democracy and – a century before the birth of the welfare state – the importance of philanthropy.

Upholding this bond of virtuous attachment in the middle of the century, as Prussia's envoy to the Court of St James's, was Charles de Bunsen, a Protestant diplomat who had charmed Henry Crabb Robinson as much as had his energetic English wife when Robinson visited their lively and bilingual home in Rome, in 1826.

Born into a poor German family in 1791, Charles de Bunsen's exceptional gift for languages became evident while he was still a child. Taught English by a pastor, he went on to master Hebrew, Greek, Danish, Icelandic, Persian and Arabic. He was planning the

further study of Sanskrit at Oxford when he was abruptly summoned to Rome, to join the historian Georg Niebuhr (founder of
the modern scientific study of history) at the Prussian Legation.
Rosy-cheeked, flaxen-haired and quietly spoken, Niebuhr's protégé soon made a good impression. The young de Bunsen was, in
the words of another eminent historian, Leopold von Ranke, 'a
winning personality respected by all'.[6]

All that Charles de Bunsen lacked in his early life was prosperity. That drawback was agreeably removed when he married Fanny
Waddington, a lively and highly educated Welsh heiress whose
mother had taught her to revere Madame de Staël. Fanny had been
taken to London to meet the famous author of *De l'Allemagne* in
1814, a year after the book's publication. Listening to her mother's
discussion with Madame de Staël was an experience Fanny never
forgot ('In my life I never was so highly gratified by conversation').

Arguably, the eloquent and voluble author served as a prime
model for Fanny's career as a hostess whose independent mind had
instantly captured the interest of the clever young Prussian who –
after attending one of Fanny's mother's 'At Homes' during a family
visit to Rome in 1817 – revised his plans to pursue a scholarship
in Calcutta. Fanny's considerable fortune may have added to her
charms as a prospective bride, but the marriage, celebrated that
year, was a long and happy one. Ernest, born at Rome in 1819,
was the first of a brood of ten.

In 1838, Charles de Bunsen and his family moved to England,
responding in part to pressure from Fanny Waddington's formidable old mother, who complained that her daughter, despite
being one of the world's most conscientious correspondents, had
not stepped foot on British soil in twenty-one years. This was true.
It was also true that Fanny, returning to England from the brilliant
skies of Italy, was not immediately eager to settle in a country
where 'the standing rule is a sort of wet blanket of sky, letting
through neither sun nor rain ... a sort of negation, moving not,
warming not, chilling not'.[7]

Fanny's complaints, while vehement, were soon assuaged by the enterprise of doing up a handsome Waddington-owned property in Wimpole Street as the first de Bunsen residence, before deciding (since money was never an issue) that the family should also rent a manor house near Pevensey Bay from their friends, the Hares.

Charles de Bunsen, by contrast to his wife, was instantly at home in England and eager to renew his friendship with Thomas Arnold, a man whom he had first met – and instantly liked – in 1827, when both fathers were pondering how best to educate their sons. In 1828, Arnold became headmaster of Rugby, and a transformer of the old-fashioned English school syllabus, to which he added mathematics, history and modern languages. An expedition to Rugby (speeded up by the brand-new railway line from Euston Station to Birmingham) was one of de Bunsen's first undertakings in England. The following year, hearing of Arnold's imminent retirement, de Bunsen took it upon himself to fire off a passionate letter in support of his friend. Why, de Bunsen wished the influential Bishop of Norwich to tell him, was Thomas Arnold, 'this great and good man' being allowed to depart from his headmastership without appropriate recognition? Why did the English not follow the German custom of giving a professorship to such a man? Did they have no respect for the great leaders of their educational system? De Bunsen's argument was effective; in 1841, Thomas Arnold was appointed Regius Professor of Modern History at Oxford.

Charles de Bunsen's primary commission in England, as in Rome, was an intricate one, requiring all of his considerable diplomatic skills. The ageing King of Prussia wanted the young English Queen's support for the establishment, in Jerusalem, of an Anglo-Prussian bishopric. De Bunsen's arguments were persuasive; Victoria gave her approval to the scheme. The German-designed church, crowned by a handsome Italianate bell-tower and displaying – somewhat bizarrely – a large Prussian eagle on its facade, survives to this day in the Christian quarter of Jerusalem.

Victoria had taken to Charles de Bunsen from their very first meeting. In 1840, the old King of Prussia was succeeded by his son, Friedrich Wilhelm IV, one of de Bunsen's most devoted friends since their early Italian days, when both Fanny and Charles had been captivated by a visit from a young man possessed of such glowingly egalitarian spirit and altruistic zeal. Newly crowned, Friedrich Wilhelm invited Victoria to choose her own ambassador to the Court of St James's. The young Queen's response was unhesitating.

From the first year of his appointment (1841), Charles de Bunsen could rely upon the support of both the English and the Prussian court for his philanthropic endeavours. High among these ambitions stood the Ambassador's desire to see a united Germany and to strengthen, by every possible means, an alliance between the two most productive – and increasingly competitive – Protestant powers in Europe.

Walking up the narrow but pretty staircase of the sole part of the Prussian Legation at Carlton House Terrace that escaped a Third Reich revamp, it's still just possible to catch the atmosphere of the happy and active years when the de Bunsen family were in residence, when the walls were hung with views of Italy, when the piano lid was always open, and Fanny's easel always offered some characterful new example of her work. Sometimes, the Ambassador, disliking formality, would open the tall mahogany entrance doors himself, perhaps welcoming in the majestic and downright prison reformer Elizabeth Fry, described by her host as 'my favourite saint'. On another occasion, the unexpected visitor might be 'My favourite and admired Miss Nightingale', a young woman who had not yet discovered her nursing vocation, and who knew that she could always turn to Charles de Bunsen for wise advice and friendly support.

The de Bunsen family letters conjure up a picture of early Victorian England at its best: erudite, cheerful, enterprising, religious and endlessly energetic. Intelligence was highly valued in this household: reading a book by Gladstone in 1838, de Bunsen told Fanny that he considered him 'the first man in England as to intellectual power'. This, from a man who told a German friend that the English were shrewd, but incapable of the German habit of deep thought ('only Coleridge has communicated something of this'), was high praise.

Sir Robert Peel was another politician who won de Bunsen's approval, notably when the Prime Minister, declaring himself to be 'a good German' (one who shared de Bunsen's own hopes for Germany's speedy unification), took Prussia's side in October 1841, at a time when the French were demanding to be given back the left bank of the Rhine that Napoleon had previously seized from Germany. ('They *shall* not have the Rhine,' Peel reassured his friend, quoting a line to de Bunsen from a newly popular German song about 'den freien, deutschen Rhein'.) Both river banks, always a contentious boundary issue, remained, on this occasion, under German ownership.

The music-loving de Bunsens had made friends with Felix Mendelssohn Bartholdy during his frequent visits to his uncle, an art-loving German consul established in Rome. A musical family, they welcomed the handsome and immensely popular young composer to their London home as tenderly as if he were their own adopted son. De Bunsen shared Fanny's anguish when Mendelssohn died in 1847, only a few months after giving a concert at Carlton House Terrace, during which the vocal contribution had been provided by Charles and Fanny's eldest son ('never did his voice sound so perfect,' a proud Fanny informed Ernest's grandmother in Wales). The Ambassador had grieved, Fanny sighed to old Madame Waddington on 12 November, 'as though he [Mendelssohn] had belonged to him by ties of blood'.

The sadness was almost universal. In Germany, hymns were sung on every small station platform at which the funeral train drew in, all along the slow journey from Leipzig to Berlin. In England, the de Bunsen family attended a memorial performance of the composer's great oratorio, *Elijah,* for which both orchestra and audience dressed in full mourning. A rare visit to the Legation from the Danish story-teller Hans Andersen, who willingly read his 'delightful' fairy-stories to cheer up the sad-faced children of the de Bunsen household, was quite overshadowed by the tragedy.

Grief was not a state that came naturally to the Ambassador's ebullient wife. Well into middle age, Fanny managed, within a single day, to whisk some exhausted German visitors around London's new National Gallery, St Paul's, the Royal Exchange and even down into Brunel's newly completed tunnel below the Thames – a risky adventure.

Less gregarious in his habits than his wife, Charles de Bunsen was happy for Fanny to perform the social niceties, while he focused upon the kind of work he most enjoyed. Thomas Carlyle discussed with him the creation of a new London Library; in 1841, de Bunsen became a founder member and a dedicated contributor of ideas at the committee meetings held at 14 St James's Square, two minutes' walk from the Legation. A glance at the titles of the books that Prince Albert donated to the new library's German collection suggests that the Ambassador himself picked out a set of books that included the great history of Rome written by Niebuhr, de Bunsen's own first patron and employer.

The suggestion of the Ambassador's involvement in Prince Albert's book choice is not far-fetched. The de Bunsens became cherished members of the royal circle from the first year of their arrival in England. An early high spot among their regular visits to the splendidly restored Windsor Castle came when Victoria invited the King of Prussia to stand godfather, in 1842, to the Prince of Wales. In Germany, where the news was received with delight, one hotelier promptly renamed his establishment the London Tavern; in Carlton House Terrace, preparations were made for celebrations on a scale that would not be matched again until the Prussian King's nephew, Fritz, travelled to England in the winter of 1857 for his marriage to the Princess Royal.

At home, in the privacy of his study, the mild-mannered Charles de Bunsen sometimes burst out in fury against the 'monstrous' life of an ambassador. Attending Windsor for the christening, however, he had no complaints. A beaming Prussian king, a radiant English queen, a fine staging of *The Merry Wives of Windsor*: all was as an Anglophile German could have wished. Fanny, meanwhile, glowed with pride when the Queen delivered a special request for de Bunsen to take her arm for a quadrille.

Fanny, unlike her scholarly husband, adored court life. Writing to her mother after a visit to Windsor in 1846, she could hardly contain the rapture she had felt on entering the great Waterloo Chamber (a scene 'such as fairy-tales present'), or in watching the round-faced little Queen promenade across the dance-floor, Victoria's face (Fanny added with proprietorial satisfaction) 'ray-onnante with that expression of countenance that she has when pleased with what surrounds her, and which you know I like to see!'

On 25 March 1848, the de Bunsens' orderly household was brusquely awakened at 8 a.m. by a hammering at the door. Revolution had broken out in Berlin and Prince William, the King of Prussia's younger brother, had been advised to flee to England for safety. Behind him, so he told an astonished de Bunsen, he had left a city in a state of uproar, turmoil and consternation in which the rebels were calling for the very thing that Charles de Bunsen himself had always hoped for: the unification of the German states. Less reassuringly, despite the King's swiftly expressed readiness to meet their demands, the insurgents were demanding a new constitution.

For the present, the de Bunsens did what was necessary. They offered a refuge to the future Emperor William I, while fondly noting that he had the same kindly and open face as his brother, the King. News came that an abdication was being discussed in Berlin; with this in mind, a series of diplomatic parties were hastily arranged for the Prince at the Legation's new and larger quarters at 9 Carlton House Terrace. Writing to his close friend Baron Stockmar after the Prince had spent two months under his roof, de Bunsen made no reference to the talk of abdication. Instead, he spoke of his hopes for a new, unified Germany towards which he was confident that Victoria and Albert would extend their warmest approval. 'There is no difficulty to be anticipated here, in the recognition of the German Empire,' de Bunsen wrote on 15 July. And then, ever prudent, he added a coda: 'when once it shall exist'.

The King of Prussia possessed, as de Bunsen knew, no history as a man of iron will. In 1848, he conceded, dithered and finally settled upon his irrevocable view: he would not support the rebels' proposals for a united Germany. De Bunsen was appalled. In December, Charles travelled out to Berlin and spent a full four hours beseeching his royal master to accept the imperial crown of Germany, but – while Bunsen lost his voice in the attempt – Friedrich Wilhelm IV remained unmoved. He would not do it. Austria's presence as the leading power (alongside Prussia) in Central Europe must not be tested by such a challenge to its authority.

Victoria, years later, looked back upon 1848 as the year when a great opportunity had been lost. That was the time when unification could first have been achieved; the time when the virtuous but weak King of Prussia had let them all down. In 1850, however, de Bunsen still believed that unification was imminent. He could not think of leaving England, he told his friend Archdeacon Hare on 29 February, not 'at this eleventh hour when all the powers of evil double their efforts to prevent this great European birth, or rather this beginning of regeneration'.

The mention of departure is revealing. From 1848 on, de Bunsen had struggled to retain any respect for the ageing Prussian ruler in whom he had once placed such high hopes. His confidence sapped by disappointment, the diplomat began to think of the homeland he had left behind, and of the scholarly pleasures that might still lie in store there for a private individual. His family's links to the beloved island he now regarded as his second home were already assured. One son, Henry, had become an Anglican clergyman; two others had married wealthy Norfolk Quakers. Both at Abbey Lodge in London, where Ernest de Bunsen lived with Elizabeth Gurney and their children, and at Old Keswick Hall, the Norfolk birthplace of Emma Birkbeck, the wife of Georg von Bunsen [sic], the de Bunsen presence in England appeared secure.

In 1854, Charles de Bunsen tendered his formal resignation; no opposition came from Prussia, where de Bunsen's efforts to enlist support for Britain in the Crimean War (1853–6) had been badly received. Returning to Germany, he devoted himself to works of scholarship, including a translation of the Bible. In 1857, on the very day of the incapacitating stroke that led Prince William to take on the role of Prussia's regent, Friedrich Wilhelm IV bestowed a barony on his faithful ambassador. That last independent action of his reign paid homage to a braver man than himself.

Baron de Bunsen died at Bonn in 1860. Fanny who survived him by sixteen years, divided the remainder of her life between winters at the quiet, slightly dull little German town of Carlsruhe, and summers at her home in the Black Forest. Here, at the Villa Waldeck, Charles and Fanny's English-born grandchildren spent long and happy summer holidays each year, in the company of their young German cousins and their cheerful, lavish, reminiscing old Welsh-born grandmother. Talking to Fanny about life at Abbey Lodge, and listening to her grumbles about the ordeal of a year's retreat to Switzerland (life for an old English lady in Germany was not considered fireproof during the Franco-Prussian war), the children slipped in and out of their shared languages without a thought. Riding along Norfolk lanes, or swimming in a lake in the Black Forest, they knew exactly who they were: two friendly cultures blended without blemish into one harmonious whole.

6

ELIZABETH FRY,
FLORENCE NIGHTINGALE
AND CHARLES DE BUNSEN'S
GERMAN HOSPITAL

(1840–52)

Elizabeth Fry's friendship with Charles de Bunsen was cemented by the marriage of Ernest, his eldest son, to her Quaker niece, Elizabeth Gurney. The friendship began through the shared interest of two dedicated reformers in creating a new public hospital for London, at a time when Britain's city slums were rampant breeding grounds for virulent disease.

This, in an age of enterprise and achievement, was Britain's dirty little secret. A horrified German visitor to Bradford in 1846 described the back streets of a thriving Yorkshire manufacturing town as a vision from hell. Young Friedrich Engels, despatched from Wuppertal in 1842 to gain some knowledge of his family's textile business in Manchester, was shown the sufferings of the city's industrial poor by Mary Burns, a radical-minded Irish factory girl who became his common-law wife. Back in Germany before he returned to England to subsidise and collaborate with his admired friend and colleague, Karl Marx, Engels published his most famous book, *The Condition of the Working Class in England* (1845), as a warning to his homeland's merchant class of the terrible consequences of industrialisation. England, as Engels pointed out in a work that (unsurprisingly) was not published in Britain until 1887, offered Germany a frightening model of what happened when social welfare was valued below economic success.

What Engels did not point out in his great book was that the people who had come to England from his own country were among the most oppressed in their new homeland, and that the conditions he had witnessed in Manchester were not restricted to that city.

In 1840, around the time that Charles de Bunsen first arrived in England, German sugar-bakers were working twelve-hour days in the infamous East End boiling houses, in conditions so bad that no Englishmen (even in the terrible decade known as 'the Hungry Forties') would undertake such labour. Consumption, caused by inhaling the sugar-scum, was rife and deadly; London's hospital beds, when compared to what was offered by other European capitals, were in short supply.

Charles de Bunsen, addressing a hospital committee about the need for immediate action in 1843, was well-fortified with the pertinent statistics, and they were shaming. Berlin, with a population of 365,000, offered 3000 hospital beds. Paris, with a population of one million, offered 20,000. London, with the comparatively enormous population of two million (of whom at least 30,000 were German immigrants who spoke no English and who relied upon a handful of overworked Lutheran pastors to communicate their needs), could supply a mere 5000 beds.[1]

Nursing in England had reached an all-time low by the 1840s, and for good reason. Readers of *Martin Chuzzlewit*, serialised in 1843–4, were not so stirred as they should have been by Dickens's characterisation of Sairey Gamp, a venal alcoholic who cares less about her work as a midwife, nurse and layer-out of the dead than ensuring her own basic comforts. Emphasising Mrs Gamp's unsuitability for her profession, Dickens neglected to mention that the hard life of a city nurse offered scant incentive for any finer standard of behaviour. Pay to a hospital nurse was negligible; training and supervision were almost non-existent. Accommodation often amounted to a straw mattress and a thin blanket, flopped at the bottom of a stairwell. Treated with such indifference, nurses could not be expected to behave like ministering angels.

Years earlier, Charles de Bunsen had successfully overseen the establishment of a small Protestant hospital in Rome. Newly arrived in London and shocked by the absence of medical provision for his poorer compatriots, de Bunsen set out to repeat his success. To do so, he drew upon his friendship with Elizabeth Fry and upon his knowledge of a German nursing institute, Kaiserswerth, that had been inspired by her example.

Theodor Fliedner, Kaiserswerth's founder, had originally entered England in 1824 as a pastor on a mission to raise funds for the German poor. A meeting with Mrs Fry had led to an invitation, a decade later, to watch this sweet but formidable woman at work as she read to a group of female convicts, in a Bible class held within the walls of Newgate Prison. Fliedner was awestruck, and inspired.

Fry's main objective was to improve the conditions of prison life for women, and to revive, by the fostering of piety among such inmates, a sense of hope. Fliedner formulated a project that was closer to the spirit of Thomas Carlyle. (An unpopular 1850's pamphlet by Carlyle, *Model Prisons*, suggested that less should be spent on the creation of smart new penitentiaries, and more on building better homes for the working poor.)

Returning to the little town of Kaiserswerth, near the Rhine, Pastor Fliedner's first pioneering venture was to create a post-prison hostel for women, a place of transition at which recently released female convicts could be trained and prepared for social service within the larger German community. The still bolder idea of a female teaching college followed on, together with the nursing institute that had so interested Charles de Bunsen. Initiated by Fliedner's second wife, who had formerly headed a surgical ward at a Hamburg hospital, the institute aimed to provide unmarried girls with three years of training in nursing and religion at Kaiserswerth, followed by practical experience, to be gained abroad. It was this final aspect of the Fliedners' programme that caught de Bunsen's attention as he began to plot the route to setting up a German-speaking hospital in London. Kaiserswerth offered a way in which to recruit a reliable supply of German-speaking nurses. All that was required now was to gather a first-hand report of Fliedner's institute.

In October 1839, Mrs Fry told Bunsen of her plan to undertake a major tour of German prisons, with the intention of bringing her forceful personality to bear on their urgent need for reform. Mrs Fry intended to travel out with her brother Samuel Gurney, a wealthy Quaker of enterprising views who would later host the first demonstration of an electrical telegraph at his home in London, and Samuel's daughter, Elizabeth. De Bunsen, having congratulated Mrs Fry upon a laudable project, urged his friend (whom he diplomatically described as 'a tall, large figure ... not plain, but rather grand than handsome') to visit Kaiserswerth, and to report back with her usual trenchant clarity.

Mrs Fry, while impressed by de Bunsen's project, was not easily persuaded. Prisons, not hospitals, were her mission in life and she had committed herself to what was already a punishing schedule for a semi-invalid, and one who was nearing sixty. It seems that a certain amount of delicate bartering took place. De Bunsen indicated his willingness to arrange for Mrs Fry to meet those royal personages under whose control the German prisons lay; letters of introduction were placed in her capable hands. In exchange, with a calm inflexibility that matched the great reformer's own determined spirit, de Bunsen insisted upon her visiting an institute, as he calmly reminded his visitor, that owed its very existence to her own splendid example. Gratified by the allusion to her influence and delighted by the entrée that de Bunsen had provided to Germany's royal circles, Mrs Fry surrendered.

Mrs Fry's 1840 trip to Germany commenced auspiciously, with a summons from Queen Victoria, who (possibly at the prompting of de Bunsen himself) delivered a short personal message of goodwill for the expedition to Germany. Mrs Fry (whose most un-Quakerish attachment to royalty did not always gain the approval of her family) was impressed.

Elizabeth Gurney, to her considerable disappointment, had received no summons to join her aunt on the visit to Windsor Castle. A lively and sharp-eyed young Norfolk Quaker who referred to herself with self-effacing meekness as 'the hem of Aunt's garment', Elizabeth went off instead to purchase a new diary from Ackermann's shop in the Strand. Its plain pages (no gilt edgings for Quakers) would record her candid impressions of Germany – and of Aunt Fry in action.

Miss Gurney's unpublished diary offers an unexpected glimpse of Mrs Fry offstage. Feeding 'Aunt' up with the requisite amount of porter and ale to keep her lively in spirits and forceful in voice throughout the trip was, so Elizabeth demurely commented, quite a business in itself. Well-nourished and constantly feted, Mrs Fry was less discomforted than her niece either by the strangeness of German meals – how peculiar, Elizabeth remarked, to begin a meal with plum pudding and end it with a joint of beef – or by the hearty kisses with which both ladies were invariably set upon by their Quaker counterparts. 'And not content with one good smack,' Elizabeth noted with dismay, 'they plan for at least four, that is two for each side . . . Aunt Fry bears it heroically.'

'I think,' the young diarist slyly added, 'she rather likes it.'[2]

A noble mission (Mrs Fry was anxious to discover whether much-heralded reforms had been put into practice in Hanover and Berlin) did not preclude the hope of some sightseeing trips for the

English visitors. Meanwhile, Elizabeth reported on various prison visits and praised the skill with which Mrs Fry persuaded ladies of fashion to adopt an eager interest in her cause. Miss Gurney shared her aunt's dismay at finding that Hanover (so closely connected by its history to England) harboured one of the worst prisons in Germany, with 400 men in chains, and all under the auspices of an unpleasant new king (Ernest, Duke of Cumberland, one of George III's least popular sons) who declared himself 'too ill' even to listen to the urgent recommendations of his English visitors. Hanover town, like its king, was very haughty and grand, Elizabeth reported with disgust. She was glad they had not dined with such a worldly man as the Ambassador, Lord Bligh.

A young woman embarked on her first trip abroad could not stay indignant for longer than an afternoon. Happy to be taken in hand by one Rudolph, their personable German tour guide, she was hard put to know what thrilled her more: the chance to sit in Luther's own chair, and there to gaze upon 'the very beer jug that he had drunk out of' (this formidable relic lay under the shy super-vision of a shabby old straw-hatted schoolmaster who stammered out that he had been reading Mrs Fry's works for twenty years), or a visit to 'the sight that all loyal English hearts cannot fail to see with interest – Albert's palace'. Here, a guide had showed off (with conspicuous triumph, Elizabeth noted) the Prince's 'really splen-did apartments – we had no idea he lived in such state'. Miss Gurney, evidently, had been taking information from one of the many English periodicals that drew attention, in the year of the Queen's marriage, to the Coburgs' lack of funds and to the pre-dicted likelihood that young Albert's impoverished relations would seek a share of Albion's hard-earned wealth.

Weimar (visited on a side-trip with her father) sounds to have marked the low point for Elizabeth Gurney, a spirited young woman whose attempts at enthusiasm ('delightful public parks and gardens . . . trees looking so lovely . . .') fail to mask her impatience with the time-worn reminiscences about Goethe delivered by the ever-hospitable Duke and Duchess, whose grandeur offered scant compensation for the fact that the aged Duchess seemed unable to hear a word that Elizabeth and her father ventured to say. But solace was on hand. Berlin lay ahead, enriched by Charles de Bunsen's promised introductions to royal personages.

Elizabeth liked Berlin. Careful record was kept of her visits to various elegant grand ladies, in boudoirs filled with exotic caged birds and a wealth of Dresden china. Note was also made of every titled person that she met, ranging from King Friedrich Wilhelm IV down to an entire galaxy of Prussian princesses. Familiarity, however, soon bred a certain degree of knowing scorn: attending a final party for '300 of the first gentry in Berlin', including 'a vast concourse of Counts, Barons, etc.' Miss Gurney told her sister Richenda that she had been introduced to 'two princes and principes', but had not been fooled. These were small fry. They were definitely 'not Royal ones'.

Awe returned, as the English party were escorted around a Berlin prison, with 'Royalty' in attendance, 'and lastly our hon-oured aunt! Oh it was a sight! . . . My Aunt looked like a Princess herself in a beautiful full silk cloak that Papa has given her . . . and a pair of light gloves and her cap. She looks', Miss Gurney was proud to declare, 'fit for any court of Europe.' Descending at the jail's gates from a magnificent carriage that Miss Gurney had been invited to share with one of the apprehensive royal party (none of whom had ever stepped inside a prison before), Elizabeth was better pleased still to see that, while Mrs Fry attracted 'huge crowds', the family of the Prussian King had attracted very limited interest.

Of Kaiserswerth, disappointingly, Elizabeth Gurney reported next to nothing. She noted that the young deaconesses wore blue uniforms and white caps, that they visited the deserving poor, that they had sole care of their patients, and that some were being pre-pared to work abroad: no more was said. Mrs Fry's admiration for Kaiserswerth, however, was unstinting. Directly upon her return to England, a new scheme for the training of nurses was set in motion. Kaiserswerth was the acknowledged German model.

Elizabeth Gurney's lesser interest in Kaiserswerth may have related to the fact that she had other thoughts than nursing reform on her young mind. It was during her tour in Germany with Mrs Fry that Elizabeth was first introduced to two of the young de Bunsens; in August 1845, she married Ernest, the eldest son of Charles and Fanny. 'Seldom can it have happened in life to have a connexion in all its circumstances so entirely satisfactory,' a delighted Fanny exclaimed of her new daughter-in-law, two days after the ceremony; her satisfaction was completed in 1854, when the de Bunsens' second, Berlin-based son, Georg, carried off the daughter of another prosperous clan of high-minded and well-connected Norfolk Quakers. Nothing, it seemed, could now sever the bond that knit the de Bunsen family into the closely woven fabric of philanthropic enterprise in England and Germany.

Charles de Bunsen was greatly encouraged by Mrs Fry's response to Kaiserswerth. In 1842, when a restless young Florence Nightingale asked him what she should do with her life, he unhesitatingly advised her to visit the Fliedners in Germany. In 1846, de Bunsen took a further step. He presented Miss Nightingale with a Kaiserswerth year-book, a volume that provided the would-be nurse with a full account of the training methods and achievements of an exemplary German institute.

Florence, who was struggling to persuade the uneasy Nightingale family that nursing could provide an acceptable career to a young lady of her social background, was impressed by de Bunsen's accounts. 'There my heart is and there, I trust, will one day be my body,' she confided to a private book.[3] In 1850, still without family approval, Miss Nightingale slipped out of England for a two-week summer visit to the Fliedners' institute.

Almost fifty years later, reluctantly sending the British Museum an old pamphlet – her first publication – that she had written in praise of Kaiserswerth, the famous and feted Florence Nightingale scribbled a note of chilling disclaimer. True, the atmosphere of the place had been spiritually pure. An endearing attention had been paid to the celebration of sick children's birthdays. As to the institute itself, however, no word, in 1897, was sufficiently harsh. The nursing standards had been poor, the so-called deaconesses were peasants (Nightingale was never an egalitarian), the hospital itself was squalid, and its hygiene standard had been a disgrace.

Reading that sour pencilled note today, it seems strange that Nightingale had returned to Kaiserswerth for a second and much longer visit in 1851, when Fliedner had commended the excellence of the results she achieved in her nursing exams.

Nightingale's later view was coloured by intervening events. By 1897, Germany's demands (massive reparations were sought from France after the Franco-Prussian war of 1870–1) had turned Florence against what she had come to perceive as a greedy upstart empire. Back in the 1850s, while pleading with her mother to come over to Germany and visit the Fliedners herself, Nightingale had written that the only happiness she lacked at Kaiserswerth was the approval of her own parents.

The training that Florence Nightingale received at Kaiserswerth provided the foundation for her later work. The young deaconesses with whom she learned the basic principles of nursing care were among the first groups who were sent out from Kaiserswerth, from 1845 onwards, to work in London at the new German Hospital. Here, they provided, from the hospital's earliest days, the high standard of care that de Bunsen and two ardent Lutheran pastors had set out to secure for the poorest members of the German population in London.

It had been hard work. In 1841, Charles de Bunsen had promised his Lutheran visitors that he would do his best to secure support and funding for a hospital that would serve the German poor. In 1843, de Bunsen summoned his first planning committee to a City pub that was regularly used, back then, for business conferences. The first Duke of Cambridge (George III's affable seventh son) was invited to become president, in part because of his strong affection for Germany and in part because he promised to make full use of his royal connections to recruit patronage and funds. Plans were made for a visit to the chosen site on Dalston Lane, where the designated buildings were set in a large garden among tranquil and almost country-like surroundings. Its closeness to the German community huddled in the East End was noted and approved. Agreement was reached for a modest start, with room for just twelve beds. De Bunsen's recommendation for the immediate recruitment from Germany of six Kaiserswerth deaconesses was passed, as was the suggestion of an annual penny subscription for all sugar-bakers, in exchange for free treatment, beds and convalescent stays. Locals, of whatever nationality and creed, were to receive free day treatment.

Helped by the generosity of the Schröder family and by contributions from de Bunsen's friends in Prussia, the Ambassador was able to push matters forward at his usual energetic pace. On 15 October 1845, the date that marked the King of Prussia's birthday, the German Hospital formally opened its doors. Appropriately, for an institution strongly linked to the Protestant faith, its inauguration began with a choir of German children singing de Bunsen's favourite German hymn: 'Nun danket alle Gott'.

The German Hospital's history of success makes for impressive reading. By 1852, when Florence Nightingale was given a tour of the wards, the nursing team was headed by Dr Hermann Weber, an expert on the then deadly disease of tuberculosis and an outstanding physician whose future patients would include Queen Victoria and five of her prime ministers. Joseph Lister, early on in his career as a pioneer of modern surgery, was acting as an advisor. The number of patients who had been treated within the first year of the hospital's opening, so Nightingale was proudly informed, numbered 10,000.

Nightingale was visibly impressed by what she was shown and told. Hermann Weber, in turn, took note of his visitor's brisk suggestions for improvements in ventilation and sanitation. Miss Nightingale's recommendations – a reminder of how conscious she was of the importance of good sanitation before she ever went to the Crimea – were swiftly adopted as standard practice in a hospital that, within a decade, prided itself upon offering the most modern standard of health service that was available anywhere in Britain in Victorian times.

7

GERMANISING ENGLAND:
THE ALBERT EFFECT

(1840–61)

By 1852, when Miss Nightingale paid her visit to the German Hospital, Victoria had been married to Albert for twelve years and was the mother of seven children. Back in 1827, when she was only eight years old, the Princess was introduced by her uncle, William IV, to two eligible German candidates for her small hand. Following the rejection of the future King of Hanover and the future Duke of Cambridge by Victoria's mother and her advisors, William tried his hand with a further two Protestant princes. The King was not a lucky picker. The Princes of Orange were extremely plain, the seventeen-year-old Victoria reported saucily to her favourite uncle, Leopold of Saxe-Coburg: 'moreover, they look heavy, dull and frightened and are not at all prepossessing. So much for the *Oranges*, dear Uncle.'[1]

Victoria had been only one year old when her father died in 1820. Leopold, the swiftly widowed husband of Princess Charlotte and, from 1831 on, first King of the Belgians, was the young girl's beloved advisor. 'He is so clever, so mild and *so* prudent: he alone can give me good advice on *every thing*,' Victoria confided to her diary in 1836, the year before she became queen.

In 1836, Leopold, acting in quiet collusion with his brother Ernst, the Duke of Saxe-Coburg and Gotha, and their sister Victoire, the Duchess of Kent, brought a third brace of potential spouses – the Duke's two sons – over from Coburg for inspection by his firm-willed niece. Victoria, while evincing an immediate preference for seventeen-year-old Albert over his less handsome older brother, was not altogether in transports. Albert, plagued by a delicate stomach that did not take well to English food, was shy, stout and serious. Asked for her reaction, the spirited Princess grew cautiously non-committal.

In 1839, two years into his niece's reign, the Belgian King arranged a second visit for his two nephews, who arrived in England with a favorite greyhound, Eos. The dog was rangily delightful and the younger boy's own puppy fat had disappeared. Albert's blue eyes shone; his uniform was impeccably tailored; he composed music and played both the organ and piano with con-siderable skill; his heavily accented English – criticised by the German-speaking Victoria upon their previous encounter – had become almost as fluent as her own. Viewing the young couple as they danced quadrilles, rode across the park at Windsor and gazed admiringly at each other (Victoria's diary suggests that she was quite overcome by Albert's muscular physique), nobody was in doubt that a decision had been made and that the scheming Belgian King was taking credit for engineering the match.

Lord Melbourne, Victoria's first and well-loved prime minister, had edited, in his youth, Madame de Staël's great book about Germany. Neither the task nor the book had shaken his dislike for a country he knew only at second-hand. Germans smoked and drank in a way that would not be regarded as civilised in the court of a lady, he objected; surely (Melbourne was too canny to come straight out and say it) an English monarch ought to choose an English peer?

Melbourne's first objections were ill-founded, since Albert drank sparingly and disliked smoking. Subsequent hints to Victoria about the bookish Prince's lack of worldly knowledge (by which Melbourne meant sexual experience) were angrily dismissed. But the Prime Minister had his finger on the pulse of conservative opinion. In 1838, even before Albert's second visit to England, *Blackwood's* had set aside its usual affection for Germany to thunder disapproval against Albert, his brother and any other grasping Coburg cousin who might be presented at court. 'Neither one nor the other is destined to espouse England's Queen,' the newly Germanophobic *Blackwood's* proclaimed, 'for she cannot and dare not enter the portals of Hymen if a nation forbids the banns . . . For the Coburgs we have paid enough . . .'[2]

The magazine's booming threats did not alarm Victoria. On 10 February 1840, she married her chosen (and hastily naturalised) consort in the Chapel Royal of St James's Palace, watched over by the motherly eyes of the Dowager Queen Adelaide and the apprehensive ones of the Duchess of Kent. (The Duchess would now have to depend upon her nephew Albert's goodwill, if she wished to regain the powers that her daughter had briskly curtailed after her own coronation.) The wedding ceremony was not especially grand. The Queen's dress had a short and untheatrical train; the carriage chosen to convey the young couple from London to Windsor, in torrential rain, was old and shabby. The Tories, having vehemently opposed this German alliance, were punished by exclusion from the celebrations. *Blackwood's* took revenge by publishing a congratulatory ode that hailed the Queen's descent from a British-born father 'In form like to the Greek's Olympian God', while ignoring the existence of her lithe-limbed German-born groom.

Hostility to the Coburg family remained strong in conservative circles and showed up in the illustrated magazines like *Punch*, where mischievous ditties and unflattering cartoons focused the attention of readers upon Albert's lack of personal wealth and decidedly un-English costumes. The nation, charmed by a youthful romance, prepared to cheer; Albert's popularity increased when the swift arrival of baby Victoria ('Vicky', the Princess Royal) was followed by a bouncing Albert Edward ('Bertie', the future Edward VII). The seven infants who duly followed on were all equally welcome to a monarchist country that saw safety in large numbers.

Most probably, Victoria was being protective when she forbade a dismayed Albert to keep any Germans in his retinue. Strong though her own attachment to Germany would become during the years of her marriage, Victoria took care to keep it out of view. Publicly, only English was ever spoken; behind closed doors, the royal couple instantly reverted to German. Visiting Albert's home for the first time in 1845, Victoria expressed delight at being among people who could speak German wherever they pleased. To the English Queen, this seemed a great novelty.

The Rosenau, Albert's birthplace in Coburg, bewitched Victoria. A pretty castle, with a ruined tower attached and an English-styled garden spread around its walls, its size approximated to an English manor house. 'I have a feeling for our dear little Germany, which I cannot describe,' the Queen wrote to Leopold (who had also grown up at the Rosenau) after this first visit. 'I felt it at Rosenau so much. It is a something which touches me, and which goes to my heart, and makes me inclined to cry. I never felt at any other place that sort of pensive pleasure and peace which I felt there. I fear I like it almost too much.'[3]

The Queen adored 'dear old Coburg . . . the cradle of our family' and she later expressed the same tenderness for Darmstadt, the anglicised home of her second daughter Alice, Grand Duchess of Hesse.[4] These were the places that best represented her idea of a country comprised of small and friendly duchies that offered no competition to the wealth and power of her own island's empire.

While German was her first tongue, Victoria always felt herself to be an Englishwoman. Albert, however, remained profoundly

German, and never more so than in his determination to reform and educate the subjects of a less enlightened land. It was a mission that would bring – at a time when many of the Prince's most talented countrymen were seeking political asylum abroad – a wealth of German talent to bear upon the task of transforming and popularising the culture of England.

On a smaller scale of ambition, Albert assuaged bouts of homesickness by helping to design two of the royal couple's favourite royal retreats. At Osborne – a new and twin-towered Italianate palace on the Isle of Wight – Albert added only an approximation of the Saxon forest in which he and his brother Ernest had hunted boars in earlier years, and a Swiss chalet in which his children could practise housekeeping (a scheme which may have contributed to their lack of affection for the family's seaside residence).

Osborne was completed in 1851; at Balmoral, the family's new Scottish estate, Albert grew bolder. The original modest house was swiftly demolished and replaced by a German variant on the Scots baronial theme. Always dreaming of his beloved Rosenau, the Prince produced meticulously drawn plans for the narrow windows, pepper-pot turrets, tall towers and castellated gables that still confer an air of kitschy charm upon an oversized block of baronial granite. Striding the hills in a green and white 'Balmoral' kilt of his own design, Albert plotted his next step: should it be a new model dairy or a forest of specimen trees?

Embellishing royal residences was the amusement of the Prince's lighter hours. Albert's greater achievements were to reform the old-fashioned English educational system, to expose the overworked and underpaid industrial poor to a world of culture that had previously been almost inaccessible and to back the noble endeavours of such socially enlightened reformers and philanthropists as the Anglo-German Schröders and those East Anglian Quaker banking families from which Mrs Fry had emerged. Albert's advisor in these ambitious ventures was Baron Stockmar, a quiet Coburgian who shared the Prince's faith in the transforming powers of education. Less visible, but always active behind the scenes, was Stockmar's close friend, Charles de Bunsen. Like Stockmar, de Bunsen's hopes for international peace were founded upon Anglo-German friendship. 'If England and Germany remain united, what can the power of evil effect?' de Bunsen asked Stockmar at the dawning of 1852.[5] The answer, to both men, appeared self-evident.

In 1847, Albert was elected chancellor of Cambridge, a position that gave him the authority he needed to overhaul a shockingly outdated system. With Albert's discreet encouragement, the university syllabus was revised to introduce – at last – technology and the natural sciences. In 1851, the first papers on chemistry and physics were marked; the stranglehold of mathematics and the classics had finally been broken.

Where Cambridge led, Oxford followed. Virginia Woolf's grandfather, Sir James Stephen, was appointed, with Albert's prompting, as Oxford's first professor of modern history. A new chair of modern literature was created for the German-born Max Müller, a close friend of de Bunsen's who believed that Anglo-German power, which he unfortunately summarised as 'the supremacy of the Teutonic race', should be based upon the shared love of a literature that had 'almost grown into one'.[6]

Had it? German admiration for England was easily identified by Müller in the devotion of his compatriots to the writings of Thomas Macaulay (to whom the Cambridge chair in modern history had been first offered), while the novels of Dickens and Thackeray 'are awaited with the same impatience at Leipzig and Berlin as in London'. Seeking similar examples in England, however, Müller was reduced to praising the Anglophile spirit displayed in the writings of his friend Charles de Bunsen, before citing Thomas Carlyle and G. H. Lewes for their 'most successful' biographies of Schiller and Goethe.

Albert is best known for another aspect of his cultural mission: an exhibition in which he intended to unite the finest that England

and Germany could offer in a display of modern inventions, designs and technology. The site, a magnificent clear-walled hall designed by Joseph Paxton and situated in Hyde Park, was named the Glass Palace, or the Crystal Palace.

The success of Albert's project was instantly apparent. In the space of half a year, in 1851, over six million people attended the great house of wonders, drawn as much by the extraordinary, glittering building itself as by its contents. The Crystal Palace was one of the highlights of the mid-Victorian age. Its purpose – to honour technological progress and strengthen Britain's export market – was achieved in an atmosphere of patriotic pride in which Albert was finally granted some credit for his achievements. *Punch* magazine, laying aside its customary jeers at the Prince's foreign ways, declared Victoria's consort to be 'a regular brick'.

Albert's late-found popularity came at a price. Flattering portraits concealed what the new daguerrotypes could not hide. His face looked heavy with exhaustion. His hair was beginning to thin. He was plagued by stomach cramps. In 1851, Albert was still only thirty-two years old.

The Crystal Palace was dismantled in 1852 and moved from Hyde Park out to a hilltop at Sydenham in south London (where it survived as a concert hall, sports stadium and exhibition centre until 1936, when fire destroyed the original structure). From the proceeds of its initial sale, Prince Albert planned to purchase land to the west of Hyde Park and create an English version of Berlin's Museum Island: a concentrated area that would bring art, music, science and technology freely within the reach of all. Culture, in Albert's noble dream, would be given, without charge, to those least able to gain access to it.

A start was made. An early form of the South Kensington Museum, better known today as the Victoria and Albert, was opened by Queen Victoria in 1857. Four years later, at the age of forty-two, and with many of his greatest hopes (the unification of

Germany loomed large among them) still unfulfilled, the Prince Consort died of typhoid. Stress, overwork and a weak constitution contributed to a tragically premature death.

Eleven years after Albert's death, Victoria was still too distraught to utter the formal words with which she intended to open the vast gas-lit rotunda of the Royal Albert Hall of Arts and Sciences by which her husband's great educational project was to be commemorated. Weeping, she stood aside while her unloved oldest son took the platform. It was one of the few occasions on which Bertie sensed her gratitude. Bertie's kindness and intelligence counted for less, in Victoria's ever-critical eyes, than all those ways in which her indolent, lecherous and pleasure-loving son conspicuously failed to resemble his glorious father.

Albert's well-known enthusiasm for culture and progress made England a natural choice of refuge for victims of the repressive measures in Germany that followed on from the riots of 1848. England – as would be the case again almost a century later – offered a new home to some of the best teachers, musicians, physicians and architects of the time. The difficulty, as in the 1930s, was that a surplus of talent exceeded the available positions. Such success stories as Johannes Ronge's Hampstead kindergarten scheme, which had trained fifty teachers by 1859, were rare. Max Müller had been rewarded with a new chair in modern literature at Oxford in 1854, but the erudite Friedrich Althaus, having arrived in England in 1853, aged twenty-four, waited twenty-one years to attain the position of professor of German at University College, London, where his sympathetic referee was Thomas Carlyle. Johanna Kinkel, whose husband had been briefly imprisoned in the Berlin fortress of Spandau as a punishment for his revolutionary activities, spoke for the majority. 'We are now a whole colony of teachers in search of pupils . . .' she wrote in 1851, 'in a condition like that after a great shipwreck: each one of us grabs a plank and entrusts himself to the waves.'[7]

Doctors fared slightly better (Sir Hermann Weber had been appointed to head the new German Hospital soon after he fled to England in 1848), but music was arguably the field in which England reaped the richest harvest from among all these cultured newcomers. Music, as early British travellers to Germany had noted, came as naturally to that country as breathing; no hamlet was too small to be without its musical society; no town was too poor to forgo an opera house or concert hall. Performances were faithfully attended by locals of all classes, often surprising smart English visitors by their universal disregard for the English tradition of dressing-up. Shabbiness, at a German musical evening, came near to being a badge of pride.

Both Albert and the older brother who became Ernst II, Duke of Saxe-Coburg and Gotha, had grown up in that world of ardent musicianship. Young Felix Mendelssohn, visiting Buckingham Palace by royal request in 1842, was naïvely astonished by the Prince's proficiency. Richard Wagner, paying a frustrating visit to London in 1855 to conduct a summer season for the London Philharmonic only to find his work rated below that of Mendelssohn and Meyerbeer, was solaced when the royal family attended one of his concerts. Victoria soothed Wagner's injured pride considerably when she expressed the rapture with which she had listened, that night, to the overture to *Tannhäuser*.

The royal couple's fondness for music certainly did nothing to dampen the warmth with which newly arrived musicians, composers and conductors were welcomed and put to prompt use in a country that stood in dire need of their gifts. The year 1858 marked the first concert given by Manchester's new orchestra under the German Charles Hallé. August Manns flourished his baton over the new Crystal Palace Orchestra (1855–1900); Otto Goldschmidt led the Bach Choir (1875–85), while Wilhelm Ganz, in 1874, took control of the New Philharmonic Society.

Karl Klindworth, the Hanover-born pupil of Liszt and an ardent promoter of Wagner, was another musical exile who came to London (in 1854) in search of freedom from repression and censorship. A music teacher during the fourteen years he spent in the British capital, Klindworth would later adopt a little English girl, Winifred Williams, and marry her off, in due course, to Wagner's oldest son, Siegfried. Ford Madox Ford's German father, Franz Hüffer, arriving in London in 1869, was a more directly influential figure in his role as music critic of *The Times*, a podium from which Hüffer missed no chance to promote Wagner's works to an increasingly receptive English audience.

The arrival in England of a number of talented German architects in the mid-century provided Albert with a team of willing collaborators in his plans for what later became known as Albertopolis, or Albert's City, in the west of London. The great Karl Friedrich Schinkel had conducted a brisk inspection tour of English industrial sites when he was scouting out new ideas, back in the 1820s. In 1850, Albert was enchanted to learn of the arrival in London of Schinkel's acknowledged heir, a man whose search for inspiration in the classical past chimed with Albert's own scholarly interests.

Gottfried Semper, driven out of Dresden for his participation in constructing barricades during the riots of 1848, had created some of that exquisite city's greatest buildings, including the legendary opera house in which many of his friend Richard Wagner's works received their premiere. His arrival in England was well timed. Swiftly recruited to create international exhibition spaces within the new Crystal Palace, Semper went on to draw up the preliminary designs for the South Kensington Museum. Offered a regular post as a professor at Albert's new Government School of Design, Semper's love of combining multicoloured brickwork with Renaissance design is still visible on the magnificent exteriors of the row of Victorian museums that march west from the Victoria and Albert's grand facade. Semper's passion for polychromy reached its zenith, however, in the Albert Hall, built by English architects as a loving tribute to the great German architect and based upon the majestic proportions of Semper's own iconic opera house in Dresden.

The swift expansion of the German Hospital contradicts any supposition that England offered a comfortable refuge for Albert's newly arrived compatriots. Many immigrants were employed in dreadful work, lived in extreme poverty and died young. Nevertheless, nourished in their German homeland upon book-learned visions of a kindly England of prosperity and benevolence, they clung to that persistent ideal. It was during the 1850s that England first saw the emergence of a new class of Anglophile émigrés who (in Ian Buruma's apt words) 'spoke English to one another, ate roast beef on Sundays, sent their sons to public schools and listened to Beethoven and Wagner'. More Anglicised than any Englishman outside the pages of the Dickens in whom they placed their trust, these carefully dressed citizens of a growing number of Little Germanys set in British cities (Manchester, for example, had 153 German firms and three Lutheran churches by 1870) admired a *Boys' Own* ideal of their new homeland. Their idealised Englishman was 'fastidious in his dress, gentlemanly in his manners and imbued with a unique sense of fair play'.[8]

The English were, on the whole, kindly hosts. Their civility was made easier by the evident gratitude of a German people who – in the admiring words of Richard Monckton Milnes (a generous benefactor to exiles from Germany, the country that had helped to educate him) – were among 'the most instructed, the most literate, the most thoughtful people in the world'.[9]

All was not sweetness and light. Albert had striven hard to improve a country that he regarded as educationally backward, but England did not wish to be seen as standing in need of improvements from abroad. It suited the requirements of national pride that German Albert, a blue-eyed scholarly Saxon, should be quietly outshone by a home-grown Saxon monarch: Alfred the educator, first king of the Anglo-Saxons and founder of the English language. German Albert, in this reading of the past, was simply carrying on the age-old traditions that had been established by an English king.

By the time that Albert had been married to Victoria for five years, the image of Alfred the Great (rather than Albert the Good) was ubiquitous. Tennyson preferred Arthur (the stories were better); Dickens, however, took care to see that *A Child's History of England*, appearing in the 1850s, had its scarlet cover stamped with the image of young Alfred reading to his mother. In 1845, when a memorial figure was being picked to stand outside the new Houses of Parliament, Elizabeth I had only one royal competitor: Alfred.

The rediscovery of England's cultural foundations in the leadership of a wise but heroic Alfred formed part of a sudden surge of interest in Anglo-Saxondom. An offshoot of that slightly weird enterprise was the establishment of a new and (in retrospect) troubling endeavour to link England to Germany. When some eighty funeral urns were disinterred near Stuttgart during the 1840s, John Mitchell Kemble, an antiquarian member of the famous family of English actors, was quick to connect the findings to others that had been unearthed near Eye, in Suffolk. A similarity in the relics (combs, tweezers, musical instruments) provided sufficient grounds for Kemble to assert that they offered incontrovertible evidence of a single racial family. Kemble's *The Saxons in England* (1849) was dedicated to Victoria with one eye unwinkingly fixed upon her husband's Saxon origins.

Ruled over by a monarch who was known to adore and revere her Saxon consort, Victorian antiquarians experienced the intoxicating sensation of actually helping to influence popular taste. And there was no denying Alfred's popularity. By the late 1850s, souvenir mugs bearing Alfred's features were churned out more regularly than those adorned with the face of any modern monarch. G. F. Watts won £500 for a project to decorate Westminster's new palace with an inspiring image of Alfred at war. Theatre-goers could take the new craze seriously, with Sheridan Knowles's *Alfred the Great*, or for laughs, with an 1859 burlesque at London's Olympic, entitled *Alfred, or the Last Minstrel*.

Alfred was everywhere, and thanks to the new vogue for that shadowy figure, Germany and England could shamelessly unite in celebration of the common heritage that they both, back in the middle of the nineteenth century, so ardently wished to find.

'We are Teuts ourselves,' *Blackwood's* had boasted to its readers in August 1841, in an article on German literature that praised Thomas Carlyle as 'a breathing incarnation of the modern Teutonic spirit', before declaring Carlyle to be 'something better than a German: his sturdiness, his raciness, his dramatic breadth of brush, seem thoroughly English'. Thirty years on, such distinctions could be swept aside. 'Engle, Saxon and Jute all belonged to the same low German branch of the Teutonic family,' John Green announced in *A Short History of the English People*: '. . . it is from the union of all of them, when its conquest was complete, that the English people has sprung'.

In 1874, when Green's confident declaration first appeared in a now long-neglected history of England, the new German Empire had been in place for a mere three years. Even so, a future emperor, Wilhelm II, the fifteen-year-old son of England's Princess Royal and Germany's Crown Prince, could already sense that he united the two countries in his very veins. A new mythology was beginning to find a dangerous form. From beneath the glowing vision of a past united through the myths of Beowulf, Tacitus and the Norse sagas from which Wagner had woven his apocalyptic vision of a master race, there had surfaced the ominous concept of two pure, strong and manly countries, linked by blood and destined to rule the world as one Teutonic supremacy.

8

TRAVELS IN A FOREIGN LAND

(1840-60)

Victoria was not the only woman to be charmed by a country that – despite the emergence in 1838 of the first of the raffishly elegant gambling casinos where a sharp-eyed George Eliot found a model for Gwendolen Harleth in Byron's great-niece, staking her future on the tables at Bad Homburg – offered quieter travellers the chance to stroll through the riverside meadows at Baden-Baden or ride a pony up into the softly wooded surrounding hills.

Some visitors settled for a restorative spa visit; others, travelling along the Rhine, identified with the enchanting 'thou' whose absence Byron had lamented in his famous fourth canto of *Childe Harold* as he gazed upon those same Rhine castles 'alone'. That the 'thou' had been the half-sister whose intimacy with the poet had caused his wife to leave home was an issue that a Victorian lady travelling to Germany preferred to overlook.

There were other options. English women who wished to combine a German holiday with self-improvement could emulate Anna Jameson, a sharp-tongued and formidably clever Irish art historian who, besides enjoying conversational skirmishes with

A. W. Schlegel and Ludwig Tieck (described by Jameson with uncustomary reverence as 'the literary colossus of Dresden'), had herself been escorted around the new Munich palace of Ludwig I by the King's favourite architect, Leo von Klenze. Mrs Jameson's enthusiastic impressions of the massive images drawn from an inspirational past with which Ludwig was adorning the city of Munich were the first to reach England.

Mrs Jameson, travelling through Germany in the 1830s, appointed herself as a go-between ambassador for culture. Having decided that both England and Germany were woefully underinformed about one another's art, she set out to improve matters. In England, she acted almost as an agent for the brilliant Dresden-born illustrator Moritz Retzsch; in Germany, she raised awareness of the work of William Blake. The German art historian Gustav Waagen was Mrs Jameson's admiring ally in these gallant enterprises; a young John Ruskin was among those who benefited from her pioneering comparisons between the Germanic approach to art (broad, expansive, myth-loving), and the English (detailed, figurative, socially nuanced).

Anna Jameson and the intrepid Elizabeth Fry were exceptions to the rule. Women visiting the Rhine and its neighbouring spas in the mid-nineteenth century were more often of the conventional kind addressed by Mary Shelley in a travel book that was published in 1844.

Mary's only previous encounter with Germany had been in 1814, when she, Shelley and her step-sister Claire Clairmont had run away to Switzerland before, running out of money, they limped home again by way of the Rhine. Returning as a middle-aged widow who had buried her disreputable past (both as the lover of a married man and the author of that shocking novel *Frankenstein*), Mary was eager to sound respectable. Demurely, she dwelt upon the charms of Heidelberg and the prettily painted tobacco pipes that she privately detested; sincerely, she praised the

German practice of granting free access for all to such glorious galleries as the one that she had visited at Dresden. Inevitably, writing for an audience of sketchbook-carrying lady travellers, her finest phrases were lavished upon the glories of the Rhine and 'the diorama ... of tower-crowned crag and vine-clad hills – of ruined castle, fallen abbey, and time-honoured battlements'.

Gushing though the language sounds, Mary was writing from her heart. She had grumbled, along the way, about dowdy locals, suffocating feather beds and unsatisfactory washing facilities. Revisiting the scenes of her young and bolder self – while reading familiar lines from *Childe Harold* (especially familiar to Mary, who had transcribed large chunks of the original poem for their author) – she was carried back to the extraordinary summer that she and Shelley had spent in Byron's company, captivated by his charm and enthralled by his friendship. Idly, she promised herself to return, and to spend a whole long summer tarrying beside the Rhine, long enough 'to penetrate the ravines, to scale the heights, to linger among the ruins, to hear still more of its legends, and visit every romantic spot'.[1]

A perfect candidate for the Mary Shelley type of travel book was Miss Mary Wescomb, visiting Germany with her sister Kitty and their widowed mother in 1843, and trailing just behind a similar party. Mrs Wescomb's friend and fellow widow, Lady Byron (she had married the poet's cousin and successor) was conducting her two very handsome and very bored sons on a tour of the picturesque scenes enshrined in their famous relation's verse. The Wescomb girls had made friends with the Byron boys back in England; the constant hope of an encounter with young George and Fred glints like silver through the pages of Mary's neatly penned journal.

Aged seventeen and eager for romance – 'who knows who I *may* meet abroad' – Miss Mary was less impressed by the Rhine scenery ('really frightful ... I expected it all to be much wilder') and the aggravations of a country where 'natives are stupid and can't understand their mother tongue' than by the excitement of running away from two saucy German officers who had laughingly pursued her at full speed along the narrow passages of a Rhineside inn.[2]

Meeting up with the Byrons at last, at Lake Geneva, poor Mary could hardly believe her ears when George and Fred announced that they thought Byron's celebrated lakeside residence, the Villa Diodati, was terribly dull. 'The Byrons have hated their tour,' Mary dolefully recorded. '[They] say they mean to return to England on Monday.'

The story does not, however, end quite there. Mary Wescomb's older sister, Lucy, married George Byron the following year, while Mary herself, aged twenty-five, married Fred. Two strong-willed, wealthy sisters for two impoverished brothers: Shakespeare might have approved the neat resolution to an improbable English comedy.

Few Germans were rich enough to take leisurely holidays in England in the mid-nineteenth century. Britain offered herself, rather, as a refuge for exiles and as a model for Germany's future as a nation state, to be led – as every Prussian confidently imagined – by mighty Prussia herself.

Theodor Fontane, a 25-year-old Prussian apothecary, made his first visit in 1844. A personable young man with curling hair and a heart-shaped face, Fontane had no trouble in making friends in England; soon, he was invited to spend a day out of London in the home of one Mr Burford, a kind-hearted stranger whose evening of family entertainments inspired one of the most delightful scenes in Fontane's *Ein Sommer in London*.

First (as Fontane told it) there had come a waltz, briskly plunked out on the Burfords' square piano by the lady of the house, and followed by Mr Burford's tuneful rendering of 'Black Eyed Susan' and 'The Girl I Left Behind Me'. Fontane, invited to respond with a German song, made one up on the spot and, following it up by a dramatic German rendering of the dagger speech from *Macbeth,* was greeted by an explosive torrent of giggles. Stepping forward to recite Shakespeare in the correct and English fashion, the Burfords' eldest boy accompanied his own speech with fierce looks and 'terrible gestures . . . [but] the family looked very proud and said that this was the style of Macready'. Fontane, courteously applauding, decided that he preferred his own performance.

Bed beckoned, but not before the honoured guest had been invited to pen a few suitable lines (his quotations from Byron and Young were well received) in the family album. Bidding Mr Burford goodnight, Fontane described his host as fulfilling his own concept of the perfect English gentleman: kind, hospitable and modest, his face marked 'with an expression of inexhaustible benevolence'.

Fontane's account of his second visit, in 1852, is written in such an easy, natural style – 'Scarcely two hours and already I was sitting in my favourite spot, up next to the bus driver' – that it's hard to distinguish artistic contrivance from pure spontaneity. The charm of the writer's descriptions – whether of snugly curling up beside a sea-coal fire with a kettle whistling on the hob or taking a day trip down the Thames – softens his harsh observation of a tougher and more mercantile climate than he had encountered eight years earlier. All exiles and emigrants are unwelcome in England now, Fontane warns his Prussian readers, since all present a threat to the overworked and underpaid English working class. Back in Prussia, a man is innocent until proven guilty; in England, in 1852, every foreigner is treated as a potential suspect.

Seeking an example of the exile's fate, Fontane describes his visit to the home of a formerly prosperous German businessman, now fallen on hard times and living with a daughter, Miss Jane, who has been reduced to taking work as a governess. Standing in for the host of cultured German women who have been forced to take what work they can find in straitened times, Miss Jane describes her new life. At dawn, she crosses the sleeping city by bus, to suffer the mockery of the pampered children of London's prosperous merchant class, before trekking home after dark. Tears fill her tired blue eyes as Fontane reminisces with her father about the old Germany she still remembers, a kindlier land, one of ease and courtesy. 'We could go there ourselves,' Miss Jane whispers to her father; saddened, Fontane joins in the pretence.

Irresistibly animated in his English prose-sketches from daily life, Fontane always had to remember that the press agency for whom he was working had required him to take notes on England's strength. How deep did national loyalty within such a country run? How well would her people protect her against invasion?

Fontane himself felt torn. Visiting Battle Abbey and imagining himself to stand on the very spot at which William, Duke of Normandy, had won his famous victory, he decided that England could never win a battle against Prussia. 'She is like the ancient Teutons. Her lances look threatening, but a man has only to puncture once the defended ring to find her vulnerable.' Just for a moment, Fontane's prose rings out cold as Prussian steel: 'Like Samson, England can be shorn.' But then, looking out across the evening fields to glimpse – with an artist's eyes – a circling flock of doves, the writer changes his tone. Here, cattle are lowing in the meadows; there, a fish starts up from a quiet pond: how could anybody wish for bloodshed in this land?[3]

Fontane's employers were satisfied with his investigations. In 1857, he was despatched to England yet again, to act as a semi-official informant to the Prussian government. Germany had united herself as an empire by the time that Fontane, aged fifty-seven in 1878, finally gave up journalism to commence on the series of novels for which he is best known – although not in England, where few of his fictions have yet been translated and only one is widely known: the haunting masterpiece *Effi Briest*.

English women became nervous about visiting Germany after the widespread uprisings of 1848. Most of the British travellers who did visit Germany during the 1850s were sturdy males: George Meredith (whose fictional hero Harry Richmond attends a German university); Charles Kingsley, who rewarded himself after ecstatic daily rambles with generous amounts of Rhenish hock (a bargain, he thought, at 9d. a bottle); and Thomas Carlyle, who paid his first visit to Germany in 1852 to tour the battlefields of his prodigious hero, Frederick the Great.

The publishers John Murray, keen to peddle their new series of guides to travellers on the Continent, did their best to reassure and allure. The Germans, they noted in an 1849 *Handbook to Northern Germany*, 'are a people who may be called our first cousins (cousins-German) whose character, manners and language more nearly approach our own than those of any other nation . . .'[4] Truth was stretched further still in 1858: English visitors to Germany had no need to study a language so closely linked to their own, *Murray's* announced. They could expect, moreover, to be greeted as persons of rank: 'Mr Count', perhaps, or even 'Your Grace'.

Charles Dickens, at whose London door Fontane observed his German compatriots queuing up for a chance to shake the great man's hand, never visited their country himself. His enthusiasm for German habits shines forth, however, in the words of Mr Bendigo Buster, addressing readers of the fortieth issue of Dickens's in-house magazine, *Household Words*. 'Look how well they educate their children,' Mr Buster declares, 'while in England forty-five out of a hundred of 'em can't read and write. That's what I call being practical.'*

Dickens made use of a whole platoon of keen amateurs to provide contributory sketches to his magazine. When a young goldsmith named William Duthie announced that he was planning to work his way across Germany while making nightly use of the guild hostels (*Herbergen*), a commission was promptly given. Duthie was presumably warned how the arrangement would work: he would

* England's literacy rate in 1850 was 52 per cent. Prussia's was 85 per cent.

supply the raw material from which Dickens himself would shape the piece.

Duthie was not the sort of traveller who was going to mind whether he was addressed as a gentleman of rank. In place of the familiar story of fashionable tourists visiting spas, museums and palaces, Duthie planned to describe the street-life realm of a journeyman.

William Duthie crossed to Hamburg on a trading schooner. Sauntering through narrow cobbled lanes that stank of river mud, he seemed to have entered the world of folk stories and myth. A stout farmer strutted past him in buckled shoes and a silver-buttoned jacket; a smiling country girl marched along in a short petticoat, her long blonde plaits braided up with scarlet bows that matched her knitted red stockings. It felt as if he had stepped back a century, and Duthie was frankly charmed.

Attending an evening performance of *Hamlet* at Hamburg's Stadt Theatre, Duthie relished Hamlet's meditation on the ease of killing his hated step-father ('Now might I do it pat . . .'), a scene that English censors considered too distressing for the stage. The curtain came down at 9.30 p.m.; by 10 p.m., an officious night-watch had cleared the streets. Tracking down the nearest *Herbergen*, an astonished Duthie tumbled into a hot cellar bursting with dancers of both sexes: 'such a scene of shuffling, whirling, shouting and pipe-smoking could scarcely be seen elsewhere'.[5] This was delightful: Duthie prolonged his stay in Hamburg for three months and announced himself in love with a country that provided operas and plays every night of the week, that allowed dancing and gambling on a Sunday and that, moreover, always offered a welcome in some snug nocturnal cavern for a song, a kiss and 'an abominable medley of waltz, smoke, wine and lotto . . .'

Duthie's account of Germany was not all so favourable. Apprentices were forced to travel for a prescribed number of years and the *Herbergen*, which were were seldom so jolly as in Hamburg, kept guildworkers apart from other men as efficiently as a system of apartheid. In contrast to England, no educational institutes served the needs of a German workman. 'His Guild is his state.'

One fact was inescapably apparent: Prussia, by 1858, the year of Duthie's journey, had become a force with which to reckon – and she knew it. Visiting Berlin, Duthie noted how the great military statue of Field Marshal Blücher on the Unter den Linden was lavishly 'crowned with laurels on every returning anniversary of the well remembered day, the 18th of June'. An ominous appetite for war hung in the air and the swaggering Prussian soldiers with whom Duthie spoke were in no doubt about who would win it. 'Prussia', he wrote in an uneasy sentence that Dickens chose not to censor, 'has progressed like a giant . . .'

The Prince Consort, preparing in 1858 to bestow Vicky, his favourite and most highly educated child, upon Prussia's future king, harboured no such fears. Albert's dream was of a progressive Germany, unified under Prussia, protected by constitutional law and allied to a powerful England. With the combination of England's invincible navy and Prussia's mighty army, there was no reason to suppose that the two great Protestant tribes of German cousins could not unite their interests. Albert's vision was to be embodied in the marriage of England's Princess Royal to the handsome, soldierly and devoted Fritz Hohenzollern.

9

THE EAGLE AND THE LION

(1858–88)

Not everybody shared the Prince Consort's enthusiasm for a closer alliance with Prussia, or for his vision of a united and reformed Germany, led by that vast northern kingdom. Richard Monckton Milnes spoke only for an informed minority in England when he used an article about Prussia to ask, in 1846, what remained wanting to 'the healthy social state of this great people? We answer, and they answer – Political development under Liberal Institutions.'[1] A country that followed the democratic lines of British liberalism would be a preserver of peace, Milnes argued, and a valuable Protestant ally for Britain in Europe.

There was another view, represented by *The Times* and by Lord Palmerston, a politician whose low opinion of Prussia's value to England was based upon its traditional deference to Vienna and the weak leadership, over a period of twenty-one years (1840–61), of a king, Friedrich Wilhelm IV, whose terror of offending Austria had played a strong part in his decision to resist unification and the imperial crown, back in 1848. For this group, including those whose livelihoods were suddenly threatened by an army of industrious German refugees, Prussia was neither to be favoured above the three Western powers (Russia, Austria and France) with whom Britain had shared the leaders' table since the Congress of Vienna (1815), nor to be trusted to lead a unified Germany.

Punch, a newish magazine specialising in inoffensive cartoons, spoke for England's sizeable anti-Prussian party in mid-September 1855, when one of its writers remarked that a Prussian eagle had been seen circling with suspicious intent over the Queen's dove-cote at Balmoral, ready to pounce and carry off a prize. *Punch*, clearly, expected Victoria to shoo this bold predator off the turrets of her Scottish home.

Time, together with the spectacle of true, spontaneous love, would end by softening even hardened opponents to an Anglo-Prussian match for the Queen's first and cleverest child.

Seldom have the desires of a young couple complied so pleasingly with the wishes of their parents as in the case of Vicky, England's Princess Royal, and Fritz (an abbreviation of Friedrich), the Crown Prince of Prussia.* Fritz was tall, principled, brave and good-looking; daguerrotypes do scant justice either to the intelligence that gleamed from Vicky's deep-blue eyes, or to her radiant smile and porcelain-pale skin. Visiting Balmoral in 1855, the young Prince was as captivated by Vicky's appealing manner as he was awed by her fluent German and well-informed interest in his country (Albert had been the chief tutor of a daughter who adored him, and who would never stop trying to live up to her father's unfeasibly high expectations). Encouraged by an ADC (Aide-de-Camp), Colonel Helmuth von Moltke, who had an English wife of his own, Fritz wasted no time in approaching Vicky's parents.

Permission was granted, but marriage, since Vicky was not yet fifteen years old, would have to wait. Nevertheless, loitering beside

---

* The term 'crown prince' is used here for convenience; Fritz did not officially become the royal heir until his father was crowned King of Prussia in 1861.

the young Princess on a hill walk around the Balmoral estate, Fritz managed to pluck and offer a sprig of heather, together with the hope, sealed by a first kiss, that Vicky would come to Prussia, not just for a visit, but for 'always'. The Princess blushed, but did not commit herself. Learning of her parents' approval, and already enchanted by Fritz's handsome face and loving looks, Vicky grew bolder, throwing herself into the young man's arms with what her approving mother described as the ardency of a grown woman.[2] An engagement was formally announced the following year.

In Prussia, the news pleased Fritz's parents more than it did Otto von Bismarck, not yet the all-dominating political figure, but one who was plotting hard, and who wanted Russia, not England, as Prussia's ally. The Princess Royal sounded to be an intelligent and warm-hearted young woman; the problem foreseen by an exceptionally wily politician was that a dutiful daughter would be more likely to take advice from her commanding mother than to listen to Prussian advisors. 'If our future Queen ... remains even only partly English,' Bismarck wrote to a friend, 'I can see our Court in danger of being surrounded by English influence.'[3]

Arrangements, despite Bismarck's forebodings, rolled smoothly forward. In the winter of 1857–58, with grim news still reaching Britain from besieged Lucknow, the prospect of a royal wedding offered welcome relief to the war-weary English press. Thankfully, The Times turned from stories of bloodshed and starvation in northern India to expressing its distaste for the greed of Queen Victoria's nastiest uncle, the elderly King Ernest of Hanover, who mysteriously chose the very month of his great-niece's wedding to lay claim to a royal hoard of jewellery and plate, treasure that the former Duke of Cumberland suspected might otherwise form part of Vicky's dowry. (King Ernest got his way; Vicky, en route to Berlin, was regaled with a Hanoverian feast presented on a splendid gold dinner service that had been destined for her own new home.) Turning to a more pleasing subject, The Times announced that the Princess would be housed within 'a splendid suite of apartments in the Royal Schloss' on the Unter den Linden. Fortunately, the paper's correspondent was unaware that, since the shabby and thriftily managed royal palace did not yet run to electricity and gas, Vicky's maid would be dressing her for state occasions by the light of a single candle.

A young German girl was among the excited observers of the elaborate procedures that occupied centre stage in London during the three weeks running up to Vicky's wedding on 25 January 1858. Countess Wally von Hohenthal (christened Walburga) was the daughter of a widowed Saxon diplomat. Exiled to England for a year after flogging a man who had dared to impugn his sister's virtue, Wally's father despatched an English governess, Miss Page, to educate his motherless child, back in Saxony.

Five years of harsh schooling (Caroline Page shared her employer's belief in the power of the whip) gave young Wally an excellent grounding in English literature, language and history. Aged nineteen in 1858, she was eminently qualified to become chief lady-in-waiting to the future Crown Princess; the post, although unpaid, provided Wally with a personal carriage, a permanent seat in the royal box and, as part of the bridegroom's wedding train, a free journey to England.

Wally liked Vicky from the start; she was as struck by the Princess's graceful manner as by her relish for a hearty breakfast of port and oysters. Vicky showed evidence of a strong personality, but this – so Wally decided – was just as well; Fritz, while courteous, kind and good, lacked confidence.

Indulged at court ('Everybody is delightful to me and I am as spoilt as I have never been before'), Wally considered Windsor Castle to be as romantic as anything she had read about in Walter Scott. The cold, however, was terrible; Wally was baffled – as were all German visitors – by the Queen's passion for a bracing gust of fresh air in every room. No wonder that the court ladies loved

87

wearing the cosy tartan jackets that were all made, as Wally couldn't refrain from complacently recording, back in Germany.[4]

Tartans were to the fore on the wedding day, with Vicky's brothers smartly arrayed in kilts, sporrans and plaids. Wally, watching from one of the best pews in the Chapel Royal at St James's Palace, was more interested in observing the heartiness with which Fritz wrung his new father-in-law's hand, while a crimson-cheeked Vicky curtseyed repeatedly, almost to the ground, before her smiling mother.

The whole affair, to the eyes both of young Wally and an appreciative crowd of reporters, had something of a fairy tale about it. Travelling on to Windsor, the smiling young couple were surrounded by a group of eager schoolboys queuing to pull their carriage uphill, with thirty in the lead and twice as many pushing behind. Fritz, praised again and again in the papers for his honest, manly face, clear blue eyes and splendid height – he towered above his tiny bride – was presented with the Order of the Garter and looked delighted, while a splendid ball held that week at the Prussian Legation enabled Charles de Bunsen's successor, Albrecht von Bernstorff, to demonstrate how thoroughly this match was approved in Germany. (Prussian press reports naturally declared that the Bernstorff ball had outshone all England's endeavours.)

One small mishap blotted the arrangements. In Berlin, a new ambassador from England painstakingly wreathed portraits of the young couple with orange blossom, unaware that myrtle was Germany's wedding symbol. Ambassador Bloomfield's guests were puzzled and unimpressed.

The Ambassador's faux pas was reported by *The Times*. Further embarrassments could not be risked, and Victoria and Albert made swift arrangements for a trusted attaché to be diverted from Vienna to Berlin. Cultivated, intelligent and sympathetic to Albert's political goals, the imposingly tall Robert Morier was to prove a valuable chess piece in the game of European diplomacy. Well placed to act as a political observer, he was expected to keep a watchful eye on the young couple who – it was reasonable to assume – would soon preside over a country that took England for its model. (For how, back in 1858, could anybody have predicted that Fritz's father would still be on the throne in thirty years time?)

It was a pity that Vicky's parents did not delegate a little more of their power to clever Mr Morier. Queen Victoria was a brilliant spymaster, but – most especially where her children were concerned – she lacked tact. A robust faith in British supremacy led to a stream of reminders to Vicky, newly established at the stiff, old-fashioned Prussian court, concerning her duty to maintain English traditions, to retain English servants and to behave – in short – in a way that was guaranteed to offend the family and country to which she now belonged.

Advising was one thing; in despatching an English midwife and nurse to Prussia, together with instructions to give her first grandchild a traditional English christening, Victoria took a step too far.

Wilhelm II, as he later became, was born a year and a day after his parents' marriage. Willy himself later blamed the English doctors and, by cruel implication, his English-born mother, for the difficult extraction that resulted in the paralysis of his left arm. Vicky, with equal injustice, blamed the German doctor, Eduard Martin, without whom, after he was called in at a late stage, both mother and child would probably have died.

Vicky, while slow to recover her strength, matched Fritz in the affection she lavished on their newborn son. Victoria, while disapproving (baby-worship was not her forte), shared Vicky's distress about the harsh methods that were vainly employed to rectify Wilhelm's defective arm: aged four, the child was encased within an iron corset with bars and a fixed helmet that was intended to strengthen his neck. Vicky shed tears; Wilhelm, while stoic, would later react violently, displaying an uncontrollable – and entirely unpredictable – temper, bewildering rages that came and went as swiftly as a shower of rain. This troubling volatility would become a lifelong hallmark of Wilhelm's complicated personality.

Victoria had shown herself to be an interfering mother; Albert, when it came to keeping his distance from Prussian politics, proved equally tactless.

Wilhelm the elder (Fritz's father) had been reluctantly forced into the position of Prussia's regent in 1858, the year during which his brother, the King, suffered a debilitating stroke. Ready to welcome a new daughter-in-law, the new Regent was less charmed when Albert appointed himself as an informal counsellor, one whose well-intended interference (expressed in the form of copious and rather commanding letters) would simplify Bismarck's route to power. Wilhelm himself was staunchly conservative in his views; he distrusted the democratic liberalism espoused by Albert and sturdily carried forward by Vicky and by Fritz. To Wilhelm, it seemed clear that all Prussia required was a programme to ensure, in times of crisis, the speedier mobilisation of troops.

The gap between Wilhelm and Albert was made dispiritingly apparent in 1861 when, in advance of his coronation at Königsberg, Wilhelm announced his wish for a feudal ceremony of homage. Albert was appalled, as were the anti-Prussian correspondents for *The Times*. Vicky, while disapproving, prudently reserved her opinions for the long and regular letters that would pass between her and her mother until the very ends of both their lives.

Three months after the accession of Wilhelm I, Vicky lost the beloved father on whom she still relied for her best counsel. Albert had been her oracle; his death in December 1861 confirmed the Prince Consort's eldest child in her determination to carry his ideals forward in Prussia, and to press for the liberal constitutions that were so dear to Fritz and herself – and so hateful to the King.

Shrewd, passionate and invincibly stubborn, Vicky's misfortune was to be ranged, from this time on, against Bismarck: a man who distrusted England and who therefore regarded Vicky herself as an inconvenient menace.

Bismarck's rise to absolute power was hastened by the feebleness of the new King. In 1862, thwarted in his plans for army reform and only a year into his reign, Wilhelm I threatened to abdicate. Vicky urged her husband to grasp this opportunity – he had strong support – to seize the Prussian throne for himself. Gentle, soldierly Fritz, overcome by the spectacle of his father in tears, backed away from any such calculated act. He could not bring himself to do it.

Here was the moment, in late September 1862, four years after their marriage, which appeared to determine the fate of Vicky and her husband. Acting against the wishes of a wife, Augusta, whom he disliked, and an heir whom he mistrusted, King Wilhelm allowed Bismarck to persuade him that abdication was unnecessary. Prussia, if placed in the proper hands, those of a loyal representative of the King, could be lovingly defended and strengthened. Newly appointed by a grateful Wilhelm as Minister President – Prussia's nearest equivalent to a prime minister – Bismarck was at last in a position to create the empire of blood and iron that was his proclaimed objective. His plans included no concessions to the gentle progress towards German unification envisaged by Vicky and Fritz.

One comfort was on hand. Vicky had conspired with her mother to arrange a German marriage for Princess Alice, the sister to whom she felt most attached. Victoria herself had been an occasional charmed guest of the Grand Duke of Hessen-Darmstadt when she visited Wolfsgarten, the family's beloved woodland hunting lodge, lying fifteen miles outside the sleepy little medieval town of Darmstadt. Prince Louis, the Grand Duke's burly heir, had courted Alice during visits to Scotland, a land for which the young people's shared fondness helped to obscure the fact that they had little else in common. Alice, like her older sister, was a conscientious girl; she had used her excellent nursing skills to care for

Albert through his last difficult days. Grieving for her husband's loss, Victoria relied upon Alice to become her secretary and comforter. It was not, however patient she might be, the ideal role for a young fiancée.

Alice married Louis at Osborne House in the spring of 1862, in a ceremony so drenched in black crepe that it was described as feeling more like a funeral than a wedding. Soon afterwards, ignoring her mother's reproaches, Alice travelled out to Darmstadt. Here, having anglicised a stuffy little court where a 4 p.m. dinner in full evening dress was still de rigueur, the Princess turned her energies toward health reform. Hospitals and nurse-training schemes were set up. When the supply of deaconesses from Kaiserswerth began to shrink, Alice was able to provide her own trained nursing teams to London's German Hospital.

Hessen-Darmstadt was a minor duchy. Nobody there minded that Alice and Louis read to each other in English, or that Louis was always popping off to England to gather information about the railways and factories that were his main interests. For Vicky, spoken of in Berlin as 'die Engländerin', life was far more circumscribed. The occasion of Bertie's marriage to Alexandra of Denmark in March 1863 offered a rare excuse for her to return home and to bring along – it was his first visit to England – Victoria's eldest grandson.

Willy's angelic appearance (he was dressed, in the preferred royal style, in Highland tartan) was deceptive. He instantly annoyed his grandmother by addressing her, without permission, as 'Duck'. Conducted to the ceremonials and placed safely out of the Queen's sightline (Victoria observed the proceedings from a private seat, closeted high above the nave), the precocious four-year-old scratched his kilted uncles on their bare calves, threw his sporran over his pew, brandished his miniature dagger and finally bit his uncle Alfred in the leg.

Willy already showed signs of turning into a little monster. Bertie's Alexandra, by contrast, made an excellent impression.

Vicky, having originally introduced the couple at Speyer, was charmed all over again by Alex's unaffected sweetness and slender beauty. The Princess's sole fault lay in her birth. If only – as Vicky had wistfully told her mother, even as she first praised the match – Alexandra had been anything other than Danish.

The Germans, significantly, had always looked upon *Hamlet, Prince of Denmark*, as their own sacred property. Nevertheless, Denmark was a separate country, linked to Germany only by two tiny Danish provinces of which one, Holstein, containing the valuable Baltic port of Kiel, also belonged to the sizeable group of states comprising the German Confederation.

Bismarck was already looking northwards with an acquisitive eye in 1863 when Denmark's new King Christian, Alex's father, put his signature to a pre-arranged treaty that bound Schleswig, Holstein's northern neighbour, to his own kingdom, so breaking both a 500-year-old pact that the two tiny provinces should enjoy joint independence under 'personal union', and a much more recent commitment (given at the 1852 Treaty of London) to let them alone. Uproar followed. Vicky's husband Fritz, duty-bound to support his friend Fritz Holstein when he, as Duke of Augustenburg, also laid claim to Schleswig, set off for the battlefield. Alex, carrying an uncomfortable Bertie in her wake, backed her father. Victoria (while privately taking the view that both small states should belong to Germany) opted for neutrality.

Bismarck, meanwhile, had reached the same conclusion. Certainly, Prussia should be involved, but only in order to acquire two valuable little states for the North German Confederation. The concerns of Vicky, Fritz and the handsome young Duke of Augustenburg scarcely rippled the surface of Bismarck's own deep calculations.

The bloody process through which Bismarck achieved the annexation of Schleswig and Holstein left no doubt of the direction in which Prussia was heading under the Minister President's control. Fritz, having shown exceptional military skill and courage, was forced to watch the outwitting of his friend the Duke (whose wife was Vicky's cousin) by a man of vastly superior political skill and unstoppable determination. Following a carefully picked squabble with Austria, Prussia's new national hero proceeded to take over Hessen-Kassel, Nassau and – following its defeat in battle – Hanover.* By 1867, only Bavaria, Baden, Württemberg and Hessen-Darmstadt remained beyond Bismarck's control.

The position of Alice and Vicky, English princesses who had married into German royalty, remained as delicate as that of two tightrope-walkers. On the one hand, their imperious mother was constantly insisting that they should remain loyal to their homeland; on the other, brought up on their father's ardent desire for a united Germany, they wanted nothing more than to see Albert's dream fulfilled.

Alice, always a peacemaker, strove especially hard to strike a perfect balance. In 1865, she told her mother about the excellent English that her children were learning from their governess, Margaret Hardcastle, and stressed the deep affection that she and Louis felt for Scotland and all their kind friends there, on the Balmoral estate ('Do tell them so always'). A year later, swept up in the war against Denmark, Alice may have pleased Victoria rather less with her vision of German supremacy: 'God grant this war, which has produced so many heroes, and cost so many gallant lives, may not have been in vain, and that at length Germany may become a mighty, powerful Power. It will then be the first in the world ...'[5] Naturally, Victoria supported her late husband's dream for German unification, but – foremost in the world?

Four years later, and the mother at last of Ernst (an eagerly

---

* Victoria provided covert support to George V of Hanover (one of the two little German Georges who had once been seen as good consort material by her uncle William IV). Funds were conveyed via Vicky to the deposed King's second home in Austria; an implicit condition seems to have been that George would make no trouble between England and Prussia.

awaited male heir to whom both Victoria and King Wilhelm stood as godparents), Alice returned to the defence of Germany. In 1870, no Englishwoman living in Germany could do otherwise.

By 1870, Bismarck had nearly achieved his goal: a unified Germany. He had created a North German Federation with Wilhelm I as its president. All that remained was to provoke a war that would bring the remaining states into line behind Prussia. In 1870, Napoleon III of France strode forward into Bismarck's open trap.

It was Bismarck who, when the throne of Spain was formally offered to one of King Wilhelm's relations from Catholic Bavaria in February 1870, urged his uneasy master to support an offer which would – and did – infuriate the French Emperor. Later, Bismarck would claim that Napoleon's ensuing decision to declare war on Prussia was provoked by his own deliberately brusque revisions to a telegram from King Wilhelm to Count Vincent Benedetti, the French Ambassador. Later evidence suggests, however, that France was already preparing for battle when Benedetti demanded Prussia's promise to stand aside regarding Spain. On 18 July 1870, France went to war against the combined and formidable military force of three Prussian armies.

The Franco-Prussian War, although bloody, was relatively short. In October 1870, following the surrender of Metz, Paris was besieged by Prussian forces and starved into submission. Thomas Carlyle, writing to *The Times* on 11 November 1870, invited England's support for the victor: 'noble, patient, deep, pious, and solid Germany'. In Berlin, urged on both by Bismarck and by the Crown Prince, Wilhelm agreed to bow to the expectations of his country – but not in order to accommodate Bavaria's status as a separate kingdom – to be named Emperor of Germany. On 18 January 1871, he was crowned the German Emperor. The ceremony took place – as the French would never forget – in the Hall of Mirrors at Versailles.

Ten days later, France formally acknowledged her defeat.

Bismarck was not a gracious victor. France was subjected to the loss of territory (all of Alsace and most of Lorraine) and to the continued occupation by German troops until five billion francs (the equivalent of a billion dollars) had been paid in reparations. This, too, was not to be forgotten by the French.

For Princess Alice, there was no doubt where her loyalties now lay. 'Everywhere,' she had written to her mother at the outbreak of the war, 'troops and peasants are heard singing "Die Wacht am Rhein" and "Was ist des Deutschen Vaterland" . . . there is a feeling of unity and standing by each other, forgetting all party quarrels, which make one proud of the name of German [sic].' Spurring her mother on in this same letter, Alice had congratulated the Queen for upholding her own shared loyalty to Albert's homeland, for 'all know that every good thing England does for Germany, and every evil she wards off her, is owing to your wisdom and experience, and to your true and just feelings'.[6]

Victoria had supported her husband's dream of German unification, but this was a difficult time for an English monarch with daughters living in Germany. Carlyle spoke for the few, not the majority. The English papers were filled with accounts (angrily denied by Alice on 14 January 1871) of Prussian atrocities. Neither Alice nor her royal mamma could force a British empire to welcome the birth of a rival in the heart of Europe. Even the Germanophile Robert Morier admitted to sharing Disraeli's anxiety about the alteration to a balance of power that had been calibrated with such delicate care in the wake of the Napoleonic Wars half a century before, at the Congress of Vienna.

Vicky and Fritz, while initially delighted at the fruition of Albert's hopes, were appalled by the rapaciousness of Bismarck's demands from the vanquished French and dismayed by the increasingly hostile tone of the English press. Secretly, Vicky must have shared her sister's relief at hearing that Napoleon III and the Empress Eugénie (of whose kindness to her before her marriage Vicky retained fond memories) had found refuge in England.

Publicly, she buttoned her lips as, all around her, the German press attacked Victoria for having dared – following Wilhelm's ascent to imperial status – to praise newly republican France as Germany's equal.

In 1872, following her engagement to the intensely Anglophile first secretary at London's first ever German Embassy, Hugo von Krause, Charles de Bunsen's granddaughter Hilda paid her own first visit to Berlin, accompanied by her fiancé, her father Ernest, and their friend Albrecht Bernstorff, the long-serving ambassador to the Court of St James's.

The visit was intended to be brief; Wilhelm I, relishing his new role as emperor, decreed otherwise. Ernest, longing to be snugly back in his London study, was commanded to build a new house in Berlin and to join the imperial circle, together with Hilda and Hugo von Krause. These were grim tidings. 'I am glad to think of the satisfaction of the dear Emperor in considering you to be secured for life to his dominions,' old Fanny de Bunsen wrote to her despondent granddaughter from Carlsruhe, before comforting her that so ardent an Anglophile as Hugo von Krause ('so English, so English') was certain to find a way to escape.[7]

Possibly, Wilhelm decided that building a vastly expensive house as a contribution to his new project to beautify Berlin was a fair price for the de Bunsen family's freedom. The house was built, release was granted and Hilda was allowed to marry her handsome Hugo back in England. A year later, von Krause died after a hunting accident and Hilda, the desolate mistress of Bendeleben, a faraway German estate that she had scarcely seen, was left alone.

While the de Bunsen family comforted the young and pregnant widow at Abbey Lodge, the house in Regent's Park that remained a haven for their far-flung family, Victoria's government approved plans to rent, as their new British Embassy in Berlin, a vacant palace on the Wilhelmstrasse. The vast edifice had been created for Bethel Henry Strousberg, a railway king of the 1860s, as a showpiece for the height of a career that had spectacularly plunged to destruction.

Strousberg's meteoric fall was part of a post-war economic crisis that almost shook Bismarck's new empire from its triumphant perch. Fortunes – including the massive French indemnities – had been lavished on glorifying the new Berlin. Fortunes had also been squandered during speculative trading in a stock market which, when it crashed in 1873, brought down everybody – in Bismarck's pungent terms – from lords to bootblacks. Strousberg's own fall did not save him from being publicly tarred, along with the bankers, as one of those Jews who were swiftly blamed for the country's economic misfortunes. Anti-Semitism had often been noted by English visitors to Germany in the past, but only as a simmering undercurrent; now, for the first time, it revealed a public face.

The country made a swift recovery, but the high-minded National Liberal Party to which Vicky and Fritz were closely attached was brutally thrust aside. For his new allies, Chancellor Bismarck reverted to his earliest supporters, the ultra-conservative Junker landowners of Prussia, whose hostility to Jews was voiced in strident calls for the head of the Chancellor's own banker, Gerson Bleichröder. Bismarck ignored them; Fritz showed a warmer heart but less wisdom when, noting that Bleichröder's daughter was being pointedly ignored at a court ball, he ordered one of his ADCs to dance with her. The result was anger from the ADC, embarrassment for the young woman and, despite his good intentions, short shrift for Fritz.

England's feelings towards Germany, despite Carlyle's enthusiastic tributes, had been improved neither by reports of Prussian atrocities during the Franco-Prussian War, nor by signs that the thrusting new empire might threaten Britain's commercial power. Relations were not improved by the discovery that several of Strousberg's investors had been Englishmen, whose fortunes were now lost. In Germany, meanwhile, the revelation that England had quietly provided arms and supplies to France throughout the recent war was considered tantamount to treachery.

A striking increase in the number of visits paid to London's German Hospital by various members of the German Emperor's family during the 1870s suggests an active desire to maintain the old relationship, and to build towards a new attachment upon sound philanthropic foundations. No hard evidence exists to prove it, but the regularity of their visits suggests that this enterprise was led by Vicky and Alice.

The German Hospital provided a perfect means for the two Anglo-German Princesses to offer help to their countrymen (both English and German) while visiting London during the relatively peaceful birth years of the German Empire. Vicky initiated this new involvement in July 1871, touring the hospital's wards before presenting as a gift from herself and her mother-in-law, the Empress Augusta, four splendid royal portraits to be hung in the entrance hall to the hospital. Alice, a far more frequent visitor, saved the hospital from collapse when – during the time that Kaiserswerth stopped supplying nurses – she sent her own over from Hesse.

Alice's connection to the many nursing foundations to which she offered unstinting support, both in Germany and England, was brought to a tragic close in the winter of 1878, when the Princess's children and husband caught diptheria. Tirelessly nursing her family back to health, Alice lost one daughter, May, and feared intensely for the survival of delicate Ernst Ludwig, their beloved boy.

Prince Ernst, who later transformed Darmstadt into a centre for art and became chief patron of the Jugendstil movement (Germany's Art Nouveau), never got over his mother's death. It was while nursing her son that Alice caught the disease and died. And, although a heartbroken Louis did his best to maintain the loving links between Darmstadt and Alice's English family, her beloved German Hospital now stood in urgent need of a new benefactor.

The Schröder family had been involved with Charles de Bunsen's great project since its beginnings. From 1878, the year of Alice's death, the Anglo-German banking family became the hospital's chief patrons. In the same year, they attended the wedding of Hilda de Bunsen to their friend and fellow banker, the Cologne-born Adolph Deichmann. Plain-faced, warm-hearted and as besotted with hunting as the Schröders themselves (they owned neighbouring hunting boxes in Leicestershire), Deichmann had also been a close friend of Hugo von Krause's. Family connections were strengthened again when his niece, Emma, married Bruno, the Schröders' nephew and heir.

Here, in a discreet little world of philanthropic bankers who loved England but retained close links to the Fatherland, Anglo-German relations continued to flourish and to prosper.

Unlike the Schröders and the de Bunsens, Emperor Wilhelm I had never got on especially well with his family. He disliked his wife; he despised his son Fritz and he mistrusted Vicky. Perhaps it was the mere giving of his name to young Wilhelm that caught a grandfather's fancy, allowing him a vain vision of a Wilhelmine future. Perhaps he wanted to counteract the influence of a daughter-in-law who never hid her pride in Britain's naval supremacy (Willy and his young friends were given a miniature British man-of-war ship to play on in the garden of the Neues Palais at Potsdam), and who wholeheartedly supported British colonialism.

Mischievous accounts of Vicky may well have leaked back to the old King from a grandson with a flair for troublemaking. Possibly, dismissive of Fritz and Vicky's idealism, the old gentleman chose to undermine it by flattering a little boy's sense of importance. For whatever reason, he forged a close bond with the child. Willy was only twelve years old when he was permitted to join the new Emperor's first triumphant entry into Berlin; from then on, the ageing Kaiser missed no opportunity to encourage his oldest grandson to see himself as a reincarnation of Frederick the Great: a figure of mythical grandeur and power, destined to lead his country towards greatness.

Bonding with young Willy, and licensed by Bismarck's unspoken approval, the Emperor continued to edge Vicky and Fritz off towards the sidelines. Possibly, he spoke of them to the boy in dismissive terms; certainly, he helped to deepen any existing rift between the parents and their son. Willy's devotion was to his grandfather. The attachment even survived Willy's unwelcome alliance, in 1880, to Dona, the virulently anti-Semitic daughter of his parents' friend, the Duke of Augustenburg.

Dona's unpleasant views caused her no harm. By 1880, anti-Semitism in Germany was beginning to spread. A card carrying the crude message 'Hurray Get Out' was on sale in Berlin. When Disraeli, a Christianised Jew, had visited the city in 1878, Bismarck's homage – 'That is the man!' – was interpreted as evidence of Germany's tolerance; in fact, it was a startling exception to the general rule.

Bismarck allowed the anti-Semitic movement to grow; its chief architect was Heinrich von Treitschke, a right-wing historian. In 1878, a wave of anti-Semitic attacks expressed anger at the growing numbers of Russian Polish Jews who were entering the country; Treitschke supported these attackers by declaring that the new, pure Germany deserved to be protected from a people generally regarded as (the dreadful phrase was not original to him) 'breeders of misfortune'.

Odious though Treitschke's opinions were, they found an eager audience. Fritz and Vicky's valiant attempts at a protest – the Crown Princess made herself the patron of a German orphanage for Jewish girls, while Fritz, dressed in full uniform, attended synagogue – won no support from Bismarck, the viscerally anti-Semitic Junkers, or even their son. If Vicky, during the 1880s, became increasingly outspoken about her admiration for England, it was because she could not bear to identify herself with the new and xenophobic Germany being forged by the Emperor's chancellor and endorsed by his government.

In England, Victoria continued to provide prudent advice and a listening ear; at a time when the mood in England was isolationist and deeply suspicious of the future plans of Europe's new dominant power, the Queen could do no more. Among the very few people in Berlin to whom Vicky and Fritz could turn to for sympathy with their own views during this period of bitter disillusionment was Lord Odo Russell, the English Ambassador who was uncomfortably occupying the ruined Strousberg's former palace on the Wilhelmstrasse, at a royal cost of 20,000 thalers a year. It was just as well for Russell that his older and adoring brother was a duke, and a rich one.

Odo Russell was one of three delightful and polyglot sons of a soldier's daughter, a forceful lady whose legendary beauty had won praise from Byron and who, while living an independent life from her husband, famously announced during the Franco-Prussian War that she herself was 'GERMANICA to the pineal gland: discipline against disorder, sobriety against drunkenness, education against IGNORANCE.'[8] Determined to give her sons an enlightened upbringing, Lady William Russell helped that project along by familiarising them with the works of Schiller, Goethe, Eliot and Carlyle. European by upbringing, the Russell boys spoke flawless English, but with a German accent.

Lord Odo came to Berlin in 1871 via Vienna, Paris, Constantinople, Washington and Florence. An acute understanding of German politics and (almost as importantly) of German etiquette made him a perfect envoy to the new imperial court.

An experienced diplomat, Russell needed all of his skill to remain on good terms with what had now become the sharply divided camps of the Emperor Wilhelm and the Crown Prince. To Vicky (for whom Odo sometimes discreetly arranged transfers of funds from her devoted brother Bertie), the kindly and clever

Ambassador was a loyal friend, one whose understanding provided welcome consolation in lonely times.

For Vicky and Fritz, high-minded representatives of the old-fashioned Victorian liberalism espoused by Albert, the showy new world of imperial Berlin was a bewildering place. Willy, their son, impatient for his own moment in the limelight ('I Bide my Time' ran the ominous inscription on a widely circulated photograph of Willy posing in a Scots kilt and plaid), thrived on the clamour and incessant parades by which Germany trumpeted her imperial role. To Vicky and to Fritz, all that side of life was anathema. Wistfully, the couple grieved for the passing of a world of high ideals, in which liberty and unity walked hand in hand, and in which voluntary public service fulfilled the role that was increasingly being diminished and usurped, under Bismarck, by the state.

Odo Russell, while respectful of Fritz's ideals, could not blame the old Emperor for favouring boisterous, modern-minded Willy. Afforded a brief chance to rule, for a passing moment, in 1875 (following an attempt upon the Emperor's life), the Crown Prince had inspired no confidence in his skills as a leader. Fritz was a brave man in battle, but he did not thrive on power; on the contrary, as Russell noted with concern, a short spell of ruling had left the Crown Prince looking tired, defeated, worried and ill.[9]

Russell himself died in 1884. The Emperor wept; the Empress Augusta told Queen Victoria that Lord Odo would never be forgotten, 'by us or by Germany'. Even Bismarck, who had occasionally taken Russell's advice, observed that the British diplomat was irreplaceable. Fritz bore his grief in silence; Vicky was visibly devastated.

During that same year, the Crown Princess lost another precious source of private consolation. Hilda Deichmann's gentle, short-sighted and scholarly uncle Georg von Bunsen, a Berlin-based diplomat who shared Vicky's own liberal beliefs, incurred the wrath of Bismarck by proclaiming those views in a form that the Chancellor perceived as a challenge. Nobody challenged Bismarck. When Georg and Emma, his English wife, next held a party at their Berlin home, they faced an empty room; the guests had been ordered to stay away. In public, Bismarck cut Georg and Emma dead; others were encouraged to follow his example. Poultney Bigelow, a half-American who had grown up as the playmate of young Willy and the Bunsen boys, Georg's sons, was horrified by the implacable thoroughness of the Chancellor's revenge on what he described as an exemplary family, hospitable to all, endearingly un-Prussianised in their 'idyllic' English home. 'No family furnished a more beautiful example of domestic happiness,' Bigelow wrote in his memoirs.[10] By the end of the year, the Bunsens had sadly decided to return to England. Willy, who had known them almost as an extension of his own family, made no attempt to change their minds.

Fritz and Vicky had waited thirty years to realise Albert's dream of a single nation presided over by a German ruler and an English princess. Fate would not be kind to them. When Wilhelm I died, aged ninety, in March 1888, Fritz was already a marked man.

A year earlier, the Crown Prince had been examined for a persistent throat infection that neither an agonising regime of cauterisation nor spa treatment could cure. In April 1887, the decision was taken to treat the condition as cancerous and perform an immediate and high-risk operation on the larynx. Fritz himself was not consulted.

While it remains unclear just how much Vicky herself had been told, it was Bismarck, surprisingly, who intervened at this point and informed the horrified Emperor of what was being planned. Wilhelm ordered a halt to the process; sullenly, the German doctors agreed to listen to an outside specialist. Nevertheless, when Morell Mackenzie, an Englishman of Scots descent, suggested less radical steps, they begged to differ.

In June 1887, Fritz was thankfully released from the care of his squabbling doctors to attend the London celebrations for Queen Victoria's half-century on the throne. Willy, also in attendance, drew less applause than his father, whose plumed helmet, great height and magnificent beard inspired comparisons to a Wagner hero. Seething at the fact that Dona had been given an inferior seat to that of the black Queen of Hawaii, Willy would have been angrier still had he known that his parents had carried three large boxes of private papers away from Berlin. These, at Vicky's discreet request, were lodged safely in an 'iron room' at Buckingham Palace.

By November, the Crown Prince's condition had worsened. Mackenzie, newly knighted and awarded the Order of the Hohenzollern, now agreed with the German doctors, while declaring that Fritz's cancer was of very recent development.

Annointed Emperor four months later, in March 1888, Fritz's first and moving action was to take the Order of the Black Eagle off his uniform and to pin it to the dress of the wife, whom he tenderly addressed as his guardian angel. Too ill, by then, even to attend Wilhelm's state funeral, Fritz permitted his son to lead the great procession of a hundred princes down the snow-mantled Unter den Linden. Willy, meanwhile, began spreading scandalous tales of his mother's affair with her court chamberlain, Count Seckendorff, and of her impatience for Fritz to die. The truth was rather different: only one person was eagerly awaiting the death of the new Emperor, and that person was Willy, his heir.

Queen Victoria, always fond of her Prussian son-in-law, had been careful to lavish affection on Fritz at her Jubilee celebrations. With sad prudence, she recognised the need to look forward and indicate support for Vicky, an isolated figure in an increasingly hostile land. In April 1888, Victoria personally travelled to Berlin and charmed a susceptible Bismarck into wearing a candy heart emblazoned with her image. The Chancellor reassured the British Queen; naturally, he would do his utmost to defend and care for her daughter. What Victoria did not know was how active a role Bismarck himself was already playing in the campaign to blacken the Empress's name.

The naïvety of the Emperor himself remained intact. On 12 June, Fritz called Bismarck to his sickroom and motioned him to clasp, across the bed, Vicky's hand. After covering both their hands with his own, the voiceless Emperor, making an indication of his trust, gently patted the Chancellor upon the shoulder.

Fritz died three days later and Willy, with indecent speed, seized control. Forbidden even to cut the traditional roses to place upon her dead husband's breast, Vicky was hustled aside while Willy's servants ransacked his parents' rooms in a hunt for the papers that might incriminate her. Nothing, to Willy's considerable disappointment, came to light; all the documents that mattered had been safely locked away in England, beyond his reach.

Matters grew worse. Willy, having refused to give his own father a state funeral, ordered his mother out of her old home, while withholding the funds for her to build a new one. (Friedrichshof, the house that Vicky would name in memory of her husband, owed its eventual existence to the generosity of a private individual, the Duchesse de Galleria.) While Bismarck spread rumours that Vicky had stolen state papers for publication abroad, Willy encouraged the publication at home of a fierce attack by two of the German team of doctors on the diagnosis made by Mackenzie, the doctor with whom Vicky, by virtue of her British background, was most easily linked. Vicky, by this route, could be implicated as a fellow conspirator in hastening her beloved husband's death. Within four months of Fritz's modest funeral, thanks to the vicious industry of Bismarck and her own son, Vicky's reputation in Germany had reached its nadir.

In February 1890, circumstances offered a scrap of grim consolation. Bismarck had announced – it was a familiar gambit – his resignation. Willy, however, seemed ready to accept it. Frantic for support, Bismarck turned to Vicky and learned, without surprise, that no help was to be had from this quarter. A month later, the defeated Chancellor paid the Dowager Empress a more dignified visit, to offer his official farewell. Determined not to gloat, Vicky wrote to her mother that there had been no harsh words: 'I should have been sorry – having suffered *so* much all these long years under the system – that it should appear as if I had any spirit of revenge, which I really have not.'[11]

Germany's great chancellor left Berlin with as little fanfare as had been accorded to Fritz's funeral. A young cousin of Willy's, Max von Baden, arrived to offer a salute; the new Emperor himself stayed at home. Writing to his grandmother in England in his finest sanctimonious style, Willy assured her that the decision to retire Bismarck had been a difficult one, but taken with the old gentleman's own best interests at heart. 'It was a very hard trial, but the Lord's will be done . . .'[12]

10

LULULAUND AND
OTHER ADVENTURES

(1880–1910)

Willy would always evince a strong dislike for the world of modern culture that thrived, despite his best endeavours, throughout his reign. He never, however, displayed the least objection to any form of art that paid appropriate homage to the Hohenzollerns and his imperial self.

In 1900 – to take but one example – Wilhelm II took time off from his royal duties to pose for an admiring visitor's portrait in the splendid Knights' Hall of the Hohenzollern Schloss. His legs were encased in gleaming thigh-high boots; the imperial crown, globe and sceptre were displayed at his feet. His uniform, adorned with every order that the Fatherland and a savvy old English grandmother who knew Willy's fondness for medals could confer, was dashingly set off by a crimson full-length cloak.

'My enamel portrait of the Emperor will be gorgeous,' an enthusiastic Sir Hubert Herkomer wrote to his students back in the village of Bushey, Hertfordshire, where he ran an art school and had built a large Bavarian schloss. The students were further informed by their ebullient tutor that the Emperor had displayed a stellar mixture of enthusiasm, intelligence, warmth and willpower: 'qualities rarely combined in one man. His suddenness of resolution delights and suits me.'[1]

The Kaiser's impetuousness charmed Sir Hubert rather less the following year. Displeased by the modest scale of an enamel portrait that, nevertheless, dwarfed the miniature originally planned, Willy declined to purchase it. Herkomer, whose vanity did not lag far behind the Emperor's, assuaged his wounded pride by smashing his artwork with a sledgehammer.

Herkomer's reaction is easily understood when we recall what his English contemporaries never forgot: that, distinguished Royal Academician and eminent former head of the Slade though the artist might be, he was not one of them. Journalists remarked upon the attractiveness of his olive skin, gleaming blue-black beard, bold manner and a certain 'kittenish playfulness': what they meant was that the polymathic and engagingly self-regarding Herkomer did not seem English.[2]

The artist himself would never have denied that he was pulled in two directions by his birthright. 'My art is English and my blood is German,' Herkomer told a friend in 1900. 'All my ways are those of a foreigner – my enthusiasm, my outspokenness, my self-possession – my life is un-English. But my art and my feeling for art will always remain English.'[3]

This announcement – as with many of Herkomer's declarations – was an attractive but limited version of the truth.

Born near Landsberg in southern Bavaria in 1849, Herkomer was two years old when his parents joined the great western exodus from Germany of those post-revolutionary years. Brought up in Southampton and London, he remembered being pursued home from school by shouts of 'brigand' and 'foreigner'. A detail he never forgot was that his father, Lorenz, a woodcarver, had sold the only cloak he owned to buy clothes for his child.

Herkomer's skill as a draughtsman developed early. Enrolled on an art course at Munich at the age of sixteen – with his uninhibited father posing nude if home-practice was required for the life study class – Hubert was twenty when he began producing regular sketches for a new illustrated weekly, *The Graphic*. Van Gogh never met Herkomer during his three-year stay in London from 1873–6, but the young Dutchman was inspired by Herkomer's powerful images of suffering and loneliness. Ten years later, an admiring van Gogh told his brother Theo how he had longed to have Herkomer for his friend ('a friend for life').[4]

The turning point in the life of an English-bred Bavarian came when Herkomer revisited his homeland with his father in 1871. Staying at a cosy lodging in sleepy, medieval Garmisch, the young artist was surrounded by the glorious Alpine landscape of Bavaria. Wandering through the great pine forests and exploring the wooden-bridged, brightly decorated villages, Herkomer experienced an epiphany. 'Something more than delight in the picturesqueness of this new ground was aroused in me,' he wrote in his memoirs. 'I felt it belonged to me, and that I belonged to Bavaria; I was of the same race, and the same blood ...'[5]

Captivated, Herkomer returned to Garmisch with his parents the following year. *After The Toil of Day*, his first entry for the Royal Academy, was sketched in England. It was completed during that long spell in Germany, where, as Herkomer frankly admitted, he looked for English subjects in foreign surroundings: 'I searched for English fruit trees and English peasants – in Bavaria!'[6]

The Toil of Day sold for £500, enough for Herkomer to buy a country home for himself and his parents at Bushey, just outside London. By 1875, his works were being shown alongside those of Alma-Tadema and Frith; by 1878, Richard Wagner was affectionately accusing him of witchcraft ('Sie hexen') for his skilful portrait from memory of the composer at work in London the previous year, when Wagner was attempting to recoup losses incurred by his first festival at Bayreuth.

By 1884, Herkomer could do no wrong. The art school he had founded at Bushey was praised and well attended; a lecture on art given at All Souls led to the rare honour of a college fellowship; Ruskin invited Herkomer to take over as Slade professor of art at Oxford.

And then tragedy struck. Herkomer was away from Bushey when his pregnant wife, Lulu Griffiths, caught sight of a village child wandering out in front of an approaching carriage. Running to the child's rescue, Lulu herself was knocked down. She died, not of her injuries, but of shock. Her unborn baby did not survive.

Publicly, the widower registered his loss in a striking portrait, as he had done at the start of their short marriage. *The Woman in White* – for which Wilhelm II put in an unsuccessful bid when it was displayed in Berlin – was now succeeded by *Woman in Black*, represented by a Mrs Silsbee, from Boston. Privately, Herkomer took consolation from summoning his relations to help create the house on which he conferred the name of his dead wife: Lululaund.

Few houses can have been created by a single family with such loving attention to detail as the sturdy Bavarian schloss built by the Herkomers just off Bushey High Street. The result was remarkable. Lululaund stood in three acres of gardens that included fish ponds, lily ponds and a small *Tannenwald*, intended to evoke the Bavarian woods. The house, based around a massive central arch, flanked by two sturdy turrets, was clad in white tufa limestone, imported from Munich and picked for its unique ability to reflect the play of light.

Within the solid walls of Lululaund, things became a little wilder. A frieze of life-size female figures hammered from copper and aluminium looked down into a rectangular well of oiled oak. The bedrooms were adorned by cupboards covered by tiny squares of pure gold leaf, while the ceiling of Herkomer's own chamber boasted the added refinement of a surface of burnished copper. A velvet-curtained music gallery overhung the drawing room and – an unexpectedly practical touch – the kitchen was located upstairs, protecting Herkomer's dinner guests from the odour of cooking.

Nothing had been overlooked; everything was designed to please the eye. Among the decorative houses that Victorian architects built for their own pleasure, Lululaund stood at the zenith, beside the London homes of Lord Leighton and William Burges. Arguably, it surpassed them.

Herkomer had intended to live at Lululaund with his beloved second wife. Instead, he shared it with her sister. In 1888, Herkomer married Margaret Griffiths in a sunrise ceremony at the Mutterturm, a hundred-foot tower at Landsberg by which, nine years earlier, Herkomer had paid homage to his Bavarian mother. Ten trumpeters and horns were imported from the Munich Opera House to play the 'Wedding March' from *Lohengrin*. The couple's son, a second Lorenz, was born the following year.

Bushey, during the years of Lorenz's childhood, was like nowhere else in England. The residential art students who worked on Herkomer's grounds in small stove-heated studios were given clear rules: students could not exhibit their work in shows and they could not imitate their teacher. For recreation, after Herkomer turned a local chapel into a theatre, students were encouraged to take part in electrically lit pageants that painstakingly recreated scenes from the artist's own paintings. On a typical afternoon, the cast might find Herkomer's friend Hans Richter conducting a thirty-strong orchestra in a Wagner-inspired score, before dashing back to London for his evening concert. On other occasions, the amateur performers might look out from a medieval street (authentic cobbles ensured that the actors walked in a convincing manner), to see themselves being watched by – in Herkomer's typically immodest words – 'the most prominent men in art, science, literature, and music'.[7]

The exaggeration was not great. William Archer, the drama critic, was a keen attendant of Herkomer's plays. Dame Ellen Terry gushingly declared that she wanted to see his second production, *An Idyl*, again and again, while her illegitimate son, Edward Gordon Craig, gathered valuable tips on stagecraft for his own future work.

Tirelessly energetic, Herkomer embraced the technology of the new century with delight. An early motoring enthusiast, he founded the world's first annual road race in 1905, providing this Bavarian event with a silver trophy that showed the driver being urged on by a naked muse. A painting of a blindfolded, near-naked girl lassoed to the front of the artist's shiny Daimler was mischievously titled *Die Zukunft* (The Future). At Bushey, Herkomer created England's first film studio, from which six films emerged, starring Sir Hubert in short episodic dramas that ranged from Dick Turpin to love in a teashop.

Herkomer died in 1914, just before the outbreak of war. Anti-German feeling had not yet seeped into the obituary pages and *The Times* declared that Herkomer's portraits could be placed beside the finest works of Frans Hals.

Today, Herkomer is a forgotten name. Even back in 1923, when the memory of war was sharp, his biographer expressed concern about the future of the extraordinary Bavarian schloss in Bushey and pleaded for its preservation.[8] In 1939, as a second war with Germany approached, a vote was taken by Bushey's parish leaders: preservation or demolition? The demolishers won by a single vote. Lululaund was pulled down. Its wooden interiors were burnt; its rubble was carted away for use at a local airfield. A Herkomer relation succeeded in rescuing a few items: the Herkomer Room at Bushey Museum still displays one handsome gilded cupboard, together with some scraps of hangings, a set of carved chairs, some film reels and a row of pewter dining plates.

The entrance arch to Lululaund survives, clamped to the front of a defunct outpost of the British Legion. The steel and glass roof structure of the old film studio is still in place, and a rose garden has been restored, following Herkomer's own design. Walking over the tangled site of Lululaund's lost estate, a visitor can still stumble across a piece of glinting white tufa, half buried in the earth.

Back in 1906, writing an article called 'Beauty in the Home' for an evangelical monthly, Sir Hubert was prepared to concede that sentiment might play as important a role in the decoration of a family home as, say, a gilded cupboard or a copper ceiling. 'The greatest decorator of a home, rich or poor,' he announced to readers of the *Home Messenger*, 'is happiness.'[9]

Herkomer's thoughts about sentiment would have won the approval of his German contemporary, Hermann Muthesius, an architect who carried home from England his admiration for the comfortable style of housing being built, around the turn of the century, for England's newly arisen and increasingly prosperous middle class.

Born in 1861, Hermann Muthesius trained briefly as a stonemason – his father's trade – before studying philosophy in Berlin and attending the city's highly regarded technical institute at Charlottenburg. A designer, architect and future historian of the Victorian house, Muthesius arrived in England in 1896 with a diplomat's commission to produce a report on English culture and technology. The task – a plum – echoed the one given to the great architect Schinkel in 1826, but, whereas Schinkel had compressed a frenetic tour of industrial England into four months, Muthesius and his equally Anglophile wife, Anna (a former concert singer), stayed on for seven contented years.

From the moment of his arrival in England, Muthesius displayed the independence of spirit that gives *Das englische Haus*, his great three-volume work, such vitality and charm. Officially, he should have resided in an extension of the German Embassy in Carlton House Terrace; instead, he and his wife set up home in semi-rural Hammersmith, where an artists' colony had grown up beside the

Thames. Here, at the Priory, Hermann and Anna created a cosily wallpapered shrine to the Arts and Crafts style of William Morris. Surviving photographs from 1896 show Anna putting her feet up by the fire, while her bearded husband (using his own little Japanese teapot) chats across their tiny table or buries his nose in a new book.

Noticeably absent from the Priory photographs are the heavy velvets and baroque swags of the high Victorian style that Muthesius detested. Praising Ruskin and the recently dead Morris for taking inspiration from medieval church architecture, he scolded them for failing to consider the expense of decorating a house in the finest Gothic style. A Herkomer could afford to indulge his wish to create a cloister or to decorate his ceiling with beaten copper panels; the egalitarian Muthesius wanted recognition for the needs of a class who wanted comfortable homes at affordable prices.

If Muthesius visited Lululaund, he must have admired the medieval ethos of communal workmanship, while frowning at Herkomer's florid taste. His own avant-garde preference was for the austerely graceful designs of a group of young Glaswegians.

Charles Rennie Mackintosh married his fellow artist Margaret Macdonald in 1900, just one year after his friend Herbert MacNair married Margaret's sister, Frances, designer of the ravishingly decorative cover of *Das englische Haus*. A friendship with the German visitors was quickly established; in his book, Muthesius championed the Mackintosh combination of sound workmanship and restrained decoration with a unifying sense of 'spacious, grandiose, almost mystical repose'.[10]

Hermann and Anna Muthesius paid regular visits to Glasgow and displayed a comforting enthusiasm for the beauty of their friends' achievements; as tea-lovers, they especially adored Miss Cranston's Willow Tearooms. But Muthesius's larger task was to carry news to Germany of the houses being built in England by Voysey, Webb, Lutyens and, above all, Norman Shaw. Here, in

Muthesius's view, were the examples from which Germany could also learn to create a sympathetic, comfortable and sometimes downright cosy environment.

For social historians, Muthesius's great book – first published in England, abridged, only in the 1970s – provides a treasure trove. No detail is overlooked in the German's courteous prowl through the Englishman's dwelling, from the nursery filled with bright picture books and cheerful jugs of flowers, through the bedroom (wooden bedsteads; immaculate dressing-table) to the ensuite bathroom that German readers were urged to replicate, with especial attention to the wonders of Victorian plumbing.

Muthesius's praises smothered a few sharp asides. The Englishman required no private study, since he had nothing to think about. His bookshelves were a sham. Bath towels were always as damp as the weather, while the ubiquitous grand piano was a waste of space, given 'a lack of critical judgment of quality in music that would be impossible in any other country'.[11]

Sharing Theodor Fontane's admiration for London's handsome parks and leafy squares – in contrast to arid, land-hungry Berlin – Muthesius also agreed with Fontane's complaints about the stifling uniformity of the terraced streets that had begun to smother London's outlying hills and hamlets. Muthesius might have had Dickens's Mr Wemmick in mind as he compared this soulless architecture of the suburbs to the charm of Raymond Unwin's pioneering and communally owned model town at Letchworth, Hertfordshire – the inspiration for Dresden's enchanting Hellerau – and honoured every English citizen's unspoken right to create 'his own little kingdom in which he may rule, spread himself and blossom'.[12]

Returning to Germany in 1903, after seven years away, Muthesius joined forces there with twelve architects of the avant-garde. Prominent among them was Peter Behrens, a recent graduate from the dynamic colony of artists at Darmstadt who worked under the enlightened patronage of Princess Alice's son,

Grand Duke Ernst of Hessen-Darmstadt. Working in collaboration with Behrens, Muthesius and a group of colleagues set out to wed traditional crafts to industrial technology, turning the decorative genius of Morris and Mackintosh into exportable artefacts with a range summed up in its ambitious motto: *vom Sofakissen zum Städtebau* (from sofa cushions to city-making). Founded in 1907, the Deutscher Werkbund became a forerunner of the amazing Bauhaus of 1913, creating Germany's first garden city at Hellerau and helping the nation forward in a bid to become the world's most successful exporter of home-produced goods. Thanks to the efforts of Muthesius and his colleagues, the English-born Princess Daisy of Pless would soon discover that it was quicker to buy an English-designed watch in Germany than back in London – and that the watch was better-made.

The cultural exchanges of the late Victorian era continued to flow in both directions. Herkomer, finding inspiration in the Bavarian landscape, imported it to England. Muthesius, enchanted both by the English style of house-building and by the new concept of the garden city that he saw at Letchworth, carried his observations back to Germany. Ethel Smyth, born in 1858 to a thoroughly unmusical family in Woking, travelled out to Leipzig in 1877 in search of a new life and the kind of musical education that was simply unavailable to an English girl at that time.

Ethel is best known today for the suffragette anthem which Sir Thomas Beecham found her conducting, with a toothbrush, from the window of a Holloway cell, when he visited her there in 1912 (Ethel was serving a two-month sentence for disruptive behaviour).

Ethel's powerful personality was already apparent when Tchaikovsky, visiting Leipzig in 1887, was introduced to Marco, the massive St Bernard dog by whom Ethel was invariably escorted to rehearsals and concerts. English women, Tchaikovsky sagely observed, must always have their peculiarities, and there was no doubting the flamboyant peculiarity of Miss Smyth.

Ethel was unnerved by the occasional displays of furious nationalism that she encountered in Leipzig, where her references to
Vicky as an English princess went down especially badly. "'She
married our Crown Prince and is a German ... A GERMAN ...
a GERMAN!! do you understand?'"[13] Nevertheless, she settled
swiftly into an intensely musical town, where the pleasures of hearing Clara Schumann execute Smyth's own fiercely demanding
piano compositions and attending splendid weekly performances
of Shakespeare at the Leipzig theatre compensated for the grimness of a muddy-booted Ball of the Professors – a snake-pit of
venomous smiles and unspoken rivalries.

Ethel had placed great faith in the treatment of her operatic
works in Germany, a country that – unlike England – would never
allow a performance to go ahead on the strength of a couple of
hasty rehearsals.

Ethel was not lucky. *Fantasio*, adapted from an Alfred de Musset
comedy, received a bad press when it premiered at Weimar in 1898
and her one-act opera, *Der Wald*, was actually hissed at its Berlin
debut in 1902. *The Wreckers* was her ominously named first full-
length work. Performed for the first time at Leipzig in 1906, it had
been so aggressively amended by the conductor that an infuriated
Ethel marched down into the pit, seized all the scores from the
orchestra and carried them off on a train to Prague, where she
hoped for – but did not find – better fortune.

Although given a performance by Beecham in 1910, the continental fate of *The Wreckers* was heartbreaking to Smyth. Mahler,
having promised to conduct the unabridged opera in Vienna in
1907, resigned his post that same year. Plans for a staging at Munich
in February 1915 were, inevitably, cancelled ahead of time.

The Wreckers became a casualty of war. The hissing of *Der Wald*
in 1902, by a sophisticated musical audience, seems less explica-
ble – especially since the orchestra had already praised the piece as
Grossartig, stupendous – until the performance is placed in the
broader context of Germany's attitude to England at the time.

Germany, at the end of the nineteenth century, was torn two ways in its view of Britain. The elite – a cross-blend of aristocrats, diplomats and artists – felt a profound attachment to a charming island: England was a pleasant outpost where they kept their hunters, did business, maintained friendships and owned agreeable country houses. A larger and more vocal group, led and abetted by an Anglophobic German press, sought a larger stage and bigger markets for a thrusting young German Empire towards which (they reasonably felt) some show of deference from an ageing Britain was in order.

Animosity, within this second group, was heightened almost to frenzy point by the Boer War. England, in her own righteous opinion, was protecting nothing more than her own imperial due (the massive gold and diamond reserves discovered in the Cape during the 1880s) when she launched a full-scale attack upon 25,000 Boer farmers. England, as perceived by the shocked read-ers of German newspapers, was behaving with unforgivable brutality towards a peace-loving minority, a minority that had strong links to Germany herself.

Visiting Munich at the turn of the century, Ethel was discon-certed to hear a boy using the words 'du *Engländer*' (the italics are her own) as an insult. Staying with friends in Berlin during 1901, she was horrified when German friends showed her a newspaper picture of an English soldier twirling a Boer baby upon the tip of his bayonet. Rebuked by Ethel in her usual trenchant tones for their credulity, the Berliners refused to yield: '*Es steht ja in meinem Blatt*: Look: it's here in my paper.'[14] Dining at the house of the German Chancellor, Count von Bülow, Smyth was assured that the Anglophobic speech he had recently given in the Reichstag was not his fault. Nothing was his fault. It was the Junkers, not he, who controlled the country. 'The German Chancellor is not der Herr Gott,' von Bülow pleaded. '. . . *I* can't muzzle the Press.'[15]

It was at von Bülow's home that Ethel first met the German Emperor, and he charmed her. True, Wilhelm II's ignorance about culture surpassed belief: 'incredible borné [*sic*], stupid, military things about art . . .'[16] But the Emperor did not strike Ethel as a stupid man. His dream of turning barracks-like Berlin into a Paris or a second London was absurd when one considered the Emperor's horror of modernity (Willy kept his distance from the underground Berlin where August Strindberg held court and Edvard Munch was exhibiting his work), but it was also touching. And who could resist the charm of a ruler who, when offered the wobbliest of curtseys as the Emperor's newest car swept past Ethel on her bicycle, responded with a cheery, thoroughly un-Prussian wave of his hand?[17] What, really, could Britain fear from a leader who – setting aside his notorious tantrums – remained so devoted to England, the country that Wilhelm spoke of as his second home?

11

THE AGE OF APPREHENSION

(1888–1901)

Alert and ramrod-backed, the small bronze figure perches at one side of a sculpted sofa that has been placed in the middle of a town square. While the fingers of one hand caress the decorative head of a carved lion, offering a hint of her legendary power to enthral and subdue, the wasp-waisted young woman in a décolleté court dress turns with an expressive smile towards the vacancy at her side, towards a space that was occupied, during her heyday, by some of the most influential figures in London and Berlin.

The town is Pszczyna, formerly Pless. The young woman who stares into emptiness with such bold eyes represents Daisy Cornwallis-West, Princess of Pless: hostess, reformer and a tireless urger of cousinly friendship between their two nations to a Francophile Edward VII of England and his volatile nephew, Emperor Wilhelm II.

Born in Wales in 1873, Daisy was eighteen and training to become a singer when an ambitious mother introduced her to a new recruit to the German Embassy in Carlton House Terrace. Hans Heinrich Pless was the thirty-year-old heir to one of the grandest titles and the greatest fortunes in Germany. Naturally, so Patsy Cornwallis-West reasoned, the Prince would wish to ally himself to her very beautiful, very young (and very poor) daughter, just as one of the richest men in England – Bendor, second Duke of Westminster – would wish, ten years later, when bent by Patsy's terrifying will, to marry Daisy's intrepid, horse-mad sister. Patsy met her match in 1900, however, when Winston Churchill's widowed American mother snapped up the handsome young George Cornwallis-West by announcing their engagement in *The Times*.

Married at St Margaret's, Westminster, in 1891, and tearfully preparing to set out for her new life in faraway Silesia, Daisy was advised by her mother's old friend, the Prince of Wales, to be sure to learn German and to show loyalty to her adopted country. Heinrich, meanwhile, studied his bride's going-away dress and observed that she had put it on the wrong way round. Hans Heinrich, as Daisy later remarked of the husband she never learned to love, always displayed 'the keenest eye for women's clothes'.[1] The implication, although delicately made, is clear: Hans had an intimate knowledge of women's clothes because he kept (and would continue to keep) mistresses.

Writing three beguilingly gossip-filled volumes of memoirs during the hardship and illness that befell her during the interwar years, Daisy Pless conjured back a world that now seems as improbable, glamorous and chilling as the *Arabian Nights*. Pless itself, chiefly inhabited by Hans Heinrich's affable father until his death in 1907, was a 600-room Silesian fortress that Daisy's husband later extravagantly converted to resemble the gigantic chateau of an imperious courtesan. Wilhelm II, requisitioning Pless for the eastern HQ of his army, picked the castle for the up-to-date comforts installed by Hans Heinrich, but also, perhaps, from fond memories of Daisy, a merrily outspoken young hostess to the vast parties of European aristocrats who convened at Pless for the purpose, principally, of slaughter. Stags, according to some mysterious local custom, were merely lassoed and released; the boar and bison that inhabited Pless's mighty woodlands were less fortunate. Daisy's first-born son, recalling his early days at Pless, would still remember in his old age the baby-like screaming of hares, shot in their hundreds each year upon the empty fields that lay in plain view of his turret bedroom.

The turret was the sanctuary and refuge of young Hansel Pless; here, he could safely carry out a quiet mutiny of his own against the massacre being executed beyond a boy's control. 'I kept a barn owl, a jackdaw, a fox terrier, two rabbits and a ferret. The smell was appalling, but nobody ever came up there. I was quite safe, and so were they.'[2]

Daisy, while capable of appearing at dinner in a sack to protest against the required five-times-a-day changes of attire, played her role with grace and style; even the stiffest of visitors found it hard to resist the freshness of a girl who, after taking them off for a midnight toboggan ride, would suggest an hour of cake walks, risqué songs and – although Daisy herself disliked alcohol – Champagne. Lady Susan Townley, recalling encounters with Daisy in Berlin during the early 1900s, remembered her as the greatest social draw in town, exuding an impetuous charm that Willy, who always put Daisy next to him at banquets, found irresistible. Who else, Lady Susan wondered, could have got away with putting on a puppet show that openly mocked the Emperor, along with all his courtiers, except for Daisy Pless?[3]

The courageous spirit so admired by Lady Susan was put to more valuable use by Daisy than for making fun of the nobility. Dividing her time between Pless and Fürstenstein, the enormous Silesian clifftop castle bestowed upon Hans Heinrich as a wedding gift from his father, Daisy became indignantly conscious of the gap separating her own semi-royal existence from that of the 20,000 miners whose labour upheld it. Down in the valley towns below Fürstenstein, where she became fondly known as *unsere Daisy* (our Daisy), the young Princess picked her way through streets of mud, where tightly packed houses with roofs made of tar paper backed onto a refuse-choked river. Complaining to her husband and receiving only a reminder of the annual tea provided to a grateful workforce, Daisy lost her temper sufficiently to point out that the miners had to trudge uphill on foot for this honour, before waiting in the courtyard for up to two hours, followed by a long walk home in the dark. Naturally, the miners did not complain. How could they, when no unions yet existed and no other source of income was available?

Hans Heinrich's father and namesake proved more willing to be enlightened than his son. Working together, the young Englishwoman and the elderly Prussian Prince initiated a programme of improvements that included two hospitals, improved housing, river-cleaning, free school milk and a pension scheme so advanced for its time that it was later adopted all across Prussia.

Daisy, slowly, came to love Germany with a deep tenderness that shines out of her account of returning to Fürstenstein from Berlin on a warm summer evening, with Hans Heinrich's English-bred dogs sprawled across the carriage floor and the hum of crickets filling the night-scented air. If she never mastered the language, the fault lay partly with a world that remained almost parodically British. Aside from reading English books and riding the Irish mares of which Prince Heinrich imported at least three a year to join his renowned stud, Daisy conversed daily with an English butler, an English groom, an English head gardener, an English valet and – although his services were hardly needed by a family who spoke English first and German second – an English tutor. If Daisy never learned to speak perfect German, it was perhaps because she never experienced the need.

Visiting England on his own for the first time, as a schoolboy of thirteen, Daisy's firstborn son, Hansel, entered a world that felt pleasingly familiar. 'It seemed', the Prince later declared, 'as if I had come home.'

And, in a more ambivalent sense than Hansel intended, so he had. Staying in Leicestershire as the guest of his father's brother, Count Friedrich Hochberg, an ardent huntsman, spiritualist and Anglophile, Hansel was introduced to Uncle Fritz's neighbours: a perfectly German circle, living a thoroughly English life. Bruno and Emma Schröder were visiting their hunting box at nearby Bicester Hall, while Count Kinsky and Herbert von Bismarck, the Chancellor's son, were staying down the road at the Garth with Adolph Deichmann and his wife Hilda. Baron Hermann von Eckardstein, a genial giant in the diplomatic world, dropped by, meanwhile, to greet Count Hochberg and to break his journey up to Chatsworth, where the Devonshires had invited him, as they frequently did, to join a party of English sportsmen.

Hansel, who later looked back on his pre-war Leicestershire visits as 'the happiest, most carefree weeks of all my life', thought his compatriots looked entirely at home jogging off to a meet through the country lanes of the English Midlands. And so they were: a painting still on display in the royal palace of Wiesbaden shows the Duke of Nassau with his pack of hounds. The Duke and his comrades are nattily dressed in the familiar costume: pink jacket, white breeches and velvet riding cap. At a glance, the viewer might mistake this Hesse hunting scene for a day out with the Quorn or Pytchley.

Daisy arrived at Pless in 1891, the year in which Wilhelm II finally condescended to visit his widowed mother at the house near Frankfurt which Vicky was patiently inhabiting until the Friedrichshof (named in Fritz's memory) could be completed.

Relations between the Dowager Empress and her eldest son had not been cordial since Fritz's death in 1888. Willy's brutal determination to diminish his father's achievement had shocked and wounded Vicky. She had disliked the way in which, during his first months in power, the young Emperor had cockily insisted that Uncle Bertie should cut short his annual stay in Vienna so that he,

Wilhelm II, might have no competition during his own, far more recently planned visit to that city. The Prince of Wales had been understandably annoyed: Alexandra, his wife, went so far as to describe Willy as 'a conceited ass'.[4]

Tact was never Wilhelm's strong point, despite a robust belief in the invincibility of his own charm. In 1889, at a moment when Germany required British support against the possible rise of a right-wing military dictatorship under General Boulanger in France, he was called upon to mend his arrogant ways. The Emperor set about it by visiting his grandmother's summer residence on the Isle of Wight with a retinue of twelve warships, and putting on a parade, for Victoria's pleasure, of 1200 goose-stepping Prussian sailors. Invited to become admiral of the British fleet by a shrewd old woman who always had the measure of her eldest grandson's vanity, Willy accepted with delight; taking the role to heart, he promptly started offering Victoria tips for improvements in the Royal Navy.

The Queen's well-judged boosts to the young Emperor's ego offered an example that her eldest daughter found difficult to emulate. Wilhelm himself did not help. He had waited three years to call upon his widowed mother; even then, he tried Vicky's patience to the limit. A last-minute telegram requested provision to be made in Vicky's modest home for thirteen servants and an imperial suite of six gentlemen that included one of the Dowager Empress's fiercest critics. 'It is really not very civil,' Vicky complained to Victoria, and added that she already wished the day were over. Wilhelm's visit was, nevertheless, an olive branch, and Vicky was in no position to reject it.

Relations between mother and son eased in 1894, as Vicky finally moved into the house that would become her beloved home for the last six years of her life. Here, at the Friedrichshof, she set out to create a comfortable feeling of England abroad, a welcoming centre for a family whose links were being loosened both by distance and by the diminishing powers of the wily old spider who still held her place at the centre of the royal web, back in Britain.

Hints of Vicky's sedate home life gleam out of the memoirs of her (slightly bored) visitors. Georg de Bunsen's tall, copper-haired daughter, Marie, wrote about the relief of retreating to the Friedrichshof's 'club-room' where she and Frank Lascelles, the British Ambassador, could smoke cigarettes (alcohol was sternly discouraged) and gossip about the nature of the Empress's relationship with her constant companion, Count Seckendorff. Daisy Pless found the Empress hungry for news of England, the country in which she had regretfully declined to settle, following Fritz's death. Her duty, Vicky explained, was to the German people, among whom she had lived for the last thirty years, and to whom – whatever her son might say to the contrary – she felt that her loyalty belonged. Daisy, uncertain how best to console a stately and sorrowful widow, but confident of her own singing skills, ventured an emotional rendering of 'Home Sweet Home'.

Vicky's real problem was that, unlike her mother, she had lost all power. The Queen, in the decade of her Diamond Jubilee, showed no intention of allowing the Prince of Wales to believe, even for a second, that he could have the final say. Vicky, adrift and functionless, enjoyed no such privilege. In 1896, as the German Empire celebrated its own first quarter-century, the Emperor himself was still a young man: trim, active and – so Willy flattered himself – in tune with the times. While Vicky sighed for an older world of high ideals and noble endeavours of the kind represented by the philanthropic institutions endowed by the Schröders, her son joined the march towards a new and hard-nosed, blustering world of colonial expansionism, aggressive markets and a fleet big enough for Germany to compete against America as the biggest trading power in the world.

Wilhelm's difficulty – one that Willy would never resolve – was that he was torn between a love of everything British, an adulation that verged upon the obsessive, and utter scorn for a country that he considered to be marooned in the past. Advising his grand-mother upon how to run a fleet that, so the Emperor emotionally declared, he loved as if it were his own, Wilhelm saw himself as an English hero: Nelson's heir (his writing desk was famously carved from the timbers of Nelson's famous flagship). Back in Berlin, the Emperor indulged his love of cabaret acts, undemanding music (Gounod's *Ave Maria* announced his state entrances) and showy statues. Visiting England, the Emperor was usually on his best behaviour and – since he spoke faultless English and loved dressing up in English uniforms – was well-liked by the crowds. Back home again, Willy would brood upon some imagined insult to his person or his empire. Always eager to challenge his less nautical royal uncle at the Cowes Regatta on his own English-built *Meteor* yacht, Wilhelm took bitter offence at the fact that Kiel, Germany's impe-rial war harbour, remained less fashionable (for the simplest of reasons, sniffed Daisy Pless: the glory of Cowes was not, as Willy appeared to think, 'something you can buy at a Woolworth store').[5]

Bertie, declining the offer of a military honour from his nephew during his first and grudging visit to Kiel, was more deliberately rude. The Prince of Wales, in Daisy's opinion, took more pleas-ure in being 'mean' to Willy than was either wise or kind. 'I am', she added, conceding that there were mistakes on both sides, 'sin-cerely sorry for both.'[6]

Wilhelm II's first serious – and knowing – misstep in his relations with England took place over the New Year of 1895. The Jameson Raid, supported by Cecil Rhodes and Alfred Beit and backed by the unwritten approval of Joseph Chamberlain, Britain's colonial minister, had been a botched attempt to provoke retaliatory action from the Boers from whom both Rhodes and Beit were keen to wrest control. German sympathies, as Ethel Smyth observed, remained firmly on the side of a people of Dutch-German origin. The Emperor, hearing of the raid's failure, despatched a telegram of congratulation to Paul Kruger, the Boer leader.

The Kruger telegram caused fury at Victoria's court and nearly brought about the resignation of Willy's embarrassed representative at the Court of St James's, Count Paul von Hatzfeldt. Willy was banned from making an official visit to England for three years, a decision which was reinforced by the news that he planned to send German troops out to aid the Boer cause. Willy's high-risk project was forestalled when the Marquis de Soveral, Portugal's suave ambassador to London, learning that the troops were to be landed at a harbour under Portugese control, promptly dictated a refusal of anchorage.[7]

In Germany, where public sympathy was already on the side of the beleaguered Boers, the despatch of the Kruger telegram triggered a fresh fusillade of anti-British reportage. Vicky hastily cancelled plans for a visit to her mother: 'if I were to go home at the moment, it might make mischief . . .' Writing to the Queen again, some ten months later, she sadly acknowledged that England, in Germany, had become a hated word.[8]

Just as her mother resisted no opportunity to deflate the portly Prince of Wales, Vicky seized the chance to blame Germany's new mood on Willy's behaviour. 'England is disliked and distrusted, which might well have been avoided . . .' she told Victoria in another letter. 'William is foolishly confident and sure of himself . . .'[9]

The captious views of an ousted mother need to be questioned. Cecil Spring-Rice joined the British Embassy in Berlin at the end of 1895, just at the time that Odo Russell's nephew-in-law, Sir Edward Malet, was replaced as the Queen's representative by the widely liked Frank Lascelles.* Thin, dark-eyed, poetic and astute, 'Springie' was a shrewd observer of Anglo-German relations during this period; his sense of England's new role as the enemy

---

* Lascelles's opposite number in London was the wise and tactful Count Paul von Hatzfeldt (1885–1901), increasingly assisted, as his health began to fail in 1898, by Baron Hermann von Eckardstein.

country ('It is curious how detested we are ... our existence is an offence to everyone ...') was that it undoubtedly pre-dated the sending of the fateful telegram.[10]

To Spring-Rice, it seemed as though the telegram helped to release and dispel the poisonous atmosphere that had greeted him on his arrival in Berlin. Writing to a friend at the Foreign Office on 11 January 1896, he noted that there was, by then, 'no real hostility', and again, on 17 January, 'no rudeness anywhere'. The press were stirring up feelings both in London and Berlin, but the people of England and Germany, especially those in mercantile life, were acutely conscious of 'what enormous interests we have in common and how fatal a war would be'.

The dread word had been set down, and Cecil Spring-Rice (who later wrote the words of 'I Vow to Thee, My Country') would allude to it with increasing anxiety over the years. Back in January 1896, he was convinced that a war could be avoided. Trade remained an arena of fierce conflict; the rapid growth of the German Navy was worrying; the press caused nothing but trouble; still, the Emperor struck Spring-Rice as a decent man who was striving to maintain good relations with his mother country. Wilhelm II had decided not to return his English uniforms (as if Willy would ever have made such a sacrifice). Instead, so Spring-Rice told Francis Villiers, his friend at the Foreign Office, on 22 January, the Emperor was boasting that he would win back all his popularity in England, 'and beat the Prince of Wales with an English-built yacht'. As for war: 'I'm sure it's correct to say of public opinion here that they regard war between us as impossible. That is the very reason for their violent abuse.' The insults, in other words, were of the kind traded between sparring cousins, too closely knit by blood to risk a fight.

Richard Seymour, a junior English diplomat, arrived in Berlin the following year (1897) for a six-month stay as an honorary attaché at the British Embassy. Less experienced than his friend Springie,

Seymour's initial dismay at being despatched to spend his first night on a sofa in a shabby back dining room at a nearby hotel (a court ball meant that all the Embassy bedrooms were taken) was deepened by the discovery that he was required to attend this event, dressed in the clean white breeches he did not possess, for his formal introduction to the Emperor.[11]

Breeches were loaned and a solemn face just about preserved, as young Seymour looked on at the stiff-legged caperings that took place at the Neues Palast that night. ('There is, probably, no person on earth less fitted to dance a minuet than a Prussian officer.') Three smart taps of a gilt cane announced, to the mandatory strains of Gounod's *Ave Maria*, the Emperor's approach. All smiles during Sir Frank's introduction of his protégé, Wilhelm asked the newcomer how he was enjoying himself in the finest city in Europe, complimented him upon an eminent grandfather – the ambassador to St Petersburg during the Crimean War – and then passed briskly on.

My grandfather enjoyed the first of his three spells in Berlin. Sir Frank was a kindly chief and life at the Embassy – even back in the days when all deciphering and message transmission had to be done by the inexperienced attachés – was seldom stressful. Seymour's account of a typical evening at 170 Wilhelmstrasse makes it sound like a gentlemen's club: large, quiet rooms, shaded lamps, the young attachés lounging over the papers in their chairs, Sir Frank off in a corner of the half-visible billiard room, a bearded courtier writing notes at his buhl desk, while puffing on his habitual Turkish cigarette in its long-stemmed amber holder. My grandfather's memoirs summon up an age when a young attaché's time off might be spent playing golf at Spandau, skating at the Tiergarten and paying sedate weekly visits to a lively old lady known to himself and Cecil Spring-Rice as Countess Tiddly-Winks (Tiele-Winckler), whose respect for England remained undimmed.

One image stands out in Richard Seymour's gentle recollections. In 1897, while still forbidden to visit England, the Emperor decided to celebrate his grandmother's Diamond Jubilee at Kiel. Travelling up by private train to Schleswig-Holstein for the occasion, Sir Frank Lascelles made what Richard Seymour later realised had been a pre-planned stop. Disembarking at a small, deserted station, well out of view of the royal party, the English diplomat ordered his team to pay their respects to a tall, shuffling-footed old man who – with a shock of excitement – Seymour recognised as the fallen Chancellor. Bismarck's health was failing, his eyesight almost gone, but he still held himself like a prince – and was saluted as such by the little English party before they continued on their way.

Welcomed to Kiel, and scolded for not having dressed in yachting attire (Willy's obsession with uniform extended to every area of official life), Sir Frank's little group were offered a pointed toast. Saluting Victoria as the wisest sovereign in Europe, Wilhelm evidently expected his emollient words to be swiftly transmitted to the ageing Queen as a peace offering. Perhaps the message went astray; certainly, no response was forthcoming.

In the summer of 1899, following strong hints from Count von Hatzfeldt and Baron Eckardstein about her nephew's desire for a rapprochement, Victoria finally relented. The Emperor was requested to visit the Isle of Wight for her birthday celebrations, but the invitation extended only to Osborne, her private home. Willy, who had been sorely missing his summer sailing jaunts to Cowes, took umbrage. Announcing that he could not dream of visiting England while his grandmother's prime minister, Lord Salisbury, stood in the way of Germany's plans to colonise the tiny Polynesian islands of Samoa, Willy presented a dollop of his own expert advice upon the handling of prime ministers, before grandly regretting his inability to travel – not to Osborne – but to Cowes.*

---

* America and England were in fierce dispute with Germany over the division of land rights in Samoa. The islands were coveted by all three countries for their strategic location.

Victoria was not easily vexed, but it did not please her to be offered advice about the handling of Lord Salisbury by her obstreperous grandson, and it pleased her even less to be so wilfully misunderstood. The words 'not to Cowes' were fiercely underscored in her response. Willy's provocative answer was to send the English-crewed *Meteor* over to compete at the Cowes Regatta, lacking only his own imperial presence on the decks. The *Meteor* won. Graceless in victory and still sulking about Lord Salisbury, Wilhelm informed the Royal Yacht Squadron (of which the Prince of Wales was the proud president) that British racing regulations were flawed (not quite up to the standards maintained in Germany).

Petty though Willy was being, the more serious dispute about Samoa did remain unresolved and Britain, in October 1899, was also at war once again against the Boers. Eager not to provoke a repetition of the Kruger telegram debacle, Victoria accepted Willy's suggestion of paying a visit to Windsor in November, together with the large suite upon which the Emperor always insisted.

In a controversy strangely reminiscent of Willy's descent upon his mother's home at Frankfurt, it was the retinue that nearly undid this second attempt at peacemaking. Bertie, who had not taken kindly to his nephew's slurs on the integrity of the Royal Yacht Squadron, was dismayed to learn that Willy intended to bring with him a certain Admiral von Senden for whom (as Willy well knew) the Prince of Wales felt a strong dislike. Pleas and warnings proved unavailing; not even the beguiling Baron Eckardstein could persuade Willy to leave the Admiral at home. Worse: the Emperor – forgetting who had requested the invitation in the first place – now threatened to cancel his visit until the issue of Germany's presence in Samoa was resolved.

Negotiations continued. Bertie grudgingly agreed that von Senden might join the gathering, so long as he kept a decent distance; the Emperor, in turn, allowed the Samoan discussions to be briefly laid aside. On 19 November, Willy and Dona arrived in England for a ten-day visit. A peculiar but carefully planned medley of Wagner overtures and Gilbert and Sullivan songs accompanied their state banquet at Windsor with the Queen. No harsh words were uttered. It seemed, to the relieved diplomats from both countries, that peace was in the air.

Good relations having been shakily restored, Willy maintained them in his own inimitable style. A gratified Daisy Pless received a contribution of £300 to her fund for the graves of British soldiers killed during the Boer War. Richard Seymour, back at the British Embassy in Berlin for a second stint, was as startled as his chief when, unannounced, 'booted, spurred and in full uniform', the Emperor bounced into Sir Frank Lascelles's bedroom, plumped himself down on the bed, unrolled his maps and delivered advice on how the new campaign in South Africa was to be conducted, with a request that his words should instantly be transmitted to London (it was 8 a.m.).[12]

Victoria, too, may have been anxious to strengthen the connection with Germany when she expressed the wish that one of her own family should preside over Prince Albert's duchy of Coburg. In the summer of 1900, 'Charlie' Albany, an Eton schoolboy without a word of German in his vocabulary, learned of his fate. Wilhelm, stepping into the role of substitute father, oversaw the first five years abroad of a bewildered exile who acutely missed his sister Alice and the happy life that they had shared at Claremont, the family home. Treating the young Duke of Saxe-Coburg and Gotha with a kindness that was not forgotten, Willy took a keen interest in his progress and even – in due course – found him a bride who was both pretty and affectionate. Gradually, with Willy's help, a very English young man learned to become a devoted German.

The Prince of Wales had never been the German Emperor's fondest fan. Nevertheless, Bertie recognised that genuine endeavours were being made. On 7 March 1900, less than a year after ridiculing Willy for his pompous habits and crass announcements, Bertie went out of his way to express gratitude to his nephew for

'the loyal friendship which you manifest towards us on every possible occasion'.

Knowing how proud the Emperor was of being an admiral of
the British fleet, Bertie even added a tactful tribute to his naval
rank, telling him that England would ever count upon Germany
as her best friend 'as long as you are at the helm'.[13]

Further evidence of Wilhelm's desire for reconciliation emerged
during this time. President Kruger's request to rally support by
undertaking a personal tour of Germany was turned down.
Instead, the Emperor attended a conciliatory meeting at the British
Embassy with Cecil Rhodes.

Initially hostile to Germany, Cecil Rhodes had revised his views
for reasons that were largely pragmatic. He had come to Berlin in
March 1899 to discuss the possibility of taking his planned Cape
to Cairo railway line through German territories: during the
course of a half-hour of private discussion with the Emperor in the
Embassy's billiard room, a second and more altruistic plan was discussed and, so it seems, agreed.

Opened three years later, in 1902, Rhodes's will included handsome funding for the Oxford scholarships that still bear his name
and that offered politically minded young Americans the chance to
study alongside English students at Rhodes's own alma mater. A
codicil added Germany to the scheme and stressed that Wilhelm II
would take personal responsibility for picking out the students he
considered eligible for the scholarships.

Why did Rhodes add Germany? It seems likely that the suggestion emerged from an encounter so amicable that Willy
(according to an attentive Richard Seymour) had expressed a wish
that Rhodes could join his own government. Certainly, Wilhelm
approved the scheme and concientiously selected students for
Oxford from 1902 until the German Rhodes Scholarships were
cancelled in 1914. (Opened again for the ten years between
1929–39, they have resumed operation without interruption since
1971.)

In the first year of the new century, the press continued to play England and Germany off against each other in a way that heightened nationalism and paranoia in both countries to fever pitch. Bertie's image of his nephew at the helm of a ship remained apt; the difficulty was that neither the German nor the British craft seemed willing to deviate from a course that had grown increasingly antagonistic and defensive.

England's war in Africa exposed weakness in her own defences and channels of information. Fears grew that the mother country was herself vulnerable to attack from the navy to which Wilhelm II had allocated an eye-watering 408 million marks in 1898, and over which, in 1899, he awarded himself complete control. The Emperor spoke of friendship – but could he be trusted?

The death of Victoria at the beginning of 1901 offered Wilhelm a rare opportunity to reassure England of Germany's friendship; it was a challenge to which he brought all of the considerable theatrical talent at his disposal.

The drama was all the more moving for being genuine. Wilhelm admired Victoria greatly; he relished his role as her eldest grandson. He was at Kiel when news arrived that she was failing; the Krupp-armed *Hohenzollern* reached harbour at Cowes on 21 January, just in time for the Emperor to join the cluster of relations who had gathered in the gloom of Osborne, waiting for the end. As Victoria faded into unconsciousness during the following afternoon, Willy took his place opposite the doctor at the royal bedside. The German Emperor's strong right arm – as muscular as his left was withered – provided a firm, unwavering support for the last two and a half hours of the Queen's life.

For once, there were no tantrums, no demands. Having measured up the corpse and placed a Union Jack on show (Victoria had rejected the use of undertakers for her funeral), Willy appeared to feel that his role as principal mourner was complete.

Tactfully, the new King Edward VII thanked his nephew by making him a field marshal as a birthday gift, three days before the funeral. Less tactfully, Willy requested (and was refused) the right to place his grandmother's body in the coffin.

The Times had mentioned the Emperor's arrival, but not his presence at the Queen's bedside. Compensation was to hand in the stately, exhaustive columns of prose that detailed every aspect of the funeral ceremonies. Readers learned that the Emperor had marched at the side of the new King, directly behind the hearse; that Willy had worn his new field marshal's uniform and had been honoured by a rendering of 'Heil dir im Siegerkranz' ('the air being the same as that of the British National Anthem', as *The Times* was anxious to explain). King Edward, courteously acknowledging his own new role as chief of the 1st Dragoon Regiment of the Prussian Guard, had paraded in the traditional blue-grey cloak and black and gold pickelhaube helmet; a uniform which, as *The Times* reassured its readers, 'did not for a moment prevent His [Majesty's] recognition by every bystander'. Such assurances were necessary; the truth was that King Edward, when attired in Prussian uniform, looked – as Bertie had always sounded – unnervingly Germanic.

Just for once, Willy failed to put a foot wrong. He talked to the crowds, delighting them with his clear and idiomatic English; he asked after the welfare of the regiment in South Africa of which he was, officially, commander-in-chief; he spoke with respectful veneration about his deceased grandmother; he wore an expression of becoming sadness when acknowledging the weakening health of his own mother.

Willy, as even the constantly apprehensive inhabitants of the German Embassy agreed, had behaved well. There was, on this occasion, no sign of the Emperor's terrifying impetuousness; no hint of that unpredictable flicker with which Willy could change from friend to foe. Mourning the end of an era, fearing the aggressive purpose for which Germany's mighty and swiftly growing fleet might be intended, the English correspondents tumbled over themselves in their eagerness to make Wilhelm feel at home and among friends. The Emperor (*The Times* pleaded with uncharacteristic humility) must have been deeply gratified by 'the cordiality of the people and their sincere desire to do him honour'. Wilhelm II, the *Telegraph* grovelled, had shown himself to be 'the true heir to Frederick the Great', while being 'largely of our own blood'. Surely, the journalistic undercurrent seemed to murmur, there was no need to rock the boat? Surely, as Joseph Chamberlain had urged to a gathering at Leicester back on 30 November 1899, England, Germany and America could now unite to preserve peace in the world? Surely, the German Emperor's deference to his royal grandmother signalled the wish for peace with a country that was so nearly his own?[14]

Willy's mother died just seven months after Victoria, following a long, painful and gallantly discreet battle with cancer. Vicky, even from the seclusion of the Friedrichshof, had always held the pin that could prick the balloon of her son's easily inflated ego. With Vicky gone, and Victoria's voice reduced to a whisper from the grave, Willy's confidence could only increase.

The women of power were dead: only his compliant Dona remained, an empress who was always ready to soothe her husband's vanity, ever willing to bolster Wilhelm's faith in himself as the imperial leader of a young, ambitious and increasingly powerful nation. In the summer of 1901, with 'IF' pinned high above his desk, Willy was ready to demonstrate that he, Emperor Wilhelm II, not the exalted gentleman whose large behind now rested on the English throne, was the man who Kipling had in mind.[15] 'If you can keep your head when all about you / Are losing theirs and blaming it on you . . .'

The fault, for Willy, would always lie in others, never in himself. Nobly, in his own turbulent and increasingly unhinged mind, he intended to gain for the great Fatherland the role that she deserved.

The Emperor Wilhelm II would reduce England to picture-book dependency: a charming island, no larger in consequence than the pretty, impoverished duchies of pre-imperial Germany. Little Albion belonged to the past. Germania held the keys to the future.

12

THE FRIENDSHIP UNDER STRAIN

(1902–10)

Wilhelm II's sense of the contrast between England and Germany at the close of his grandmother's long reign was hubristic, but it was not entirely wrong.

Back in the 1820s, Germans had come to England to observe and learn from a country that was deploying a combination of engineering skills, industrial power, a formidable navy and a surge of entrepreneurial spirit to transform itself into a super-power. During the first years of the twentieth century, it was the English who were sitting up to take note of the fact that Krupp, employing over 20,000 people at its Essen works, had become the world's largest industrial company; that the north German shipyards at Danzig, Hamburg, Kiel, Wilhelmshaven and beau-tiful, Parisian-styled Stettin were on target to produce (at the urging of Admiral Alfred von Tirpitz) thirty-eight battleships by 1919; that the Stettin-built *Kaiser Wilhelm der Grosse* (named for Wilhelm I) was both the world's first four-funnel transatlantic liner and a pioneer user of the Marconi wireless system for trans-mitting rescue messages; and that Albert Ballin, taking charge of the great Hamburg-Amerika line in 1899, was overseeing the launch of the world's first cruise ship, proudly named for the Emperor's daughter: *Prinzessin Viktoria Luise*. In 1902, it may also have been wistfully noted that Germany had a vigorous, morally upright and relatively youthful leader, while England was led by a stout, indolent and philandering bon viveur whose best-known source of pleasure (next to love-making and gambling) derived from the cigars named in his honour.

Moral rectitude did not save Wilhelm II from being mocked, at home and abroad, both for his lack of culture and for his faith in the power of official art to inspire and uplift the German people. It was with this goal in mind that the Emperor presented the city of Berlin, in 1901, with his own addition to a handsome boulevard that had been constructed back in 1896, to honour Germany's military triumphs and to give pleasure to Sunday strollers in the Tiergarten park. The original Siegesallee had been well received; the Emperor's addition of almost a hundred marble statues, with prominent placing for his own Hohenzollern for-bears, was ridiculed as 'Puppets' Alley' or the 'Plaster Walk'. Wilhelm, undaunted, used his opening of the transformed boule-vard to express imperial disapproval of 'ugly art' (in comparison to a double-banked row of quasi-classical figures). Ugly art, in Willy's opinion, included the dangerously gloomy works of Cézanne, van Gogh and Edvard Munch that were being simulta-neously displayed in the city by the Berlin Secession group, led by the great Impressionist painter Max Liebermann, and the dealer Paul Cassirer. What, the Emperor Wilhelm demanded, was the point of increasing people's misery by showing them such dreary work, when the purpose of art was to raise people's hopes above their modest expectations?[1]

The new Siegesallee was derided in Berlin, as were the Emperor's views on modern art. Neither were the Emperor's efforts to burnish his country's image as a dynamic modern power helped, in the sphere of music, by Willy's old-fashioned preference for Verdi and Gounod over Wagner, for whose work his appreciation was confined to borrowing the thunder motif from *Das Rheingold* for the horn of the imperial automobile.

Wilhelm's philistinism did not equip him well for his dream of turning Berlin into the German Athens. It was Wilhelm, nevertheless, who presided over the gradual transformation of his home city from a dusty collection of military parade grounds into an elegant metropolis of broad streets, handsome department stores, new theatres and the smart restaurants at a precursor of which an astonished Matthew Arnold, lunching out in Berlin in 1885, had found himself sharing a table with two elegantly dressed tarts. Such a triangle, by the time that Berlin's new Adlon Hotel opened its doors in 1907, would have widened no Prussian eyes at all.

The spirit of Berlin in 1902 was, despite lingering traces of an older world, keeping company with the 43-year-old Emperor's jaunty sense of himself as 'a man of the future'. London, by contrast, seemed locked, together with its new but ageing king (Edward was Wilhelm's senior by eighteen years), into the past.

The past – that Pickwickian England so dear to the Emperor himself – held considerable power over German Anglophiles. The attractions of foxhunting in the Shires had seduced other German grandees besides Hansel Pless's two Hochberg uncles to settle in England; many others paid regular visits. (One German officer claimed to know Yorkshire's hunting fields well enough to name every blacksmith's forge in the three Ridings.[2]) Count Friedrich Schulenburg, posted to London as a military attaché from 1902–06, was sufficiently bewitched by English ways to persuade his wife, Freda Marie von Arnim, that their children must be granted the sense of a dual heritage. Life at Tressow, the Schulenburgs' Mecklenburg manor house, was effortlessly bilingual; their daughter Tisa remembered English books and German books being read as interchangeably as the two languages of this large and lively household were spoken.

The wish to maintain a bond between Germany and England

was most easily granted to the families of people like Hansel Pless, the Schröders and Hilda Deichmann, who were lucky enough to have inbuilt connections to both countries.

The author Robert Graves belonged to this privileged group. Visiting Laufzorn, his grandparents' atmospheric manor house in Bavaria, during the long Edwardian summers of his early boyhood, Graves formed a keen respect for the bushy-haired old gentleman who was greeted by a warm 'Grüss Gott, Herr Professor!' when they drove out from his home and through the neighbouring villages.

Admired by young Robert for the atheism and rebelliousness of his early years, when his part in the Prussian uprisings of 1848 forced him to seek refuge in England, Heinrich von Ranke had studied medicine in London. Having served as a regimental surgeon at the Crimea, von Ranke went on to supervise paediatrics at the German Hospital in Dalston, while helping to set up the Great Ormond Street Hospital for children. Subsequently, having married the 'tiny, saintly, frightened' Danish daughter of the Greenwich astronomer, Graves's grandfather returned to Bavaria. Here, in the process of becoming one of Munich's most eminent paediatricians, von Ranke acquired Laufzorn and developed the habits of a respected country squire, while insisting – like Wilhelm II, whom he greatly admired – that his children should speak English in their family life, and look to England always as 'the centre of culture and progress'.[3]

The warm feelings for England that Graves found among his German cousins endeared them to him. So, too – although Graves described German as a language in which he felt instantly at home – did the fact that his Bavarian cousins were fluent in English. Setting those benefits aside, it's still hard to overstate the sense of settled contentment conveyed in Graves's wistful recollections of those early summers in Germany: they were, he wrote, 'easily the best things of my early childhood'.

The rural arcadia evoked by Graves was grounded in simple, accessible experiences: picking fruit in an orchard filled with greengages and plums; jumping on springy hay in a high, raftered barn; picking mushrooms in the woods; diving under a waterfall in the bright green Isar; paying visits by train to a castle up in the Bavarian Alps, where an eccentric great-uncle (Baron Siegfried von Aufsess) teased the credulous young visitors with craftily placed chocolate drops among the pathway pebbles that he urged them to devour.

All sounds innocuous and almost bland, until we remember that Graves was writing in 1929, and that he had fought against these same cousins in the war. Peppering the benign accounts of a distant past are reminders of the aftermath. Uncle Siegfried, serving on the Emperor's staff of officers, was killed and lost. His body was never recovered. Wilhelm, a favourite cousin and a dab hand at picking off mice in the attics with his airgun, was 'shot down in air battle by a schoolfellow of mine'. Conrad, another cherished cousin, with whom Graves remembered having gone skiing near Zurich in January 1914, is described as 'a gentle, proud creature, chiefly interested in natural history [and] studying the habits of wild animals; he had strong feelings against shooting them'. Conrad von Ranke, so Graves tells his readers, went on to win the Blue Max (the German equivalent of the Victoria Cross), for his bravery. 'Soon after the war ended, a party of Bolsheviks killed him in a Baltic village, to which he had been sent to make requisitions.'[4] Looking back across ten traumatised years, Graves made no attempt to conceal his bitterness at the futility of war; at the pointlessness of Conrad's death; at the horror for any soldier of having known – and loved as part of his own family – the enemy he was under orders to destroy. The experience was not an unusual one; Graves's compellingly bitter war memoir, *Goodbye to All That*, describes a company mess in which the majority of British officers had German mothers or naturalised German fathers.

Robert Graves, born in 1895, belonged to a younger generation of Englishmen than Ford Madox Ford. Their bond was the dilemma of belonging to families with a dual heritage.

Ford, as buttercup-haired and blue-eyed as his father, the Wagnerian music critic Franz Hüffer (a name that had been swiftly exchanged for the more English-sounding Francis Hueffer), was seven years old in 1880, when he was despatched from home to learn German at a private school in Folkestone. Married at eighteen to Elsie Martindale, two years after the loss of his beloved father, Ford's affair with Elsie's sister led to social ostracism. In the autumn of 1904, following a nervous breakdown, Ford left England for five months, to make the acquaintance of his father's Münster-based German family and to discover – between some eccentric courses of spa treatment recommended by his sympathetic cousins for three further nervous collapses – what the intelligent, unhappy and highly strung young writer described in his letters to England as a most wonderful sense of having come home.

Aside from his breakdowns, Ford was exceptionally happy in Germany; writing (somewhat tactlessly) to his wife and to their friend Olive Garnett, he compared the sorrowful rootlessness that he had come to feel in England ('the tremendous feeling of loneliness and the end of the world that I had latterly') with the sense – one that was novel to him, and quite delightful – of being accepted. 'I am treated here like a duke,' Ford told Olive Garnett. '... I feel I'm really liked and understood by everyone.'[5]

In 1906, Ford paid a second visit to Germany, taking Elsie and their young daughters from Heidelberg to Münster, where the girls, following their father's own earlier conversion and with the warm approval of their Hüffer relations, adopted the Catholic faith.

Four years later, while visiting Germany in the summer of 1910, Olive Garnett's son David bumped into a faultlessly dressed Ford enjoying a Rhine tour in the company of his mistress, Violet Hunt. Conducted to Nauheim, the beautiful Jugendstil spa created under the patronage and close attention of Ernst of Hessen-Darmstadt, Hunt was struck by the gentle Grand Duke's courteous manner; Ford's pious Aunt Emma, less politely, refused to let her nephew's lady friend enter her German home.

Violet was at her lover's side again later that year when he paid a memorable visit to Marburg Castle, the setting for Luther's unfaltering defence of Christ's corporeal presence in the communion sacraments. Marburg gave Ford the setting for a key scene in the celebrated novel that he published five years later.

The Good Soldier was written and published in wartime. No hint appears in the novel of the author's own German connections. Instead, the depth of Ford's love for the nation to which he half belonged is artfully submerged in a cast of American and English protaganists who, staying at Nauheim at the turn of the century and mired in the unhappy complexities of their personal relations, respond to their surroundings only as tourists. Dowell, the unreliable narrator, views his surroundings with eyes that reject – or are incapable of seeing – any beauty in a German landscape. If Ford felt any lingering affection for the country he had once looked on as his true home, writing the novel that he had first wanted to call *The Saddest Story* seems to have helped him to kill it.

The advent of war ended Ford's wish to connect himself to the Münster Hüffers and even to the German writers among whom he had once felt so happily at ease. In 1919, he relinquished the surname Hueffer; France, not Germany, would become his chosen home in a Europe to which the newly named Ford Madox Ford belonged, by temperament and blood, more closely than to the England of which he wrote, increasingly, with the romantic, idealising pen of a visitor from abroad.

In March 1905 – the year after Ford's first visit to Germany – 26-year-old Morgan Forster arrived at Nassenheide, the Pomeranian schloss near Stettin to which he had been invited from England as a tutor to the children of Count Henning von Arnim, a tall, balding, impecunious – and cheerfully unliterary – Prussian landowner,

and Elizabeth Beauchamp, his tiny, energetic and intensely literary Australian wife.

Forster had never been to Germany before; his first impressions
of the celebrated setting of *Elizabeth and Her German Garden*
(Countess von Arnim's first and massively successful book had
been anonymously published in 1898) were not good. Recalling
his arrival, over fifty years later, Forster described how a farm
worker had led him through a muddy farmyard to a dimly lit
house at which, until Elizabeth herself hurried down to greet him,
the newcomer was received with bewilderment (a German housemaid, not an English tutor, had been expected at the schloss).

The homely gabled manor house of Nassenheide won Forster's
heart during his four-month stay there, as did its inhabitants. The
Count, despite an unnerving fondness for rinsing his false teeth
during meals, proved both kind and courteous; the German tutor
already in residence was a jovial beer-drinker; the pupils were
entertaining and playful. One daughter, Trix, when asked by
Forster to write an essay upon which country she would wish to
win if England and Germany went to war, answered that she
would not care: 'I should run away as fast as I could.'[6]

Elizabeth herself lived up to her self-chosen motto: *parva sed
apta*: small but effective. Indomitably competent and hard-working,
she wrote twenty-one books, read voraciously and spoke her husband's tongue well enough to pass as a native. Elizabeth was also,
according to Forster, a merciless tease and disciplinarian who, after
informing the young tutor that his work-in-progress made her
want to take a bath, ordered him to finish it.

That book, Forster's first novel, was *Where Angels Fear to Tread*,
in which no hint of his German experiences can be detected. In
1908, back in England and with two further well-received novels
to his name, Forster began work upon a fourth. He called it
Howards End.

It is possible to interpret the story of the German Schlegels, the
British Wilcoxes and Howards End (the house that binds them

uneasily together) as an anti-war book. Forster's novel also offers a personal tribute to the country that had so enchanted him during the months he spent at Nassenheide, visiting pretty, elegant Stettin and exploring the birch woods and the broad fields that stretched away from the windows of the Pomeranian manor house.

Criticisms of Germany, despite Forster's fond recollections of life with the von Arnims, were not withheld. Mr Schlegel, looking wistfully back to the gentle world of the little princely courts and denouncing the new spirit of pan-Germanism, is endorsed in a way that suggests Forster himself may have shared the old-fashioned outlook of his former Prussian employer. Two haughty Schlegel cousins, visiting England from Stettin, are ridiculed for their firm belief in Germany's God-given right to rule the world; another visitor, Frau Architect Frieda Liesecke, does not show to advantage when, invited to admire the Schlegel sisters' favourite view across the Solent to the Isle of Wight, she registers only a muddy harbour (Poole) and the dreary bulk of distant hills.

Forster balances his mockery of the visitors against the ardent sincerity of the Schlegel girls, proudly described by their German-hating aunt, Mrs Munt, as 'English ... English to the backbone.'[7] In fact, while belonging wholly to neither country, Margaret and Helen display a powerful attachment to the country in which they have their first encounter (while visiting Heidelberg) with the hard-headed and philistine Wilcoxes. The Wilcoxes see little in Heidelberg to charm them; the Schlegels see much. 'The German is always on the look-out for beauty,' Margaret Schlegel declares, defending herself as well as her paternal heritage. 'He may miss it through stupidity, or misinterpret it, but he is always asking for beauty to enter his life.'[8] Helen, revisiting the countryside around Nassenheide on Forster's behalf, praises the landscape in words taken directly from the novelist's own observations: 'She spoke of the scenery, quiet, yet august; of the snow-clad fields, with their scampering herds of deer ... [of] real mountains, with pine-forests, streams, and views complete.'[9]

It would be ambitious to read a direct comment upon the broadening rift between England and Germany into Forster's famous words, spoken by Margaret Schlegel: 'Only connect the prose and the passion . . . and human love will be seen at its highest. Live in fragments no longer.'[10] It would be careless to dismiss the likelihood that Forster, writing a book about English and German attitudes at a time when war had become a looming probability, was making the case that he would argue more overtly in his political essays of the 1930s. Margaret's statement can be read as a writer's plea both for the thoughtful use of words (as opposed to the inflammatory language of the pre-war press) and for taking the larger view, for what Forster described in *Howards End* as 'that interest in the universal which the average Teuton possesses and the average Englishman does not'.[11]

Howards End was published in 1910, the year that Henning von Arnim died, just one year after the sale of his beloved Nassenheide. The possibility of war hung like a cloud in the air; Elizabeth von Arnim, publishing a novel in 1909 about a German baron's visit to England, had warned readers of *The Caravaners* that Prussian eyes were already sizing up their 'plump little island' and that the Prussian Junkers ('that chivalrous, God-fearing, and well-born band that upholds the best traditions of the Fatherland') had gathered in spirit, 'like a protecting phalanx around our Emperor's throne'.[12]

Protecting the Emperor from whom, precisely, von Arnim did not say. An assertion made elsewhere in *The Caravaners* that the Prussian eagle will always hold its place at the head of the European tree shows that England was not the only imagined aggressor. Encirclement, Germany's fear of being trapped within a noose of unfriendly and allied powers, was much discussed in the circles in which the von Arnims moved.

Back in 1907, while paying one of her occasional visits to England, Elizabeth met up with another clever young novelist, Hugh

Walpole. She invited him to take on the role that Forster had briefly occupied two years earlier, as an English tutor to her children. The meeting with Walpole took place over a lunch at a women's club called the London Lyceum, the brainchild of a remarkable Birmingham-born woman called Constance Smedley who made a valuable contribution of her own to strengthening the Anglo-German connection.

Smedley was attending a conference in Berlin in 1901 when she noticed, with the disapproval of a staunch feminist, how many German women were still confined to the infamous triangle of the three Ks: *Kinder, Küche, Kirche* (Children, Kitchen, Church). Keen to help emancipate them from such a restrictive definition, Smedley shared her thoughts with Countess Harrach, an influential and progressive *Palastdamen* (lady-in-waiting) who divided her time between Berlin, her husband's Silesian estate and her own family castle in Switzerland (Oberhofen). Together, the two women set to work.

The Berlin Lyceum opened its doors on 4 November 1905. The report in the *Berliner Tageblatt* of the following day mentioned only that the new club's public spaces were gaily decorated; quite probably, the blueprint was taken from London, where Smedley offered thirty-five female members a library, an art gallery, a once-a-month book-club dinner and a monthly concert of modern music. Countess Harrach had prevailed upon the usually stodgy Empress Dona to support the project, with the result that the opening night included a large delegation from the court. The recently bereaved English Ambassador, Frank Lascelles, brought along his sister, Lady Edward Cavendish; his American counterpart, the gloriously named Charlemagne Tower, came with his wife. Speeches (all of which were faithfully reported by the *Tageblatt*) included one in which Constance Smedley expressed her ardent hope that the new Lyceum might become 'a bond of union between Germany and England'.

And so, working together with its London counterpart, it did. No insuperable divisions between the two countries existed in the

Samuel Taylor Coleridge as he appeared to his new friends at Göttingen in 1798.

Theodor Fontane in 1843, aged 23, the year before his first visit from Prussia to England.

AN.ELECTION.BALL

Prince Pückler-Muskau seeks a rich English bride with the blessing of his devoted German wife, and provides a good-humoured target for British cartoonists.

Sarah Austin, who translated Pückler-Muskau's travel-writings and fell in love with their author during the process.

In 1894, Victoria visited Darmstadt, following the stage-managed marriage of a favourite grandson, Grand-Duke 'Ernie', and the engagement of Ernie's sister, Alix, to Tsar Nicholas, standing left, just behind Wilhelm II. Wilhelm's mother, the Empress Friedrich, stands beside her mother, the Queen.

Prince Albert as a proud Scot.

The Princess Royal ('Vicky', later the Empress Friedrich) at Osborne in 1855.

Lululaund, the Bavarian home named for the artist's late wife and built by the Herkomer family in Bushey, Hertfordshire, in the 1890s.

Never reticent, Sir Hubert Herkomer paints a landscape while preparing to speak into a phonograph.

As well as painting, directing plays and films, and setting up an art school, Herkomer launched one of the world's first motor races in Germany and designed this sexy image to promote it.

The Welsh-born Princess of Pless (Daisy Cornwallis-West) sits second left beside her father-in-law (Vater), and behind her husband, in a houseparty at Pless for the Grand Manoeuvres of 1905.

One of the young princesses from Hesse with shrimp pail and boater during one of the family's summer-long stays at Eastbourne, which they loved.

Privileged, artistic and intent on preventing a war between the two countries to which he belonged, Count Harry Kessler – seen here as a boy – was the son of a Hamburg banker and an Irish beauty who caught the eye of Wilhelm I. Kessler rejected suggestions that the Emperor was his father.

A photographer in 1891 captures the very uncordial relationship between an annoyingly youthful Wilhelm II and his worldly – far wiser – Uncle Bertie.

Prince Louis of Battenberg married one of Grand-Duke 'Ernie' Hesse's sisters and became a respected German Sea Lord of the British Fleet (de László 1910)

Wilhelm II adopts a proprietorial position standing just behind his cousin, George V, in a gathering of Europe's royal leaders, in 1910.

Hilda de Bunsen, later Baroness Deichmann (painted by Herkomer), was the English-born mother of a (English-born) son who fought for his Fatherland in 1914.

Hilda's brother, Sir Maurice de Bunsen, grandson of a Prussian diplomat, British ambassador to Vienna in 1914.

Frieda (von Richthoven) Weekley at Irschenhausen in Bavaria in 1913, during her first months as the lover of D.H. Lawrence.

Prince Karl Max Lichnowsky, a most unhappy ambassador when he left England, a country he adored, in 1914.

Mechtilde (Arco-Zinneberg) Lichnowsky, writer, art patron and diplomat's wife. The Omega workshops fabric shown behind the princess was named 'Mechtilde' in her honour.

Sir Edward Goschen, the music-loving British ambassador to Berlin who was there when war was declared in 1914.

Daisy Pless doing her bit for the wounded in 1915 as a Red Cross nurse stationed in Germany.

LT. GOSCHEN HOME.

SIR EDWARD'S PATIENT WAIT FOR HIS SON.

George Goschen ('Bunt'), a talented pianist who was the much-loved companion of his widowed father at the British Embassy in Berlin. Accompanied by one of the cuttings that announced the return of Goschen's son, George, following his capture and imprisonment.

shared world of culture, and it was from this deep mutual well that Smedley's Lyceums drew their most valuable support. Max Liebermann, his nephew Walter Rathenau, the art patron and bibliophile Count Harry Kessler and the playwright Gerhart Hauptmann (an Anglophile who hungered for – and obtained – an Oxford doctorate to crown his German achievements) were recruited by Countess Harrach to assist and advise on the Lyceum in Berlin. In England, Smedley's impressive committee included C. F. A. Voysey, Laurence Alma-Tadema, William Rothenstein, Frank Brangwyn, Sir John Lavery and Walter Crane. In Berlin, an exhibition of art by British Lyceum members went on show in 1905 before touring Germany. In London, at the suggestion of William Rothenstein, a corresponding show of works by twenty-five new German artists was organised under the aegis of the Lyceum in the winter of 1906 and displayed in a specially con-structed hall at the (now entirely forgotten) Prince's Gallery in South Kensington. From Berlin, the half-Irish Harry Kessler advised on which German artists should be included; the opening was followed by a slap-up banquet at the Savoy, attended by G. B. Shaw and presided over by that ardent Germanophile and most avuncular of political intellectuals Richard Haldane. Haldane's younger sister, Elizabeth, the first translater of Hegel's lectures into English in 1892, was also present.

Men like Harry Kessler and Richard Haldane were acutely con-scious of the growing rift between their countries. They were not alone in their concern (Henry James was only half joking when he told an American friend in 1907 that he believed the Kaiser was training his cannons to fire on the chimney-pots of his own little Rye residence). An Anglo-German dinner held by Constance Smedley in December 1905 attracted a formidable list of guests which included the Earl and Countess of Aberdeen, the entire diplomatic staff of the German Embassy, the Lord Mayor of London and the editors of two of the more level-headed organs of

British public opinion: George Prothero from the *Quarterly Review* and Austin Harrison from *The Observer*. Speeches, given by the German Ambassador, Count Metternich, by Prothero, Lord Aberdeen and Smedley herself, focused on the urgent need – in Prothero's words – for those 'who write, and who address great masses of persons, to do all they can to quench the flame of enmity'. Smedley herself pleaded that night for England to remember that Germany was not merely a commercial nation, but the land of art and literature, 'of Beethoven and Bach, of Handel and Wagner, Strauss, Schubert, Schumann ... That is the Germany we love ...'[13]

Both the dinner and the speeches were reported upon the following day – and warmly commended – by the *Daily Telegraph*, the *Morning Post* and the *Daily News*. To the surprise of none, Smedley's gallant endeavour at peacemaking passed without note from either *The Times* or the brand-new *Daily Mail*.

Of these two Germanophobic papers, Alfred Harmsworth's venture, the *Daily Mail*, was the more active as a troublemaker. Erskine Childers, back in 1903, had written the widely read *Riddle of the Sands*, a naval thriller warning of danger from a foreign power. Struck by the magnitude of Childers's success, Harmsworth commissioned a spine-chilling account of England under siege from the Huns.

The Invasion of 1910, published in 1906, was brashly advertised by the appearance in Oxford Street of a band of touts in Prussian uniforms, proclaiming evil tidings to the guileless shoppers. A German invasion was imminent! Details were available only in the *Mail*'s new giveaway book! Harmsworth's idea was an instant hit. William Le Queux's novel was translated into twenty-seven languages, including a pirated German version. Selling over a million copies, the book enriched the author and vastly increased the circulation of the *Mail*.

The Times, so sober in the appearance of its enormous, closely printed pages and small, sedate headings, was less cynical and –

because of its august reputation – far more dangerous. The problem here was simply that the newspaper's chief correspondent in Berlin, George Saunders, was fiercely anti-German (Houston Stewart Chamberlain, an English-born Anglophobe, later remarked that Saunders should have been hanged for the damage that he wreaked on Germany). Thanks entirely to Saunders, friendly opinions of the kind that were regularly expressed by such newspapers as the Anglophile *Köln Zeitung* never reached England. *The Times*, trusting in Saunders to tell the truth, actively contributed to England's fears of a hostile, power-hungry empire on the make, building up its massive, armour-heavy navy not – as the German Emperor would always insist, to protect his Baltic coastline and provide a useful backup to Britain in the Far East – but for attack and destruction.

Fears were growing. Daisy Pless, taking charge of all social arrangements at the German Embassy in London during the residence there of the deaf, shy and quietly appreciative Count Metternich, had noted in her diary for 23 April 1905 that the English kept asking her whether the Germans hated them, or their country, or both.[14] Cecil Spring-Rice, following what amounted almost to a diplomatic incident during that same year – the Emperor, sulking because Uncle Bertie had sent his son, the Prince of Wales, over to visit Berlin in his place, had forbidden his own eldest son to visit the King at Windsor – told the American President's wife that 'the indications are most threatening'.[15] Hermann Muthesius, lecturing on the glories of the Glasgow School in Berlin in 1907, was so outraged by a command to stop praising British art that he withdrew from the association that had rebuked him and joined, instead, the group that subsequently formed the state-sponsored Deutscher Werkbund and that included Peter Behrens, Mies van der Rohe, Richard Riemerschmid and Henry van de Velde.

Daisy Pless, who knew the rulers of both countries well enough to have persuaded them to stand as joint godparents to her eldest boy, Hansel, exerted all of her considerable personal charm in the endeavour to reconcile volatile Wilhelm with his royal uncle. Harry Kessler took a more radical approach. He launched a public appeal.

The son of a rich Hamburg banker and a beautiful Irishwoman, Alice Blosse Lynch, the dapper, diminutive and passionately artistic Kessler stood in a perfect strategic position to create a bridge between the countries. Educated in England and France, he went on to university in Germany, studied art history and – at the age of twenty-four – undertook a lecture tour of America. In England, where he formed strong links with the art world through William Morris, Augustus John and the Rothensteins, he took time off, in 1902, from studying typefaces at the British Museum to attend both boxing matches in the East End with his friend Aristide Maillol and theatres in the Haymarket. Impressed by the dramatic setting of a play – it was Ibsen's *The Vikings* – directed, in 1903, by the startlingly handsome Edward Gordon Craig, Kessler invited Craig to work, at Weimar, with Hugo von Hofmannsthal (a disaster) and then with Max Reinhardt (another disaster).

The friendship between the two men survived such disappointments, finding its fullest artistic realisation in Craig's illustrations for an edition of *Hamlet* printed by Kessler's Cranach Press. That commission did not come until 1913; back in 1905, Kessler's attention was focused on destroying the vitriolic influence of another form of press: the anti-German British newspapers represented by *The Times* and the *Daily Mail*.

On 5 January 1906, a remarkable document appeared in the Letters columns of *The Times*. It was a plea for peace; a reminder that – in Kessler's own words – 'A war between the two powers would be a world calamity for which no victory could compensate either nation.' Its request, directed at the very paper in which it appeared, was that *The Times* should desist from 'attributing to Germany sinister designs against England, and thus sowing sentiments that in an emergency would render difficult and perhaps impossible the task for those responsible for the peace between both countries'.

The message was clear. A list of signatories from Germany included Richard Strauss, Max Liebermann, Ernst Haeckel, Elisabeth Förster-Nietzsche and Siegfried Wagner, while the English side was represented by Thomas Hardy, Jane Morris, John Lavery, Walter Crane, Edward Elgar, Gilbert Murray, C. H. Shannon and Isaac Zangwill. Harry Kessler's staunchest ally, the Bradford-born (to German parents) artist William Rothenstein, was among the first to sign his name.

In the short term, Kessler's appeal proved effective. On 8 January 1906, just three days after the letter's publication, *The Times* informed its readers of an assembly of several thousand peace-seekers in Munich, headed by the British Minister in Residence, Sir Reginald Tower, and Munich's Mayor, Herr von Borscht. The purpose of this gathering, so *The Times* reported with uncharacteristic cordiality, was to demonstrate a wish for 'friendly relations'.

The new mood was short-lived. At the end of the month, the royal launching of Britain's first and massively expensive *Dreadnought* battleship prompted the tiresome question of cost and justification. *The Times* was ready to help out. The German Emperor's recent birthday was alleged to have been celebrated by speeches which – according to the Germanophobic George Saunders – had adopted a stridently military tone and had been received with cheers. Anti-German feelings in England, *The Times* rumbled, were now running very high indeed.

The commissioning of the *Dreadnought* had been sparked off by a brief summer visit that King Edward paid to his nephew at Kiel in 1904. Daisy Pless was present, observing the ceremonies from the comfort of the Vanderbilts' yacht. (American yachtsmen were regular visitors to the Emperor's favourite harbour, where they annually defeated him in the battle of the waves.) The Princess took the view that the King's visit, however small a gesture, demonstrated good diplomacy. Uncle Bertie had been at his most affable, offering nothing but admiration as Willy showed off the results of his shipbuilding programme. (The four funnels of the gigantic *Kaiser Wilhelm der Grosse* are just visible in paintings of the occasion.) Taking his departure, the King of England was all smiles. By the end of that year, however, word reached Berlin that Britain's new First Sea Lord, Sir John Fisher (a man for whom the sea-loving Emperor professed great respect) was overseeing the construction of a ship intended to dwarf and intimidate all rivals. The *Dreadnought,* built in secrecy, was launched into the English Channel in 1906. Its appearance marked a new and worrying stage in the battle of the big ships, and an increasing chill between the kingly and the imperial courts.

On a domestic scale, the Emperor decided to treat Britain's new war-craft as a joke. 'Our British dreadnought' was the name Willy playfully bestowed upon Ethel Topham, the governess appointed to teach English to his daughter Viktoria Luise and his son Joachim.

Miss Topham (whose charges already spoke better English than her German) waited until 1926 to publish her recollections of life at the Prussian court. Her account throws fascinating sidelights upon one of the most unfortunate episodes in the pre-war history of Anglo-German relations.

Edward VII, following his 1904 expedition to Kiel, waited three years to offer Wilhelm the further olive branch of the first family visit to Windsor since Victoria's death. Reluctantly undertaken in November 1907, when the Emperor was suffering from one of his unpredictable fits of Anglophobia, the excursion proved a huge success. The Empress Dona, who did not like England, was won over by a Christmas shopping tour of Harrods in the affable – and hugely pro-German – company of Richard Haldane. The crowds showed their usual appreciation of the Emperor's delight in donning English uniforms for every possible occasion. Wilhelm, to the relief of all, was on his best form. While Dona and their accompanying suite returned to Berlin, Wilhelm, concerned about a polyp in his throat, decided to take a private rest-cure at Highcliffe, a Hampshire castle (with a view towards Cowes) owned by Colonel Edward Stuart-Wortley.

It seems to have been by mere coincidence that Highcliffe was owned by a cousin, through marriage, of a man whom the Emperor had begun to venerate as the voice of truth: Houston Stewart Chamberlain. Stewart Chamberlain's particular skill, odiously apparent in his grovelling letters to the Emperor, was to combine gobbets of handy erudition with deferential tributes to Willy's genius and majesty. Colonel Edward Stuart-Wortley was less complex. Eager to do his bit towards improving England's relations with Germany, he asked only the honour of being permitted to remain on hand. The sole condition that Stuart-Wortley requested to be imposed during Wilhelm's visit to Highcliffe was that the Emperor would permit him to listen and, perhaps, to advise.

Wilhelm's mood swings were always extreme; playing the bluff English gentleman of leisure for his host at Highcliffe Castle, he grew ecstatic. Everything delighted him: the pretty manners of the castle's estate children; the beauty of the unspoiled coastal landscape; the decorous habits of an old-fashioned household; the nonchalant sportsmanship, even, of a local clergyman who boxed as well as he played cricket.

Back in Berlin, Dona read Willy's joyful letters aloud, compelling her court ladies to hear about that 'indefinable something which English homes alone possess of comfort'. Feelings about the Emperor's disloyalty took the form of cross looks cast at poor, English-born Miss Topham, or small, ironic bows.[16] Discomfited, Miss Topham nevertheless glowed with pride: these letters, she believed, offered proof of 'how intensely he [the Emperor] loves and admires English life as apart from English politics'.[17]

The Highcliffe interlude prefaced a disaster that almost led to Wilhelm's abdication. Colonel Stuart-Wortley, having paid a return visit to Germany the following summer as the Emperor's guest at Metz, wrote an article of which an advance précis went to Berlin. It was seen both by the Emperor and his chancellor, Count von Bülow. No revisions were made.

On 28 October 1908, the 'Highcliffe' article appeared in the *Daily Telegraph*. It quoted Wilhelm as having described the English as 'mad, mad, mad as March hares' and of presenting himself as the man of peace who struggled to defend an ungrateful little Britain from the wrath of the great Fatherland. ('The prevailing sentiment among large sections of the middle and lower classes of my own people is not friendly to England,' Wilhelm had allegedly declared to his English host.)

English readers reacted with mild amusement to the Emperor's airs; the Germans were outraged. A further scandal erupted. News of the sudden death – while prancing about in a pink tutu – of one of Wilhelm's generals (the Emperor had been an enthusiastic observer of the performance) broke together with the first revelations of homosexuality in the circle of men who habitually addressed the Emperor as 'Liebchen' ('Darling'). Abdication was discussed. Miss Topham, attending silent lunches under the rococo garlands and naked deities of the Apollo Room, noted that the Emperor looked pale and crushed and that his wife was always in tears.

Chancellor Bülow, forced to shoulder the blame for the *Telegraph* article, was sacked and replaced by the tall, scholarly, musical and eminently trustworthy Theobald von Bethmann-Hollweg.

Harry Kessler's 1906 appeal for peace had produced no lasting results; the shipbuilding race was underway; talk about the inevitability of war had become commonplace. The Highcliffe interview added the frosting to a relationship that was already turning glacial.

In February 1909, the ailing British King decided to contribute what he could towards alleviating the situation. A show of family unity was required; an act of homage to the Emperor's court would be an act of good diplomacy.

Edward's 1909 visit to Berlin was undermined by illness and mishaps that started at the station when the royal train steamed to a halt at the wrong platform and Wilhelm, grandly waiting to receive his guest at the far end of a long red carpet, had to run like a hare to catch up. Escorted to the finest of Willy's royal carriages, the British King and Queen were forced to get out and walk to the palace after two of the elegantly caparisoned coach horses went on strike. A frightening collapse by the King during lunch at the Embassy ('We all thought it was the end,' Sir Edward Goschen's private secretary, Benjie Bruce, confided to his diary) was followed later that day by an even more worrying moment. Miss Topham, who was present at the ballet performance of *Sardanapalus* (forming the first part of an interminable evening), noticed that King Edward, jolted from slumber by bangs and flashes of light from the stage, evidently thought the opera house was on fire. He looked, the governess thought, both panic-stricken and ill. Back at the palace and settling down for a cosy gossip with Daisy Pless, Edward suffered a second seizure. His eyes stared, his breath came in short gasps, the cigar fell, unlit, from his fingers to the floor.[18] A philandering man might suffer a worse fate than to expire in the arms of Daisy Pless, but Daisy was not the only one who blanched at the unimaginable consequences if the King of England dropped dead during a state visit to Berlin.

Death held off until the following year when Edward VII, aged only sixty-eight, was struck down by a series of heart attacks. Wilhelm, invited to stay at Buckingham Palace by the widowed Queen, was charmed by Alex's friendly manner, and impressed by the dignity and evident sadness of the quiet crowds who turned out to line the streets for the ceremonial procession.

Competition for attention was now stiffer than it had been in 1902. Wilhelm's ranking as a mere nephew impressed reporters less than his role, back then, as Queen Victoria's eldest grandchild. Faced by the hooded camera, and flanked by seven competing monarchs (most of them rather younger than himself), Wilhelm still managed to seize the position directly behind the new King, allowing him to conceal his left arm from view, while gazing out over George V's head with an air of quiet authority.

On film, if not in life, the Emperor would present (to the eyes of a hopeful Germany) her place as the friendly power behind – but never against – the English throne.

13

THE RIFT WIDENS

(1906–14)

In 1911, Sir Ernest Cassel, the formidably astute and philanthropic Cologne-born financier (and grandfather of the future Edwina Mountbatten), donated £200,000 for the creation of an Anglo-German Institute. Its admirable purpose, honouring the reputation of Cassel's friend, the late King Edward, as a peacemaker, was to promote mutual understanding through the study of the cultures of the two great nations, while providing funds for unemployed workers who found themselves adrift in either country, England or Germany.

Acting in the same conciliatory spirit, King George V, a month before his coronation in June 1911, invited his cousin the German Emperor to pay another visit to London. Wilhelm had appreciated the warm welcome he had received during his attendance at Edward VII's funeral in 1910. It had felt, he announced at the time, like a homecoming; his current stay in England – and his first in the satisfying role of elder statesman, now that Uncle Bertie was gone – proved equally gratifying. George and his Germanic wife, Mary of Teck, were carefully affable; their British subjects, separating the rising fear of an imminent German invasion from the amused regard in which they held the German Emperor, were positively enthusiastic.

Was the Emperor's attention caught, during the ceremonious unveiling of the monumental bulk of the Victoria Memorial, by the sculpted prows of four mighty marble ships, thrusting forward, as if putting out to sea, under the supervision of his imperial grandmother? If so, Wilhelm chose not to comment upon the placing of such a brazen declaration of England's naval supremacy directly between Buckingham Palace and another brand-new testimony to the confident stance of a seafaring nation: Admiralty Arch. That particular designation, as the Emperor would surely have been aware, reinforced the symbolism of the four ships sailing out to battle from beneath Victoria's rigid skirts. Britain, not Germany, still ruled the waves.

In 1911, the battle of British and German shipbuilders had temporarily slowed down. England, nevertheless, remained apprehensive of Germany's intentions, and angry about the prodigious expense required to maintain her own traditional supremacy. Wilhelm, when he was not arguing the case for his vastly augmented fleet as a necessary form of national defence, rhapsodised about the eventual prospect of a shared alliance, with rich mutual rewards. England could keep her empire; all Germany would ask in turn was a free hand with the rest of the world. (The Emperor's proposals were not entirely unlike those that Hitler would produce, a little over twenty years later, when seeking Britain's support for his raids on Nazi Germany's neighbours.)

Set within the context of such a grand global vision, the tiny current issue of England's support for French rule in a (theoretically) independent North African country seemed almost unworthy of mention. Shortly before leaving London, however, Wilhelm raised with his cousin George the topic of Germany's own interest in Morocco and expressed his hope that no harm would be done if Germany made that interest plain. George, or so Wilhelm persuaded himself after their chat, was reassuring:

Germany could do as she wished. She should not fear interference from England.

Wilhelm was good at hearing only the answer that he wished to hear. King George had not consented to stand aside, and he was in no position to do so. In 1904, Edward VII, had negotiated an *entente cordiale* with France that – as an integral part of the deal – agreed to offer British support of the French in Morocco so long as the French didn't disturb Britain's own presence further along the coast of North Africa, in neighbouring Egypt. Possibly, George did offer some bluff words of sympathy for Wilhelm's concerns about Morocco, a country that provided crucial access to Germany's own cluster of African colonies.* Sympathy required no action.

In the first week of July 1911, less than three months after Wilhelm's visit to London, Edward Grey, King George's tall, patrician and country-loving foreign secretary, was urgently recalled to London from a fishing holiday by a message from the German Ambassador.

Count Metternich's news was disturbing. Wilhelm had despatched a gunboat, the *Panther*, with armed troops on board, to anchor off the minor Moroccan port of Agadir. Officially, the *Panther* had arrived to offer protection from the predatory French to a cluster of Hamburg merchants who lived in Agadir. (Later reports disclosed that a lone German merchant had been despatched to the port and ordered to settle in as quickly as possible.) In fact, as the armed troops indicated, the *Panther*'s arrival lodged a pointed threat. Germany was questioning the French presence in Agadir and offering an implicit deal (or gunpoint blackmail). Either France could withdraw her demand for a protectorate in Morocco, or Germany should receive, whole and entire, France's vast holdings in the rubber-rich Congo.

To Grey and his anxious colleagues (the British Chancellor,

---

* Germany held Togoland, Namibia and Kamerun (Cameroon) in West Africa, and Burundi, Rwanda and Tanzania in East Africa.

David Lloyd George, promptly began urging England to prepare for war), Germany's aggressive stance seemed preposterous. Did the Emperor not remember his humiliation at the Conference of Algeciras, back in 1906, when, championing Morocco's right to reject French control, Wilhelm had managed to receive the support of only a single country out of fourteen (and that one was Austro-Hungary, which had no option but to side with Germany)?

For a second time, Wilhelm's bluff was called. The *Panther* was compelled to withdraw and the Treaty of Fez in 1912 saw Morocco placed – with Britain's blessing – under the divided protection of Spain and France. True, a sizeable portion of the Congo was transferred to German ownership, but that was mostly a diplomatic sop, and the Emperor knew it.

The Second Moroccan Crisis had more enduring consequences than the wound to a vain man's self-esteem. For the first time, England had experienced serious alarm. On 20 July 1911, England and France concluded an agreement to maintain their mutual safety. If Germany should offer a future threat to either country, an immediate joint mobilisation of 150,000 troops would be put into action. Three years later, that agreement, significantly, remained in effect.

In Germany, where face had been lost, Kiderlen-Waechter, the foreign secretary responsible for despatching the *Panther* in 1910, remained in office (he died the following year). Instead, the blame was laid upon the German Ambassador to Britain, Daisy Pless's friend, the peace-loving and honourable Count Metternich. In May 1912, Metternich was unhelpfully replaced at the Embassy in London by the non-English speaking Baron Marschall von Bieberstein, a grim elder statesman unswervingly committed to Admiral Tirpitz's clarion call for greater efforts to be devoted to building up Germany's war fleet.

The German Navy – as viewed by a glowing-eyed young Anglo-Irishman who went straight from English public school to the Rhineland, aged just seventeen – played a crucial role in strengthening Germany's national morale.

Stranded in Germany as a lonely teenager during the earliest years of the twentieth century, Evelyn Wrench was bewitched by the friendliness of the German people upon whom, as an ardent young imperialist, he inflicted his arguments in favour of the Boer War. Entranced by the glamour of the military ('capes of pale grey worn with all the air of Henry Irving in a Shakespeare play'), young Wrench was more impressed still by Germany's attitude to her navy.[1] Any German sailor, however low his rank, was treated as a king, Wrench wrote. When boats came down the rivers, their masts and funnels were festooned with garlands; stepping ashore, a sailor could expect to be greeted by wreaths, feasts and the applause normally reserved for royalty. Thriving on such treatment, Germany displayed 'all the confidence of successful youth', or so Wrench recalled in 1934. 'Her rise to prosperity and world fame had been meteoric . . . All Germany had to do was to sit tight.'[2]

Despatching hundreds of brightly coloured souvenir postcards to friends and family had occupied Evelyn Wrench's spare hours in Germany; home again, he set up a postcard business before landing the job of overseas editor at Lord Northcliffe's new *Daily Mail*. His heart lay elsewhere. Attending the funeral of Edward VII in 1910, Wrench introduced himself to Philip Kerr and Robert Brand, two brilliant members of the group known as Milner's Kindergarten, men whose work towards South African union after the Second Boer War had led Kerr to set up the influential political group named (Camelot-style) the Round Table. Wrench played no part in the Round Table's 'moots' and he never joined the high-minded coterie linked to it, that was already beginning to congregate at Cliveden, the newly acquired riverside estate of William Waldorf Astor. Nevertheless, the encounter with Brand and Kerr thrilled Wrench. 'We talked imperialism,' he noted in his diary on 5 October 1910. 'It is splendid to think that there are young men like Kerr devoting themselves to the Empire.'[3]

That conversation with Milner's protégés gave Wrench the confidence to embark upon his own grand plan. He aimed – 'aflame with enthusiasm' – to create 'a great Brotherhood of Service, which would be to the Empire what the German Navy League was to Germany, a kind of "Imperial" Salvation Army.'[4] Working in alliance with his cousin, Frank Yeats-Brown, Wrench had recruited 300 members by the following year (1911). At its peak, over 12,000 imperial enthusiasts would join the Royal Over-Seas League.

Since Evelyn Wrench was ardent in his desire for friendship between England and Germany and inspired by what he had seen of the German Navy, it is not surprising that one of the greatest heroes of his youth was the German-born prince who, by 1912, had achieved the position of first sea lord of the British Navy.

Described by one shrewd admiral, Lord Selborne, as 'the cleverest sailor I have met', Prince Louis of Battenberg (born Prince Ludwig Alexander von Battenburg) grew up at Hessen-Darmstadt, back in the years when Princess Alice was despatching teams of Protestant nurses to the German Hospital in London.[5] Always kind to the young, Alice became a second mother to a quiet, clever boy whose parents were not rich and whose own Polish mother was not royal.

In 1868, the effortlessly trilingual prince reached fourteen and discovered his enduring passion for ships. Alice, aware that Germany possessed as yet no navy of her own, pulled strings to enable her intelligent protégé to join the British fleet.

Naturalised, transformed from Ludwig into Louis, and trained as a cadet on Nelson's old flagship, the *Victory*, the handsome young man was just twenty when he gained the best marks ever recorded in his exams for seamanship. A favourite with both sexes, Louis's philandering days were put behind him when he married Princess Alice's eldest daughter. When Louis's equally good-looking brother, Henry ('Liko'), married Queen Victoria's youngest daughter, Beatrice, the position of the modestly born

Battenbergs (of which 'Mountbatten' was a later, neat translation) stood secure within the royal circles of both England and Germany.

For Edward VII, Louis Battenberg was the perfect family diplomat, one who was always able to calm the easily aroused feelings of the German Emperor. (He proved his value in this respect during the awkward stationing of the *Panther* at Agadir.) Louis's tact, as much as his naval skill, resulted in his steady promotion through the British ranks. In December 1912, just as feelings between England and Germany settled into a dreadful awareness of the likely consequences of creating two over-burdened and vastly expensive war fleets, Prince Louis reached the pinnacle of his career. As first sea lord, he occupied a role that placed a German at the head of the entire British naval service, including defence.

Few questioned the authority of a man who was widely liked and respected. To Admiral 'Jacky' Fisher, Prince Louis was 'Moses and Aaron rolled into one'. To an observant German naval attaché, he seemed an impressively modest man, one who combined a wise prudence with 'the inborn German thoroughness of a systematic worker'.[6] Prince Louis epitomised, in fact, what was best in both the English and the Germans.

To the Emperor Wilhelm's engaging younger brother, Prince Henry of Prussia, visiting England in the autumn of 1912, Louis was the ideal person with whom to discuss politics. Henry wanted to find out what, if anything, Britain would do if war broke out in Europe. Alarmed by the Prussian's airy confidence in British neutrality, Louis reported the conversation back to the King. George, who had already warned Henry that England would support either Russia or France if Germany attacked 'under certain circumstances', shared Louis's concern. Henry was delightful, but he shared the dangerous tendency of his older brother for hearing only as much as suited him.[7]

George V was not a linguist, but the conversation that took place between Louis and Henry in 1912 could have been held in either of the languages that they spoke with equal ease. From discussing diplomacy, they could have turned with mutual pleasure to an informed argument about which was the finer: a German Daimler or an English Rolls. Henry, almost certainly, would have opted for the British car.

Anglicising the German royals with a view to strengthening the bond to their own mother country was a task to which both Vicky and her sister Alice had applied themselves with diligence and success. Prince Henry, Vicky's second son, was as entranced by English cars as the Emperor was by English-built boats. Vicky's youngest daughter, Margarete or 'Mossy' (nicknamed for her short and springy hair), confided to Daisy Pless that England was the only place in which she felt free to be herself.[8] Wandering around the house that Mossy had inherited (much to the Emperor's annoyance) from their mother, Daisy saw evidence everywhere of the friendly Princess's sincerity. Friedrichshof, while less rigorously run than in Vicky's day, still looked and felt like an English home in which English was spoken in preference to the German language.

Anglophilia went deeper still. Several of Willy's offspring took long, regular holidays at Eastbourne on England's sunny south coast and educated their children at nearby schools. Mossy's third son, Prince Philipp of Hessen-Kassel, playing truant from one such establishment at Bexhill-on-Sea, found that Germany was not, after all, so very far removed. Local landmarks showed where the gallant Hanoverian soldiers of the King's German Legion had defended the coast from Napoleon; it must have occurred to Philipp that by calling its magnificent new pier the Kursaal, Bexhill was showing pride in its German connections.*

Prince Philipp of Hessen-Kassel, royal-born and speaking English with only the faintest trace of an accent, suffered from no

---

* The connection survived the war. The Augusta-Viktoria College at Bexhill was German-funded and attended by the daughters of German industrialists with British connections (MAB Mallender-MS, December 2012). Meanwhile, the Kursaal was demolished, largely on account of its German name.

Germanophobic unpleasantness during his pre–war schooldays on the south coast.

The young Robert Graves, arriving at Charterhouse in 1909, at the sensitive age of fourteen, faced a very different experience. At Rokeby, the London prep school where he had previously enjoyed three happy years, the young Graves had been urged to take pride in his Bavarian connections, encouraged by a headmaster who admired German culture. By 1909, the mood had altered. Signed onto the Charterhouse school list under his full name, Robert von Ranke Graves, the new boy was identified, from the start, as one of the enemy. 'Businessmen's sons, at this time, used to discuss hotly the threat, and even the necessity, of a trade war with the Reich. "German" meant "dirty German." It meant: "cheap, shoddy goods competing with our sterling industries." . . . It also meant military menace, Prussianism, useless philosophy, tedious scholarship, loving music and sabre rattling.'[9]

Understandably – forgivably – Graves decided that the time had come to suppress his German links. The 'von Ranke' of his mother's family, a name in which he had previously taken immense pride, was dropped. Dropped, that is, until the young author elected, in 1929, to write his memoir of the war and to speak up for the enemy country to which a large part of his own family belonged.

The youthful Robert Graves, within the confined walls of a public school, was made personally aware of a spirit of hatred that was rising against Germany in the England of 1909. Attendants of the fiery lectures being given at Queen's College in that same year by a fiercely moustached and scholarly Scottish historian, John Cramb, experienced at firsthand just how easily that spirit could be inflamed.

Constricted by the difficulties of caring, on a modest income, for a crippled son and an invalid wife, John Cramb's chief solaces were music and literature. Wagner was his favourite composer; in

1911, Cramb was a devoted attendant at the great *Ring Cycle* that Thomas Beecham (aided by the family fortune that derived from Beechams Powders) sponsored at Covent Garden. Beecham himself, having given Richard Strauss's magnetic operas *Elektra* and *Salome* their successful British premieres the preceding year, was naturally on the podium.

Cramb's love for Germany was of a singular kind. His lectures at Queen's College, illustrated by lurid quotations from the tales of the Nibelungen, conjured up a world in which battle, conducted upon a titanic scale, became a glorious inevitability: a manifestation of 'the world-spirit in the form most sublime and awful that can enthral the contemplation of man'.[10]

Cramb's mind, although brilliant, was to become increasingly deranged and his hunger for imperialism went far beyond Evelyn Wrench's idealistic quest for a unifying sense of national purpose. But Cramb's more troubling obsession, towards the end of his life, was with the need for a great and cleansing war. His death in 1913 cut short his projected series of lectures on the likely outcome of an imminent and, in Cramb's view, desirable clash between England and Germany.

Cramb sounds, on first acquaintance, to have had much in common with the dreadful – and far too influential – Houston Stewart Chamberlain. But the Scottish academic was not an evil man; unhappiness, combined with fierce intellectualism, had led an essentially noble mind into taking a disastrously wrong course. Chamberlain, a globular-eyed distant relation of the English political family, was a far less benevolent figure.

Married in 1908, to Eva Wagner (by arrangement with her mother Cosima), Chamberlain achieved what he had long desired: a controlling position at the summit of Wagner-land, among the complex and unhappy clan who lived upon the hill of Bayreuth. Driven by a hatred of Britain that was only exceeded by his loathing of all Jews, Chamberlain's successful endeavours to gain control in the Wagner family and to influence the Emperor have been outshone, posthumously, by our knowledge of the awe in which this dangerous man was later held by Adolf Hitler, a pall-bearer at his funeral.

Shunned today by even the most rabid of right-wing apologists, Chamberlain was widely admired in his own time for a book which argued that the early Germanic people had, by over-running Europe, saved it from Jewish domination; that the Germanic races belonged to the world's most highly gifted group, the Aryans, and that the Germans themselves, representing the physical and mental peak of this group, could justifiably regard themselves as the lords of the world.

First published in German in 1899, Chamberlain's *Foundations of the Nineteenth Century* became an immediate success, selling 10,000 copies in its first ten days and 87,000 by 1914. In England, the 1910 translation was provided with a glowing introduction by Lord Redesdale, an erudite peer and former diplomat who had written authoritative works on early Japan. Thanks in part to Redesdale's own excellent connections, the book received a hand-ful of admiring reviews; English interest never, however, matched the veneration accorded to Chamberlain's *Foundations* in Germany.

Chamberlain did not expressly advocate war, as Cramb had done; nevertheless, he played an important part in bolstering a sense of entitlement in a people to whom his book granted the idea of racial superiority. Convinced, as Prince Henry became, that England would never stand in the way of German expansion in Europe, Chamberlain made use of his sycophantic corre-spondence with an easily flattered emperor to reassure Wilhelm on this point. The events of 1914 came as a shock to the hilltop occupants of Bayreuth. 'You can't imagine the deep grief England's declaration of war has caused me,' Chamberlain wrote to a German friend: 'shame, anger and despair'.[11] Disillusionment did not, however, lessen his confidence in a victory for Germany, his chosen country.

*

Viewed through Chamberlain's supercilious and Anglophobic eyes, it seemed clear that a waning imperial power like England would never have the courage to oppose German might. Ida Wylie, a British novelist whose later works helped to create the modern image of strong, independent women in the Katharine Hepburn mould, shared that view. Growing up in an England that bristled with suspicions of the German aggressor, and putting her own visits to the Rhineland and the Black Forest spa towns to good use, Wylie published *My German Year* in 1910, when she was just twenty-five. Her chosen audience were the English householders who, as avid readers of the *Daily Mail* and *The Times*, dreaded that they might one day awake 'to find themselves overwhelmed by German airships, German Dreadnoughts, German soldiers, and – worst of all – German policemen; in other words, to find that their dear Motherland has been transformed into a German colony ...'[12]

Keen to calm the fervour of imaginations that had been overheated by the press, Wylie based her account of Germany on personal recollections of tranquil, orderly Carlsruhe, the former winter habitat of old Fanny de Bunsen. Germany, she wrote, was a homely country, aglow with pride in her army (little mention was made of the mighty navy) and the lovingly preserved traditions of regional rule. The German, Wylie's readers learned, was not really interested in nationalism; his attachment was only and always to 'his own particular little Fatherland, his own particular Sovereign'.[13]

Later, Wylie became a strident champion of German supremacy. In 1910, she was seeking to restore a peaceful friendship between two cousinly nations. England and Germany had fought together, blood-brothers, at Waterloo, she pleaded; why, then, should they quarrel? 'Two nations, who, time after time, have fought shoulder to shoulder, who together saved Europe from her greatest danger, related in blood and in all the highest virtues of courage, and tenacity, and loyalty, should surely go forward in the future united as in the past ...'[14]

*

Wylie sought to preserve the peace by reminding her readers of a shared, harmonious past. Ford Madox Ford, in 1908, began making use of his new publication, the *English Review*, to give German authors a voice in England. He had, during his visits to Germany, formed a great admiration for Levin Schücking, a writer who bore an uncanny facial resemblance to the late Stephen Crane, Ford's friend and literary neighbour. Schücking was happy to contribute an essay about Shakespeare, beloved in both countries.[15] Joseph Conrad, Ford's former collaborator, meanwhile agreed to hand in a friendly appraisal of the German Emperor.

Appearing in Ford's magazine at the same time was a young English writer who needed no converting to the cause of Anglo-German friendship. D. H. Lawrence, at the time when Ford began to publish the young man's first poems and stories in the *English Review* (1909), was already studying German and even writing a novel, *The Trespasser* (originally titled *The Saga of Siegmund*), with a Wagnerian theme.

Lawrence was not only a brilliant mimic but a gifted linguist. Following his mother's death in 1910, his aunt, Ada Krenkow, newly married to a scholarly German and living in a remote part of the Rhineland, had a suggestion to make to her young nephew. Lawrence desperately wanted to escape from his roots in the mining village of Eastwood; why did he not consider making his future in Germany, where he could supplement his fledgling writing career by teaching? Ada Krenkow's husband was himself an academic; doors could be opened for a clever young man, if he chose to settle in a new country.

Some scheme along such lines had begun to shape Lawrence's plans for his future by February 1912. He could have sought the advice of Ford, whose German connections were excellent. Instead, Lawrence went to lunch at the family home of one of his teachers at Nottingham University College. Professor Ernest Weekley was a fluent Germanist; it had possibly occurred to Lawrence – a collier's son with a powerful streak of snobbery – that Weekley's wife, the well-born Baronin Frieda von Richthofen, could provide introductions to a grander German circle than those inhabited either by Ford's friends or his own Krenkow connections.

All occurred as planned – and as had not been planned. The gaunt, fiercely sincere young man fell in love with the Professor's blonde and buxom wife; Lawrence's sedately charted journey towards a new life as a teacher and writer was transformed into a runaway escapade with a woman who, in these early stages of their romance, had no intention of enjoying more than another brief fling, an affair of the light kind that enlivened the tedium of her married life.

Frieda and Lawrence left England on 3 May 1912. Weekley, receiving confirmation of their relationship a week later, declared the marriage to be over and that he would take the children into his custody. Lawrence, having spent an impatient two weeks with Krenkow's family at Waldbröl, sped joyously to Munich (the hometown of Frieda's family) to embark on a new life with the woman he adored.

Lawrence's summer in Germany, although punctuated by emotional storms, proved to be a time of exceptional happiness. Spending the Whitsun holiday at an inn near the River Loisach, he grew rhapsodic about strolling with Frieda through flower-spangled meadows to a lake, beside which they sat, putting Frieda's rings on their toes and dabbling their feet in the pale-green water, 'to see how they looked'.[16] Later, assisted by Frieda's elder sister, Elsa, and her lover, Alfred Weber, the runaways settled into a Bavarian home at tiny Icking, set high above the River Isar and looking out towards the Alps across fields sprinkled with the brightly coloured square farmhouses inhabited by members of Der Blaue Reiter painting school. (Lawrence, who became one of the school's earliest English admirers, was thrilled to be confronted by one of Franz Marc's great horse paintings when he visited Alfred Weber's Munich home.) Later, helped by Elsa's husband, Edgar Jaffé, the couple moved to Irschenhausen, where a woodside chalet offered another glorious

Alpine view and the daily company – so the nature-loving Lawrence wrote – of tumbling squirrels and wandering roe deer.

Living in rural bliss, Lawrence could not entirely escape a glimpse of the future in a country where large-scale army manoeuvres had become a feature of everyday life. His witnessing of these ominous preparations provided the material for one of his finest early stories, 'Honour and Arms' (Lawrence's editor shrewdly changed the title to 'The Prussian Officer' in November 1914, strengthening the tale's relevance to a country newly at war with Germany). For the most part, however, despite the evident hostility of Frieda's autocratic father, Lawrence enjoyed his time in Germany. He never – as the most notorious of his later works shows – ceased to admire its culture.

Sexually incompatible though Sir Clifford Chatterley and his wife appear to be in the revolutionary study of sexual appetites that Lawrence wrote during his last years, they can commune through a shared attachment to Germany. We learn that Connie (having been hurried home to England from her Dresden school on the outbreak of war) had been 'profoundly thrilled' by the German way of life, the music and the talk ('The endless talk about things had thrilled her soul . . .'). Sir Clifford Chatterley, although seriously injured during the war, retains a quiet and stubborn sympathy for the enemy: 'the young intelligent Germans who were, like himself, caught up in the huge machine that they hated'. During periods of leave, he reads aloud to Connie from the works of Rilke and Gerhart Hauptmann.

For Lawrence to have written in this way during the late 1920s, in years when the merest reference to Germany could provoke a British snarl of abuse, testifies to the strength of the English novelist's own feelings for a country where he had known great happiness.

Back in the summer of 1914, Frieda and her lover returned to England, but only to get married. Their plans, already settled for a return to Europe, were overtaken by events.

Had there been no war, it's entirely possible that Lawrence might have settled in a country where he, like Ford, felt instantly at home. Post-war, his visits to Germany were brief and circumscribed by the demands made by Frieda's mother, living out her widowhood near Baden. It was during the last of these visits, in 1929, that the terminally tubercular Lawrence wrote one of his greatest poems, inspired by a jar of sea-blue flowers that had been placed in the dying man's room, there in Germany.

'Reach me a gentian, give me a torch!
Let me guide myself with the blue, forked torch of this
    flower
down the darker and darker stairs, where blue is darkened
    on blueness.'

'Bavarian Gentians' charts Lawrence's descent into the underworld. Reading the poem today, it's tempting to intuit that a dying man had been granted a prescient, dreadful glimpse of the darkness (the 'sightless realm') that lay ahead for Germany, a country that he loved.

The plans that Lawrence had initially made, back in 1912, for his future as a teacher in Germany were not seen by his friends as reckless or eccentric. It is only with hindsight that the signs of impending war glare out from the terrifying summer of 1911, when Germany's challenge to Agadir, a French port in Morocco, suddenly threatened to compel Britain to fulfil her promise to support France in times of war. The signs were certainly there, but only a small circle of people were conscious of what was at stake and how urgent the situation had become.

Sir Maurice de Bunsen, a shrewd observer of events in Europe from his position as British ambassador to Spain, had been among the first to sense where the kindling match might be lit. Back in 1908, while the English papers filled their columns with details of the Highcliffe interview and the German Emperor's gaffes, Sir Maurice took anxious note of the furious response in Serbia to Austria's annexation of Bosnia and Herzegovina. In February 1912, Wilhelm II was visiting Pless when he discourteously informed his English hostess that her countrymen were due for a thrashing. Daisy had shuddered when Willy added, with a glare, 'and they'll get it if they don't take care'.[16]

De Bunsen and Daisy Pless inhabited the social and political spheres in which every avenue was being explored for ways to avert an oncoming crisis. Richard Haldane, England's formidably prudent and long-serving secretary of state for war, was despatched in February 1912 on a secret mission to Germany (Sir Ernest Cassel, making use of his friendship with the German shipbuilder Albert Ballin, was a prime mover behind the scenes) to negotiate for a mutual reduction in the pace of shipbuilding. The news that Haldane brought home to England was not good. Germany had no intention of deviating from the increased naval programme that Admiral Tirpitz had set in motion. Germany's intention, so it seemed, was not to attack Britain, but to intimidate her: the Emperor and his advisors wanted no interference from the English in Europe. A strong navy would hold a troublesome island at bay.

Out in the eastern wilds of Silesia, in the summer of 1913, Daisy Pless's teenage son, Hansel, was offered another portent of the future when he came across an unmarked aerodrome and a line of flimsy, wire-strung biplanes drawn up, all ready for action. Later, strolling homewards, a startled Hansel witnessed the final stages of an army manoeuvre as, in a scene that seemed to belong to another century, a line of magnificently uniformed Prussian cavalry officers came charging out of a wood, to a blast of golden trumpets.

War was in the air, but only a few had caught the acrid whiff of smoke. While Lawrence felt confident enough to start plotting a German future for himself in 1912, a wealthy young violinist who had already left England to make her home in Bavaria began laying plans for her personal contribution towards the preservation of peace.

Germany, in the years before the war, remained the pinnacle of aspiration for young English musicians. When Mary Portman discovered her vocation, at the age of eighteen, she asked nothing more of her parents than to be allowed to go to study music (like Ethel Smyth, whom she greatly admired) in Germany.

The tenth child of the aristocratic owner of Bryanston House and large tracts of land in north London, Mary was expected to tread the traditional route towards a good marriage, a fine house and the production of an heir. It took a persistent daughter fifteen years to be granted her wish for independence and freedom. In 1910, Mary moved to Bavaria. Armed with her violin and impressed by the openheartedness of a musical nation that was ready to pay tribute to her compatriot, Beatrice Harrison, as the greatest cellist of all time (Harrison performed a tour of Germany in 1912, to rapturous reviews), Mary developed an idea.

A century later, in 2009, an ancient inhabitant of Garmisch-Partenkirchen was still relating the tale of his family and their momentous encounter with Miss Portman. Back in those long-ago days before the First War, his parents had been out walking together through the beautiful local valley known as 'the Golden Round' when they met a solitary Englishwoman. She was looking for Schachen, Ludwig II's secluded hunting lodge, and – having lost her way – seemed transfixed by the beauty of her surroundings. She asked the couple what the valley was called. When they told her, she smiled and announced that she had found what she had sought. 'Here,' Mary grandly declared to the two puzzled Germans, 'here, I will build my house.'[17]

The Portman House, as Mary's ambitious project rapidly became known, was to be no ordinary home. Designed by the Arts and Crafts architect Detmar Blow in the style of an Anglo-German castle, with high, stepped gables, its principal feature was to be the immense concert hall at which, in Mary's vision, an international community of musicians would be drawn together in a setting of almost mystical serenity. Here, in the meadowlands of Bavaria, Germany and England would reaffirm their friendship. On 8 September 1913, the sum of 4,192 marks was paid by Mary into a bank in Munich: the first step had been taken towards the realisation of a magnificent dream.

14

DEBACLE

(1913–14)

The German Emperor, despite his threatening words to Daisy Pless at the beginning of 1912, had remained anxious to maintain cousinly relations with Britain ever since her alliances with France (1904) and with Russia (1907) had raised the spectre of encirclement.

Securing the presence of a German-friendly British ambassador on the Wilhelmstrasse became one of Willy's personal missions. In 1908, as Sir Frank Lascelles stepped down after thirteen years of service, the Emperor asked for him to be succeeded by Sir Maurice de Bunsen, who was then at Madrid. It would be pleasant to conjecture that Willy was seeking to compensate Maurice for his own failure, back in Bismarck's day, to rescue Maurice's Uncle Georg – the Emperor's childhood friend and playmate – from the wrath of a vindictive chancellor. It is more likely, however, that Willy was viewing a man whose grandfather had served as Prussia's ambassador to the Court of St James's as a potential ally.

Willy's request was not granted. In 1908, Lascelles was replaced as British ambassador in Berlin by Sir Edward Goschen. In 1912, Wilhelm lost out once again when George V recalled Sir Maurice from Madrid and despatched him – greatly to de Bunsen's relief – to Vienna.

Vienna was everybody's favourite posting in those pre-war years. Richard Seymour, serving there under Sir Edward Goschen before the 1908 transfer to Berlin, thought Vienna the most captivating city in the world. Goschen himself – as a violin-playing music-lover who (despite his tubby figure) adored a waltz – remembered his time in Austria with wistful joy. Berlin offered a poor substitute to a man who disliked most Germans and took no pride in his own descent from an eminent Leipzig publisher. If the Emperor made a point of staying away from the British Embassy during Goschen's six-year stint on the Wilhelmstrasse (1908–14), it cannot be said that his absence was much mourned.[1]

One sound reason for posting the reluctant Sir Edward to Berlin was that he was able, through his close friendship with Edward VII – and their shared fondness for taking long summer breaks at the spa towns of Baden and Bad Homburg – to act as a discreet supplier of information about Germany's escalating programme for armaments and shipbuilding. Doubtless, Goschen also kept the King posted about the latest ideas whirling through the brain of the King's volatile nephew. The Ambassador established no personal friendship with the Emperor, but his contacts in the Wilhelmine circle (the Anglophile and music-loving Chancellor Theodore von Bethmann-Hollweg, became one of Goschen's closest friends) were excellent.

Possibly, noting Goschen's closeness to the British monarchy, the Emperor decided to take a leaf out of his royal uncle's book. In the summer of 1912, when the elderly Marschall von Bieberstein died after only three months in office, Wilhelm looked about for a new ambassador to the Court of St James's who could act as his own personal representative and informant. Searching, in particular, for a man whose winning ways would gain England's trust, his choice fell upon Prince Karl Max Lichnowsky. The Prince's credentials (perfect manners, exquisite English and a fond first cousin in

Count Benckendorff, the Russian ambassador in London) seemed to Wilhelm easily to outweigh his old friend's lack of experience as a diplomat. Endorsing Lichnowsky's suitability for the post on 3 October 1912, the Emperor was delighted by this personal step towards restoring good relations with England.

The English shared Willy's enthusiasm. The German Embassy had become a little dull during Count Metternich's day, enlivened only when Daisy Pless stepped in to act as the bashful Ambassador's social hostess and to preside over a diplomatic dinner party or an embassy ball; Marschall Bieberstein's residence, while brief, was also dour. Now, only George V's old-fashioned wife complained about Princess Mechtilde Lichnowsky's insistence on plastering the walls of Carlton House Terrace with works by Franz Marc, Picasso and Kokoschka, while a few strait-laced peeresses raised their eyebrows at a pretty young woman who kicked her way through autumn leaves, in public parks, while wearing white socks and – far more shockingly, in those days – no hat ('hutlos').[2]

The critics were in a minority. Daisy Pless found that the Prince grew a little gruff when she prattled on, while Sir Edward Goschen, sharing a car with Mechtilde and a motley crew of cats, children and dogs after visiting the Lichnowskys' Silesian shooting estate, pronounced the Princess to be 'ein bisschen sauvage' ('a bit crazy').[3] But the English were, for the most part, entranced by the friendly Lichnowskys and their romantic history (Karl Max's ancestors had housed and funded Beethoven, who repaid them with the *Moonlight* and *Pathétique* sonatas). How could they not be charmed by an impetuous blonde princess who declared herself bewitched by the beauty of London's mist-drenched parks and terraces of rose-red brick?[4] How could they not be beguiled by a kindly and still handsome prince who spoke with such evident conviction – based on Lichnowsky's absolute faith in the Emperor's assurances to him – of Germany's desire for a harmonious partnership with England?

On 3 June 1914, an ardent Anglophile's happiness was crowned by the presentation to him of an honorary doctorate at Oxford, during which the Public Orator saluted Lichnowsky as a true representative of the spirit of his nation ('Totam Germaniam animo salutamus'). At a dinner held in his honour that same evening, the Prince took the opportunity to declare that 'the whole of humanity would be best served if the Teutonic peoples were brought nearer together and would join hands for the purpose of spreading their civilization to distant regions'. Reporting upon the event the following day, the *Berliner Tageblatt* wondered if one gallant ambassador might yet preserve the friendship between England and Germany. The writer did not, however, sound entirely hopeful.[5]

Three weeks later, Prince Lichnowsky (who disliked sailing) was a dutiful guest on the Emperor's yacht as the *Meteor* put into Kiel to welcome a carefully scheduled visit by three light British cruisers and four mighty dreadnoughts. Georg von Hase, appointed by the Emperor to act as ADC to their honoured English guest Admiral Warrender, never forgot his first glimpse of the British ships, ten miles out at sea from Kiel, advancing through a swirling mist: 'On came the formidable giants, the greatest warships in the world . . .'[6]

In a visit that was intended to be conciliatory, the evidence of mutual suspicion was hardly concealed. The British declined to reveal the secrets of their wireless rooms. The Germans kept their guests away from the submarine production yards. 'Whatever you do,' a colleague warned von Hase, 'tell them nothing about our U-boats.'[7]

Superficially, the tone was resolutely cordial. The Emperor, while furious with Sir Edward Goschen and his underlings for appearing in top hats instead of yachting caps, accepted the *Meteor's* defeat by a British ship with reasonable grace and apologised for the absence of his wife (the Anglophobic Empress disliked the etiquette of Kiel, a place in which women took second place to the boats, only marginally less than the idea of shaking the hand of a British admiral).

All went well. The weather was magnificent. Garden parties and playful tugs-of-war between English and German sailors took place in the town. When local girls ran short, men twirled and trotted together around the hall of the Imperial Dockyard while, on board the boats, gay groups of dancers moved from the deck of the *George V* to the *Viktoria Luise*. News that the Emperor of Austria's heir and his wife had been murdered in Sarajevo on 28 June, the fourteenth anniversary of their wedding, barely rippled the surface of the festivities. Wilhelm ordered flags to be lowered as a mark of respect, but only gentle Edward Goschen shed tears for the death of the unpopular Archduke, a man whom he had counted as his friend.

Nothing, on 28 June, seemed to threaten the carefully established new relationship between the mighty navies of England and Germany. Glumly setting off the following day to offer his official condolences to the Habsburgs, the German Emperor bade Admiral Warrender a warm and public farewell. Steaming away from the Baltic port, Warrender despatched a radio signal of similar warmth back to the German fleet: 'Friends In Past and Friends For Ever.'[8]

Certainly, there had been a large degree of stage-management at Kiel; certainly, the messages of friendship proffered on both sides expressed hope rather than commitment. Nevertheless, the encounter – the British Navy's first official visit to Kiel in ten years – had augured well. A month later, one of Goschen's colleagues at the British Embassy could scarcely believe how many terrible shifts had taken place within so short a space of time. 'When I think of Kiel and now!' Horace Rumbold wrote on 30 July 1914, 'It seems almost incredible.'[9]

At the time of the Kiel rapprochement, Sir Maurice de Bunsen had been stationed at Vienna for half a year. 'We were delighted by the prospect of Vienna and wished for nothing better,' his English wife, Berta, wrote in the diary she kept of that memorable time.[10]

Neither the shabby British Embassy nor the glorious city quite lived up to the magnificent expectations of an intensely sociable ambassador's wife. Berta could not conceal her disappointment when a ball at the Schönbrunn Palace ended at suppertime, enabling the ancient Emperor to totter off to bed and leaving no time at all for the British Ambassador's wife to display her waltzing skills. Neither did Berta relish the proximity of the British Embassy to the residence of Count Heinrich Tschirsky, the German ambassador. The Count, as Berta irritably noted, never missed out on a chance to explain Germany's need to attack Russia 'before she grew too strong'. What Berta did not grasp in those early months was that Germany was merely biding its time, waiting for the chance that came its way on 28 June.

The assassination at Sarajevo of the Archduke and his consort caused few tears to be shed in Vienna. Writing to his sister, Hilda, back in England, de Bunsen remarked that the younger Habsburgs had been generally disliked, and that the Emperor of Austria was well aware of the danger of despatching his heir to Sarajevo, known to be a Serbian trouble spot. Berta noted that the Viennese even went out in the streets to dance with joy after the news came through.[11]

On 24 July, taking courage from a private assurance of German support, Austria made her formal response to the Archduke's assassination. An ultimatum was delivered to Serbia with such provocatively ferocious conditions that refusal seemed certain. Serbia, however, capitulated, surrendering on all but one minor point. One point was all that Austria – and Germany – required. Austria declared war on Serbia. Germany, as planned, fell in behind her.

To a dismayed Maurice de Bunsen (he told Berta that the situation was the worst he had ever known), the undoubted local villain of the piece was their neighbour across the street. Count Tschirsky, as Maurice de Bunsen anxiously advised the Foreign Office in London, had been a prime supporter of Austria's aggressive approach. Citing Count Benckendorff at London's Russian Embassy as his authority, de Bunsen explained Tschirsky's tit for tat strategy. If Austria attacked Serbia, then Russia would come to the latter's defence. Germany, as Austria's ally, would thus have obtained the pretext she needed for going to war against the Tsar.[12]

Maurice had confided to his wife his fears of an imminent and appalling crisis well before the Austrian ultimatum was issued. England was not yet involved, but Berta's considerable sangfroid began to crack on 27 July, the day that a tight row of armed guards suddenly sprouted along the front of every embassy in Vienna. Five days later, she heard that German troops had been mobilised for action on two fronts, against both Russia and France. In Vienna, the mood grew fraught. 'Panic is seizing people,' Berta wrote on the evening of 2 August. 'I got tonight a wild letter from Baroness Fould Springer ... begging me to take her children to England.' The de Bunsens' Austrian chauffeur had already been despatched to fight the Serbians; on the morning of 3 August, his German replacement set off in tears to join the troops assembled on the Western Front, while declaring that 'he would shoot high or low if he were asked to shoot at English or French'. Meanwhile, the Embassy's Parisian cook, Raymond, under marching orders from France, found time to prepare a splendid last dinner for his sombre employers and their guests.

On the morning of 4 August, a haggard Count Tschirsky ventured out of his door across the street to enquire of Ambassador de Bunsen what the chances were of England staying neutral. 'Maurice said he did not know yet. Then Tschirsky said: "If England comes in, then we *are* crushed."'[13]

Events were moving too swiftly to be absorbed. All around her, Berta de Bunsen saw the shattering fragments of the cosy, reliable world into which she had settled a mere eight months earlier. An Austrian friend, Count Larisch, unofficially passed along news contained in a letter from his son in Berlin. It spoke of a 'great move forward' planned by Germany on 10 August. The fact that the Austrian Larisch's son was privy to the news showed that his country would be fighting against France and Russia on Germany's side, and that – as Berta noted with sick dismay – 'we may be forced to fight against these nice people'.

On 4 August, England declared war on Germany, but not, as yet, on Austria, although the atmosphere in Vienna clearly foretold what was to come. An outraged Berta learned that the German wife of one of Maurice's own diplomatic colleagues, Theo Russell, had secretly been celebrating the sinking by German mines of an English cruiser, the *Amphion,* on 6 August (the *Amphion* had sunk a German mine-layer, a hastily converted Hamburg holiday ship, on the previous day). It troubled her more to contemplate the perilous futures of the innocent English people who resided in Vienna. In her diary, Berta singled out a Miss Congreve and her widowed sister, Baroness Oesterreicher, as dear old ladies who had inhabited the city of Vienna for decades and knew no other home; Maurice was praised by his proud wife for helping wherever he could to give money and to facilitate escapes.

On 12 August, the news that the de Bunsens had been dreading reached Vienna. England was now the official enemy of Austria, as Germany's ally. Orders were clear: departure must be immediate, by whatever route the de Bunsens could manage to find.

Packing up as many possessions as could be crammed into the single saloon car provided for their hasty exodus, the de Bunsens gave one last glance across the street at the shuttered windows of the German Embassy. Bitterly, Berta imagined Count Tschirsky peering out through a chink in the panels, gloating at a departure during which the de Bunsen's slow-moving vehicle was pelted with rocks. Reaching, finally, the safe haven of neutral Switzerland, Sir Maurice and his wife settled into the same hotel as another new exiled diplomatic couple. Jules Cambon, formerly the popular French ambassador at Berlin, was ready to provide a first-hand report of events at their own British Embassy on the Wilhelmstrasse.

The Cambons themselves had not fared too badly during their last hours on enemy territory; Sir Edward Goschen had been less lucky. Angry Berlin crowds had hurled stones and bricks at the Embassy's bleak facade, breaking eleven of the former Palais Strousberg's large windows. Some of the bolder members of the mob had clambered onto the sills to try to force their way inside, while flying cobblestones crashed into the Embassy's hastily vacated reception rooms on the ground floor.

Leaving the following morning, Sir Edward Goschen was obliged to lug his own trunks out into the street while the German staff, having torn the British insignia off their uniforms, stood by with folded arms. One staff member had apparently spat on the Ambassador's valise. A parting salvo had been delivered from the Emperor, who wished the Ambassador to know that he was forthwith divesting himself of any British titles bestowed upon his imperial self by treacherous Albion.[14]

The Emperor's injured tone was sincere. The discovery of how little his opinions counted in a time of crisis had come as a considerable shock.

Realisation of his powerlessness had begun to dawn on Wilhelm II during a fraught exchange of telegrams with his cousin Nicholas II, the Tsar, between 28 July (when Austria declared war on Serbia) and 1 August (when Russian troops mobilised along Germany's eastern borders). The following day, Wilhelm's chief of staff, General von Moltke, had been forced to explain that the Emperor's peremptory command to call off the invasion of France, while sending German troops back east to face the Russians, could not be obeyed. By 2 August, it was already too late. His troops had occupied Luxembourg and were only awaiting the outcome of England's ultimatum to Germany before following their orders to march through Belgium into France.

Germany and Russia were now formally at war. England, to the horror of both the Emperor and his chancellor, Theobald von Bethmann-Hollweg, was preparing to stand by the treaty that, faraway back in 1839, had pledged her always to support a threatened Belgium. Counting on his own firm friendship with Goschen, the Chancellor pleaded with the British Ambassador that England was being absurd. *Why* should she abandon neutrality for 'a mere scrap of paper' (the 1839 Treaty)? *Why* would Britain not honour the understanding of neutrality that she had given to Germany, her cherished sisterland?

Emperor Wilhelm, like his anguished chancellor, had become certain that Britain would not interfere in a European war. Seeking where best to lay the blame for that misplaced conviction, the most evident and recent culprit appeared to be his own well-meaning brother.

In July 1914, Prince Henry was yachting at Cowes and relaxing at Eastbourne in the company of his sisters Sophie and Mossy when news came through of the Austrian ultimatum to Serbia. The moment seemed right to make use of family connections to discover England's attitude. Visiting Buckingham Palace informally on 26 July, Henry asked King George what England's line would be. Fatally, once again, the Prince drew a wrong conclusion.

What George actually said in July 1914 – according to his own account on a half sheet of paper preserved in the Royal Archives at Windsor – was that a German war against Russia and France would make it impossible for England not 'to be dragged into it'. Prince Henry, writing to his brother Wilhelm on 28 July, had heard differently. The King, so Henry informed the German Emperor, had offered an almost unequivocal reassurance to his cousins: 'We shall try all we can to keep out of this and remain neutral.'[15] That message was just what Wilhelm had wanted to hear. Germany could do as she pleased; England, on the pledged word of her king to a member of his own family, would stand aside.

Prince Henry's subsequent actions suggest that he was less confident than he sounded. Directly after paying his hasty visit to London, and having urged his alarmed sisters to pack their cases for immediate departure to Europe, the Prince returned to Germany. These were not the actions of a man who placed much hope in England's future neutrality.

One man continued to believe, until the very end, in a compromise that could somehow save England's friendship with Germany. Possibly, the bestowing of his Oxford doctorate a mere month earlier had caused Prince Lichnowsky to become unrealistic in his views; possibly, he interpreted too much from his own close friendship with the Germanophile family of Prime Minister Asquith. 'Mediation', strikingly, is the word that crops up in every Foreign Office reference to discussions with the Prince. He could not give up hope.

'Maybe he'll finally accept it,' the Emperor coolly noted in the margin of a note from the Prince that reached him on 4 August, acknowledging – at last – that a break was imminent. 'Poor Lichnowsky.'[16]

Wilhelm's marginal annotations to diplomatic communiqués were notoriously erratic; nevertheless, his impatience with the romantic Prince was, on this occasion, understandable. Only four days earlier, the Prince had despatched the glad news to Berlin of Sir Edward Grey's personal assurance that Britain would not intervene. The English Foreign Secretary, a kind-hearted man, had perhaps weakened in the face of Lichnowsky's evident despair. It is more likely that Lichnowsky, like Prince Henry, heard more than was promised and dashed off a report before coming to his senses.

On 2 August, the day after his discussion with Grey, Lichnowsky paid a final visit to his friend Asquith, an encounter during which both men shed tears.

On 3 August, Edward Grey made his celebrated speech to

Parliament. The tired-eyed Foreign Secretary now declared that the only hope of escaping war lay in an ignoble casting aside of Britain's long-standing commitment to defend Belgium. 'We cannot do that,' Grey stated, to a cheering House. In that one sentence, England's grounds for war were given and understood.

A few still hoped for a miracle. Daisy Pless, back in Britain on a visit to her English family, cabled King George with a heartfelt request: 'Your Majesty please remain now and forever at Germany's side so that all Europe may be protected . . .'[17] But Daisy's plea, like a sheaf of others that begged, on the eve of war, for peace at any price, had come too late. German troops were already marching across the Belgian borders. Britain's ultimatum had been ignored.

On the evening of 4 August, Lichnowsky received a sturdy package from Sir Edward Grey. The contents were self-evident from its bulk; in order to leave England, the Ambassador and his staff would need the passports that were always held by the Foreign Office. Retiring to his dressing-room, the Prince put on his pyjamas, turned on the pink-shaded light and stretched out upon his bed. Below the Carlton House Terrace windows, he could hear a great roar and the cheering of the crowds along the Mall as the King, together with the Queen and the Prince of Wales, emerged onto the balcony of Buckingham Palace, following the official declaration of war. ('It is a terrible catastrophe, but it is not our fault,' the King consoled himself that night as he offered a prayer for the safety in action of his own dear Bertie, his younger son.[18])

Crowds were still surging along the shadowy Mall later that night, as a junior Foreign Office official, entering the German Embassy by a small side door, was ushered up to the dressing-room in which Lichnowsky lay. Here, murmuring his regrets, Harold Nicolson unobtrusively exchanged the note contained in the previously delivered – and seemingly still unopened – packet (in which an exhausted Grey had erroneously informed the Ambassador that Germany had declared war on Britain) for a second, and correct, statement of the facts. Lichnowsky, courteous to the end, signed for the receipt, apologised for having had his light off and sent his regards to Nicolson's father, Sir Arthur.

On 5 August, Daisy Pless came across Mechtilde Lichnowsky, quietly weeping as she wandered for a last time around the sandy pathways of St James's Park. Walking across the Mall, Daisy was greeted at the German Embassy by the distracted Prince. A team of London workmen were hard at work; the imperial eagle had already been brought down from its proud perch above the entrance. King George, so Daisy gathered, had sent a few kind words via his private secretary, Frederick Ponsonby; he had even apologised that etiquette prevented him from saying a personal farewell.[19]

Lichnowsky's love of England was widely known and sympathy for him was considerable. The Asquith family called at the Embassy on 5 August, the day of departure. Grey, inviting Lichnowsky to visit his rooms in Richard Haldane's home at Queen Anne's Gate, seemed 'deeply moved' and anxious to offer reassurance. 'We don't want to crush Germany,' Grey told the Prince, a declaration that Lichnowsky dutifully passed along to Berlin.[20]

Painful though the departure felt, everything was done with a respect that went straight to Prince Lichnowsky's tender heart. A special train was laid on to conduct the Ambassador, his family and his staff to Harwich, where a Guard of Honour stood by to salute as the evacuating Germans stepped on board a British ship. 'I was treated', the Prince wrote with forlorn pride, 'like a departing Sovereign.' Travelling later towards Berlin, on board a German train, the Lichnowsky party were passed by a troop train crowded with laughing boys on their way to the front, their necks hung with garlands of flowers by proud families and friends. The Prince waved to the young soldiers until they were out of sight, when he burst into tears.[21]

Visiting the shuttered German Embassy in London a few weeks later, as part of an official clearance group, a young man called Shane Leslie found its interior in chaos. A silver half-filled cigarette case still lay open on the Ambassador's desk. Books were scattered everywhere. Mechtilde's rosary beads lay strewn across the bedroom floor. Abandoned toys were tumbled in heaps around the children's nursery.

Leafing through the books, the young officer opened a copy of Marcus Aurelius's *Meditations*. A final gift of consolation to the Prince from Margot Asquith, the Prime Minister's wife, it carried the date of her last visit: 'the day of war'. Out across the breadth of the little flyleaf, the impulsive Mrs Asquith had scrawled her last words of tribute to a well-loved friend.

Concluding his account of a distressing commission, Shane Leslie mused on the strangeness of a world in which he was now bound by law to regard a gentle German diplomat as his enemy. 'To the most true and honourable of men' were the words that Mrs Asquith had written on the flyleaf of the *Meditations*; copying them into his report, Leslie added a comment of his own: 'which I believe he is'.[22]

As the desolate German Ambassador left England, Sir Edward Goschen and his son returned home.

Goschen adored his younger boy. Always known, for some reason, as 'Bunt' to a loving father, the Oxford-educated and Wagner-loving George Goschen had been the Ambassador's chief companion in Berlin following the sudden death of Hosta Goschen from a brain tumour in 1912. (The Emperor Wilhelm, ever tactful, had chaffed Sir Edward on having killed off his beloved wife by knocking her about; the Empress, more graciously, sent a remembrance card upon each anniversary of Lady Goschen's death.) Bunt had been there to support the first sociable venture that his father tremulously undertook as a widower – a musical evening at which Cambon, the French ambassador, and his wife, were among the sympathetic guests. Bunt was at his adoring father's side again, duetting in a Bach sonata, on the night in March 1913 when news came through to the Wilhelmstrasse of the assassination of the King of Greece, brother to England's Dowager Queen Alexandra. A few days later, when the composer Puccini paid a visit to the Embassy – and astonishingly revealed his absolute lack of music-reading skills – Bunt was on hand to strum the scores. In April of that year, 'my dear old Bunt' took up his first diplomatic appointment, at Cairo, at £300 per year. It was, so his proud father noted, a splendid start.

Edward Goschen had kept no diary through his frightening last hours in Berlin; life left no time for it. Safely home in England, however, he resumed his journal at the end of the year. He noted that he and Bunt had been playing Mozart's Violin Sonata No. 6 on the evening of 15 December, when the news that he had dreaded came through. Bunt, a peace-loving and dreamy young man of twenty-seven who had completed just one month of army training, was required to join his regiment.

Two weeks later, Sir Edward recorded the news of Bunt's death as brokenly as though he could not see the page for tears. 'That darling darling boy – who has been such a loving, bright and always cheery companion to me, so full of bright hopes, of promise, of talents – and such Joie de Vivre . . .'[23]

15

VICTIMS OF CIRCUMSTANCE: ENGLAND IN GERMANY

(1914–18)

'To Germany'

You are blind like us. Your hurt no man designed,
And no man claimed the conquest of your land.
But gropers both through fields of thought confined
We stumble and we do not understand.

CHARLES HAMILTON SORLEY

In January 1914, Charles Sorley was an eighteen-year-old school-boy, with two terms left to go at Marlborough. Before taking up his scholarship place at Oxford, the young Scot decided to follow the example of his father, an eminent Cambridge academic, and spend some time in Germany. His hosts, the Bentin family, lived at Schwerin, up in the remote north of the country, in lovely, lake-studded Mecklenburg.

Sorley was a friendly young man. It didn't take long for his hosts to learn that their good-looking guest was every bit as enchanted by their country as they were by England. 'Encourage your people to send you to Germany,' Charles wrote to a school-friend, Alan Hutchinson, on 7 February. 'They are a delightful people ...' To his parents, he urged the wisdom of despatching his younger brother, Kenneth, to follow in his footsteps.[1]

On 20 February, shortly before leaving Schwerin to study at Jena University, which Professor Sorley believed would give his clever son a better grounding in German language and culture, Charles met with an experience that he found unforgettably moving. Returning to the Bentins from a day trip into the Mecklenburg countryside, he came across a band of soldiers, singing their way home from a day of field manoeuvres of the kind that were being regularly undertaken all over Germany in those last years before the war. The roar, so Sorley told his parents, 'could be heard for miles ... simply flung across the country, echoing from Schwerin two miles away. Then I understood what a glorious country it is ...' Writing to the headmaster of Marlborough (whom Sorley treated almost as a second father), he spoke more candidly. The songs themselves were probably 'contemptible jingo'; the emotion had gone straight to his heart. 'And when I got home, I felt I was a German, and proud to be a German: when the tempest of the singing was loud enough, I felt that perhaps I could die for Deutschland ... and I have never had an inkling of that feeling about England, and never shall.'[2]

Nothing occurred during the next seven months to diminish Charles Sorley's enthusiasm for a land he described as his new-found Canaan. At Jena, where he wrote delighted accounts of romantic castles, narrow cobbled streets and – everywhere – the headily sweet scent of lilac blossom, he found the German students more cultured and more liberal than their counterparts back in Britain. A version of *The Merchant of Venice* that he watched in Weimar presented Portia as a merciless vixen, out to crush every last vestige of the ageing Shylock's pride: what English company would dare to offer such an interpretation? Sorley's parents, joining him for their summer holiday, in June 1914, shared their son's delight at seeing *A Midsummer Night's Dream* performed – to Mendelssohn's music – in a real woodland glade ('the most harmonious thing I have ever seen'). But Sorley was equally impressed to discover that both Wilde and Byron, dismissed at home because of their private lives, were revered in Germany as among the greatest writers that England had produced. In that pinched, provincial attitude to art and morality, in Sorley's opinion, 'England is seen at its worst . . .'

On 28 July, shortly after sharing these unpatriotic thoughts with a Marlborough schoolfriend, Sorley set off for a walking tour of the Moselle Valley. Four days later, Germany and Russia were at war over Serbia, and France was under threat of invasion. Imprisoned at Trier, Sorley was hastily released; fortunately for him, Britain was not yet involved.

Returning home to England, a dutiful young man put off his Oxford studies in order to sign up as a fresh recruit for Lord Kitchener's New Army.

On 5 October, 1915, crouched in a limboland between the rattling railway and the death-fields of the Western Front, Sorley scratched out a letter – a risky one to send in those times – to Arthur Watts, an English friend who was still living out at Jena. Half deafened by the clatter of the rail trucks and the roaring of the guns, the twenty-year-old captain described for Watts the happiness he had felt, just over a year earlier, on one perfect picnic day near Schwerin – '(where they are very English)' – in a farmhouse set above a little English-style fishing town.

Champagne had arrived in a tureen at 3 p.m. The meal, presented by Sorley's kindly hosts, the Bentins, had been a simple mixture of freshly caught fish and game. Throughout the afternoon, the sun shed a steady glow over the broad fields that sloped away to the sea. Everything had been at peace. That German picnic was, the young soldier confided to Watts, the most wonderful meal of his life: 'a wedding of the elements . . .'

Eight days later, Sorley died at Loos from a sniper's bullet. In his pocket was a poem that he had just completed.

> When you see millions of the mouthless dead,
> Across your dreams in pale battalions go,
> Say not soft things as other men have said,
> That you'll remember. For you need not so.
> Give them not praise . . .

Sorley's verses would speak, from the heart of his own divided anguish, to the parents of both armies, for all their dead young sons.

One son, most unexpectedly, had survived. On 30 December 1914, Sir Edward Goschen had received the news of his son George's death. Eleven months later, late in the afternoon, an anxious Sir Edward arrived at Fenchurch Station to welcome home his lost boy.

Reporters were also present, ready to witness Sir Edward's nervousness as he paced for an hour beside the barrier, and his relief when a tall khaki-uniformed figure emerged from among the evening throng of homebound city workers. Bunt, whose handsomeness and height were much remarked upon, wore the expression of one who had experienced considerable suffering. He was accompanied by a doctor and walked slowly, with the use of a stick. The two Goschens shook hands – one reporter was astonished by such restraint – before, leaning on Sir Edward's arm, Bunt was driven hastily away to a private hospital. Word was given out that visits would not, just at present, be advisable.

Bunt was home, but he never recovered his former health and high spirits. One old friend who still remembers him recalls how, in the middle of some cheerful gathering, Bunt would suddenly burst into tears, weeping like a child. He never spoke about his experiences in Germany. The papers, however, reported that

Lieutenant Goschen had been kept in confinement, with 'specially restrictive conditions', as part of the German government's reprisal policy for treatment accorded by the British Admiralty to German crews.[3]

Charles Sorley was among the many whose loyalties were divided, or who were unlucky enough to find themselves living in the wrong country at the wrong time.

Frederick Delius was born to German parents in Bradford. Trained at Leipzig, he was championed in Germany long before Thomas Beecham (in 1907) appointed himself as the composer's lifelong British devotee.* In Germany, Delius's music was dropped at the outbreak of war and never publicly played there again during his lifetime. In England, where Delius spent the war years, the composer's only chance of survival was to disappear from public view. Writing about Delius for the *Musical Times* in 1915 (the year when the sinking of the *Lusitania* heightened anti-German feelings in Britain to hysteria) a fellow composer, Peter Warlock, went out of his way to stress how little of a threat his colleague posed: 'He holds no official position in the musical life of this country ... He never gives concerts or makes propaganda for his music, he never conducts an orchestra, or plays an instrument in public.'[4]

No German music was played on Britain's concert platforms during the war. In Munich, plans for a 1915 performance of Ethel Smyth's monumental *The Wreckers* were brusquely cancelled. Mary Portman, the English violinist who had dreamed of creating an international haven for music in Bavaria, suffered a still harsher fate.

On 5 December 1914, the *New York Times* reported that Viscount Portman's daughter was being held under arrest in Germany, having failed to pay money due to the Bavarian building team who had

---

* Beecham was buried, in 1961, close to Delius, the composer he so admired and of whose music he became the most celebrated interpreter. Delius died in 1934.

been working on her new house. What the newspaper omitted to explain was that Mary's bank accounts had been frozen overnight when war was declared, and that – since all financial transactions between England and Germany were formally severed – nothing could be done to help her.

Mary Portman's release was finally procured by the intervention of the American consul in Munich (America suffered no difficulties in dealing with Germany until she herself entered the war). Back in England, Mary was too distraught and depressed to contemplate returning to Bavaria and her beloved project. The half-completed Portman House never acquired the great concert hall that she had planned to make into an international home for music. Today, the handsome, step-gabled bulding forms part of Das Kranzbach, an opulent Bavarian country hotel.

While classical music suffered from an excess of wartime patriotism, the attitude to popular music remained ambivalent. Sefton 'Tom' Delmer, a British schoolboy in wartime Berlin, was utterly unfazed by the lyrics to Germany's new songs, so long as the music was fun. 'To tell the truth,' he confessed later, 'I loved singing the German victory songs ... particularly when we marched around the gymnasium roaring joyfully at the top of our voices ...'[5] Back in England, however, even remote Cornwall was not distant enough for D. H. Lawrence and his wife Frieda to escape being marked down as potential traitors when they sang German folk songs in the privacy of their own kitchen.

Out in the brutal world of the soldiers, the songs of the music halls offered a coded way of displaying friendly feelings. Robert Graves, newly arrived at a dugout on the Western Front, was fascinated by the way that courtesies at stand-to were exchanged in Morse ditties. 'Meet me down in Piccadilly,' the English announced. 'Yes, without my drawers on,' the Germans cheerily rattled back.[6] A wounded English soldier spoke to Daisy Pless's mother about how he heard the enemy singing 'It's a Long Way to Tipperary' across the battle lines. Sneaking that account out to her daughter in Berlin, Patsy Cornwallis-West told Daisy that the young man's earnest enthusiasm had been quite moving. The German soldiers had sung it quite beautifully, he told her, 'all the voices together'.[7]

Expressing empathy with the enemy while serving at the front was a risky enterprise. In some cases, it amounted to little more than a gesture. Harry Kessler, while serving as a German officer in Belgium during the early stages of the war, refused to give up either reading English newspapers or drinking the finest tinned turtle soup from Fortnum & Mason. Yet Kessler had no doubts where his loyalties lay when twenty German soldiers were massacred. It was entirely acceptable to shoot, in response, 200 innocent Belgians at Seilles: 'one has the right', Kessler noted.

The sudden evidence of a common bond could colour a soldier's feelings for the rest of his life. The novelist Henry Williamson remembered how, during his first Christmas in the trenches, a group of German soldiers sang 'Silent Night' around their newly erected Christmas tree before persuading the English lads to cross the barrier lines and join them. Gifts were exchanged, and family photographs proudly displayed. ('A nice German had one of Princess Mary ... "Ah, schöne, schöne Prinzessin!"') Games of soccer were followed by a general trading of addresses. Threatened with court-martial if they didn't return to duty, the men vowed – like Berta de Bunsen's German chauffeur – that they would fire high in order not to kill.[8]

Williamson, a German-speaker with a Bavarian grandmother, lived on until 1977 without ever forgetting that extraordinary moment of wartime camaraderie. Edward Hulse, a 25-year-old British captain, died just ten weeks after describing the same Christmas experience to his mother. 'Words fail me completely,' Hulse wrote. But – 'here goes!'

Hulse's account of the festivities is even more startling than the scenes recalled by Williamson. Rounds of 'It's a Long Way to Tipperary' were met by a jolly roar of 'Deutschland, Deutschland'

from the German side before – following a swapping orgy of cigarettes, souvenirs, photos and handshakes – both sides linked hands
('English, Scots, Irish, Prussians, Würtembergers, etc.') to boom
out 'Auld Lang Syne'. The entire group then set off into No Man's
Land to shoot hares, which were later roasted and eaten at a shared
supper. The whole experience, Hulse wrote, had added up to 'the
most extraordinary Christmas in the trenches you could possibly
imagine . . . absolutely astounding'.[9]

Acts of defiance did not only occur on the battle lines. They
could be tiny. Two Englishwomen with German husbands managed to smuggle an old copy of the *Daily Mail* into that
caravanserai of exotic exiles, the Esplanade Hotel in Berlin. Far
more bravely, Margot Asquith, the British Prime Minister's wife,
not only refused to sack the old German governess who had shared
her family's home for almost twenty years, but, when visiting a
group of German POWs, had the nerve to address them in their
own language.

Daisy Pless, hungrily gleaning every scrap of news that she
could gather about a country that she was now forbidden even to
mention, announced that she admired Margot Asquith 'more than
I can say' for her behaviour.[10] Back in Germany, where Daisy herself earned strong criticism for what was perceived as disloyal
activity, she found firm allies among the German royals.

Disloyalty or courage? Daisy herself never stopped to give a
name to the humane impulses that sprang from a warm and generous heart. Sitting with the heartbroken Mossy in the muffled
chambers of the Friedrichshof, Daisy comforted the Princess on
the loss of her two eldest boys and admired a little photograph
of the younger son, Max, that had been sent over by a sympathetic Queen Mary. Was it right for the Queen of England to be
sending gifts and letters to the German Emperor's sister during
a war? Was it treacherous for Daisy herself to share the grief of
an old German duchess over the sinking, in 1916, of the ship
carrying Lord Kitchener, the man in charge of Britain's war

effort? Was it wrong of the Duchess's Anglophile grandson, 'Freddy' Mecklenburg-Strelitz, to go around distributing copies of the *Daily Mail* to any English prisoners-of-war that he could find? Or to elect, in the middle of the war, to start building himself Parkhaus, a Georgian-style manor decorated entirely in the English style, complete with sporting prints?

The young German died before the completion of his English home. In February 1918, two years after the death of his adored grandmother, Freddy drowned himself in a canal on the family estate at Strelitz. Daisy, who included a soulful photograph of the young man in her memoirs, blamed a divided heart.

'I think', she wrote, 'the loss of his grandmother, the apparent endlessness of the War, his heart in England and his home in Germany, and the two countries fighting with each other, just tore him to pieces and he could stand it no longer.'[11]

Freddy's agonised sense of the war as something that had torn apart the fabric of his own life was not unique. Tisa Schulenburg, a Prussian child who had been cared for by English nurses and educated by English governesses, saw the despair in her father's eyes when he brought home the news that they had never expected to hear: '"England has declared war ... Everything is lost."'[12] Count Schulenburg was speaking not from a fear that England would win, but from the sense of having lost their family's own cherished ties to a beloved land. Tisa's brother, Fritz Dietlof, had been born in England. Tressow, their pleasant house in Mecklenburg, was crowded with English mementoes: chintz chair covers, carpets purchased on London's East India docks, sturdy tweed coats, bone china tea sets. Nothing was put away; throughout the war, the house reminded Tisa's parents of the time that they wistfully recalled as 'the happiest years of their lives': their years in England, now the land of the enemy.[13]

The Schulenburgs had been deprived only of the precious sense of a connecting strand; for others, the loss was more acute. Count Münster, an affable Anglophile who had been married since 1890 to Lady Muriel Drummond Hay, forfeited the Sussex estate on which he had been tranquilly residing for over twenty years. Old Prince Blücher, a contented resident of the British island of Herm, where he reared kangaroos, was brusquely ordered home to Silesia. Blücher's son, after living in England for seven years with Evelyn, his English wife, was forced to travel back to Berlin in the same sad convoy as the weeping Lichnowskys, to camp out in the palm-thronged limboland of the Esplanade Hotel. Evelyn was still living at the Esplanade the following year when the sinking of the German *Blücher* (a ship that she herself had helped to launch from Kiel back in 1908) left her wondering whether to weep or to rejoice. Living in Berlin with a German husband whom she adored, to which side did a patriotic young woman from Lancashire now belong?[14]

The case of Daisy Pless's elderly German brothers-in-law was more pitiful. Fritz Hochberg, like his brother, Conrad, felt no great affection for Germany. The brothers had long ago chosen England as their homeland. By 1914, they had almost forgotten how to speak German. Sent back to Silesia in September of that year, they immediately began laying plans to return for the next English hunting season, following what promised to be the briefest of skirmishes between two friendly powers. The Austrian Count Kinsky, meanwhile, adopting a more pragmatic view, sent orders back to his groom at Melton that his English hunters were to be shot. The groom refused, and reported Kinsky's instructions to the police.*

In 1915, still trapped in Germany and impatiently awaiting their permission to return home, the Hochberg brothers learned that the new 'Trading with the Enemy' Act had deprived them not only of their English homes, but of all they owned. Prince Lichnowsky had abandoned books and children's toys when he

---

* The information about Count Kinsky appears in the unpublished section of Berta de Bunsen's diary (Broughton Archive).

was forced to flee from the German Embassy in London: the Hochbergs, more trusting still, had left behind everything they possessed. It was not only their houses that had now vanished, but every vestige of the cosily hospitable way of life they had enjoyed for over thirty years. Family photographs in silver frames; tailor-made tweed suits; chess boards and Crown Derby dinner plates; prayer books and Bibles (both brothers were intensely religious); even the Hochbergs' cherished hunt caps, riding boots and walking sticks were now the property of the English Crown.

Stranded in their Fatherland, the heartbroken brothers adamantly declined to behave as if they were German. Fritz, talking to his English sister-in-law in the summer of 1917, told Daisy that, after donning his favourite old English hacking jacket one morning, tears had come to his eyes, 'and such a rage to my throat I could have knocked people down for the mere reason that they were Germans'.[15] News of the death of his old English valet, who had given him eight years of loyal service, brought on another storm of emotion. Lying in bed on a quiet summer night, Count Hochberg caught the fragrant echo of an evening in England's New Forest – and wept again. 'Oh, that precious beloved country,' he sighed. 'The only country in the world.'

Rebelliously, he changed the words to a song that would become (in 1922) the anthem of Germany: 'England, England, über alles . . .'[16] Conny, with similar defiance, gave orders that, if he died in Germany, the funeral service must be conducted in English, with songs from the English hymnal.[17]

The Hochberg brothers were staunch supporters of Daisy Pless's endeavours to help her home country. Fritz Hochberg loaned his own coach, and himself as an escort, when the Princess set off, late in 1914, to offer solace to the British POWs being lodged at Döberitz, a field camp outside Berlin. Fritz approved of Daisy's loyalty, but her husband and German friends were outraged to learn that the Princess had addressed the prisoners in English, offered to get their family letters out by her own special route (the American diplomatic bag) and lingered on to glean news about the sons of her closest friends in England.

Rebuked by her husband, and issued with a stern warning by the Emperor from Pless (Daisy's former home had become a very luxurious eastern HQ for the German Army), the Princess continued to follow her own heart, and not the orders that were handed down. In 1916, a malicious neighbour reported her for daring to wear a Red Cross uniform in church; by 1917, Daisy could only visit Fürstenstein if she stayed out of sight in her faux-Trianon garden cottage. When the young Grand Duke of Mecklenburg-Strelitz drowned himself in 1918, scandalous stories of Freddy's (entirely unproven) relationship with the beautiful English Princess prompted a fresh storm of scandal.

'Mother', in the bemused opinion of Daisy's eldest son, Hansel, 'was trouble!'[18] Hansel, reminiscing in his old age, felt that Daisy had behaved imprudently and that she should have been more aware of the embarrassment that she caused to Hans Heinrich, an officer on the imperial staff. Yet the Princess was no traitor to her husband's country. She travelled as a working nurse three times to Serbia – and at considerable risk – on a Red Cross train that had been converted into a travelling hospital. She set up a convalescent home for the mothers and children of German soldiers. Characteristically, given her strong views about social reform, Daisy also paid a visit to the Emperor to insist that his smart new hospital for officers at Bad Salzbrunn, close to Pless, should also provide first-class care to enlisted men from the lesser ranks. Wilhelm was not pleased, but the hospital – formerly an elegant hotel – belonged to the Plesses, as did the enormous castle that the Emperor was comfortably occupying. Permission was reluctantly given. Sixty-two privates were given beds at Bad Salzbrunn and – to Daisy's delight – were offered exactly the same treatment and benefits as the officers whose life they now shared.

For Daisy, living in Germany, as for Maurice de Bunsen's sister,

Hilda, living in London, a particular anguish lay in knowing that they, as the English mothers of German sons, had no right to question the decision of those sons to fight for a nation that – although neither woman could describe Germany as the enemy – threatened the England to which they themselves belonged. Here, hearts and loyalties were torn in two. We can smile at the vision of Hilda Deichmann as she solemnly requested the depleted wartime staff of Abbey Lodge to choose each morning whether to pray for the 'poor dear Emperor' or for the 'poor dear King'. For Hilda, as for her little Anglo-German workforce, the question was one that raised profound concerns. Hilda's brother was a high-ranking British diplomat. But where, as the widow of two German husbands, did her own allegiance lie?

For Hansel Pless, however, as for Wilhelm, Hilda's son, the question was easily answered. As the sons of German fathers, they owed their loyalty to the Fatherland.

Young Hansel Pless was living at Fürstenstein, his family's preferred home, when word reached the castle that Germany was at war. For Hansel, the first brutal glimpse of what that war might mean was the overnight emptying of the paddocks and loose-boxes under the sorrowful orders of Albert, the English head groom. Not one animal could be kept. Horses were needed to serve the cavalry and to haul the cannons into line; over eight million animals would die in the service of the war machine.

The taking of the horses told Hansel where his duty lay. If they could go into battle, then so could he. He announced that he was going to Berlin. Once there, 'tired, dirty and bedraggled, I went straight to the Hotel Bristol on the Unter den Linden and into the room where my father stood with his back to the door'. Informed of his son's wish to fight, Prince Hans Heinrich laughed. Despatch a mere child to the front? Did Hansel not understand that his social rank might well require him, a boy of fourteen, to lead a regiment of grown men?[19]

Two years later, Hansel proudly pledged his allegiance in the traditional fashion (one hand on two crossed swords; the other raised to vow his solemn oath of loyalty to the Emperor) and marched out to join – not to lead – the cavalry regiment to which he had most ardently aspired: the glorious and famously chivalrous band of the Lifeguard Hussars.

A quintessentially modest man, Hansel Pless said less in later life about his own courageous acts than about the pride he took in the survival, after service on both the Western and Eastern Fronts, of his two English hunters, Ernest and Malcolm. Brought home at last to Fürstenstein, the rescued horses were by then so weak from hunger that their girthbands and bridles had to be hooked to the roof of the stable, in order to keep their gaunt bodies from outright collapse. Asked about his own experiences, Hansel shrugged aside the hardships and praised instead the kindness shown to him by Prince Eitel Friedrich (the Emperor's second son), who was in command of the regiment. The Prince, conscious of young Hansel's dual heritage, would often ask him to visit their headquarters – usually stationed in a French farm or some outbuildings – at the end of the day. 'And, then, after I had reported in, he would shake me by the hand and talk with me in English, inquiring after my father and my relations in England and saying how glad he was to see me . . . but only a great gentleman like Prince Eitel Friedrich could have behaved in such a manner.'[20]

Interviewed in later years, Hansel Pless also offered a cameo from one solitary afternoon when, riding alone at dusk through empty fields in France, he came across an abandoned British battery. The gunners were all dead; a single, badly wounded officer was staggering among the strewn corpses, too stunned even to hear Hansel's offer of help. Riding slowly on, the young Prince came to a field where a group of English soldiers were being held as prisoners. Among them, he spotted the bedraggled uniform of a sergeant from his uncle George's regiment: the Rifle Brigade. Dismounting, the young German officer walked over for a chat, and to see if he could gather any comforting information for his mother.

The news of George Cornwallis-West was good; when the sergeant had last seen him, Daisy's brother was leading a small British troop that had been stationed, in reasonable safety, not far from Antwerp. Lingering on, Hansel finally decided to venture his opinion of the war. The British sergeant shared his view: victory for either side mattered less than an end to the slaughter.

'We both agreed,' Hansel wistfully recalled. 'What mattered was that this terrible war should have stopped a long time ago.'[21]

Hilda Deichmann's son was old enough to have been Hansel's father. Born in 1874 and educated at Dresden and Balliol, Wilhelm served in the British Army before taking a further degree at Berlin. In 1903, he adopted the time-honoured profession of his mother's family and entered the diplomatic service. The difference was simply that, while his uncle, Sir Maurice de Bunsen, became an ambassador for Britain, Wilhelm became an envoy for Germany.

Diplomacy ran in his family's veins. Wilhelm spent seven happy years in the service, working at Rome, the Hague and, finally, at Athens. In 1911, however, Hilda Deichmann decided that she was too old to run two households, one at Abbey Lodge, in London, and a second (far bigger and more complex) at Bendeleben, in Thuringia. Wilhelm, after resigning from his post in Athens, had been running the German estate himself for just three years when war was declared. His duty was clear; abandoning Bendeleben, he offered his services to the Emperor.

Nothing is known about Wilhelm's war experiences before the moment that, captured in France in 1916, he was sent to a camp in Brittany for German POWs.

It was at this point that Wilhelm von Krause decided to put his dual nationality to use. Announcing his intention of acting as an English language teacher to his fellow German prisoners, he attracted the interest of a group of Americans. The YMCA arranged for the camp to receive a large wooden hut that could be used as a school room and lecture space. By the end of his first two years of captivity in France, von Krause had succeeded in educating his comrades well enough for them to find work, after the war, as teachers of English. What none of Wilhelm's prisoner-pupils could guess at the time was that a teacher's language skills would prove more valuable when they returned home than the great estates – ruined, sold or confiscated after the war – that these former landowners had left behind.[22]

16

VICTIMS OF CIRCUMSTANCE: GERMANY IN ENGLAND

(1914–18)

'Little Germany's Farewell'

The German steamer "Titania" sailed from St Katharine's Dock on Saturday night amid memorable scenes. Her German passengers, Reservists and private families, sang their National Anthem. Then a fair-haired German boy leant over the rails and, waving his hat, cried, "Three Cheers for Great Britain." The cry was taken up with great fervour.

EAST LONDON OBSERVER, 8 AUGUST 1914

The fate of the expatriated Hochberg brothers, the Lichnowskys and the Blüchers was unfortunate, but these members of noble families were not, in 1914, in dire financial straits. Painful though it was to be deprived of all their English property and personal possessions, they had other resources. Count Hochberg, owner of Schloss Halbau, was still in a position to drive Daisy Pless out to the Döberitz camp in his splendid family coach. The Blüchers moved out of the Esplanade Hotel, following the death of Count

Blücher's father in 1916, but only so that they could take up residence at Krieblowitz, a magnificent Silesian castle overlooking woods and lakes. The Lichnowskys, in 1914, still owned Schloss Kuchelna, a shooting estate at Gratz and one of the most remarkable art collections in Europe. Daisy Pless's cottage refuge ('Ma Fantaisie') in the gardens of Fürstenstein, while dwarfed by the Pless family's castles, had four bedrooms and only one occupant. The sufferings of these men and women were deeply felt, but they were not of the kind that shortens lives.

Robert Graves's first glimpse of what it meant to be at war was of the German side. Despatched to Lancaster in the autumn of 1914 to help guard the people who suddenly found themselves identified as enemy aliens, the nineteen-year-old Graves discovered an internment camp filled with bewildered school children, tailors, small shopkeepers and – arriving in a later convoy – forty middle-aged German waiters who had been rounded up by an efficient Manchester police force and brought to the camp in chains.

Internment was the fate of most working-class Germans, belonging to a group who had often previously acquired English citizenship, but who were now regarded as too dangerous to remain at large. The fate of those who had not yet been naturalised was not much better. Rendered unemployable and unwelcome, a legion of German bank clerks, waiters, governesses and tutors were summarily ordered to depart the country. Governesses sometimes received as much as ten pounds to cover the cost of transporting themselves to wartime Berlin. Waiters and bank clerks were seldom so well treated.

Strolling the dusty length of London's Tottenham Court Road on the sultry morning of 10 August 1914, a *Manchester Guardian* reporter took note of the sort of people who were waiting in line to obtain the vital permit for departure. (A mere two weeks had been granted, following the declaration of war, during which to obtain these precious documents.) The mix was eclectic: 'quiet looking old ladies, probably teachers, young German girl students, tourists caught without money, barbers, stockbrokers, shipping clerks . . .'

These were still the early days and the reporter's tone was sympathetic. In the autumn of 1914, D. H. Lawrence foresaw no difficulties about dedicating his new novel, *The Rainbow*, to Frieda's sister. (Advised not to increase a provocatively frank work's chance of being censored, Lawrence eventually compromised by dedicating his book to Elsa von Richthofen by her first name only.) In September, *The Times* still saw no harm in reporting that newly interned German soldiers were grateful for presents of cigarettes, ginger beer, apples and cake.

Attitudes were about to change. In Germany, throughout the war, it remained possible for the King of Bavaria to amble across a public street in Munich to ask the British-born wife of his musical friend Clement Franckenstein whether she had received 'good news from home'.[1] In England, by the summer of 1915, such behaviour, demonstrated in public, and by a public figure, had become unthinkable.

Propaganda, as the Germans soon learned, was handled with considerably more skill by London than by Berlin. The propaganda masters' task was not hard. Germany's aggressive occupation of Belgium in 1914 (the scenes of destruction at Louvain were strikingly captured by an English camera) led to the precipitate and not entirely welcome arrival in Britain of some 150,000 homeless refugees, all of whom needed to be housed and fed. In the early hours of 16 December 1914, three massive German warships shelled three Yorkshire fishing towns, acting on the mistaken assumption that they were of military value. Hartlepool's normal protective force of several light destroyers was not, due to bad weather, in position; Scarborough and Whitby were, as usual, completely undefended. The casualties (137 dead and 592 wounded) were reported by the newspapers as the first victims of military action in England since the Battle of Sedgemoor in 1685. Germany had handed its adversary an invaluable gift.

For Germans still residing in England, the final public relations disaster came in May 1915, when German torpedoes deliberately sank a passenger ship bound from the US for Liverpool. Of the *Lusitania's* 1,959 passengers and crew, 1,195 drowned; the ship's secret cargo, a gift to Britain from the US of 1,248 cases of shrapnel and Remington shells, remained unreported. Five days later, the Bryce Report was published.

Viscount Bryce, a former ambassador who had been educated at Heidelberg and decorated by the German Emperor, was a man whose distinguished record lent authority to the detailed account of German atrocities in Belgium that appeared under his name. The report itself, while based entirely on second-hand evidence, took care to distinguish the kindly German civilian from the brutal actions of the Prussian military; the allegations made against Belgium's occupying force and listed in an appendix, were, nevertheless, extreme. Monstrosities were said to have included the slicing off of women's breasts; the disembowelment of living victims; the shooting of sons in the presence of their fathers, and the bayoneting of women and babies.

Ten years after the war, Robert Graves wrote dismissively about 'highly-coloured accounts of German atrocities in Belgium' and declared the Bryce Report's accusations of 'rape, mutilation and torture' to have been mere fabrication.[2] Sassoon, his comrade at the front, also scoffed at the absurdity of some of the myths that had been allowed to pass for truth: 'Everyone had been talking about the hundred thousand Russians who were supposed to have passed through England on their way to France.' But neither man denied that the more gruesome tales had been believed. Just as the German newspaper readers of 1901 had dutifully absorbed the ghastly image of British soldiers twirling Boer newborns on sabre points and rifle barrels, so the British readers of 1915 accepted the possibility that German soldiers might do the same, and worse. 'The newspapers informed us that German soldiers crucified Belgian babies,' Sassoon recalled. 'Stories of that kind were taken for granted; to have disbelieved them would have been unpatriotic.'[3]

It was possible, until the summer of 1915, to preserve a degree of rationality as an English civilian. Winston Churchill could get away with drinking German hock and joke that he was only interning it. Evelyn Blücher's parents could feel safe enough to offer a guest room in their Welsh house to Ernest Ratibor, the princely survivor of a torpedoed German submarine. Early in 1915, Rudyard Kipling could still venture a subversive twist to 'Mary Postgate', his story of a woman who, after deliberately allowing a wounded German airman to die as punishment for a death that he, paradoxically, may not have caused, treats herself to a long, hot bath and comes downstairs looking – according to her bemused employer – 'quite handsome'. The self-righteous, so Kipling's terrible tale suggests, knew no qualms.

Humane treatment of Germans living in England had become brave and rare by the summer of 1915. Hilda Deichmann, living at Abbey Lodge during the first years of the war, admired the few English ladies who were prepared to visit an old friend whose son was serving in the German Army. Meanwhile, beyond the tranquil purlieus of Hilda's family home, anti-German feelings escalated into displays of public violence. Writing in a May 1915 issue of the *Daily Herald*, the socialist paper he had founded in 1912, the celebrated pacifist George Lansbury pleaded for leniency towards 'the helpless men and women whose only crime is that of being descendants of Germans'.[4] In Parliament, speaking two days earlier, Prime Minister Asquith urged the need to prevent 'serious injury and irreparable hardship to individuals'.[5]

Following the sinking of the *Lusitania* and the publication of the Bryce Report, even the most complacent of English-born Germans took fright. Five hundred had already changed their names, and a popular East End pub had transformed itself – with the deft flick of a brush over an inconvenient 'P' – into the Russian Flag. Tragically, the new surge of Germanophobia also secured the downfall of a chancellor who, in his previous incarnation as secretary of state for war, had done more than any other man in England to give Britain an army that was fit for battle.

Richard Burdon Haldane's pro-German stance had come under attack even before the outbreak of war. Haldane's achievements, both during his service as war minister (1905–12) and, subsequently, as a lord chancellor who quietly continued to run the War Office of which Asquith became the titular head in 1914, had been immense.

Working alongside Alexander Haig, Haldane had given England a fledgling aeronautical industry and set up the Territorial Army. He had also turned the British Expeditionary Force (BEF) into what was considered, in August 1914, to be the best fighting force ever to have come out of Britain. All of this mattered less than the fact that Haldane had privately declared his enduring affection for a remembered lecture room in Göttingen, and that he refused to disclose the contents of an entirely innocuous personal letter from a friend, the great German shipbuilder Albert Ballin. By 1915, even the news that Haldane owned a dog named Kaiser confirmed his treachery.

Booed in public, reviled in the right-wing press, targeted by letters of abuse and mocked from the stage in a music-hall ditty, Haldane offered to resign. Asquith, who had known and loved Haldane since boyhood, refused. A few allies rallied around. 'We have to search our memory in vain', an anonymous writer pleaded in the *Westminster Gazette* of 8 January 1915, 'for an attack on a public man which has been more ungenerous, more ungrateful and more unfounded.'

The supporters were in the minority. By February 1915, Haldane's two chief enemies in the right-wing press, Arnold White of the *Daily Express* and Leo Maxse of the *National Review*, were congratulating each other upon the support they had received from the Unionist Party for their increasingly vicious attacks upon the Chancellor. Writing to Maxse on 4 February,

White told him that three leading Unionists (Edward Carson, Andrew Bonar Law and Walter Long) were eager for the moment 'when the plump body of the Member for Germany swings in the wind between two lamp posts'.[6]

It is possible that Asquith changed his mind without any outside influence being exerted upon him. It is also possible that he sincerely believed Haldane's poor health and the pressures of a hostile press might render retirement welcome. It's even possible that he did – as Asquith later assured his dismayed wife, Margot – indeed put up a last stern fight to retain the services of his long-serving ally. The truth has never been entirely clear. However, when a new coalition government came to power in May 1915 – with Andrew Bonar Law leading the Conservative element and Asquith clinging on as the Liberal prime minister – it was announced that Richard Haldane was to be replaced as lord chancellor by the almost entirely insignificant figure of Stanley Buckmaster.

Hostility towards Haldane did not diminish during the war. In 1918, after the former chancellor had been advised not to show his face at the Victory March, one celebrated fellow Scot decided to demonstrate his allegiance. Calling at Haldane's London home that evening, dressed in all the splendour of his field-marshal's uniform, Alexander Haig presented a book of dispatches. It carried a personal tribute, written on its flyleaf, where Haig had expressed his admiration for 'the greatest Secretary of State for War England has ever had'.

Haig's view has, for almost a hundred years, held true.

Richard Haldane was not alone in being sacrificed on the altar of Germanophobia. In October 1914, Winston Churchill, as first lord of the Admiralty, had to undertake the disagreeable task of asking the First Sea Lord to resign. Prince Louis of Battenberg's undeniably German origins had become too controversial an issue for him to stay at the helm of a British Navy. Comforted by the assurance that he would return to his old position after the war,

Louis took his leave and embarked on writing a three-volume history of naval medals. In January 1919, he gracefully acknowledged that a German sea lord – even one who now bore an English name – remained, after the war, an unacceptable proposition to the British nation.

Louis had shown more humour than most of his royal relations when the news came, in 1917, that a change of names was in order. Visiting his son, freshly transformed into the Earl of Medina, the new Marquess of Milford Haven offered a skittishly astute response in the family's guest-book: 'Arrived Prince Hyde; departed Lord Jekyll.'[7]

Name-changing had nearly become de rigueur among Germans living in England since the autumn of 1914, when some 500 German families underwent a hasty process of Anglicisation. In 1915, Ford Madox Ford dropped his father's Germanic 'Hueffer' and turned to his pre-Raphaelite grandfather (Ford Madox Brown) for a new identity. Robert Graves's regimental colleagues performed the task for him themselves, converting the 'von Ranke' that had given such pride to Graves as a boy into the jocular 'von Runicke'.

The wonder was that it had taken three long years of war to bring about a similar alteration in the country's leading family. Understandably, Victoria and Albert's descendants remained attached to their traditional titles; still, as Wilhelm II would mischievously observe, a staging of *The Merry Wives of Saxe-Coburg and Gotha* was unlikely to inspire confidence in the English crown. Plantaganet, York, Lancaster, Fitzroy and England had all been put forward as candidates for a more British sounding family surname; Windsor, connecting the monarchy to the only home for which their loyal subjects felt real enthusiasm, won the day.

The family member who was hit hardest by the overnight transformation was the one who had no option but to be excluded. Charles Edward, Duke of Saxe-Coburg and Gotha, was thirty-three in 1917. Following in the footsteps of Grand Duke Ernst of Hessen-Darmstadt, Charlie Coburg (as he was known to his friends) had refused to take part in a war against his own family. His reward for loyalty was to learn that King George V had, acting with extreme reluctance, disowned the Duke as a member of the family. By July 1917, Charlie Coburg's strong connection to England had shrunk, through no desire of his own, to a discreet correspondence with Alice, his sister (newly transformed into the Countess of Athlone). As mementoes of far-off times, the Duke still possessed a Claremont bed and a painting of himself, aged seven or eight, parading as a miniature Scotsman for the enter-tainment of Queen Victoria, a doting grandmother.

Name-changing offered little help to the large number of prominent financiers and bankers who had settled in England long before the war. While the Prussian-born Sir Ernest Cassel survived with his honours and property untouched (Cassel had contributed to the British arms industry by overseeing the amalgamation of Vickers-Armstrong), Sir Edgar Speyer, a generous funder of Scott's 1912 expedition to the Antarctic, was driven out of the country by a hate campaign. Speyer returned to America. In 1921, he was stripped of his honours, following unfounded allegations of his having traded with the enemy.

Hilda Deichmann belonged to this group by virtue of the immense banking interests she had inherited following Baron Deichmann's death in 1907. Hilda, up to the very eve of war, had enjoyed a life of considerable social prestige. On 22 July 1914, she gave a dinner party for the Lichnowskys at which the Prince, still elated by his Oxford doctorate, had talked about the improvement in Anglo-German relations 'with great satisfaction'.[8] Three days later, Hilda lunched at Eastbourne with two of the German Emperor's sisters, leaving only after she had promised to visit the friendly Princesses at their respective homes in Greece (Sophie) and Germany (Mossy). And how – she wondered sadly, looking back – just *how* could any of their happy little group have imagined the crisis that was about to tear that comfortable – and, in retrospect, complacent – little world apart?[9]

The impact upon Hilda's personal life was not immediate. By May 1915, however, she realised that several old friends were keeping their distance. By 1916, it was deemed unsafe for the mother of a German officer to live alone in central London. Abbey Lodge was closed up, while Hilda, gladly accepting an invitation from her husband's niece, Emma Deichmann, moved into the comfortable house that Emma and her husband Bruno Schröder inhabited at Englefield Green, on the edge of Windsor Great Park.

The move proved timely. Hilda would have found it devastating to be alone when her brother Maurice came to deliver the terrible news that her only son had been killed in action. (News of Wilhelm von Krause's survival and capture by French troops arrived later in the year.) Hilda was equally thankful for the companionship of the Schröders when it was reported that some awkward questions were being raised in the House of Commons, and that they concerned the legitimate status of the Deichmann bank, of which Hilda was now the owner.

Confiscation was a useful strategy for raising funds in wartime. Hansard's Parliamentary Report for 16 November 1916 demonstrates the shocking vindictiveness with which attempts were made to enforce that policy. Sir Henry Craik, rising to question Mr Pretyman (parliamentary secretary to the Board of Trade), proposed that Horstmann and Co, formerly under the ownership of Adolph Deichmann and now owned by his wife, should have its licences withdrawn, prior to immediate confiscation. It was pointed out that two of Baroness Deichmann's daughters were married to German officers, while her son had fought in the German Army. It followed, Craik thundered – his tone is clear from the report – that Horstmann and Co were actively serving enemy interests.

Mr Pretyman, feebly defending Hilda's interests, chose to retreat into technicalities. The licences had been issued in December

1914, when there was a German partner, who had since resigned. Sir Henry was not satisfied; Mr Pretyman himself sounded ready, at a pinch, to throw Hilda and her bank to the wolves.

Law, nevertheless, was on Hilda's side. Mr Pretyman, rallying at last, pointed out that the Baronness herself had been born in England, to an English mother and a half-English father. (Oddly, he failed to mention that Hilda's brother was an esteemed British ambassador.) Adolph Deichmann, her late husband, had also taken British citizenship just before his death in 1907. Since there was no German involvement in the bank at the present time, a licence was not required. The licence could not, therefore, be removed. Sir Henry, floored and furious, sat down.[10]

The family bank was safe, for the time being, but the ferocity of Sir Henry Craik's attack served as a sharp reminder to Hilda of just how tenuous her position in English society had become. In her post-war memoirs, she expressed heartfelt appreciation for the unfailing support of her brother Maurice and his forthright, kindly English wife during what she called a 'terrible' period. 'Terrible', from a mildly spoken woman of Quaker background, was a strong word.

Hilda, by 1917, knew that Wilhelm was alive but imprisoned. No such comforting news was on hand for her hosts at the Dell. In the summer of 1914, Emma and Bruno Schröder's eldest boy had gone straight from school in England to receive six months' training at the Hamburg branch of the family bank. When war broke out, the young man was conscripted for the German side. Captured near Vilnius on the Eastern Front in 1916, the Schröders' son was never seen or heard of again.

Bruno Schröder's own bank escaped confiscation, in part because Bruno himself had prudently acquired British nationality ahead of time, and in part because his long-standing business partner, Frank Tiarks, was British. Nevertheless, despite the fact that five of the Schröders' British-born bank staff were killed in action while fighting the Germans, Bruno himself was perceived as one

of the enemy. Helmut, his younger and surviving son, was persecuted at school. At Englefield Green, the decorative hothouses
used for the cultivation of rare orchids were destroyed by vandals
who claimed, most unconvincingly, that the Schröders had been
using the buildings for their secret hoard of coal.

Rumour, once started, proved hard to quell. The walls around
the Schröders' estate were eyed with suspicion. Was it possible that
they concealed a battery of guns, all trained upon the windows of
Windsor Castle? Richard Haldane's nemesis, Leo Maxse, started a
hare in the *National Review* by declaring Schröder to be a leading
supporter of the Unseen Hand, an evil – and entirely imaginary –
group of foreign financiers who planned to broker a secret and
lucrative deal with Germany.

Nothing could have been further from the truth, but it was
undeniable that Bruno Schröder, as much as Hilda Deichmann,
felt torn. In 1915, ordered to make a public declaration of his allegiance to England, Bruno confessed that he found it impossible to
choose which country was dearer to him. 'I feel', he said with desolate candour, 'as if my mother and father have quarrelled.'[11]

Throughout the war, Bruno Schröder continued to invite anger
and suspicion by his quiet determination not to be bullied out of
either his loyalties or his beliefs. All of the English-based financiers
gave funds to help the German internees, of whom there were
some 33,000 by the end of 1915. Edgar Speyer donated £5,600;
Ernest Cassel produced a generous £27,833. Schröder, dwarfing
their contributions at a time when both his bank and home
remained at daily risk of confiscation, gave £92,000: a staggeringly
generous sum.

The Schröders' chief act of wartime philanthropy was to
ensure the survival of the great London institution that their
family had supported from its earliest years. In 1914, as war was
declared, an emergency meeting was called at the German
Hospital and agreement reached to receive patients of all nation-
alities. The attitude taken by the English towards the hospital

proved, in turn, to be surprisingly enlightened. The German nurses were granted permission to remain at their posts and Sir Hermann Weber's son Frederick (Parkes-Weber) served as a consultant physician throughout the war. When doctors from captured German ships were brought into the country, several of them took up the offer to provide their services to a sturdy working hospital that shone out, in hateful times, as a beacon of humanity.

Among the few records to have survived from the hospital's war years, one offers a memorable cameo account of a German patient and his own small attempt at reconciliation.

Baron Anton von Horst, like Edgar Speyer, was a German-born American. In 1914, he was returning with his family to Germany. Unfortunately for Horst, the liner had just docked at an English port when war was declared. Interned as an enemy alien, Baron Horst nevertheless managed to get his children and wife sent safely home to Coburg (where he would eventually rejoin them). Meanwhile, having been afflicted by a form of paralysis during his lengthy internment, Baron Horst was eventually brought to London and given remedial treatment at the German Hospital.

It's likely that the Baron was simply missing his own children. The hospital records report only that, following his partial recovery, and when the weather permitted, Anton Horst would hobble down to the front gate of the hospital. Here, he became beloved by every small slum child in that impoverished area of London for his willingness to shell out the princely sum of two shillings apiece, to be earned by any girl or boy willing to compete in a race along the short stretch of road leading from the hospital to Dalston Lane. All the children got prizes: winning – outside the field of mortal combat – played no part in this tiny Olympics. Every entrant was a victor.[12]

Here, at the centre of a world engulfed in hatred, misery and all the horrors of war, a tiny echo can be detected of the behaviour of that good-natured old King of Bavaria, a man who never forgot to cross the road in wartime Munich, just to ask a wistful member of the enemy nation whether she had received good news from home.

17

PAY-BACK

(1918–19)

The silver coins distributed to children living in the shadow of London's great German Hospital earned Anton von Horst no favours in an enemy country in 1916, two years into a war in which almost five million people would die, while the wounded comprised almost twice that amount. Subsequently transferred to Knockaloe on the Isle of Man, where 24,500 internees were wearily marooned during the last years of the war, Baron Horst was one of a considerable number of Germans who were only released six months after the signing of the armistice agreement on 11 November 1918.*

Hindsight suggests that Germany's fate was sealed on 6 April 1917, the day that Woodrow Wilson brought America into the war. Nevertheless, on 4 June 1918, when American reinforcements were pouring into France at a rate of 10,000 men a day, Prince Heinrich of Pless could still stand on a French hillside at

---

* Repatriated in 1919, Horst rejoined his family in Germany, set up a hop-producing business and, in 1933, briskly joined the newly elected Nazi party.

the side of a splendidly uniformed Wilhelm II and join him in anticipating the destruction of Paris, 'so that not one stone will be left on the other, simply wiped off the face of the earth ...'[1] In point of fact, as the Prince informed his dismayed wife back in Germany, everything, at the end of a long war, was going 'marvellously well'.

Prince Heinrich's brother, Fritz Hochberg, was also eagerly anticipating a swift conclusion to hostilities, although the Count had no idea of who would win. What, really, did it matter, so long as release was at hand? Writing to his beloved English sister-in-law during that same month, Fritz told Daisy of his own peaceful fantasy: 'we'll take the next boat and sail for our beloved little island'.[2] In fact, neither of the Hochberg brothers ever saw England again.

Daisy – ignoring the orders given both by her husband and by the Emperor himself to try to stay quiet and out of sight – was working too hard on her own humane projects to humour the unrealistic notions of the Pless family. In October 1918, determined to make a contribution wherever she could, the intrepid Princess set off on a long journey, via Belgrade, to establish a new convalescent home for wounded soldiers at Constanza, in Romania.

Daisy's timing was terrible. Europe, towards the end of the war, was in a state of meltdown. Rebel troops had blown up the one bridge leading to Constanza; the only option was to abandon her brave project and turn back. A twenty-hour return journey to Belgrade got the exhausted Princess there just in time to be rushed onto the last steamer leaving for Budapest. Arriving on 18 October, Daisy found the city in a state of uproar. Confronted by rioters, bonfires and bombs, she locked herself into a hotel room to sit events out until – on the very day that Germany's own home revolution began at Kiel – the exhausted and terrified Princess finally abandoned all hope for her plans.

On 4 November, Daisy Pless joined the hordes of refugees who were streaming across Europe, through countries that trembled on the verge of disintegration, fleeing back into a nation that was simultaneously facing defeat in France and revolution at home, as the German sailors led the call for an end to imperial rule. Eleven days later, having been warned to stay away from Pless and Fürstenstein because of local riots, Daisy reached Berchtesgaden. Here, in a resort that had long been favoured by the German aristocracy, the Princess found that her pretty alpine villa had been taken over by members of the new revolutionary Workers' and Soldiers' Council. Daisy, approving of this turn of events, promptly set about providing them with cigarettes and beer. 'They are very very nice to me,' she confided to her journal on 15 November and added that she supported the rights of these gallant soldiers, last protectors of a threatened nation: 'as I see things clearly coming, they are our only defence against Bolshevism'.

All in all, while initially unnerved, Daisy Pless believed that the new and fiercely nationalistic Germany deserved support. Her awareness of the hardships suffered by the miners at Pless and Fürstenstein had come early on in a privileged marriage. The news that these same workers and their comrades now sought to establish their rights troubled the Princess far less than the news that Patsy Cornwallis-West, now widowed and frail, was calling for her daughter to come back home and nurse her. The British government forbade any such course of action. Regarded as a traitor to her husband's country because of her friendly behaviour to English POWs, Daisy's thoughtfulness for the wounded soldiers of Germany now cast her, in her own land, as one of the enemy. There could be, in 1918, no question of making a return to England.

Hansel Pless had scarcely set eyes on Daisy since 1916, the year in which he set off, as a proud sixteen-year-old, to fight for his father's country. Following Germany's victory over Russia and the subsequent signing, in March 1918, of the ferocious reparations treaty of Brest-Litovsk,* the young officer was transferred from Galicia on the Eastern Front to France, where, so Hansel later recalled, life in dugouts had been made a daily nightmare by the attacks of the French and the Americans. (Loyal throughout his life to his mother's country, the Prince refused to allocate any responsibility for his discomfort to British troops.)

Hansel was sharing a dugout near Sedan with his most recent commander, Count Eulenburg, when the news came through on 9 November that the German Emperor had been forced to abdicate.

Eulenburg, whose father, Philipp, had been one of the Emperor's closest friends and advisors, stood high among Hansel Pless's canon of military heroes. The Count was a man adored by his troops, a stickler for etiquette who, while crossing a burning bridge, once stopped to reprimand a frightened soldier for failing to deliver the correct salute. Gravely wounded on seven occasions, he himself had never complained. But now, informed of the Emperor's degradation, Eulenburg shed public tears and then called for one last round of applause from his men. 'I've never heard them cheer louder,' Hansel remembered.[3] Two days later, under Eulenburg's command and in spite of the announcement that armistice had been agreed, his weary troops made a final – and futile – attempt to recover their lost position, just outside Sedan.

Eulenburg's behaviour was not unusual. So many promises had been made and broken. To the men at the front in November 1918, an armistice announcement amounted to no more than the latest piece of worthless propaganda.

News of the spreading revolution reached Hansel while he was

---

* The 1918 Treaty of Brest-Litovsk gave Germany one-half of Russian industry, nine-tenths of her coal mines, six billion marks' worth of financial reparations and one-third of her people (constituting all German-speaking members of the Russian population). The treaty provides a disturbing hint of what Germany would have sought from the Allies had she emerged victorious.

still at Sedan and suffering from the so-called 'Spanish Flu', the deadly influenza that choked more people to death in a year than died during the entire terrible process of the war.* Recovered, Hansel became part of that German Army who were now summoned home to act as heroes and patriots, defenders of a country in which 'Deutschland über alles', when sung at Weimar in December 1918, would signify victory, not over the Allies, but over the dreaded spectre of the Bolsheviks.

The rebellion had begun early the previous month, at the Emperor's favourite sailing harbour. Ordered to carry out a suicidal attack upon the British Navy in the last weeks of a lost war, the sailors of ration-starved and battered Kiel rebelled. By the afternoon of 4 November, the town was controlled by 40,000 mutineers. Four days later, the revolutionaries' call for peace and a new democratic government had spread to Hanover, Brunswick, Frankfurt and Munich. At the very same time that the armistice was agreed and signed at Compiègne, in France, internal preparations were being made to sweep away the last vestiges of imperial Germany. Would Germany follow imperial Russia's fate? Would the sailors and the powerful anti-war movement known as the Spartacus League (it became the Communist Party, or KPD, in December 1918) seize the reins?

One thing was clear: at the very moment of defeat, Germany's army faced a new challenge which could, if shrewdly handled, become a life-saving salvager of national morale. In this scenario, there had been no defeat; Germany had simply elected to return home to face battle with a greater enemy. 'Our field-grey heroes return to the Heimat undefeated . . .' ran the official press release.

Similar words would be used by Friedrich Ebert, the short and plain-faced socialist moderate who had been singled out by

---

* Between twenty and forty million people were killed in 1918–19 by the most devastating epidemic that the world has yet experienced.

Wilhelm II's last chancellor (his nephew, Max von Baden) as the man best suited to take the Emperor's place and yet uphold the rule of sanity. 'I salute you,' Ebert declared to the soldiers, 'you, who return unvanquished from the field of battle.'[4]

Germany, as her new leader-in-waiting was eager to stress, might have lost two million men on the battlefields, but she had never been occupied and she had not been crushed. A greater cause had brought her valiant armies home. Challenging the world mattered less than protecting the threatened Fatherland from destruction by her own people.

For Hansel Pless, the return offered a chance to demonstrate how well he had learned the duty of a German officer to serve his country and his leader. Proud still in his old age, he recalled how, during the march to Potsdam, a mob of revolutionaries had called for his blood: '"Tear his epaulettes off and kill the bastard!"' Turning towards them, Hansel prepared to defend himself. There was no need. 'They were quite a crowd, but when they saw a Cavalry Officer with an Iron Cross, aged just eighteen, and quite ready to kill them if they attacked, they all shut up.'[5]

Hansel had been taught to offer his allegiance to the throne. Harry Kessler had earned his title as 'the Red Count' from his left-leaning sympathies. Nevertheless, back from acting as an unofficial German cultural attaché in Switzerland and doing his bit for the November Revolution as a part-time 'Red' policeman, the dapper Kessler was shaken by the size of the crowds and the violence of the riots that he witnessed in Berlin on 9 November, the day of the Emperor's abdication.

Count Kessler had no time for the notion that Germany remained undefeated. It was his country's loss to the Allies that made this, for him, 'one of the most memorable and dreadful days in German history'. Nevertheless, he shrank from the sight of the rebels who booed the returning troops of gaunt-faced soldiers who wore their wreaths of flowers as if 'festooned in melancholy'. Neither could he see why the mob needed to destroy the personal correspondence of the imperial family, while plundering the palace of the absent Wilhelm.[6]

A tweed-suited, softly spoken, aristocratic aesthete whose swiftly blinking eyes – they were sometimes compared to camera shutters – missed nothing that passed under their scrutiny, Harry Kessler was a divided man. He admitted that he disliked the hooliganism of the men whose politics he wanted to endorse. Such fastidious reservations, however, would only have caused Kessler doubly to deplore a young Hansel Pless for taking part (under orders that could not be disobeyed by an army officer) in the dawn attack on the headquarters of the left-wing newspaper *Forwards* (*Vorwärts*). The attack was followed by the arrest and covert murder of Rosa Luxemburg and Karl Liebknecht, the revolutionary leaders of Spartacus.

Friedrich Ebert, meanwhile, indicated his implicit approval of the killings by refusing to allow the assassins to be court-martialled. For Ebert, who had initially opposed the Emperor's abdication, what mattered most was to broadcast the fact that a newborn and wholesomely republican country would stand firm against the threat of Bolshevism. Republican Germany must never suffer Russia's recent fate.

Tisa Schulenburg was not among the little band of girls attending the select Stift Heiligengrabe boarding school who shed tears over the Emperor's departure.[7] Gleefully defiant of their nun-like uniforms, Tisa and her own coterie of rebels decked out their hair with scarlet ribbons, put on an anti-monarchist play and announced that they would no longer curtsey to their teachers. Back home at Tressow (as she later remembered with a twinge of guilt), Tisa marched around singing, 'Smear the guillotine with the aristocracy's fat', purely for the pleasure of terrifying her mother's old-fashioned lady's maid. Countess Schulenburg, doubtless to her daughter's disappointment, did not oppose Tisa's displays of republicanism. Known in the neighbourhood of Tressow as 'Red Maria' on account of her strong and active social conscience, the Countess was treated with respect by local insurgents. This was a woman who, while she fed her own family on a strict wartime diet of bread and turnip soup, had chopped up old Schulenburg uniforms (an act of desecration equivalent to Mrs Woodrow Wilson ripping up the Stars and Stripes), in order to make jackets for the threadbare and starving villagers. Such acts had not been forgotten. The officially delivered command for just one Schulenburg family shotgun to be removed from the Tressow premises was no more than a token gesture by the well-disposed local authorities. Meanwhile, when grand visitors bewailed the loss of their homes and possessions to the villainous Bolsheviks, Tisa shared with her mother the secret sense that justice was being done.

Tisa's father was less eager than his daughter to embrace the birth of a republic. General Schulenburg had been with the Emperor at Spa on 9 November. Speaking as a man who believed with passion in his country and his duty, the General had begged Wilhelm to follow his chancellor's recommendation to step down, but not to flee.

Wilhelm gravely shook General Schulenburg's hand and pledged his firm commitment. The risk of suffering the fate of his cousin Nicky, the Tsar, proved, however, too terrifying for Willy to contemplate at a time of crisis. Within hours of that commitment, and accompanied by a train of fifty-seven carriages loaded with his personal effects – they included every film that had ever shown Willy on camera – the dethroned Emperor slipped across the border, fleeing into Holland.

Schulenburg, years later, paying a single reluctant visit to the Emperor's Dutch manorhouse at Doorn, was rewarded with a memento: a block of wood upon the surface of which Wilhelm had neatly carved not Schulenburg's name, but Willy's own.

Tisa Schulenburg's experiences of harsh rationing at Tressow were duplicated all across Germany. Starvation conditions were savagely extended through the decision to keep Britain's naval blockade in place until full reparations from Germany had been agreed.

In January 1919, an Eton-educated member of Margot Asquith's extensive and largely Germanophile family was despatched on a mission to Berlin. Officially, young Ernest Tennant was supposed to be ascertaining whether the armistice conditions were being observed. Unofficially, he smuggled in as much as he could carry in the way of fodder (dried beef and soup tins) to feed the needy. Prepared for disturbing scenes, Tennant found himself horrified. 'What I saw in Berlin in January 1919, especially the starvation of small children, had a considerable influence on my later life,' he recalled in 1957, 'because it made me think that another war with Germany was quite impossible and that now we should endeavour to be friends.' Eventually, this view would lead Tennant to become one of Hitler's most ardent advocates; back in 1920, a well-founded concern for Germany's fate inspired him to plead with the Economic Council that help should be extended to a suffering nation.[8]

Hilda Deichmann owed her own post-war visit to rations-starved Germany to the timely return to England, late in 1918, of her brother Maurice, covered in glory for his success in the rallying of troops from the British dominions to assist in the war.

Maurice de Bunsen stepped ashore just as Hilda, together with her third and youngest daughter, was being despatched to an internment camp as an enemy alien. Maurice, acting with his usual quiet dexterity, obtained permission for Hilda and young Marie Therese to intern themselves more agreeably at Bendeleben, the beautiful Thuringian estate that Wilhelm von Krause had dutifully abandoned in 1914, to fight for his country.

The journey from Holland to Thuringia was, of necessity, a slow one. Few trains were in service and Hilda was disconcerted to see that flimsy sheets of paper had been tacked across the glass-less windows of the carriages. She was shocked far more than this by the sombre spectacle, wherever she looked, of the lines of

frail-boned, gaunt-faced children begging for food; of the shuffling rows of men, their faces pinched to skulls; of shabby old
officials, mere skeletons within the bulk of their once splendid
pre-war uniforms. Staying at an immense hotel at Hanover, she
paid a quite staggering sum for the privilege. The reason was
soon apparent: there were no other guests.

In May 1919, Germany was still in a state not far removed from
civil war. Hilda witnessed no violence during her journey; nevertheless, arriving at Bendeleben, where a single maid and a lone
housekeeper were on hand to welcome her, the Baronness soon
learned how life had altered since the days before the war. The
farms stood in ruins; the horses were gone; the pastures were
derelict and the cattle were dead. The farm-workers, while desperate to earn some money, were too weak and underfed to
perform any active tasks; the local Communist leader, although
quite unthreatening when he paid his formal visit, had no solutions to offer. Visiting a few of her formerly grand neighbours to
glean news and helpful ideas, Hilda found the elderly Grafins
down on their hands and knees, their skinny bodies garbed in
threadbare clothes, scrubbing floors. When Wilhelm, gaunt and
prematurely grey-haired, finally returned from his long imprisonment in 1920 and married Princess Lieven, Hilda was relieved
to discover that the Princess's sturdy teenage daughter had only
one dream: to spend her days working on a farm. Such a wish, as
Hilda dryly observed, was one fancy that was not difficult to grant
at Bendeleben.[9]

Conscious, everywhere she looked, of poverty and hunger, and
of the contribution that was still being made to that misery by
Britain's naval blockade, Hilda Deichmann was astonished by the
lack of hostility shown towards herself as an evidently well-off
woman whose German, although fluent, was spoken with a strong
British accent.

Likewise, the British Army, who began their post-war occupation of the towns along the Rhine in 1919, as stipulated in the

armistice agreement. An army of 13,000 soldiers, few of whom spoke German, had taken up residence; yet the artist William Rothenstein, briefly billeted in Bonn early in 1919, detected no evidence of resentment or aggression. On the contrary; the grateful and surprised British soldiers were regularly offered gifts and invited to join the Rhinelanders at their family meals. Violet Markham, whose officer husband was stationed on the Rhine from 1919–20, confirmed Rothenstein's impression. Tom Delmer, last met as a schoolboy chanting victory songs in a Berlin classroom and subsequently taken to England in 1917, was overjoyed to exchange grim, soot-blackened London and a school where he had been mocked for his tubbiness and a foreign accent for Cologne, a cheerful riverside city where the defeated citizens welcomed his German-speaking family like long-lost friends.

In England, doors that had slammed shut in August 1914 were beginning to creak ajar. At Covent Garden, Beecham put *The Meistersingers* and *Tristan and Isolde* back on the programme in 1919 and drew packed houses. On 8 March 1919, a mere six months after the armistice had been signed, Geoffrey 'Robin' Dawson, a former editor of *The Times*, attended a large party being given for the King and Queen at Londonderry House and found Prince and Princess Lichnowsky there among the guests. Lady Londonderry herself was known to be as ardent a Germanophile as Margot Asquith, the former prime minister's wife; what startled Robin Dawson more was the fact that King George himself had approved the addition of two German visitors to the guest list.

Overtures of friendship were cautiously being made. Nevertheless, the naval blockade remained in place, purposefully contributing to Germany's hardship until reparations were signed into the Treaty of Versailles. The date for that signing was set, with meticulous care, for 28 June 1919, precisely five years from the day on which the shooting of an unpopular minor royal had led to the outbreak of war. The setting for the signature – the Hall of Mirrors at Versailles – was selected with equal care. France, still smarting from the vicious reparations that had been imposed after her defeat in the Franco-Prussian War, wanted Germany to savour that ashy taste on precisely the same spot that Prussia had triumphantly proclaimed Wilhelm I as the German emperor.

The choice of location was vindictive, and many felt that the French demands for compensation from a ruined neighbour were excessive. (Certain American delegates were heard to remark, during the course of heated pre-treaty negotiations, that they wished they had fought for Germany.) But it was an Englishman, Philip Kerr, who wrote the fateful memorandum from which – as Article 231 – the issue of Germany's responsibility emerged into the spotlight. Germany might feel, within herself, that she had not been vanquished. Article 231 (subsequently known as the war guilt clause) left no doubt that Germany was to be identified as both the perpetrator and the loser of the war. Great though her present suffering might be, Germany alone had brought it upon herself. She must pay the price.

Philip Kerr would spend the rest of his life reproaching himself for having contributed to the economic destruction of a Germany that desperately needed encouragement and support. Kerr, a brilliant and high-principled man who had come to Paris as the Prime Minister's put-upon private secretary, was too hard on himself. The daily sharing of a cluttered and over-heated suite of rooms with Lloyd George, alongside the Prime Minister's unofficial mistress and his daughter, Megan, was not the ideal working scenario for a quiet but highly strung man whose nerves began to creep into the shrillness of his voice. Kerr was responsible for a memorandum, but not for the terms of the treaty. And the Treaty of Versailles, however guilty Kerr and others felt about it afterwards, was no harsher in its demands than those that Germany herself had issued to France in 1871 and to Soviet Russia (at Brest-Litovsk) in 1918.

The treaty's conditions were undeniably tough. They were made far worse because the new and socially conscientious republic could not bring itself to impose further miseries upon a suffering nation. The bulk of the German Navy had been scuttled at Scapa Flow instead of handing it over to Britain (with a possibility of continued employment for the sailors who now had none). Seven-eighths of the German Army had been dismissed in compliance with the treaty's demands. Friedrich Ebert, the fledgling republic's first president, was in no position, therefore, to keep his well-meant promise of offering work to all willing and able-bodied German citizens.

The problem of unemployment was less immediately apparent to a country in the throes of financial crisis than the question of reparations payment that was raised at the Treaty of Versailles and ratified in 1921. The bill for war amounted to an eye-watering ten million pounds (later reduced to a mere £6,600,000).

Nor was that all. Rolling stock, train engines and all forms of military transport were to be immediately surrendered to France, while the restoration to France of Alsace and German-speaking Lorraine launched a crippling attack on German industry, principally located in Lorraine. The immense coalfield of the Saar was to be ceded to France for fifteen years, after which a plebiscite would decide its future. The Rhineland was to be occupied not only by the British Tommies, but by 25,000 soldiers imported from the French colonies. Far more problematically, the newly independent state of Poland was to be given a route through German territory to the port of Danzig (Dansk), now nominally under international control. East Prussia found itself suddenly marooned and portless, while the coal-rich estates of such mighty Silesian magnates as Prince Hans Heinrich of Pless were placed within the grasp of Polish control.

Philip Kerr, writing to an anxious Violet Markham in 1920, told her that the treaty's conditions were far too stringent.[10] Lloyd George himself seems to have felt an occasional qualm and showed it when he argued, without success, for Upper Silesia's right to choose whether to be governed by Poland's new republic.*

Philip Kerr had been thinking about Anglo–German rivalry since 1909, when he was sharing a London flat with Robert Brand, an All Souls fellow who, like Kerr, had belonged to Alfred Milner's South African Kindergarten of ardent imperialists.

Prevented by a nervous breakdown and acute rheumatism from taking part in the war, Kerr was nursed back to health by Nancy Astor, the formidably self-willed American wife of Waldorf, owner of Cliveden. Converted from Catholicism to Christian Science by Nancy at a time when his faith prevented him from marrying the Protestant Lady Minna Cecil, Kerr's contribution to the war had been purely cerebral: some eighteen articles in which he addressed the causes and likely effects of the war. Robert Brand, meanwhile, having been despatched to Washington in 1917 as a liaison officer for the supply of US munitions, married Nancy Astor's divorced sister, the former Phyllis Langhorne from Virginia.

Newly arrived in Paris in the spring of 1919, and preparing to discuss the future of Germany, a country he had never yet visited, Kerr found himself once again in the company of Bob Brand, representing the interests of Lazard's Bank and acting as an advisor to Lord Robert Cecil, head of the Economic Council. Brand's own farsighted opinion was that little benefit could be gained from ruining a potentially valuable business associate. That view was shared and expressed with a forceful eloquence to which Brand never aspired (Bob Brand's writings were as thoughtfully dull as his personality was charming) by a younger and far more articulate

---

* A plebiscite vote that was supposedly rigged both by the French and the Poles brought no easy answers to an area on which Poland, under Marshal Pitsudski (the hero of the Ukranian-Polish defeat of advancing Soviet troops in 1920), imposed ruinous demands. By 1924, the Pless mines were under Polish management teams; the stamp of the White Eagle on the furniture soon clarified any doubts about who now owned the contents of Fürstenstein and Pless.

colleague. John Maynard Keynes's book, *The Economic Consequences of the Peace*, would offer a first and devastating critique of the Treaty of Versailles, laying the majority of the responsibility for its failings upon a vengeful Clemenceau and an ageing, increasingly incompetent Woodrow Wilson.

John Maynard Keynes was thirty-six years old when he came to Paris in 1919. Born into an English family that had always looked to Germany as a model for enlightenment, he shared Robert Brand's view that the way forward was to help build a defeated Germany up, not to inflict further damage upon an already devastated nation.

The cause of Keynes's most immediate concern was the spectre of famine. The German people were starving; 270,000 tons of American food was being withheld from them. The French were objecting to its release because the cost of purchase would reduce the amount that could be taken from Germany for reparations payments. Keynes thought this was unjust. So, among the row of silent gentlemen ranked on the opposite side of the debate (Germany was granted no voice in the discussions), did Dr Carl Melchior, a financier from the Hamburg branch of Warburg's Bank.

In 1920, the year after his return from Paris, Keynes wrote a remarkable tribute to Melchior, a small, thin man who dressed – unlike Keynes himself – with immaculate formality in a dark suit above which a high white shirt collar rose to frame a pensive, intelligent face. Melchior alone appeared to Keynes to lend an aura of poignant dignity to Germany's defeat. Privately (the essay about Melchior did not appear in print until three years after Keynes's death), the British economist wrote that his feeling for the German banker had come close to love.

Talking ardently together, the two men sought and found a compromise. Germany should have her provisions; the payment for them (the suggestion came from Keynes) would be the surrender of what remained of Germany's interned – and currently redundant – fleet. Melchior approved. 'We pressed hands, and I hurried quietly on into the street.'[11]

Keynes, disgusted by the scenes and the atmosphere to which he had been a witness during his five-month stay in Paris, resigned from the British Treasury on 5 June and went home. Shielded from worldly intrusion at Charleston, the Sussex home that Clive and Vanessa Bell shared with Duncan Grant, Keynes began to express, at a rate of a thousand well-picked words a day, his pessimistic view of what would be the likely outcome of imposing harsh conditions upon a large, nationalistic and financially straitened Germany. 'If we aim at the impoverishment of Central Europe,' Keynes warned in the book that would make his name, 'vengeance, I dare predict, will not limp.'[12]

Harry Kessler, witnessing the ratification of the peace in Paris on 10 January 1920, echoed the British economist's despondency that day in his journal: 'A terrible era begins for Europe, like the gathering of clouds before a storm.'

Germany's Foreign Minister let his thoughts be known by a premeditated gesture of disgust. Leaning over the document that he was required to sign, he laid upon it, in silent protest, a single pair of mourning gloves.

PART TWO

From Versailles
to the Verge of War
(1919–40)

18

LOVE AMONG THE RUINS

(1919–23)

The challenge facing the modest and quietly spoken Friedrich Ebert as the first president of Germany's new Weimar Republic was considerable. In 1920, the President was briefly deposed during a right-wing coup supported by Erich Ludendorff, an embittered general who dreamed, ahead of Hitler, of a vastly expanded Germany, filled with soldiers and emptied of Jews. In 1922, it was Ebert's task to calm the country after anti-Semitic right-wingers assassinated, in open public view, Germany's foreign minister, Walther Rathenau. (Rathenau, a remarkable man, was the nephew of one of Germany's greatest artists, Max Liebermann.) In 1923, Ebert and Gustav Stresemann, his able and intensely Anglophile new Chancellor, struggled to retain control during the terrifying inflation surge, when family fortunes were destroyed overnight and when Germany faced starvation for a time. President Ebert faced a challenge of a different order in the November of that year when Adolf Hitler embarked on his first attempt to seize power for the emerging Nazi party, in a Republic where support for the right remained strong and the swastika was already becoming a familiar symbol of the union, in wavering times, between firm conviction and brute force.

Hitler's name was still unknown back in the Berlin of 1920, where a twenty-year-old Hansel Pless was studying for his law exams. Up at the family homes of Fürstenstein and Pless, a dinner jacket remained essential attire even for a quiet supper alone with the ageing Prince Heinrich, while a ventured remark about powder-headed footmen being just a little out of date could lead to a growl of contempt for such 'Bolshevik' notions. In Berlin, Hansel found lodgings with a hard-up widow ('a very kind and intelligent Jewess') whose brilliantly academic sons, when not entertaining Professor and Mrs Einstein to tea, cordially addressed each other across the table as 'You so-and-so Jew'. Hansel, while initially startled, decided that he preferred such directness to the ornate courtesies required at Pless.[1]

Hansel was a young man who took life as it presented itself. He didn't consider it especially odd that a young man whose family castle had served as the eastern headquarters of the German Army was welcomed, during his time in Berlin, as a daily visitor to the British Embassy. Here, when no official event was in progress and no legal lectures required Hansel's attendance, Lord D'Abernon and his guest passed the time by playing badminton in the vast and chilly ballroom, pausing only when Ribbentrop, the Ambassador's obsequious wine merchant, paid an unscheduled visit and, unwanted, lingered on.

As the half-English son of a German prince, Hansel took his own welcome on the Wilhelmstrasse for granted; later, he came to appreciate that Lord D'Abernon's friendly manner had been part of a general endeavour to help the cause of reconciliation. Recalling his years at the Embassy in Berlin in 1929, at a time when Germany faced a new financial crisis, Edgar D'Abernon urged readers of his memoirs to forget the past and to treat Germany 'as a great power and not as an outlaw'. Paying tribute to Gustav Stresemann, Germany's wise foreign minister since 1924,

D'Abernon praised the Weimar Republic's leadership as both 'reliable and strong' and added, warmly, 'What greater praise is there?'[2]

Friendships between the young in both countries had already begun to heal the wounds. Siegfried Sassoon's post-war friendship with the fallen Emperor's nephew, Prince Philipp of Hessen-Kassel, was inspired by the fact that Philipp had grown from a shy schoolboy at Bexhill into a handsomely bisexual young man. It also sprang from a conscious decision (Sassoon had narrowly escaped court-martial in 1917 for his anti-war pronouncements) to embrace – quite literally – the enemy. Sassoon made this thought explicit by requesting Philipp to send a special photograph of himself in battledress, as he would have appeared across the lines of war. The Prince, nothing loth, obliged.[3]

The friendship began when the two men met, in 1921, at a dinner in Rome, given with who knows what ulterior motives by Harold Nicolson and his wife, Vita Sackville-West. Three days later, Philipp moved into Sassoon's rooms. Back at the grief-drenched Friedrichshof, where his mother was still in mourning for her two lost sons, Philipp wrote wistfully to dear 'Sig' of the kindness that the gods had shown, and of the happiness he had experienced in two small hotel rooms ...

One reason for Sassoon's interest in Philipp was a sense of kinship that bridged the trenches (both young men had lost beloved brothers in the war). Another was culture. Sassoon, moving politically to the left after the war, had been appointed as literary editor of George Lansbury's *Daily Herald*. He was thus able to act as a patron of literary and artistic work that he admired, but about which he was conscious of being underinformed. Help was at hand.

Philipp, at the end of the war, had gone to study art and architecture at Darmstadt, while being housed by his Anglophile (and half-English) Uncle Ernst of Hessen-Darmstadt. Here, in the course of almost forgetting German, since Ernst preferred to speak English, Philipp had acquired an old-fashioned appreciation of

Greek sculpture and mythical figures. Sassoon, an instinctive traditionalist himself, was happy to be guided by his friend's artistic preferences and reassured to see that Philipp met with the approval of Gerald Berners and the Sitwells. On 29 July 1922, Sassoon announced that he wanted his charming German prince to become 'my link with Europe'.

Perhaps it was as well for the poet's own future reputation, given how deeply committed both Philipp and his brother Christoph would become to Adolf Hitler, that Sassoon, shortly after this grand declaration, started to cool off. By September, he was expressing disapproval of the young German Prince's fondness for 'cocktail bars' and for listening to what the English poet primly referred to as 'filth stories'. A month later, Sassoon ended the relationship, in part, so he confessed, because he was bored by Philipp's romantic obsession with his own royal lineage. (A portrait of the Prince by the society artist, Philip de László, depicted him as a seventeenth-century nobleman, dressed in a doublet and ruff.)

Easygoing by nature and gentle in his personality, Philipp bore no grudge and suffered no heartbreak. In 1925, while studying art in Rome, he became betrothed to Mafalda of Savoy (a daughter of Vittorio Emanuele III, King of Italy), and – like Sassoon – applied himself with reasonable success to becoming a family man.

Sassoon, during the warmest phase of friendship with his fellow officer Robert Graves, made romantic plans to join him, after the war, in one of those rural communes about which young men from both sides dreamed as they murdered each other in ravaged landscapes. While that project remained unfulfilled, Rolf Gardiner, after inheriting an uncle's Dorset farm in 1927, was able to bring a similar fantasy to practical fruition. Back in 1922, however, a youthful Gardiner was taking time off from reading modern languages at Cambridge to lead a group of English folk-dancers on a tour of Germany while looking for links between the old songs of England and Germany.

Rolf Gardiner would pay many more visits to Germany, but it

was during this first adventure that he became fascinated by the various German youth movements, and by the interest that their followers shared – in times of great privation – in bestowing upon themselves the muscular bodies of athletes. Gardiner, a devoted reader of D. H. Lawrence, was both impressed and inspired. Back at Cambridge, he began to edit *Youth* magazine and to spread word of the cult that was spreading like wildfire across a starved and myth-fed Germany, of the pure spirit in the perfect body.

The hand of friendship that Charles Ball extended to Germany in 1923 was more pragmatic.

Born in 1893, Ball had been one of Robert Graves's contemporaries at Charterhouse. After studying engineering and being sent out to Gallipoli with the Royal Artillery, Ball travelled to post-war Germany as a member of the grandly named Inter-Allied Commission of Control. His dispiriting task was to investigate and then dismantle the impeccably preserved chemical factories of the Rhineland. Ernest Tennant had already put in a plea that the factories should not be destroyed; Ball carried out the orders for demolition, while shrewdly calculating a way to be of assistance both to his host-land of Germany and to the country that he represented.

Stationed at Gallipoli during the war, Ball had noted with fascination the uncommon resilience of a shard of spent shell, of German origin. It interested him so much that he took it back with him to England. Later, talking to some of the industrialists whose factories he had been sent to the Rhineland to destroy, Ball learned more about 'the miracle metal' and discovered that it was a magnesium alloy.

Returning to England in 1923, as inflation spiralled out of control in Germany, Ball had no difficulty in attracting German backing for a Manchester-based plant at which he promised to employ only German workers. Their job would be to produce the miraculous alloy once again, but for use by the British military. In the summer of 1939, Ball was still employing a German workforce whose loyalty was entirely given to the country that had become their homeland. The wartime order for their deportation could not be gainsaid, but Ball, talking in later life about his past with members of his family, spoke with unshaken affection and respect about the German engineers and metalworkers alongside whom he had worked in Manchester for sixteen years.[4]

The enlightened attitude of Ball, Gardiner and Sassoon was representative of a cultured group, not a multitude. Few visitors to post-war Munich were charmed – for example – by the sight of Ernst 'Putzi' Hanfstaengl, a cheerful giant with the drooping cheeks of a bloodhound, bellowing Harvard college songs as he wove through the town centre on an old Swift bicycle dating back to the Boer War.

Half-American, half-German, from a family who had served as privy councillers to the Dukes of Saxe-Coburg, Putzi's fifteen years in America had come to an abrupt halt in 1921, when Germanophobia led to the vandalising of his father's elegant art gallery (an offshoot of the family's main business of publishing art books). Returning home to Bavaria with his American-born German wife, Helene, he became reunited with a favourite sister, Erna. (The entire tribe of Hanfstaengl siblings had been given names that began with an 'E' in deference to Ernst II, their father's ducal patron.)

Putzi was plotting a new future as a popular historian and looking into the story of Count Rumford and Munich's English Garden (Rumford designed it) when a chance commission changed his mind. American diplomats, during that volatile post-war period, were gathering reports on local politics in Munich. Putzi was asked by a friend from the Embassy to go to a political meeting and take stock of a right-wing demagogue who seemed to be attracting increasingly large crowds.

Later, Hanfstaengl would credit Adolf Hitler with 'a miraculous throat construction' that allowed him to hold a crowd enthralled until they fell into a state of unified ecstasy. Attending that early speech in a *Bierkeller* on the evening of 21 November 1922, Putzi was himself enthralled by the visionary words of a mesmerising orator who held out a prospect of hope to a broken and embittered Germany.

From 1922, Ernst Hanfstaengl began to plot how best to offer help. The nascent Nazi party had no money and no obvious access to funding; Putzi, while personally short of cash, possessed a formidable range of contacts who included both the wealthy Bechstein family (makers of the celebrated pianos) and their friends, the even more famous Wagners.

One of Putzi's greatest charms, for his Wagner-loving protégé, would always lie in his willingness to sit down at the piano and thunder out, with tireless good will, snatches from the great overtures and *Lohengrin* – the opera by which a youthful Hitler had first become enthralled, or so he himself claimed. Putzi, together with the Bechsteins, was quick to see the value in promoting a friendship between a man whose gift for oration far outranked his modest education, and the family whose name represented the cultural Parnassus of Bayreuth. The Wagners, to put it plainly, would add the touch of class and credibility that a scruffy and poorly mannered Hitler, back in 1922, visibly lacked. It was perceived by all as a bonus, at a time when the bridge to England was being rebuilt, that Siegfried, the composer's son, possessed an English wife, while his sister Eva was married to the English-born Houston Stewart Chamberlain.

Putzi – witty, shallow and well born – inspired no more than a flicker of mistrust among England's post-war visitors to Munich. Even blessed with more sterling attributes, he might still have found it hard to gain acceptance, back in the twenties, in their homeland.

Portents for reconciliation had boded well, in 1919, when Edith Londonderry welcomed the Lichnowskys to a grand reception and Beecham put Wagner back on the concert programmes. Sadly, the

Germanophobic attitude represented by Barty Redesdale's second, surviving son, David, father of the Mitford gang, proved to have a loyal following. When Lexel Pless, Hansel's younger brother, was permitted to visit his dying grandmother in England after the war, a butler threatened to quit rather than serve food to a German schoolboy. At Bushey, not a voice was raised or a hand lifted as the late Sir Hubert Herkomer's film studio, rose gardens and splendid house fell into disrepair. Attending the State Opening of Parliament in 1921, young Loelia Ponsonby expressed her approval of how resolutely the English peeresses turned their backs on the wife of Friedrich Sthamer, Germany's new ambassador. Harry Kessler, visiting England in 1923 to seek help in desperate times for homeless children from the Ruhr, was told by the Quakers, famous for their philanthropic ways, that no assistance could be provided. The explanation was blunt: 'a part of the nation, although a dwindling one, still remains in a wholly belligerent frame of mind'.[5]

Count Kessler was shocked, and understandably so. Back at home, all the signs pointed towards a genuine desire for rapprochement with a once cousinly nation. English had recently replaced French on the German school curriculum; *Charley's Aunt* (first performed in London in 1892) was playing to capacity in Berlin; asked to name their favourite writers, Germans of the early post-war period regularly cited Mark Twain, Jerome K. Jerome and George Bernard Shaw. Joseph Goebbels, no Anglophile, was using every-day parlance when he drawled into his diary, 'Nur Mut, Old Boy' ('Chin up, old boy').[6] Surely, Kessler thought, England would not abandon a country to which her bonds had always been so close? Surely, England would not fail to understand the peril in which Germany now stood?

Britain's economists and bankers, while not necessarily the most soft-hearted of men, had been viewing Germany's predicament with concern ever since the signing of the Treaty of Versailles.

Both Maynard Keynes and Robert Brand paid regular visits to Berlin during the post-treaty period, armed with a clear remit to advise on the need for currency reform. Keynes took the view that swift action was required; Brand disagreed. Harry Kessler's proposal for a loan to Germany of five billion gold marks was dismissed out of hand; writing to his wife, Phyllis, from Berlin, Brand simply said: 'We shan't.'[7]

Bob Brand hatched a plan of his own. His proposal for a two-year moratorium on Germany's reparations payments came, however, with a sting in its tail. In exchange for Brand's first Standstill offer (his better-known six-month version would be implemented for a later crisis in 1931), Germany must cut back on spending and raise taxes. Such a notion horrified the anguished leaders of the Weimar Republic. Cut spending? Raise taxes? Had a country in utter chaos not suffered enough?

Nothing was done.

The threat of massive inflation was already looming over Germany in January 1923, when France moved 60,000 troops into the Ruhr as a punishment for the non-delivery of newly mandated supplies of coal and timber. When industrialists like Fritz Thyssen decided on a policy of passive resistance (a refusal of any co-operation with the French workers who came in and tried to run the factories themselves), angry Germans across the nation demonstrated their approval. Terrified of further disturbances, Ebert's government fell into line, selling the country's borrowed funds to support a crippling policy of stasis. In the spring of 1923, the German mark, already plunging, crashed. Hyper-inflation ensued, with inevitable – and terrible – consequences.

Hilda Deichmann, visiting Wilhelm's family from England that year, found that discussing money 'in millions and trillions' had become the unnerving order of the day. The local Thuringian shops had all closed down; everything in the countryside around Bendeleben – including concert tickets, which cost two eggs per seat – had to be purchased by barter. Banks locked their doors;

great houses stood empty. 'We heard of sad suicides,' Hilda wrote, 'the result of ruin and despair.'[8]

Robert Brand, paying a concerned visit to Dr Marten, a distinguished German doctor with a former practice in London's New Cavendish Street, found his elderly friend famished and shivering in the unheated farmhouse rooms he now shared with a railway contractor, a tailor and a mechanic. Stories were told of mothers allowing their children to trade the use of their bodies for a loaf of bread, and of great works of art being exchanged for a couple of sacks of rye. In Silesia, the Lichnowskys sold Picassos and Kokoschkas, along with their Old Masters, in order to pay for winter fuel. Up at Tressow, Tisa Schulenburg experienced not just the sense of daily hunger, but the despair of daily helplessness as her father turned once again to the subject from which there was never an escape. 'The nation was now seen in a romantic, a religious light. For ever, the talks revolved around one theme: Germany. The loss of the War. The result of this loss.'[9]

Hints of what lay ahead glint through the recollections of a strong-willed young woman who was torn between the high ideals of her conscientious mother and her own shamed eagerness to get away from the poverty and the endless desire to look back, as if – Tisa reflected – the old imperial world had been, after all, truly worth fighting for. How pleasant, she thought, as she gave English lessons to Fritz Dietlof, the brother nearest to her in age, to go away and live in England and hear no more about Germany's woes. 'We even toyed with the idea that he [Fritz], born in England, might claim English nationality whenever he wanted.'[10]

No invitation to England was forthcoming.

Despatched, instead, to learn the practicalities of housekeeping from two old ladies in Lemgo (one of the Hanseatic trading towns), Tisa was overjoyed when the order came for her to join a political youth group – the Deutsch-National Jugendbund – belonging to the extreme right. Politics counted, at this point, for less than the opportunity to escape a drab existence. Dancing barefoot, while singing the haunting songs of the Wandervogel (the hikers who embodied the spirit of freedom among the youth of post-war Germany), and wearing, in approved *völkische* style, a cotton dress that was dyed saxe blue, Tisa joined in the group's discussions of a topic that was becoming disturbingly popular: it was not the Allies who had brought misfortune upon a great nation, but the Jews.[11]

Tisa's memoir ducks the question of what her own contribution might have been to these discussions. Given the fact that her future husband, Fritz Hess, would be Jewish, it seems unlikely that she supported the anti-Semitic faction.

It was during this intensely volatile period in Germany's history that Adolf Hitler made his first, abortive stab at seizing power. On 26 September 1923, orders were given by Germany's new chancellor, Gustav Stresemann, to end the disastrous policy of passive resistance in the Ruhr. To the eyes of the far right, mostly established within Bavaria, it seemed that Germany was knuckling under to the French; this, to the sixty or so small parties who shared the Nazis' unwaveringly nationalistic outlook, was unforgivable.

Later that same September week in 1923, a short, plainly suited man with a slick of brown hair and a penetrating, almost glaucous blue stare, addressed a crowded hall at Bayreuth. This was Hitler's first speech in the town that would embrace him with such fervour. His theme was dictatorship: the need to replace endless parliamentary hagglings with a single voice of truth. Hitler's voice, self-trained to ascend from a stern but calming monotone to a sustained crescendo shriek, compelled an emotional response. The Bayreuthers, revved up by a well-planned day of marches and parades, reacted with enthusiasm. Climbing the hill to a roar of acclaim, Hitler was ushered into the room where Houston Stewart Chamberlain, syphilitic, bed-ridden and venomous as ever, was waiting to confer his blessing: 'with you all parties disappear, consumed by the flame of love for the Fatherland'.[12]

At Wahnfried, the hallowed home of Wagner's comatose but still conscious widow, Cosima, an awed Hitler was introduced to another immediate convert. Winifred Williams had been brought over to Germany by the Klindworths, ardent Wagnerians who, in 1914, had readily supported a match between their adopted seventeen-year-old English daughter and Siegfried, Wagner's 45-year-old heir. The marriage, while not passionate – Siegfried's lengthy bachelorhood tells its own tale – nevertheless led to four children, all born by the time that Hitler visited Bayreuth.

Winifred's response to Hitler was immediate and intense; Siegfried, who seldom disagreed with his handsome and forceful wife, shared her conviction that they had met a remarkable man. Within days, Hitler had confided in the couple about his plans for the overthrow of President Ebert on 9 November 1923, the fourth anniversary of the abdication of the German Emperor. The message would be clear: a rightful successor had appeared. The Wagners, thrilled, arranged to travel to Munich and witness, at first-hand, the triumphant ascent of their new friend.

On 8 November, the intended coup got off to an impressive start. Hitler's ally, Ernst Röhm, leading 600 stormtroopers, hijacked an evening address being given by the emergency leader of Bavaria; Hitler, seizing the platform, won applause (he even gained the support of the deposed speaker) after announcing that he had received the personal blessing of General Ludendorff. By the following morning, however, brisk orders from Berlin brought Bavaria's dazed government back to its senses.

Hitler's own confidence in his success is apparent from the fact that he was wearing a tailcoat under the shabby clothes in which (accompanied by Putzi Hanfstaengl, Ernst Röhm and the two war heroes Hermann Goering and Erich Ludendorff) the aspiring leader paraded ahead of his faithful troops through the centre of Munich on the morning of 9 November. An ambush had been set. Sixteen Nazis and three policemen were killed during the gunfire that caught the rebels by surprise. Hitler, fleeing to the Hanfstaengls' home for refuge, was captured two days later and convicted in March 1924. The swift commuting of an appropriate five-year sentence to a mere eleven months says as much about the lenient attitude of a powerful Old Guard in Germany towards rebellions on the right as it does about the weakness of a faltering government that was still – just – being led by Friedrich Ebert. (Ebert died in office the following year.)*

The eleven months of Hitler's imprisonment at Landsberg-am-Lech (home to Hubert Herkomer's gold-topped medieval turret of maternal tribute, the Mutterturm) were both fruitful and pleasant. Surrounded, according to Putzi Hanfstaengl, by reverent visitors and enough luxury food to set up a small delicatessen, Hitler was gratified (as the months wore on) to learn that his request had been met for a new grey Mercedes-Benz to be held ready for his release. The car helped to inspire thoughts for a new and more contemporary look: a smartly belted motoring coat, set off by knee-high boots and a riding crop.

Hitler's principal reading matter during his stay in prison seems to have been the autobiography of Henry Ford, whose depressingly popular book, *The International Jew*, was also on Hitler's reading list. Possibly, Ford's self-regarding writings were intended to focus the prisoner's thoughts on the autobiography that had been promised to his eager publishers.

The searing life story of a rising young politician was what

---

* The old judges of the empire kept their positions after the revolution. Mostly from privileged backgrounds and with close links to the right and the officer class, these men were notoriously biased. Thus, between 1918 and 1922, seventeen of twenty-two assassinations by left-wing elements in Germany were punished by harsh sentences. Ten merited the death penalty. In the same period, of the 354 murders committed by right-wing extremists, one resulted in a serious sentence and none were punished by the death penalty.

Hitler was expected to produce. What the publishers got instead (dictated by Hitler and taken down in prison by one of his most ardent admirers, Rudolf Hess) was *Mein Kampf.*

Everybody has a vague idea of what *Mein Kampf* (*My Struggle*) contains: that it champions an Aryan race and that it explains how – by reducing their status from that of citizens to subjects – Germany's Jews are to be deprived of all their rights. Less generally known is how much Hitler looked to England's most recent prime minister as his model for powerful leadership. Lloyd George was singled out, not for his achievements, but for his skills as a demagogue. Truth, as Hitler was never afraid to state, was unimportant: what mattered for Hitler, as for his Welsh-born hero, was to kindle his listeners' emotions.

The other aspect of British politics that attracted Hitler's interest was the quality of ruthlessness. Ruthlessness, so he asserted in *Mein Kampf*, was always allied to self-interest; a ruthless England would therefore gladly join forces with a Germany that shared, but did not encroach upon, her own ambitions for world dominion. England, so Hitler declared, could keep her empire; Germany would ask only for a free hand in Europe. And Britain, safely protected by Germany's regained might from the looming threat of Soviet Communism, would not object.

Living the life not of a prisoner, but a prince-in-waiting, Hitler warmed to his vision of an England of which he had no personal knowledge (he spoke no English), but which, strategically, in his opinion, 'can be compared to no other state in Europe'. The conclusion that he drew was clear and would not change. For the Germany he intended to create, 'the last practicable tie remains with England'.[13]

Myth had become an intoxicating substitute for religion in the literature of a desolate post-war world. Here, in the mad vision of Hitler's terrible book, myth found its darkest form. Britain's ruthless Beowulf was to ride forth to battle at the side of Germany's unsullied Siegfried. United in self-interest through their shared faith in the Aryan supremacy, two great nations would conquer and rule the world.

19

RECONNECTING

(1924–30)

'It is not freedom they are out to find, but communal bonds.'

HUGO VON HOFMANNSTHAL, SPEAKING IN MUNICH, 1927

Hitler entered Landsberg's elegant Art Nouveau fortress on 1 April 1924, when Germany was in ruins. Released in the early spring of 1925, he walked out into a transformed land.

Affection for a once powerful Germany had played less of a part than pragmatism in the decision, led by America, to come to the aid of a stricken nation. The Dawes Plan generously reduced the scale of Germany's future reparations payments and imposed a four-year freeze in the interim. Less generously, it opened the way for American and British banks to compete against each other in offering their former enemy short-term loans at high interest rates. By the summer of 1925, thirty-three billion marks' worth of foreign loans had been accepted and Berlin was filled, once again, with smart carriages, wealthy shoppers and a non-stop round of party-going for those who didn't choose to ask from just where the money had come. Germany had experienced, according to one leading American economist of the time, 'one of the most spectacular recoveries in the world's entire economic history'.[1]

A hint of unfinished business still lingered in the air. 'The English are easy and agreeable to work with,' the president of the Reichsbank, Herr Schacht, was heard by Britain's ambassador to remark before adding, with pointed care, 'provided you do not question their position and hegemony.'[2] Peaceful relations, however, were slowly being restored, smoothing the way for Germany to resume her place among the great powers who had controlled Europe since the defeat of Napoleon.

Symbolic of the new mood of rapprochement was the private meeting that took place in London, on 1 December 1925, between King George V and representatives of the German government. The setting was the magnificent, if rather shabby, 'Golden Room' of the British Foreign Office at Whitehall. Lord Londonderry, an ardent Germanophile who was thrilled to be present (if only as a humble privy councillor in Stanley Baldwin's second Conservative government), made his own effort to smarten up the walls by producing a portrait of Lord Castlereagh, his illustrious ancestor, to supervise proceedings and conjure up auspicious memories of the Congress of Vienna.

The occasion was the signing of the Treaty of Locarno, by which reciprocal vows of support were pledged – Soviet Russia stood aside – while Britain and Italy committed themselves to protecting Germany's new post-war boundaries in the West. (Few signatories, in 1925, troubled themselves with what Germany might wish to do in the East.) To Edgar D'Abernon, Locarno was long overdue. As ambassador to Berlin, he had tirelessly spoken out for the need to forgive and forget. Now, so it seemed to him, Britain had rightly made acknowledgement of that necessity. 'It has', the kindly Ambassador rejoiced, 'been a wonderful negotiation.'[3]

The Dawes Plan and the Treaty of Locarno had eased Germany's pain. Easement was not, however, good news for an ambitious representative of the far right, emerging from prison into a more hopeful and relaxed country than the desperate land over which he had aspired to seize control in the autumn of 1923. Communism, Hitler's most conspicuous adversary, remained a valuable bogeyman: in 1925, Berlin was teeming with the largest population of Communists of any city outside the Soviet Union. Nevertheless, on the May morning in 1925 when the 78-year-old war hero Field Marshal Hindenburg stepped briskly into President Ebert's shoes (the unpretentious and increasingly unpopular Ebert had died in his mid-fifties), the chances of a Nazi leadership in Germany any time soon seemed remote.

Help was on hand from Hitler's two most ardent supporters, both of English birth. Houston Stewart Chamberlain was still able to place a trembling hand upon the head of the man he considered most fit to lead the German nation towards Aryan supremacy. Winifred Wagner, a devoted visitor to the Landsberg during Hitler's confinement, offered to provide hospitality to her hero, while he planned his future strategy, at Bayreuth.

Officially, Hitler was banned from giving political speeches for two years after his release from prison. Unofficially, haranguing the hired mobs who were regularly bussed in to make a show of party strength, he continued to deliver the fiery orations which left no doubt of his uncommon powers, both among his supporters in the Wagner clan, and in the fervent mind of a new recruit, Joseph Goebbels.

Germany's new foreign secretary, Gustav Stresemann, had infuriated Goebbels during the Locarno negotiations by his tacit acknowledgement of Germany's wartime defeat. 'How can a modern German statesman accept these shameful statements!' Goebbels raged in 1925, the year the pact was signed. 'Stresemann is a perfect rogue!'[4] Goebbels, educated in literature at Heidelberg (by two Jewish professors), had lately fallen under the spell of Dostoevsky and had only recently abandoned Marxism. Hitler, while far to the right of his own personal ideology, now appeared to be the only public figure with the charisma and the energy to rescue Germany from the humiliations of the recent past.

Goebbels himself could speak for four hours without stopping to an audience that, while always attentive, was seldom enraptured. It was not Hitler's stamina, but his ability to arouse and then manipulate a group spirit in his listeners that enthralled his new admirer. Offstage, Goebbels found the 36-year-old demagogue captivatingly informal: 'Hitler like a boy,' he noted on 19 April 1926, 'riotous, singing, laughing, whistling.' Together again four days later, the two men celebrated Adolf's thirty-seventh birthday, inspiring Goebbels to offer secret homage to his hero: 'Adolf Hitler, I love you, because you are both great and simple ... A genius.'

Visiting Bayreuth in Hitler's company later in the same month, Goebbels was introduced to Stewart Chamberlain. The experience overwhelmed him, just as it had Hitler. Chamberlain, so it seems, was similarly affected: 'Broken, mumbling, with tears in his eyes ...' Goebbels noted. 'Trail blazer, pioneer ... he weeps like a child.'* Winifred, graciously showing off Richard Wagner's room while the new visitor recovered from his emotion, proved dazzling: 'a thoroughbred woman ... a fanatical partisan of ours ... We are friends in no time.'

Winifred was impressive, but it was to Hitler that Goebbels was in thrall. Fascinated, he noticed the way that Hitler worked over speeches, rehearsing not what he said, but how to deliver the words until, as 'a born whipper-up', he had it off pat: 'a wonderful harmony of gesture, histrionics and spoken word'. Helping to rally the troops for a Weimar speech-fest that summer, Goebbels was awed all over again. Hitler's speech on this occasion was 'deep

---

* Making the most of a good press opportunity in which Goebbels played a part, Hitler arranged to be present in Bayreuth the following year, joining brown-shirted stormtroopers as they carried Stewart Chamberlain's coffin through the streets (one of which bore Chamberlain's name until long after World War II).

and mystical. Almost like the Gospels . . .' The crowds (trucked in for the event from a couple of Nazi strongholds) roared for more. A cynic might wonder if these same applauders had stood among the 13,000-strong mob who, back in 1922, earned themselves a few groschen as movie extras by hailing Ernst Lubitsch's gilded ruler on the gigantic Berlin film set of *The Loves of Pharaoh*. If so, the experience had given them a taste for leader-worship. 'The Third Reich is appearing,' Goebbels exulted on 6 July 1926. 'Germany is awakening . . .'[5]

Despite Goebbels's excited reports and the energy that he now began to devote to shaping the image of his chosen leader, Germany's recovery in the mid-twenties marked the quietest period in the gradual ascent of Adolf Hitler. Prosperity offered no pulpit to extremists. As the incoming tide of foreign loans was invested in transport and housing and – less ostentatiously (while ardent youths drilled for future combat within the country's dark concealing forests) – in the costs of rearming a depleted country, Germany was prospering as never before.

Prosperity, to a left-wing aristocrat like Count Harry Kessler, evoked complicated emotions. Visiting England as a tourist in 1925 (his hopes of being made ambassador to the Court of St James's had been thwarted by a governmental decision to retain the services of the quietly reliable Friedrich Sthamer), Kessler decided to explore the impoverished north. Oxford had depressed him with its air of monkish rectitude, but Manchester put Kessler in touch with 'an archaic grandeur, grey and sombre, a soul compounded of coal dust, and yet with a hard, untameable energy . . . This is the real England, without the mask . . .'[6] The decision not to replace Sthamer with Kessler had been prudent: a man who felt moved, in 1925, to hail medieval Durham as the hallowed cradle of white supremacy might not have served his country's public image well.

A happier move by Kessler was the decision to resume his

nation-bonding pre-war enterprise of publishing a magnificent new German edition of *Hamlet*, freely translated by the revered Gerhart Hauptmann and magnificently illustrated with eighty expressionist woodcuts by Edward Gordon Craig. Back in Berlin, the impish Count amused himself by inviting Josephine Baker to his home to watch her gyrate, as one goddess paying homage to another, around the voluptuous curves of one of his collection of Maillol sculptures. Art, rather than politics, was Harry Kessler's natural habitat.

Chameleon-like in the way that he was able to adapt to changing times, Count Kessler stood in direct contrast to Tisa Schulenburg's father, a military aristocrat of the old-fashioned school. By 1925, however, General Schulenburg had joined the Reichstag and pledged himself to serve a new and nationalistic Germany. His sons, all but the youngest, enthusiastically joined their father on a road that would lead them straight to becoming early supporters of the Third Reich. Wayward Tisa, meanwhile, having been refused parental permission to embroil herself with the futuristic enterprises and (as perceived by her conservative father) radical politics of the Bauhaus at Dessau, took herself off to study art and sculpture in Berlin.

Always keen to demonstrate her left-wing views, Tisa expressed dismay about the grimness of the concrete slums that had grown up on the outskirts of the city. Her own life soon led her elsewhere. 'I courted lechery ... Sealed doors, sealed lips, sealed conscience.'[7] Later, naming no names, Tisa was willing only to say that she had spent a good deal of time at the house of Hugh Simon, a banker and art patron whose circle of friends included, in 1926, some of the best-known artists and writers of the time.

Countess Schulenburg, in search of informed opinion about the evident talent of her schoolgirl daughter, had long ago introduced Tisa to one of Germany's greatest painters, Max Liebermann. Visiting Hugh Simon, Tisa met the ageing Liebermann again and began to make up for her lost youth in Mecklenburg by mixing with – among others – Bertolt Brecht, Erich Remarque, Thomas Mann and the Viennese Zweig brothers. Tisa, in the year before she married Fritz Hess (a wealthy, charming man with a magnificent collection of modern art), was having the time of her young life in Berlin, a city where the lights were never turned off and from which, even in those early days of aviation, a plane from Tempelhof Airport could whisk a traveller in a blink to any of fifteen foreign cities. To a wild, good-looking and adventurous young woman, Berlin, in 1926, felt glorious.

Daisy Pless, estranged from her husband since the Prince's return from the war, had fared less well.

For an English wife, it had proved impossible to forget or forgive the relish with which a German husband had written to her, throughout the war, of his contempt for her countrymen and his desire for England's defeat. It did not much grieve her when, in 1921, the philandering Hans Heinrich began proceedings for a divorce.

Daisy, aged forty-eight, was undergoing an experience of a far more terrifying kind: gradually, she was losing the ability to walk. (Her condition, not fully understood at the time, marked the rapid onset of multiple sclerosis.) Hans Heinrich, back in 1921, felt prosperous enough to guarantee a secure future for a woman who had grown tiresomely hysterical in her constant references to ill-health. Guided by Hansel, and eager to be rid of Daisy and her complaints, the Prince's lavish promises included the maintenance of a villa (Les Marguerites) on the French Riviera, and sufficient funds to build a new town house in Munich, to be furnished from Daisy's splendid former rooms at Fürstenstein and Pless. A lady's companion would be hired to take care of Daisy and her league of ailments. Finally, a generous monthly income would guarantee that the status of a Silesian princess was maintained.

Inflation, combined with the imposition of increasingly stringent

Polish taxes on what had formerly been Upper Silesia, swiftly reversed these lavish plans. By 1923, Daisy had become very frail indeed; by 1924, her ex-husband, hit by hyper-inflation and struggling to retain his legal ownership of the immense Silesian mines that now lay within the boundaries of Poland, was no longer willing to help or to provide more than the minimum of funds. The promised car and chauffeur were out of the question; deprived of transport, and with her legs now almost completely paralysed, Daisy was housebound and helpless. By the end of 1924, unable to cover even the cost of renting lodgings until the new house was built, she was threatened with eviction.

The villa in France was sold; the new home at Munich, when finally completed, was furnished with just two bedsteads. Nothing more, so the Prince's representatives regretted to declare, could now be spared from His Highness's homes. In letters that were invariably signed off by Pless's new Polish administrators, Daisy was chillingly referred to as 'a woman'. Ena FitzPatrick, an impoverished Irish cousin who had initially jumped at the opportunity to earn some money by nursing Daisy, began writing plaintive appeals to Pless for help, along with the wages that remained unpaid. Receiving only a cool recommendation to teach the improvident Princess to practise greater frugality in her housekeeping, Ena abandoned Daisy, to try her luck elsewhere.

Help came at last, but not from Pless. Young Hansel, put in charge of dealing with Pless's Polish administrators because of his legal expertise, found it impossible either to convince them that his mother's requirements were urgent, or to dissuade his father from continuing to live in a style to which Croesus might not have objected. Edgar D'Abernon, visiting Pless in 1924, was staggered by the grandiose standards that were still being upheld there. Taking a second wife in 1925, Hans Heinrich celebrated his new alliance with impenitent opulence. (Clotilde, the Prince's 26-year-old Spanish bride, later married Hansel's youngest brother, Bolko, and produced the two children that Hans Heinrich craved to carry on the family line.)

Daisy's continuing problems are apparent from the heartfelt gratitude with which, in 1924, she accepted a cash gift of £300 from her former brother-in-law, the Duke of Westminster. In 1925, she received a more enduring offer of assistance, one that would transform her life.

Dolly Crowther was a sturdy young Englishwoman who had looked after Patsy Cornwallis-West during her last bedridden years. Informed that Patsy's daughter was in urgent need of care, Miss Crowther didn't hesitate. Never having left England in her life, the resolute Dolly crossed the Channel, booked herself onto a train to Munich, tracked the Princess down and offered her services. Money was never discussed and a wage seems never to have been paid. Dolly, effectively, took over and, with quiet discretion, ran Daisy's life. When Hans Heinrich's advisors suggested that Daisy could be more economically housed above the gatehouse of Fürstenstein, all arrangements for the move were supervised by Dolly Crowther.

A solution of sorts had been found. Daisy, restored to familiar surroundings and greeted kindly by the nearby townspeople who had always liked 'unsere Daisy', grew happier. Money, however, was still pitifully short, and would remain so while Hansel, having taken Polish nationality (together with his father and brothers), struggled to appease both the tax-hungry administrators and the wage-starved workforce of miners.

Hansel's endeavours to save the estates, care for the miners and dissuade his mother from spending the modest pittance she received on subsidising Lexel, Daisy's second and favourite son, made a young man feel old before his time. Like his Hochberg uncles before him, Hansel dreamed of an escape to England. He remembered, with longing, the pre-war summers of hunting in the Shires. He thought of the cheerful English friends with whom, despite the war, his friendship had survived intact. England was where he belonged. 'England!' Hansel exclaimed with passionate conviction. 'England shall have my bones!'[8]

Hansel Pless was still young enough to imagine himself setting forth on a new life. Hilda Deichmann, having seen her third, English-born daughter married to a suitable German spouse in 1921, toyed with the idea of settling on the picturesque Thuringian estate that, however dilapidated, had welcomed her back with such kindness after the war. Visiting Bendeleben in 1923, during the worst of the economic crisis, Hilda changed her mind. Nearing seventy, she went home and raised funds for Wilhelm by selling Abbey Lodge, that last family link to a gentler age. In 1925, Hilda moved, together with her unmarried sister, Marie de Bunsen, to a modest abode near the Thames. Here, in Chelsea, entertaining their Norfolk Quaker cousins and undertaking the quiet acts of charity to which the de Bunsen family had always felt themselves bound by conscience and by duty, two rather grand old ladies lived out their days in peace, their German origins long since forgiven by an affectionate band of English friends.

For Hilda's niece, Emma Schröder, life at Dell Park had also begun to resume its old-fashioned pre-war pace by the mid-twenties. The Schröder Bank, whose annual revenue had plummeted to a dismaying £18,000 at the end of the war, climbed back, in 1924, to a million pounds a year. Bruno Schröder, having meticulously restored his wrecked hothouses of orchids and seen to the survival of his beloved hospital (funds from Germany had been severely depleted by the country's fallen economy), embarked on a new mission. Rescuing medieval church masterpieces from their now destitute German owners, Bruno Schröder created, for England, what remains to this day one of the finest collections of European silverwork in the world. In 1930, demonstrating once again the spirit of philanthropy that had provided such a powerful bond between England and Germany in the past, the Schröders celebrated the marriage of their son, Helmut, by presenting – at the suggestion of Helmut's bride – a handsome radio set to all the blind people in Gloucestershire, where Meg Darrell had worked as a volunteer. Many, poignantly, were former soldiers.

Visiting England in 1919, when they were entertained to dinner by the Londonderrys, Prince and Princess Lichnowsky had been heartened by the warmth of their welcome; enough so to decide that their son (like Gustav Stresemann's) should finish his university education at Oxford, in the England for which both Mechtilde and Karl Max felt a profound affection. Back at home in Silesia, the Lichnowskys' lives were as drastically affected as those of the Pless family by the war, by inflation and by the re-drawing of national boundaries. The great paintings were steadily sold off; the former friends who – with some justification – blamed Lichnowsky's published admission of Germany's war guilt for the outcome of the Treaty of Versailles, took care to keep their distance.

The Lichnowskys were not, however, forlorn. Certainly, their fortunes had fallen, while their vast network of social friendships had shrunk to the level where the high point might be the welcoming of a local pastor for his weekly game of chess with the wistful Prince. But, while Karl Max suffered a great deal from the sense of being cold-shouldered by his former peers, comfort was on hand in the form of his wife's avant garde circle of intimates: the writers, musicians and artists with whom the Princess had made friends throughout her life.

Skilful caricaturists with a sharp and witty turn of phrase, both Mechtilde and her sister Helene (a gifted sculptor's wife) had been brought up to embrace the modern world. Resuming her preferred form of life in Germany, Mechtilde continued to write memoirs, along with novels and poems, while maintaining a vivid correspondence with the great Viennese satirist Karl Kraus, to whose magazine, *The Torch*, she contributed drawings. With Kraus, Max Reinhardt, Alban Berg, Max Liebermann and Elias Canetti among the Lichnowskys' friends and visitors, life at Kuchelna maintained the tradition that had begun over a century ago, when the ageing Prince's forebears had taken under their gilded wings a prodigiously gifted German composer: Ludwig van Beethoven.

In 1928, Prince Lichnowsky died. His eldest son took over the depleted estates. Mechtilde – disgusted by the violent methods and the hate-filled speeches of a political party that was becoming increasingly visible in Germany – began to withdraw into a life abroad, and to rebuild her former English friendships.

Culture – coming to the rescue of the ageing Lichnowskys during a decade of political disgrace – had provided one of the first connecting strands between England and Germany after the war. In 1920, after devouring *Blick ins Chaos*, which included Hermann Hesse's essay about Dostoevsky, T. S. Eliot cited it in *The Waste Land* and invited Hesse to contribute essays on German poetry to his brand-new English quarterly magazine, *The Criterion*. D. H. Lawrence, in 1926, made a point of stressing how the Chatterleys' respect for German culture had remained unshaken by the experiences of war. But it was cinema that provided one of the most potent of all links, at a time when the vast glasshouse studios of UFA at Babelsberg, just outside Berlin, began to produce, in the years of Germany's greatest despair, some of the most remarkable films that the world had yet seen.

In London, an official ban prevented German films from being shown until 1922. Solutions could always be devised. In 1919, members of the Royal Automobile Club were invited to attend a private showing of *Dr Mabuse the Gambler*, Fritz Lang's vision of a world controlled by a criminal mastermind. Visiting the home of the press baron Lord Beaverbrook in 1922, Duff Cooper was treated to a screening of the German horror masterpiece *The Cabinet of Dr Caligari*.

Even back in the years of war, Germany had provided the spark that ignited one remarkable career in English film.

Lieutenant James Whale had already completed a four-year

course in Arts and Crafts when he enlisted. Following his capture by the Germans, Whale was sent to Holzminden, a prison in Lower Saxony that is best-known for one of the largest successful escape missions during the war. Whale, seeking a refuge from the bullying and the tedium that dogged his own four years at Holzminden, decided to put his pre-war training into use. Directing prison plays provided him, so he later remembered, with 'a source of great pleasure and amusement', while the enthusiasm of the (literally, captive) audiences proved 'intoxicating'. Whale had discovered his metier.

Ten years later, a play written by R. C. Sheriff, starring a young Laurence Olivier and directed by James Whale, was being advertised along the side of every bus and train in the London area with the nifty slogan: 'All roads lead to *Journey's End.*' Whale's subsequent film of the play attracted interest in Germany, where, starring Conrad Veidt and still set in an English dugout, it was remade as the short-lived *Die andere Seite*. Whale, meanwhile, directed perhaps the greatest of all versions of *Frankenstein*, in a film that reveals in almost every shot the influence on its maker of German expressionist cinema.[9]

In England, following the end of the boycott, the new wave of German cinema caused few ripples. When Fritz Lang's keenly anticipated triad of *Nibelungen* films reached England in 1924 as *Dragon's Blood*, viewers fell asleep, waking up only when the largest mythical beast that had yet lumbered onto any film set in the world prepared to do battle with Siegfried.[10] Alfred Hitchcock, despatched in 1924 by Gainsborough Films to work on an UFA-based film called *The Blackguard*, was unstirred to observe that a massive chunk of *Nibelungen* forest scenery had been destroyed to make room for a new set (involving scenes from the Russian Revolution).

It was in Germany, as Hitchcock gratefully acknowledged, that he learned many of his most characteristic techniques. *The Lodger*, a 1927 thriller set in London, opens with an angled through-the-keyhole shot that he took directly from German expressionism; the famous shower sequence in *Psycho* borrows from one of the most terrifying images in Murnau's 1922 classic vampire film, *Nosferatu*. Like his spoken German (which remained impeccable until the end of the British filmmaker's life), the skills and methods that Hitchcock brought back to Britain from his pivotal apprenticeship in Germany were never forgotten.

Cinema stood high among the attractions that were bringing a new and specifically post-war category of visitor to Berlin. Charles Ball and Ernest Tennant had travelled out to Germany from motives of duty and social concern; John Heygate, arriving in 1923, was among the first of the flood of rebellious young who wanted to distance themselves from a war that had not been of their making and in which they themselves had played no part.

Nothing in Germany was as John Heygate had been led to expect. His father talked at home about "'the hated Huns'"; the son found it impossible to reconcile such violent words with the quietly respectable people – 'this mild bespectacled man ... this Frau with her hair done in a high bun ...' – that he met along the way. Such couples seemed as if they might have been his own parents, while the family with whom Heygate first lodged in Berlin impressed him with their quiet dignity, taking in lodgers and showing no envy of the tourists who – thanks to hyper-inflation – could live like kings.[11]

Heygate loved Germany for its people and for its culture. As a keen young motorist, he was also delighted by the new ruler-straight roads (many of them laid out by Russian POWs) that offered such freedom after the winding lanes, hay carts and high hedges of Old England. Most of all, returning with his friend Anthony Powell in 1929, Heygate relished the mixture of squalor, sex and danger offered by Berlin. It's 'a beast of a city', he wrote with glee: 'utterly inhumane, and yet I love it'.[12] Loelia Ponsonby was fascinated, on her first visit to Berlin, by the spectacle of two

sedately rouged old German gentlemen executing a neatly dex-
terous tango together (an image that evokes the vicious caricatures
of George Grosz); another visitor from England in the late twenties watched a row of caviare tubs bobbing their way across a
luxurious swimming pool (the occasion was a party being given at
one of the elegant diplomatic homes near the Tiergarten).

Heygate and Powell, while no strangers to the charms of the
erotic dance clubs and exotic cabarets, preferred the informal tran-
quility of an afternoon spent sunning themselves beside one of the
city lakes, where families of Berliners and clusters of young people
casually stripped off to swim, to lounge, or to offer a lithe display
of gymnastics. This was the genial, seedy, cosy and frequently violent metropolis with which Isherwood, Auden and Spender – and
a young Hardy Amies, enjoying time off from teaching English in
the Rhineland – fell in love; the recollections of Heygate and
Powell serve as a useful reminder that having sex with azure-eyed
German boys, at a time when homosexuality remained taboo in
England, formed only a part of the charm of Berlin.

Back home in Britain, by contrast with the exuberant sense of
freedom they could find in Berlin in 1929, the young felt trapped
in a staid world of the past. The war had shaken the established
world and slaughtered its children – and for what? For a mere
nine months, in 1924, England had accepted a government
of the left; for a paltry nine days, in 1926, she had experienced
the thrill of mutiny: a general strike. Promises had been made.
Nothing had been gained. In 1929, the year that Powell and
Heygate left for Germany, Britain's miners, if working at all,
were actually receiving less money for longer hours. Ramsay
MacDonald's brief moment of Labour rule had been followed up
by five slow years of Stanley Baldwin and the Tories. In England,
life at the end of the twenties smelt of prudence and the past; in
Germany, the scent of progress was as heady as the novelty of
diesel fumes.

Progress was in the air; progress, here, felt to the visitors as if it had reached up to the airy heights of the magical, futuristic city sketched out at the Bauhaus in 1923 by Paul Citroen, a drawing from which Fritz Lang borrowed the image for his 1927 cinema masterpiece, *Metropolis*. And, as in that extraordinary film, down below the glittering surface and the ultra-modern skyscrapers, there lay an underworld of anarchy, poverty and exploitation.

In 1928, a young English aristocrat, Tom Mitford, was studying law in Berlin. Visited by his sister, Diana, and her husband, Bryan Guinness, Tom announced that if he were a German, he would want to be a Nazi.[13] By 1928, the Nazis were already linked to acts of extreme aggression, including public cudgellings and brutal private killings. Asked by his gentle brother-in-law how he felt about the violent tactics of his chosen party, Tom coolly answered that their tactics had nothing to do with him. It was, so Diana remembered her brother saying, 'their own affair'.[14]

Their own affair. Nobody else's affair, and most certainly not the affair of an English visitor to a country about which Tom – and so many like him – entertained feelings of deep guilt, engendered by what seemed to almost everybody, back then, to have been a most vicious treaty.

Tom Mitford's declared determination to stand aside, to let Germany do whatever she wished, so long as England was left out of it, exactly matched the image that Hitler had so confidently projected in *Mein Kampf*: a tacit understanding for the division of power to suit both countries, leaving Germany in control of her own destiny in Europe, and with nobody to gainsay her across the Channel, in Britain.

Today, we call that dangerous posture of knowing – and increasingly culpable – laissez faire, for lack of any better word, 'appeasement'.

20

FALLING IN LOVE AGAIN:
TOM MITFORD

(1909–45)

Tom Mitford was born in 1909, the year before his doting grand-father, Lord Redesdale, wrote an admiring introduction to the book that would become a sacred text of the Nazi Party. Barty Redesdale's own published view was that the Jews had greatly enriched and improved the civilised world; nevertheless, he thought highly enough of Houston Stewart Chamberlain's *Foundations of the Nineteenth Century* to mail copies of the new English translation to his friends. Edmund Gosse approved. Richard Haldane did not. In 1912, however, Redesdale was able to inform the author that his niece's husband, Winston Churchill, had spoken of it with 'unmea-sured praise'.[1]

In 1912, when his family were still dividing their time between London and Batsford Park – a mansion that he had built in the grounds of the family's old Gloucestershire estate and surrounded with magnificent trees named in honour of various Mitfords – Lord Redesdale's mood was still sufficiently pro-German for him to approve the decision by Jack, his youngest son, to take a job with one of Germany's greatest coal magnates, Baron von Friedlander-Fuld, and to welcome Jack's subsequent engagement to the rich Baron's daughter.

The extreme brevity of Jack's marriage cannot be blamed on the war, since Annie left her husband in May 1914. Nevertheless, a marriage that lasted only five months must have hurt his father's pride. The following year, Clement Mitford, Jack's eldest brother and his father's favourite child, was killed in action in Flanders, aged thirty-eight. Now cursing the Germans with a passion that he passed on to his soldierly second son, David (along with the heavily encumbered estate), a heartbroken Bertram Redesdale died in 1917.

Tom, like his sisters, had fond memories of Batsford Park. His grandfather had doted on him, especially since Tom, even as a little boy, showed signs of having inherited the exceptionally handsome features of the Mitford males. David Redesdale was no scholar. When the family left Batsford in 1918, to settle more modestly into an Oxfordshire manor house a few miles away, at Swinbrook, Tom, aged nine, was put in charge of choosing which books should be saved. In 1918, Germanophobia was at its height. The new Lord Redesdale hated the Germans to a degree that would later provide splendid comic opportunities for the lethal pen of his first-born, Nancy. Nevertheless, young Tom scrupulously – and rather courageously – chose to preserve the collection of German books that had meant so much to his grandfather.

Erected in a separate building from the main house and equipped with comfortable sofas and a piano, the Asthall library became a favourite refuge for the younger Mitfords. Nancy, the eldest child by five years, knew the bookshelves well enough to observe – in a collection of essays entitled *The Water Beetle* – that the German section was poorly equipped in poetry and fiction, but not so well as to remember correctly the name of 'Stewart

Houston Chamberlain' [*sic*]. Pamela, the Redesdales' second daughter, showed a keener interest in her grandfather's books and later married Derek Jackson, an ardent Germanophile. Tom, during his school years at Eton, was sufficiently interested in them to work his way through Kant (translated by his erudite grandfather) and to discover a taste for Schopenhauer. Tom also claimed to have liked Gibbon's *Decline and Fall* so much that he read it through three times.

At school, where he enjoyed several homosexual liaisons, Tom displayed an unnerving combination of confidence, careless beauty, considerable musical talent and a merciless wit that his young second cousin, Randolph Churchill, was taught to fear. ("'My *dear* Randolph!" he would cry in his loud tenor voice, very Oxfordish in intonation. "I have heard a great many stupid remarks, but this is a *masterpiece* of its kind.'"[2])

Home for the holidays, Tom paid his less-educated younger sisters (Nancy would have scorned such condescension) a shilling each to practise the art of debate that formed part of every young Etonian's training. Quite possibly, the debating classes presided over by an idolised brother fuelled the interest that Tom's siblings began to display, from an early age, in radical politics.[3]

To inherit an estate, especially from a father like David Redesdale, whose idea of financial management was to go gold-prospecting in Canada or to gamble – with more success – on the Grand National, was not viewed as a blessing by the younger generation of the post-war years. (A well-known *Punch* cartoon showed an elderly land-owner taunting his languid heir with the ultimate threat: 'Stop fooling about or I'll leave you The House!') Behind the depressing silliness of the twenties' treasure hunts, pranks and masquerades lay a desperate impulse to escape responsibilities of the kind that had fallen so heavily upon young Hansel Pless.

For Tom, a bright and thoughtful boy who had taken the top musical prize during his final year at Eton, the moment of decision came in 1927. All the family loved sleepy, pretty old Asthall

Manor, but David, remorseful about the loss – incurred by death duties – of Batsford, had recklessly decided that it behoved him to restore the family to finer surroundings. Swinbrook – promptly renamed Swinebrook by the unenthusiastic young inhabitants – was built to David Redesdale's own design, to look down upon the village, church and winding river from a haughty height that quite eclipsed secluded little Asthall. Swinbrook, not Asthall, was to represent Tom's inheritance, and Tom hated it. With a remarkable lack of foresight, given his son's passion for music, Lord Redesdale had even neglected to leave space for a piano.

The expectation must have been that Tom would go to Oxford, marry, sire an heir and settle down to the business of running Swinbrook. Instead, aged eighteen in 1927, he requested to be allowed to go to Vienna, to study music and German culture.

Vienna, at least, was not Berlin. Assent was unwillingly given; Tom's next news (sent from Vienna) was that he wanted to move out of the city and rent rooms at the home of a new and captivating friend called Janos Almasy, an 'extremely clever' Hungarian count, aged about forty, who lived with his crippled wife in a hilltop castle called Schloss Bernstein. 'I have never seen a view to approach it,' Tom pleaded, 'and being on the top of a small but steep hill, it looks out in every direction.' Staying with the Almasys would also, as Tom artfully added, be a real economy: 'money does trickle away so in a town'.[4] Never able to resist their son (Diana Mosley described how irresistibly Tom could make his voice 'sag with desire' when he wanted something), the Redesdales gave their approval.

There is no doubt that the English-educated Count Almasy was both charismatic and fascinating. (His brother, László, an explorer and much decorated pilot, was the model for the mysterious hero of Michael Ondaatje's novel *The English Patient*.) Diana Mosley remembered Janos as 'intellectually stimulating and with a Don Juan-like temperament. He took Tom to all the neighbouring castles . . .'[5]

Dwelling, with the most graceful of hints, on the effect that a handsome young Englishman might have had on the wives and daughters of Count Almasy's neighbours, Diana Mosley skirted the trickier subject of politics. Almasy, at the time that Tom arrived at Schloss Bernstein, was already committed to the burgeoning Nazi Party.

Almasy proved a powerful mentor. Tom was studying law in Berlin when his sister Diana, together with her first husband, Bryan Guinness, paid him a visit in 1928 and heard not only that Tom approved of the Nazi Party, but that he was willing to over- look the violence of their methods. Back in England the following year, however, Tom was less forthcoming. Attending a fancy-dress party given by Diana and Bryan, he appeared as Bruno Hat, a black-wigged and heavily accented German artist whose works, catalogued by Evelyn Waugh and painted by Brian Howard, seem to have been poor pastiches of Otto Dix. Hindsight might cause us to wince when we remember how the Nazis would soon be treating the makers of 'degenerate' art; at the time, according to the social columnists, Tom's prank seemed quite clever.

In 1930, the Nazi Party won its first major victory and cele- brated it with an attack that targeted the big Jewish-owned department stores like Wertheims, Tietz and Nathan Israel. Harry Kessler and the Jewish journalist Bella Fromm were dismayed. Did Tom approve? If the paper trail ever existed to reveal his thoughts – and the lack of family letters from Tom is, even for a dilatory cor- respondent, quite remarkable – it seems not to have survived. The solitary published letter from Tom in 1930 blandly shares with his mother the fun of going on a pier-hopping plane trip with some chums, along the south coast of England. But Tom, according to his fond youngest sister, Deborah, was not a man who ever both- ered to pick up a pen. That's how it was, she has said. 'Tom never wrote.'[6]

It seems, in a family of ardent correspondents, a little unlikely. And while proof is hard to demonstrate by its absence – in the form of letters that may have been tucked out of view – it is clear that Tom Mitford, by demonstrating his own approval, paved the way for two of his admiring sisters to embrace the Nazis during the first years that they came to power.

Officially, the connection between the Mitford sisters and the Nazis began when Putzi Hanfstaengl attended a party given by the mother of two of London's most effervescent socialites, the Jungmann sisters. Introduced to the exceptionally beautiful Diana Guinness (already in thrall to Oswald Mosley), Putzi painted an enticing picture of the warm reception that would be offered, should she wish to visit his country and see – so he assured her – how well the Jews were treated there, despite a few unpleasant items in the papers. Unity, who had been planning a holiday in France or Italy, was easily persuaded by Diana to change her mind and accompany an admired older sister on the first trip that either girl had ever made to Germany.

It was Putzi who provided the invitation (although not, on this occasion, the promised introduction to Hitler); it was Tom who helpfully provided his sisters with the chaperones for their German adventure. And it was Tom who, when Lord Redesdale expressed his furious opposition to any connection between his girls and the Nazis – a party he considered to be a 'murderous gang of pests' – promised Diana that he would exert what she described as Tom's 'enormous influence' over a father who always gave in where his son was concerned.

Diana was right. Lord Redesdale could never resist Tom's charm; Tom himself, while sternly disapproving of the way that Diana had abandoned her kindly and cultivated husband for an intensely promiscuous married man, found it equally impossible to resist his sister. Reassured by their son's calming words, the Redesdales duly visited Munich and (despite Lady Redesdale's refusal to pay homage at the hallowed shrine of the Nazi martyrs of the 1923 putsch) did not embarrass their daughters.

In the summer of 1935, when Unity was completely under

Hitler's spell, Tom encouraged a further step. The Redesdales were persuaded to offer tea, at the House of Lords, to a Nazi director of Daimler-Benz. Tom, who seems to have engineered the occasion, was present in the role of interpreter. 'I talked with him most of the time,' Tom reported to an excited Unity, 'and he told me what a high opinion Hitler has of you and how unusually intelligent he [AH] thinks you are.'[7]

Tom, clearly, was taking pains to give happiness to an impressionable young sister whose love for Hitler had become the most dominant emotion in her life. A few weeks later, Tom allowed Unity to introduce him to her hero. Briefly, at least, Tom seemed impressed. Unity, while gratified to hear from Diana that Hitler thought Tom was 'ein fabelhafter Junge' (a wonderful young man), was less sure about her brother's response. At the time, it had seemed that Tom 'adored the Führer', but later? Wistfully, Unity confessed her suspicion that 'he will have cooled down by the time he gets home ...'[8]

Did he? Tom had declined, back in 1934, to attend the rallies at which an increasingly outspoken and anti-Semitic Oswald Mosley endorsed the murderous 'Night of the Long Knives' in Munich as a welcome cleansing of the Nazi regime. Even Nancy Mitford, while hating Mosley's politics and mocking them in her first novel, *Wigs on the Green*, dutifully showed up for an Oxford rally that year. Gerald Berners, a family friend, (while warning Mosley to tone down his remarks about Jews and homosexuals) contributed 'a dreary little tune' to the event. Tom stayed away. In 1936, however, the year of the Nazi Olympics, Tom attended the annual Parteitag and even an al fresco dinner given by the SS and presided over by Himmler; the following year, Tom was present at the Parteitag once again, and with him came Almasy. An inscrutably handsome figure, standing at Diana's side, Tom Mitford – as a sister with whom he shared all his secrets was fond of pointing out – could pass for her twin.

In 1938, Tom gave his coveted pass to the annual rally to a

friend, Robert Byron, who (as Tom was mischievously aware) viewed the Nazi regime with abhorrence. In 1939, however, having dutifully signed up with the Rifle Brigade to fight for his country, Tom donned his new uniform to stand, on 16 July, beside Diana and Unity at the biggest peace meeting that had ever been held in England. The speaker, Oswald Mosley, asked the audience to back his mission to protect England from becoming involved in what he memorably dismissed as 'a Jews' quarrel'. Randolph Churchill walked out. Tom Mitford raised his arm in the fascist salute. Two days later, a delighted and almost disbelieving Hitler hailed Mosley's speech as England's voice of reason, raised against the pernicious influence of 'Jewry'.

Tom Mitford's first loyalty was not to a party, but to his family. In September 1939, it was Tom's friend Almasy, described by Diana Mosley as 'the faithful Janos' (and to whom Unity had become extremely close during her last two years in Germany), who accompanied that pathetic young woman's stretcher, following Unity's attempt to shoot herself in the head as a forlornly egotistical demonstration against the outbreak of war. (Hitler, who seems to have been genuinely fond of Unity, would provide an ambulance train to Switzerland, where Lady Redesdale arrived in December, to collect her now unrecognisable child and take her home.) But it was Tom who came to the rescue the following year.

The Mosleys, not least because of Diana's many visits to Germany and her friendship with Hitler, were judged dangerous enough, in the summer of 1940, to be seized and imprisoned. Diana, still feeding a month-old baby (Max), was taken to Holloway, while Mosley himself went to Brixton. David Redesdale could have chosen to plead with his cousin, Winston Churchill, for a gentler fate; in the end, it was the irresistible – and perhaps implacable – Tom who convinced the Prime Minister that the couple should be given married quarters, and in conditions of uncommon comfort. (The Mosleys were not only given a small garden, but were permitted to recruit fellow prisoners to work for them.) While impossible to prove a connection, it would seem likely that Tom also had a hand in persuading a normally cautious Home Secretary (Herbert Morrison) to sign the permission that granted an intensely unpopular couple's early release in November 1943.

How deep was Tom Mitford's commitment to the Nazis? Tom gave his own answer by electing to fight in Italy and North Africa. Returning to England in 1944, he visited a greatly diminished Unity in the company of James Lees-Milne, a friend from Eton days. Talking to Lees-Milne (who was struck by, and could not get out of his mind, the absolute sadness of his former lover's gauntly handsome face), Tom expressed his personal horror of the anti-Semitism espoused by Unity and Diana. And yet, he still could not bear the thought of fighting against a Germany, and a German people, that he had loved so much. 'All the best Germans are Nazis,' Tom told Lees-Milne at that encounter, echoing his words to Diana and Bryan in 1928, 'and if I were a German I would be one.'[9]

On Good Friday, 30 March 1945, while serving in Burma with the Devonshire Regiment, Major Tom Mitford died of his wounds, having been shot by a Japanese sniper. He was thirty-six years old. 'His loss', Diana Mosley wrote, 'was something from which I never recovered for the rest of my life.'[10] David Redesdale, who also never recovered from the death of his only son, arranged for an oval memorial tablet to preserve Tom's memory in the tranquil little church at Swinbrook. Placed above the pew that commemorated Clement Mitford's death in the previous war, it mourns Tom as 'a perfect son and brother'.

Beloved by his family in his lifetime, Tom Mitford has almost vanished from public memory, buried by the loving hands of a clan of sisters who did not, perhaps, wish others to consider just how far the obsessive anti-Semitism of Diana and Unity had strayed from the ideals of the brother they had revered and followed. It was diminishing of Nancy, years later, to refer to Tom as 'a fearful old twister', meaning that, having no true views of his own, he simply adapted to reflect the views of those around him.[11] It was also untrue. For Tom to tell Diana and her husband, back in 1928, that he espoused the Nazis (and to repeat that sentiment in 1944) was, contrary to Nancy's declaration, unprompted and uncompromisingly direct.

It was Tom who led the way from Swinbrook to Germany and who, moving in the musical circles of Vienna, reached the view that it was intolerable to be anti-Semitic. That view has a value in the Mitford story; the deliberate reduction of Tom to a ghost on the sidelines has, while preserving him from harm, skewed the angle from which we stare at the six sisters. More sadly, it has robbed a remarkable young man of his significant position within a complex clan.

21

ENTERING THE ABYSS

(1928–34)

'We must remember the most elementary truth: "this past did not know what we now know."'

FRITZ STERN, *FIVE GERMANYS I HAVE KNOWN (2006)*

'People who wanted to know could find out about it early, in the beginning.'

TISA SCHULENBURG, *MEMOIRS*

Hitler became chancellor of Germany on 30 January 1933. London's Foreign Office had already been warned what to expect.

In the summer of 1928, Horace Rumbold, a seasoned second-generation diplomat with the blinking gaze of a sleepy koala bear and a mind as sharp as a needle, replaced Edgar D'Abernon as British ambassador to Berlin. During the four years of turbulence, despair and radical change that preceded Hitler's appointment to the chancellorship, Sir Horace never faltered in his articulately expressed reservations about the Nazi Party and its leader. Sir Robert Vansittart, Permanent Under-Secretary at the Foreign Office in London – and thus the man in charge of Britain's international diplomacy between 1930 and 1938 – took Rumbold's bulletins seriously. Vansittart's own anxiety about the rapid growth and rise in Germany of the Nazis, the violent extremists of the right, was shared, back then, by Sir John Simon, Secretary of State for Foreign Affairs.

Rumbold's previous stay at the British Embassy, working under the affable leadership of Sir Edward Goschen, had ended abruptly in 1914, with rocks splintering the windows along the street side of the Embassy building. In 1928, Britain's new ambassador to Germany returned to a Berlin flush with money, hot with politics and still – despite the handsome injection of foreign loans – fiercely resentful of the reparations payments from which Chancellor Stresemann had deliberately made no attempt to extricate his nation at the Treaty of Locarno. (Stresemann was, nevertheless, trying to get the payments reduced.)

Harold Nicolson, stationed at Berlin as a chargé d'affaires in 1928–9, took a dim view of his superior at the Embassy. Sir Horace, who was nearing sixty, struck his younger colleague (Nicolson himself was an active forty-two) as being both slow and dim: 'an old bumble-bee' was the actual phrase used in his diaries. When placed beside Etheldred (Ethel) Fane, his horse-faced wife, Rumbold seemed to his worldly compatriot 'so appallingly English that it is almost funny'.[1] Harold Nicolson may have come to repent a carelessly formed judgement. Bella Fromm, an attractive and well-born Jewish society journalist who worked for the massive Ullstein Press in Berlin, proved more astute.

It took only one visit to the spacious British Embassy (Bella especially admired the splashing fountains in the grand two-tier marble entrance hall) for the Nuremberg-born writer to detect that the kindly Rumbolds were not the simple creatures that they seemed. Both husband and wife, for a start, spoke impeccable German. Lady Rumbold, a diplomat's daughter, made no secret of her anger at the way that Nazi thugs had already begun, in 1930, to target Jews; Sir Horace indicated where his sympathies already lay by offering Bella immediate and privileged access to visiting foreign diplomats. Such access, during a time of increasing censorship in Germany, would enable at least one journalist in Berlin to tell the nation how Germany was being viewed from beyond her boundary lines.[2]

Horace Rumbold was not alone in his concern about where Germany was heading during the final years of the Weimar Republic. Robert Bruce Lockhart (a former diplomat who had set up an anti-Bolshevik spy network during the first years of Soviet Russia) was working as a banker in Central Europe during the late twenties. In September 1928, Lockhart recorded his belief that a second war was already on its way. Talking to Gustav Stresemann the following year, Lockhart noted that the Chancellor thought Germany's only chance of maintaining peace in Europe ('for a hundred years') lay in a change back to the pre-war Polish border with Germany. This reversion, as Stresemann acknowledged (and as Lockhart agreed), was unlikely to happen. How could Germany expect Poland, a geographically vulnerable new republic, to surrender its protecting corridor and the crucial access that it provided, for a land-locked country, to the sea? To ask such a sacrifice, as both men understood, would be tantamount to requesting Poland to commit suicide.[3]

Germany's jovial, port-swilling Chancellor died in 1929. With him, in the increasingly apprehensive view of Harry Kessler, Germany had lost both its last great statesman and its hopes of a secure future. On 3 October, Count Kessler soberly recorded his belief that the ascent of the Nazi Party, leading to a dictatorship, had become unstoppable.

Events of the next three years would confirm Kessler's fears. As America's Depression struck home, panic-stricken US banks began recalling their German loans. A new chancellor, Heinrich Brüning, was briefly licensed by President Hindenburg to rule without control by the Reichstag. Desperate to save the Reichsmark at a time when Germany had no reserves upon which to draw, Brüning dared not devalue. Instead, taxes were raised, while wages were cut. The result was a disaster. Between 1929 and 1932, devastation swept across rural Germany. Unemployment figures in Berlin alone increased by a terrifying 2000 per cent. By 1932, six million Germans were out of work and the country was once again experiencing the miseries of 1923.

Industrialists like Fritz Thyssen, whose steel works in the Ruhr had been badly affected during the Weimar years, shared the furious feelings of many Germans about the Treaty of Versailles and welcomed the prospect of working with the Nazis; by 1932, Hitler's backers also included a substantial number of landowners and several of the former Emperor's clan. (The Emperor's most cultured son, Auwi – August Wilhelm – had joined the Nazi Party early on, as had Siegfried Sassoon's former lover, Philipp, and his brother, Prince Christoph of Hessen-Kassel.) Their interest was self-serving; the Nazis appeared to offer no threat – as the Communists most certainly did – to the estates that the Junker landowners, of whom Hindenburg himself was one, continued to guard with jealous zeal. While uncharmed by the rough habits of his followers, these aristocrats placed their faith in Hitler as a friendly little chap who could be easily controlled. Lady Rumbold, disgusted, observed the ease with which the Nazi leader took them in. Hitler had, she told her mother, both a 'very human' smile and a genius (possibly borrowed by a known film enthusiast from Chaplin's famous Tramp) for gracefully conveying 'the courage of the little fellow ... They all feel they want to protect him and help him on his difficult way.'[4]

The first hint of how the Nazis might behave when in power came in September 1930, six months into Brüning's chancellorship, when the pain of withdrawn funds from abroad was being acutely felt – and a scapegoat sought. That month, 107 brown-shirted Nazis gained seats in the Reichstag. Marching along Berlin's Leipziger

Strasse in broad daylight, twenty of the new delegates paused to hurl cobbles through the windows of – and only of – the Jewish-owned stores. Asked to explain themselves to their stunned – but troublingly uncritical – colleagues, the Nazis coolly declared that these 'spontaneous outbursts' had taken place in response to attacks by Communists. Bella Fromm, who had begun to write her diary on flimsy sheets of paper that she could safely conceal in letters to friends abroad, expressed her scepticism about that dubious explanation.[5]

The 'Standstill' (by which a six-month moratorium was imposed on repayments, leaving only interest to the loaning banks to be kept up) came too late to stave off trouble.* It helped to stem the flight of money from Germany. It failed to halt the nation's steady movement to the right, in search of the authoritative command that only Adolf Hitler – freshly boosted by massive injections of funds from multinational concerns like I. G. Farben, and from magnates like the steel baron Fritz Thyssen – seemed able to offer at his increasingly well-orchestrated rallies.

Robert Brand, as a prime mover for the Standstill, was obliged to make regular visits from Lazard's Bank out to Berlin during the early thirties. Shocked by the evidence of escalating violence, secret beatings-up and even murders, Brand expressed his fears about the increasing dangers of a Nazi-governed Germany. A young Welsh journalist called Gareth Jones issued more inflammatory warnings, publishing them in the American press.

Jones, a lively, dark-haired and attractive young man, had already been noticed by the circle of politicians and economists among whom Robert Brand moved when visiting his wife's sister at

---

* It remains debatable whether the annual renewal of the Standstill Agreement (it remained in place until shortly before the Second War) was motivated by appeasement or, closely linked to appeasement, by the realistic awareness that Hitler had no intention of repaying loans that implied 'War-guilt'.

Cliveden. In 1930, Jones had been appointed as private secretary to Lloyd George and given a useful introduction to *The Times* by Philip Kerr (newly become Lord Lothian and the uneasily left-wing owner of a raft of glorious country homes). Writing for the *New York American* on 29 November 1931, Jones warned that the economic annihilation of Germany's most stable force, its influential middle class, pointed towards the imminent rise of 'a Nazi dictatorship'. Jones's only error was to suppose that the Nazis would be in power by the spring of 1932.[6]

Jones predicted Hitler's rise to dictatorship in November 1931. Five months earlier, a chance encounter occurred that might easily have swept Adolf Hitler from sight.

Neither a darkening political scene nor the daily tragedies brought about by a financial crisis could impede the steady arrival in Munich, Berlin and Dresden of a horde of fresh-faced boys and girls from England. Most were straight out of school and eager for a stimulating combination of culture, sport and socialising, spiced by the occasional sense of a peril that threatened no harm to these guileless innocents from abroad. Among the summer's intake was John Scott-Ellis, a cheerful eighteen-year-old who had three months left to fill (he had just returned from inspecting family estates in Kenya with his father) between leaving Eton and going up to Cambridge.

A week or two into his summer sojourn at Munich, Scott-Ellis purchased a small, scarlet Fiat. His driving skills were shaky. Haupt von Pappenheim, a rosy-faced and newly hard-up Nazi aristocrat, offered his services as a guide on a practice drive around the city.

Edging cautiously up the Ludwigstrasse, the inexperienced driver turned into a side street too fast. Down, right under his wheels, sank a small, toothbrush-moustached man who seemed to have blundered straight off the pavement without seeing the car. The man got up and, although displeased, appeared unharmed; John's passenger offered frantic apologies. Hands were shaken;

partings taken. Told that his victim was a man called Adolf Hitler, John registered only that Haupt Pappenheim had been appalled by the incident. Sweating hard by the time they reached John's Munich lodgings, the self-appointed driving instructor beat a rapid retreat.[7]

While Pappenheim's reaction indicates how powerful Hitler had become by 1931, a more intriguing question is posed by the uncharacteristic absent-mindedness of a politician famous for the obsessive care with which he avoided danger. One possibility presents itself as an explanation.

A few weeks after the brief encounter between young Scott-Ellis and the future dictator, Hitler's niece, Geli Raubal, co-habitant of his princely Munich apartment at 16 Prinzregentenplatz, shot herself, using her uncle's revolver, at their flat. The precise nature of the intimate relationship between Hitler and his half-niece remains unclear, but a domestic drama had surely been reaching crisis point if a preternaturally cautious man was too distracted to spot the approach of a bright-scarlet foreign car in a city where, especially in straitened times, private motor vehicles remained rare.

This author's own German connection owes everything to John Scott-Ellis's first visit to Munich, a city that never ceased to charm my uncle with its airy informality and its glistening distant views of the Bavarian Alps. Today, walking through the neglected garden of the charming new house on Biedersteiner Strasse that a sculptor (Hans Albrecht Harrach) and his wife Helene (Mechtilde Lichnowsky's artistic sister) moved into during 1926, it's still possible to come upon a circular pool, presided over by Anadyomene, a graceful naiad sculpted by Hans Albrecht himself. This little pond was a favourite meeting spot for the young English visitors who, as paying guests, were given cultural tours of Munich by one of the Harrachs' five daughters. Scott-Ellis, invited over by one of the guests for a swim, conspired in a prank. A large live fish was purchased and surreptitiously slipped into the pool as a surprise companion for the giggling bathers. John's punishment for such impudence was to be invited to return the following day and join the family for a lunch made from their 'catch'.

The fish, in hard times, provided a splendid feast; Irene, the Harrachs' youngest daughter, made an impression that John Scott-Ellis would never forget. She was cleaning the stairs, Cinderella-style, when he walked up the house's steps and in through the columned entrance. For a shy young man, gazing at an exceptionally pretty young woman across a large, bright entrance hall filled with Hans Albrecht's sculptures (his head of Helen Keller had won tributes at a recent exhibition in New York) and Helene's witty drawings and sketches, it was love at first sight.

Between 1931 and 1934, John became a regular visitor to the Harrachs' home in Munich. Sadly, an affable man's good-humoured memoirs and family recollections reveal little of a city that was experiencing extraordinary times. Conversations with Count Harrach about Keyserling, whom Hans Albrecht admired, and Spengler, whom he mistrusted, were vaguely mentioned. (John himself became sufficiently interested in Spengler to give a talk about him at Cambridge.)

One memory lingered. Driving through Bavaria on one of his regular visits to Munich, the young Englishman lost his way. Motoring through deep woods, he blundered upon a military exercise that was being conducted with armoured tanks. Back in England, his reports were laughed away. The tanks were of a kind that the German Army (in theory) did not then possess.

Otherwise, for John – as for the majority of bright-eyed youngsters who visited Munich and Berlin during the early thirties – Germany presented itself as a country seen through thick protective glass. They were there to enjoy themselves. The country's politics were not their affair.

In August 1932, President Hindenburg had fiercely refused Hitler's demand to be given the chancellorship. Half a year on, a mentally enfeebled President (as a despairing Bella Fromm noted on 10 April 1933: 'he grasps nothing') endorsed Hitler's appointment as chancellor of Germany. The date was 30 January 1933. A month later, the Reichstag went up in flames and a young Dutch Communist took the blame. Many suspected a set-up (there had been rumours of a planned fake attack on Hitler's life), and that an excuse was required for the vicious reprisals that were swiftly carried out as leading Communists were swiftly rounded up for beatings, imprisonment, or both.

On 23 March, President Hindenburg put his signature to the Enabling Act. Back in 1930, Chancellor Brüning had been allowed to rule without the Reichstag during a period of financial emergency. The 1933 Enabling Act removed the need for such emergencies: Germany's new chancellor was free to make what laws he wished, and without consultation.

All resemblance to a normal life in Germany now started to unravel with alarming speed. Jewish tombs were vandalised. Churches erected swastikas on their spires. In Berlin, Bella Fromm watched her own chauffeur from Ullstein shouting death to the Jews as he marched down the street. Back in uniform by the end of the day, the same chauffeur opened the limousine door for his 'Miss Bella' and not a word was said.

On 1 April, a national boycott was imposed, backed by the watchful presence of bully-boys in uniform, on all Jewish-owned shops. (Ethel Rumbold made a point of shopping at the Jewish stores in Berlin that day.) On 6 April, citizens learned that German literature was to be purified by fire; on 10 May, Nazified students and teachers joined in the fun of hurling books from the windows of schools and libraries and then setting them ablaze. Among the 25,000 books considered important enough for incineration were the works of Ernest Hemingway, Lion Feuchtwanger, Jack London, Heinrich Heine, Helen Keller, Heinrich and Thomas Mann, Bertolt Brecht and Erich Maria Remarque. The writings of Helene Harrach's sister, Mechtilde Lichnowsky, joined the pyre.

'Spontaneous protests' meanwhile guaranteed that the film of Remarque's classic anti-war book, *All Quiet on the Western Front*, followed the fate of *Die andere Seite* (the German remake of *Journey's End*) in taking a swift departure from the German screen.

The union of state and party as a single unit ('Partei und Staat sind eins') came on 1 December, following the suspension of all parties other than the Nazis. All this had been achieved in less than a year.

The exodus, not surprisingly, had already begun.

Hitler had become chancellor at the end of January 1933. Within less than a month, Tisa Schulenberg's Marxist sculptor friend, Emil Fuchs, heard that his life was in danger. 'We had laughed at the small man's desire at marching about in a queer brown shirt,' Tisa Schulenburg stated in her memoir, but she did not laugh when a terrified Fuchs knocked at her door just after the Reichstag fire, begging for sanctuary and for a car to get him away before the police arrived. (Fritz Hess drove their friend to the borders; the SA arrived at Fuchs's house a few hours later, and moved on to conduct a thorough search of Tisa's studio.) That same month, warned that his passport was about to be seized, Germany's leading theatre and literary critic, Alfred Kerr, left without a moment's hesitation (his family followed him within the year). Harry Kessler, tipped off in March about an imminent arrest, fled to Paris; in April, he learned that a trusted servant had discovered an old flag, rolled up in the Count's attic. It was enough. Harbouring non-Nazi icons had become evidence of treason. Kessler's house was confiscated the following year. With it went all his treasures: the books, the paintings, the Maillol sculptures among which Josephine Baker had once gleefully danced.

In Paris, on 7 June 1933, Count Kessler and Count Keyserling, a fellow exile, could still ponder whether Hitler might yet restrain a party that seemed hell-bent on destruction.

Horace Rumbold suffered from no such illusions. Devastating in the quiet moderation of his tone, the British Ambassador despatched reports that left the Foreign Office in London in no doubt of the extremes to which Germany's new leaders were prepared to go. Unlike the optimistic Prussian Junkers, he did not believe that Hitler would endeavour to hold them back.

In March, 1933, Rumbold told Robert Vansittart and his colleague Sir John Simon that law and order had been suspended in Berlin; that Bruno Walter had been forbidden to conduct; and that Einstein's house – contrary to Wyndham Lewis's confident declaration in 1931 that the Nazi leaders would always cherish the geniuses among the Jews – had been ransacked.*[8] A month later, on 5 April, Rumbold informed the Foreign Office that all non-Aryan Germans were now excluded by law from taking paid employment; that large camps for Jews and other 'unsuitables' had been erected; and that one, Dachau, built over the grounds of a former artists' colony close to Munich, was designed to hold 5000 prisoners. Writing more informally to Margot Asquith that same week, Rumbold passed on the news that Marxists and pacifists now qualified as common criminals and were being sent to Dachau. Tisa Schulenburg, meanwhile, learned from her old school head at Heiligengrabe that the women who did the cleaning for a nearby prison camp complained about regularly having to wash clothes that were sodden with blood.[9]

Even theatregoing had become a crime for Germany's newly created underclass. Writing to his son on 23 April, Rumbold described with disgust how a Jew attending a fundraising concert conducted by Furtwängler had been forced to his feet and elbowed out of the building by a couple of Nazi guards. Nobody protested. The risk of being seen to do so had become too great.

Rumbold's last effort to persuade Britain to pay attention came

---

* Wyndham Lewis's enthusiastic short life of Hitler (1931) had been commissioned by Lady Rhondda, the right-wing extremist who owned *Time and Tide*.

in what is known as the '*Mein Kampf* Despatch'. Sent to Sir John Simon on 26 April and read by both Ramsay MacDonald and Neville Chamberlain, the 5000-word document argued that *Mein Kampf* offered a clear blueprint for the Germany that Hitler had now begun to create. Racial purity; forceful repossession of lost territories; the creation of a powerful military machine: all of this had been proclaimed in a book that Rumbold (wrongly, in this respect) imagined that a Hitler grown 'cautious and discreet as he was formerly blunt and frank' would now wish to bury.* Hitler stated that he wanted a ten-year peace; Rumbold believed that the decade would be spent in re-arming Germany. 'The outlook for Europe is far from peaceful,' he warned, 'if the speeches of the Nazi leaders, especially the Chancellor, are borne in mind.' Rumbold did not ask Britain to intervene; what he implored was that England's leaders should pay attention.[10]

The reward for Rumbold's strenuous endeavours was not what he might have anticipated. The Foreign Office ordered the Ambassador home that summer and replaced him with a potentially more malleable figure: Robert Vansittart's own brother-in-law, Sir Eric Phipps.

Sir Eric Phipps, a decent man whose own increasing distaste for the Nazis would lead to a similar recall within a couple of years, must have wondered what he had done to deserve such a fate. On 28 June 1933, on the verge of his departure from Berlin, Rumbold confessed to a personal friend, Clive Wigram (private secretary to George VI) that 'many of us here feel as though we were living in a lunatic asylum'. Addressing the Foreign Office for the last time two days later, Rumbold grimly observed that Hitler's good fortune was to preside over a people who, desperate for a moral leader, no longer cared what that morality might be.

---

* *Mein Kampf*, made mandatory reading and encouraged as a suitable gift to wedding couples, became a useful source of revenue for Hitler.

'There is no doubt,' Rumbold added, 'that the persons directing the policy of the Hitler Government are not normal.'[11]

Fond though Sir Horace's playful half-brother Hugo was of entertaining John Scott-Ellis's parents and their friends by dressing up
as a duchess for dinner parties, the Ambassador himself was a man
of conventional habits and tastes. It's unlikely, although they were
in Berlin at the same time, that Sir Horace ever encountered the
clever, cultured, left-leaning group of young men who appear,
thinly disguised, in Stephen Spender's *The Temple* (begun in Berlin
in 1928) and in Christopher Isherwood's poignant evocation of a
vanishing world, *Goodbye to Berlin* (1939).

Isherwood, invited to Bremen by a donnish cousin in 1928, was
lazily beguiled by a schoolboy-annual world of rose-brick walls,
bicycles and yachting caps. 'My vision of Germany is utterly the
boys' country,' he wrote in his diary on 21 May; the following
year, still struggling to master the language, but fascinated by the
people, Isherwood settled into a room near Berlin's Tiergarten.
Stephen Spender, urged on by a German-speaking grandmother
who wanted him to visit her cherished homeland, settled nearby.
Together with their friends Wystan Auden and John Lehmann,
who paid regular visits from Vienna, the young Englishmen
savoured the freedom of a society in which homosexuality was not
yet a crime (the Nazis would soon make it a criminal offence) and
in which, before censorship set in, the culture was headily diverse.

Politics came far below sex for Isherwood during the time he
spent living in Germany; Spender, ranging excitedly between
Hölderlin and Goethe, Reinhardt and Brecht, focused on culture,
while saving an occasional sigh for the hardships being imposed on
Berliners by the economic slump.

Had Isherwood, Auden and Spender fallen under the spell of a
man like Janos Almasy, it's possible that they, like Tom Mitford,
would have opted for a state of political detachment that leaned
towards favouring the Nazis. Instead, they met Wilfrid Israel.

Tall, fair-haired, softly spoken and spectacularly rich, the London-born Israel owed his impeccable English to the fact that his mother, Pauline Solomon (also born in England), refused to have German spoken at her table. At the time that he met up with Auden, Isherwood and Spender, all of whom were a shade younger than himself, this cultured and enigmatic man was beginning to take over the family empire. (Nathan Israel was one of the largest and most respected department stores in Berlin, employing over 7000 people, among whom a modest 10 per cent were Jews.) A collector of Oriental art, Israel was a pensive dandy and aesthete of dual nationality. At the time that he met the young English writers, Israel was beginning to ponder how he could best use his own privileged position as a dual national to help the vulnerable majority of Jews who were more directly threatened than himself by the new and ugly politics of Germany's ultra-right wing.

Spender, partly Jewish himself, instantly recognised Israel's exceptional qualities. ('Dass Sie für diese Welt zu gut seien,' Einstein would write to Wilfrid on 7 June 1939, at the time of his escape: 'You are too good for this world.') Isherwood, put off by the air of elusive detachment, portrayed Israel as the impassive aesthete Bernhard Landauer in his novel about Berlin and, when he came to revise the portrait in 1977, still failed to inject the character with any warmth. (It seems almost as though Isherwood, who had so artfully impersonated detachment through his literary motif of the camera's eye, felt threatened when he met the real thing.) Wilfrid Israel, however, liked the clever and appealing young English writers enough to meet up with them both in Berlin and – travelling up to the fringes of the North Sea in 1932 – in the silvery, pine-scented oasis of Rügen Island that had enchanted Elizabeth von Arnim during her years in Germany.

Isherwood later politicised his memories of Rügen by adding the striking image of a small naked boy carrying a swastika flag along the sandy shore and singing 'Deutschland über alles' to the groups of cosy Germans who snuggled deep within the wicker hives of their wind protectors, out by the side of an oyster-grey sea. But Rügen, above all, was a place for doing nothing: day after day, the young men from England sunbathed, read, talked and went for strolls. Occasionally (if Isherwood's fiction is based on fact), they fell into conversation – and maybe something more – with Nazi boys who loved their Führer and burned to please him.

It was at Rügen, in 1932, according to Stephen Spender's rec-ollections in *World Within World*, that Wilfrid Israel first persuaded him to study the Nazis' literature. Whatever Israel produced as reading material (Spender's account is not specific), it proved effec-tive and determining. Finally, the visitors from England were compelled to take notice of a programme that amounted to some-thing far more dangerous than random bullyings and a bit of censorship.

It can't be claimed that Auden and his friends took up a position of marked nobility at a challenging time. It can, however, be noted that the young writers grew less detached and more attentive after the Rügen holiday. John Lehmann, watching the Reichstag go up in flames, understood enough to see an omen of future confla-gration. A few months later, Stephen Spender recorded with dismay the transformation of Germany's traditional midsummer bonfires into a series of witches' sabbaths at which even Erich Kästner's innocuous books – newly identified as a threat to racial purity – were cast into the flames. Only *Emil and the Detectives* escaped destruction, thanks to its immense popularity among German readers.

For Christopher Isherwood, there may have been as much self-interest as heroism in his endeavours to get a young Jewish lover, Heinz Neddermeyer, out of the country in the summer of 1933, but Isherwood was already making a record of the bullyings and ill-treatment, the racism and the violence, that he saw taking place around him. ('How quickly fear set in,' wrote Fritz Stern, remem-bering the shock he had felt on learning from his family that he himself was one of the newly designated inferior race: a Jew.[12]) Isherwood's observations, first published in magazine form between 1935–7, were later incorporated into his novel *Goodbye to Berlin,* but the last chapter of an earlier work from 1935 (*Mr Norris Changes Trains*) had already provided a powerful account of a society headed for terminal breakdown.

Isherwood left Germany in 1933. A year later, Wystan Auden and two friends crossed Germany during the hot August weeks that followed the octogenarian President Hindenburg's death. His successor, already hailed as 'Your Majesty' by the bewildered old man, had wasted no time in seeking divine rights. Two hours after Hindenburg's death, on 2 August, Hitler announced his self-appointment as Germany's first all-in-one chancellor and president. What Auden witnessed – as did a bronzed young Patrick Leigh Fermor, striding through a swastika-spattered Fatherland on his colourful pilgrimage to Constantinople – was the utter lack of freedom with which Germany yielded an enforced consent, in the summer of 1934, to the apotheosis of Adolf Hitler.

Auden may have had Wilfrid Israel to thank for the lucidity with which he recognised an atmosphere not of joy, but of terri-fied compliance: 'every house waves a flag like a baby's rattle ... Every shop has pasted a notice, "We are all going to vote yes."' A hotel owner, hearing the advancing stamp of the Labour Corps, broke off from chatting to his English visitor to throw open the window and beam out. The moment had arrived, Auden wrote, for a prudent businessman 'to show a welcome face'.

Auden failed, however, to grasp the situation's full gravity. This was the summer during which a horrific massacre had recently taken place in Munich (the Night of the Long Knives, catchily named after one of Hitler's favourite marching songs). And yet, the English poet was still ready to compare the Nazi assassins to 'the sort of school prefect who is good at Corps'. Listening to one of the most menacing speeches of Hitler's career, Auden could only come up with another schoolroom image: a boy gabbling phrases learned off by rote.*[13]

The fact that they had little direct dealing with Germans except within the intimate world of personal friendships enabled Isherwood, Auden and Spender to keep out of politics. John Heygate, returning to Germany in 1932 to work at Babelsberg as a supervisor on British films, registered events from a less detached angle.

Good-looking, amoral and enterprising, Heygate had already taken a couple of motor jaunts around Germany when the invitation came to work at UFA. Heygate's autobiographical novels suggest that he revelled in the glamour of working alongside Laurence Olivier's elegant first wife and the effortlessly bilingual and German-born Lilian Harvey, while the male stars interested him rather less. He loved being entertained at a movie mogul's sumptuously modern home in Berlin's Grunewald; he relished cabaret evenings spent watching Jean Ross (Isherwood's Sally Bowles) crooning to bemused businessmen in a raucous cockney accent, while presenting them with an act that, as Heygate noted with amusement, 'was their idea of Piccadilly and Broadway with a touch of Harlem rolled into one'.[14]

Heygate's novels, while less successful than those of his friends Anthony Powell and Evelyn Waugh, have the merit of being written by somebody who was not an outsider (as were Isherwood, Spender and Auden), but who was working among Germans, in an industry that employed a great many Jews. In *Talking Picture* (1934), Heygate is speaking from experience when he describes how the new ban on Jewish workers has thrown the film studio into panic. One cameraman, however, looks quite jaunty: 'Braun

* Back in England the following year, Auden performed the more useful service of marrying Erika Mann (Thomas's lesbian daughter) – a ceremony that took place during a lunch break at the country school where he was teaching. Auden's motives were mixed: while glad to save a member of the Mann family from potential persecution, the alliance also provided a valuable literary link for an ambitious writer.

jumped to his camera ... he was one of the only pure Aryans in the studio and had nothing to fear from Hitler.' The Babelsberg film sets are put to fresh use in the novel, offering memorably symbolic images of a country locked in the bitter grip of winter's rule. Behind the wreckage of *Front Line 1918*, a street of summery flowers from *Vienna* lies buried deep in snow. Nearby, on Fritz Lang's old *Nibelungen* sets, reduced to a wilderness of tangled power cables and planks, the lake in which Siegfried once battled with the dragon has become an ice-bound wasteland.

Writing in 1934, by which time Germany had experienced a full year of rule by ruthless force, Heygate refused to romanticise his feelings for a country that had once enchanted him. Asked by two anxious stormtroopers what people in England think about the brave new Germany, the narrator offers them no reassurance. For himself, he has no choice but to quit a country that now fills him with dismay. 'The road – the road to England opened before me. There was no other.'

The narrator never went back, but John Heygate did. Returning for the Nuremberg Rally of 1935 with the ardently pro-German novelist Henry Williamson at his side, Heygate was still keen to register his disapproval. Typically, English visitors to the Nazi rallies praised the clockwork precision of the marching troops; Heygate, pointedly, dwelt upon the beauty of the old medieval city. Comparing national anthems, he observed that while Britain aspired only to rule the seas, Germany 'says that she will rule the world'. Shown a torture instrument similar in design to the legendary iron maiden, Heygate saw a perfect symbol of the new Nazi soldier: lean, soulless, and brutally efficient.[15]

It is harder for a novelist to send clear signals of current affairs from abroad than for a foreign correspondent working for a major paper.

Gareth Jones had begun visiting Germany on walking tours in 1923, when he was eighteen years old and reading French, German and Russian at the Welsh university of Aberystwyth. A star reporter for one of Britain's largest provincial papers, the *Western Mail*, Jones was offered the chance to speak to a wider audience when Philip Lothian, having heard Jones speaking authoratively about his impressions of Stalinist Russia, provided an introduction to his friend Geoffrey Dawson, the long-standing editor of *The Times*. Dawson, advised by the Foreign Office not to antagonise Soviet Russia, rejected Jones's firsthand 1932 reports on famine in the Ukraine. Nevertheless, when Jones expressed a wish to report on the rise of the new Germany, Dawson promised to do what he could.[16]

Six years after his first visit to Germany, there was still no doubting Gareth Jones's affection for the country. 'Hurray! It is wonderful to be in Germany again, absolutely wonderful,' he wrote to a family who were used to such characteristic outbursts of enthusiasm. (In one charming early letter, Jones had fantasised about sending his favourite Welsh aunt's fine cake around all the great houses of Germany, for a special tasting in which they would all share his own relish for her cooking, and hail the finest cake-maker in the world.)

Jones put his connections with *The Times* to good use during his time in Berlin. Invited by Putzi Hanfstaengl to accompany Hitler on a plane trip from Berlin to Frankfurt, the young Welsh reporter found himself sharing the honours with Sefton Delmer, putting his own fluent German to good use as a correspondent for the *Daily Express*. Delmer's chatty report focused on the presence on the *Richthofen* (Germany's fastest plane, travelling at 142mph) of Auwi von Preussen, Emperor Wilhelm II's third son, morosely eating his way through the chocolates that Hitler, always terrified of being poisoned, refused to touch. Jones was more intrigued by the presence of a giggling, twinkling Goebbels, and by the transformation of the private Hitler (a pale and flabby introvert) into the public figure who climbed out of the plane: the man whose oratory 'is in colour one blazing red which makes the people mad'.[17]

Jones suffered from no illusions about the man who had taken control of Germany. From the moment of Hitler's election as chancellor, he spoke out with a clear warning to his British readers. 'The personality of Hitler arouses no confidence in the calm observer,' Jones wrote on 9 February 1933. 'It is hard to reconcile his shrieking hatred of the Jews with any balanced judgement.' In the months that followed, the young journalist sent home accounts of the bonfires of books, the banning of Jews from public jobs and the corrupt rewriting of German history to fit the deceits of propaganda. He wrote about the military music that was played through every hour on the radio and relayed through megaphones into city centres, beach resorts and public parks. He described, as a personal witness, the power of the speeches for which he rated only Hermann Goering as comparable to Hitler in his eloquence.

In June 1934, Jones's tone grew more urgent. He wrote that German newspapers were boasting of the 10,000 planes that stood ready for action on every frontier. On 22 August, he described the ongoing creation of a military monster: 'a super-regimented, forcefully cemented people, who are to speak with one voice, think with one brain, and march at a single command'. On 3 October, describing what he called 'a cleansing', Jones added, in chilling understatement, as if he feared to say more: 'There is a lot going on under the surface.'[18]

The *Western Mail*, proud of their star Welsh reporter, published every one of Gareth's articles. Geoffrey Dawson, sharing the Foreign Office's anxiety not to offend the new Germany, published none of them. *The Times* would prove equally reticent in 1935 when Jones, whom Stalin had banned for life, was kidnapped by bandits while travelling through Mongolia with a German journalist. The German was released. Jones, who had just turned thirty, was murdered. No obituary, nor even a mention of Jones's death, appeared in *The Times*.

Yet Gareth Jones had made his mark. Writing for the *Berliner Tageblatt* on 17 August 1935, a German journalist mourned the untimely loss of a 'splendid' man and seized the chance to plead for more of such honest reporting on Germany's tragic situation.

'The International Press is abandoning its colours,' Paul Scheffer declared, '– and in some countries more quickly than others ... The causes of this tendency are many. Today is not the time to speak of them.'

Such a mildly measured statement, published in a prominent German newspaper, by the summer of 1935, was enough to lose an author his liberty, and perhaps his life. Sadly, Scheffer's muted words had no noticeable effect on Geoffrey Dawson, an editor who had committed himself, where both Soviet Russia and Nazi Germany were concerned, to a policy of suppression and censorship.

It was Jones's misfortune that he had been given an introduction to *The Times*, rather than to the *Daily Telegraph*, the far more open-spirited newspaper for which Graham Greene's cousin, Hugh, started writing from Berlin in 1934.

The Greene family had proudly asserted their German links throughout Hugh's life. Two tall tribes of Greenes had grown up in the Hertfordshire town of Berkhamsted as cousins and friends. Hugh and Graham belonged to one clan; the other, thanks to their Brazilian-born German mother, Eva Stutzer, an ardent pacifist, had been taught German as their first language.

Ben, Eva's eldest boy, had led the way in 1920, when he followed up his studies at Berlin University by travelling around Germany, before briefly joining a Quaker aid-mission in Soviet Russia. Graham, during his studies at Balliol, had paid a fact-finding visit to the Ruhr in the company of an Oxford chum, Claud Cockburn, who shared Graham's impression that the French strategy for post-war occupation was calculated to inflict maximum discomfort on a defeated nation. (The presence of a large number of black Senegalese troops struck the two young men as especially inflammatory.)

In 1928, an eighteen-year-old Hugh Greene went to Marburg, where he fell in love simultaneously – and enduringly – with

German cinema and German girls. Five years later, Hugh returned to Germany to act as a stringer in Munich for Kingsley Martin at the *New Statesman*. In 1934, the long-legged, myopic and astonishingly curly-headed young man was given the journalistic plum he craved: a job writing for the *Daily Telegraph* from Berlin.

Greene's timing was impeccable. The thirties was a golden decade for the foreign correspondent, and Hugh arrived in Berlin alongside William Shirer, Edgar Mowrer and H. R. Knickerbocker. Norman Ebbutt, working for *The Times*, was an old hand, widely regarded as the best reporter of them all. Ebbutt, resigned to the fact that his own reports were invariably spiked or rewritten by Dawson as soon as they reached London, was happy to share some of his most remarkable scoops. Hugh Greene, throughout the Nazi years, was delighted to make use of them.

Ebbutt and Greene were returning from a city tennis match one morning in late June 1934 when the two journalists spotted something untoward: Goering's state police were herding a group of Ernst Röhm's stormtroopers into a van, before rapidly driving away. It was the eve of the massacre in Munich.

Events developed at speed. Hitler, travelling to Munich, announced that action must be taken to forestall an attempted coup. Ernst Röhm was killed in his bedroom; Kurt von Schleicher, the chancellor who preceded Hitler and whose attitude had remained critical of the Führer, was lunching at home with his wife when a group of SS officers burst in and shot them both dead.

Officially, the victims had been planning a revolt. Unofficially, it was apparent that the SA were not popular with the German Army and that Hitler, preparing to seize power from Hindenburg – and unaware that the ancient President was about to die from natural causes – had done a deal with the military. In Germany, Goebbels praised a heroic act by a great leader who had dared to venture into the traitor's den; on 13 July, the official explanation for Röhm's death was announced in one of Hitler's most truculent speeches. Delivered in the Reichstag, it was broadcast across the nation. Unity

Mitford, horrified for the Führer (he had just honoured her with a personal salute during one of his regular teatime visits to Munich's Carlton Hotel), thought he had been tremendously brave. '*Poor* Hitler. The whole thing is so dreadful.'[19]

Foreign journalists had not, as yet, been killed in Germany; expulsion, however, was always possible. With considerable courage, Hugh Greene wrote and sent off his despatch. Appearing in the *Daily Telegraph* on 4 July (a full week before Hitler made his official announcement at the Reichstag), Greene's report described a brutally executed set-up. It was, he wrote, splendid for Goebbels to describe Hitler as having bearded savage lions in their den, but what courage was needed to kill families at their lunch table or sleeping in their beds? And what kind of conspirators employed no guards and trustingly opened their doors to strangers?[20]

Hugh's report was ill-received in Berlin. The following week, all copies of the *Daily Telegraph* in Germany were confiscated. Temporarily forbidden to listen to Hitler's speeches in the Reichstag, and informed on 14 July that the *Telegraph* was to be banned from circulation in Germany for a further fortnight, Hugh was unfazed.

Hindenburg died, obligingly, on 2 August. Hugh's account of the carefully orchestrated state funeral did full honour to the ironies of the occasion. Beginning with an account of the black-draped building and the massing of the troops, the young reporter described how Hitler had dedicated a great president to his rightful place in Valhalla before – as a rousing chorus of the 'Horst Wessel Lied' was sung in honour of the Reich's favourite martyr – a massive hawk that had been hovering over the cere-mony like a presiding spirit rose with a shriek into the sky. The hawk, as Greene later cheerily admitted, was a touch that had been added by a London editor; he himself had taken pains to shape his account into a warning of the new Germany that was coming into being. The sheeted building had loomed up 'like some sinister dream of the future'; the tightly ranked parading troops had offered an image of complete invincibility: 'uniformed strength'.[21]

Goebbels, while launching furious attcks on what he called Greene's 'revolver journalism', allowed Britain's most outspoken correspondent to remain in place for a further five years. Hugh himself believed that his fate was sealed on the day in 1939 when, standing on a station platform in Berlin, he was afforded the pleasing spectacle of a burly guard scooping the tiny Minister of Propaganda up in his arms and popping him through the carriage window of a departing train 'with his short legs kicking in the air'.[22]

The knowledge that his humiliation had been witnessed, and by an English journalist, was too much for a vain man to bear, or so Hugh Greene avowed. Ordered to leave the country in May 1939, the ebullient young journalist departed in style, waving a fencing foil and shouting to his friends that he intended coming back – 'als Gauleiter!'[23]

22

NIKOLAUS PEVSNER:
THE ODD ONE OUT

(1929–33)

Nikolaus Pevsner's reputation rests chiefly upon his passion for English architecture and upon the thirty-two (he co-authored a further ten) guides to England's monuments that are today known simply by his name. It's possible to imagine that, with such enthusiasm, Pevsner might have been among the few German Jews who were able to accommodate themselves to an enforced change of nationality. Nothing could have been further from the truth. The young Pevsner was not in love with Britain. On the contrary, despite having an Anglophile mother, he positively disliked England.

Born in 1902, Pevsner grew up in Leipzig's elegant Music Quarter, where families such as his own lived in handsome apartment blocks (the Pevsner flat comprised well over twenty rooms). Visiting his mother's parents in West Hampstead as a small boy, Nikolaus was oppressed by the confining spaces of their modest home in Sumatra Road. He left London with an enduring and horrific memory of an outing during which the family became trapped inside the lift – more like a mineshaft – that plunges deep into the earth at Hampstead tube station. Later in life, Pevsner showed scant interest either in talking about his late grandfather, a Talmudic scholar who spent most of his days at the British Museum, or – with the exception of an occasional brisk visit to a Victorian church – in visiting north London.

Pevsner's detachment from his Jewish grandparents in England becomes more understandable when seen in the light of his later career. Aged nineteen in 1921, he found that the academic quota system restricted the number of Jews in Germany who were allowed to hold academic posts. Pevsner's solution was a simple one: he converted to Lutheranism. Two years later, he married – taking a step up the social ladder – Lola Kurlbaum, the daughter of a charming, cultured, eminent Leipzig lawyer. (It did not, at the time, seem of any significance that the Lutheran Alfred Kurlbaum had married a Jew, since Lola had followed her father's faith.) The devotion to scholarship that Pevsner would show throughout his life was already apparent from the fact that his honeymoon suitcase was neatly packed, not with clothes, but with art books.

An encounter with English art in 1926, when Pevsner was working as an intern at the Dresden Art Gallery during the city's celebrated international show, did nothing to increase an opinionated and highly strung young man's enthusiasm for his future homeland. Always intrigued by the idea of communal work, Pevsner was more excited by the brilliant palettes of the Dresden-based pre-war group Die Brücke (Ernst Kirchner, Emil Nolde, Max Pechstein) and their Bavarian contemporaries of Der Blaue Reiter (Franz Marc, August Macke, Alexej von Jawlensky) than by the muted tints of the English contributions. Duncan Grant's paintings were conceded to be almost French in their colouring (which Pevsner intended as a compliment); the works of Gwen John and Stanley Spencer, when placed alongside the French and German entries, were dismissed as 'no more than middling fare'. The best, in fact, that Nikolaus Pevsner could say about the

English works on show at Dresden was that they were measured and correct.[1]

For a man whose name has become part of English art history, this was an unpromising start. The change began in 1929, when the tall, fair-haired and fiercely scholarly 27-year-old was given the post at Göttingen University of *Privatdozent*, an unsalaried tutor who was paid directly by his pupils.

Pevsner was not immediately thrilled by the prospect of teaching at a provincial university whose reputation – in terms of its art history course – stood far below those of universities in Munich and Berlin. But his revered teacher and mentor, Wilhelm Pinder, had recommended the move and the posting proved unexpectedly congenial. John Ratcliff, a cheerful young Welshman who was studying art as a pupil on Pevsner's course in 1932, sent home delighted accounts of Göttingen, a friendly, broad-streeted town lapped by wooded hills that reminded him of north Wales; Pevsner, too, soon reconciled himself to – and even came to love – a university at which his students adored him, while his colleagues all offered him their enthusiastic support.[2]

Göttingen's links with England, which were unusually strong, dated back to the founding of the university by King George II, Elector of Hanover. George III had presented the university with some 300 of the artefacts brought home by James Cook from his voyages in the South Pacific. The college library, founded with the inauguration of the university, was also committed to emphasising Hanover's connections with Britain. With such a history, it was not surprising that the university required Pevsner to teach, as part of his curriculum, a course on the art and architecture of England. It was a subject on which Pevsner felt woefully underinformed. 'I was supposed to give every semester a one-hour-a-week lecture on some aspect of English art and architecture,' he told an interviewer, 'but then found I couldn't really do it.'[3]

Pevsner was being too modest about his early achievements. In December 1929, delivering his first Göttingen lecture, he chose for his topic 'Community Ideals in Nineteenth-Century Art'. According to the reports that appeared in Dresden's newspapers, Pevsner's hour-long talk caused a sensation, while offering plenty to gratify an Anglophile community.

Proposing to chart out a moral chain in art, Pevsner established a line that closely linked England to Germany. Beginning with the group of German-speaking Nazarene artists who had lived in Rome back in the time of Charles de Bunsen, Pevsner reminded his audience of how that influence had come to England and then travelled (via Ford Madox Brown and the Pre-Raphaelites) to William Morris and the Arts and Crafts movement. From there, it was an easy step to demonstrate how Hermann Muthesius, while visiting England in the 1890s, had become a devotee of the great Arts and Crafts' architect Norman Shaw. A German audience was not displeased to learn that – thanks to Muthesius – the chain of influence had finally returned to Germany, to flourish afresh under the leadership of Walter Gropius at the Bauhaus.

To such a loyal son as Nikolaus Pevsner, Germany was the country in which this moral chain of art had to complete its circle. Nevertheless, wishing to pursue the subject and investigate it more deeply, Pevsner realised that he would have to go back to that unloved island across the sea and look with his own reluctant eyes for examples that would bear out his thesis. (He had, until giving his lecture, relied upon the opinions of Gustav Waagen – Waagen was a contemporary of the Nazarene painters, and one who had spent time in England – and, a little more recently, upon the opinions expressed by Hermann Muthesius in his monumental pre-war work *Das englische Haus*.)

Pevsner's visit to Britain, paid in 1930, was successful both in enhancing the young art historian's knowledge and in inspiring his enduring fascination with the guilds of anonymous woodworkers and stonemasons who had ornamented the precious treasury of abbeys, minsters and parish churches that he discovered for himself on his first journey through England. The tour achieved little, however, in warming Pevsner's feelings about a country that he would have been horrified to envisage as his future home. Writing to Lola, his long-suffering wife, he complained about England's poor-quality spa towns (something in which Germany excelled), the disgusting food, the insufficient heating and the garrulous guides. (Visiting English country houses as part of his tour, Pevsner was unimpressed to find himself being conducted around by owners who seemed less interested in the historic detail of their homes than in the milk yield of their cows.)

The German visitor's temper was not improved by the fact that he suspected the English of laughing at him. 'What is it?' Pevsner asked his wife. 'The hat? The socks? The horn-rimmed glasses?' Pevsner – as one of his best biographers, Stephen Games, observes – seems not to have grasped just how much entertainment might be provided by a lanky, binocular-carrying German academic taking copious notes on public buildings, while arrestingly garbed in knickerbockers and patent leather pumps. (Pevsner, characteristically, had been more concerned about packing the right books for his tour than the appropriate clothes.)[4]

The visit to England was, despite strongly felt reservations about the nation's backward state, a success. Home again at Göttingen, where Pevsner began restructuring his courses to increase the time devoted to English art history, he persuaded an English-based colleague to visit Germany and lecture (while unwittingly fascinating the students by cloaking himself in an English don's black gown) on medieval painting. Delighted by the success of his expanded courses, the heads of department praised Pevsner as one of the most gifted art historians of his generation. He must, they said, be granted a salaried position for what he had achieved. Göttingen, thanks to Nikolaus Pevsner, could now boast that its English art history course was the best in Prussia.

Pevsner's downfall as a young man with a brilliant future in German academia owed a little to the fact that the number of candidates greatly exceeded the number of professorial posts available at a limited number of art history departments. It owed far more to the rise of a radical politician for whom Pevsner himself entertained a high regard.

With hindsight, Pevsner's confidence about his prospects in a Nazi-run Germany appears to have been breathtakingly naïve. Talking to Pallister Barkas, an English Quaker colleague at Göttingen, during the run-up to Hitler's election as chancellor, Pevsner dismissed *Mein Kampf* as empty propaganda: 'It's not to be taken seriously.' Pressed further about the Nazis, Pevsner praised them for helping to rebuild Germany's self-confidence. As a Lutheran convert who admired church architecture and who kept a three-foot-high porcelain crucifix in his home, it never occurred to Pevsner that any of the unpleasant constraints beginning to be applied to Germany's Jews could affect his own career. Even on 7 April 1933, the day when a new law was introduced to exclude 'non-Aryans' from employment by government-funded bodies (including universities and schools), Pevsner did not object. Admiring the Reich and loyal to the Fatherland, he believed himself to be entirely safe.[5]

Göttingen had been among the first towns to embrace Nazism; the new edict was immediately enforced. The Quaker Barkases were dismayed when one of their closest academic friends, a man who had fought for Germany in the war, lost his job. Pevsner, too, had forfeited the right to teach. And yet, allowing himself to be interviewed anonymously by Barkas's English sister-in-law, Francesca Wilson, for her home-town paper (the *Birmingham Post*), Pevsner continued to defend the policies of the Nazi Party. 'I want this movement to succeed,' Pevsner told Wilson. He added, for good measure, that he still honoured Nazi ideals, respected the party's projects for curing unemployment and believed that Hitler 'has the courage and will to do what he says'.[6]

The Nazi policy, nevertheless, had thrown a massive spanner into a career that had been moving smoothly upwards. Being a Lutheran was of no use if Nazi officialdom could track down

Jewish ancestry. The university, while valuing Pevsner, dared not take the risk of offering assistance; Lola's father, while sympathetic, was stymied by the fact that he himself had a Jewish wife. The Barkases had suggested that they might be able to find a clever young art historian some work in England; Pevsner, having vainly applied to Oxford's newly established Academic Assistance Council on 5 July 1933 for an offer of work 'at any university in the world', received instead a generous £250 stipend towards finding employment in England, the country that he so disliked.

Reluctantly, Pevsner took up the offer. In October, he travelled to England. By December, he was back at Göttingen, ready to make a last attempt at gaining himself a place in the Germany that he profoundly loved, working for a party that he continued to revere. Having written an article about the future of art in a Nazi-governed country, he signed the piece off with an Aryan pseudonym and sent it to a magazine closely linked to Hitler's new regime. Pevsner must have hoped that, following publication, he could disclose his identity and be welcomed back into the halls of German scholarship. This was again naïve. Identifying the true author and fearful of compromising himself, the editor of *Kunst der Nation* declared Pevsner's article to be too long, and sent it back.

A final door had closed.

Nikolaus Pevsner's uneasiness about restarting his career in England was understandable at a time when the history of art was still regarded as a superfluous discipline. The fact that Pevsner favoured modernism at a time when even the calm orderliness of the late Charles Rennie Mackintosh's designs seemed avant garde to British eyes did not improve the German academic's chances of success.

Nevertheless, largely due to the kindly intervention of Pevsner's Quaker friends in Birmingham, an eighteen-month research fellowship was arranged, complete with lodgings, at the city's university. Pevsner, a man who detested cats, cigarettes and – above all – untidiness, was to be given accommodation at the cosy refugee-filled home of Francesca Wilson (a woman who cheerfully pleaded guilty to all three of Pevsner's aversions).

Quiet, merry and completely unfazed by her new lodger's protests about the manner in which she chose to live, Francesca Wilson provided the home – and the company, while Pevsner's family were still out in Germany – that helped a lonely, awkward man to settle down and reconcile himself to making the best of his drab and wretchedly uncultured new homeland. The university fellowship, meanwhile, provided the new exile with the time to write his first and highly significant book, while mastering a language in which, thanks to his usual perseverance (as well as the lightness of his Saxon accent), Pevsner was soon able to pass himself off as a rather comically precise Englishman.

It's a mark of Pevsner's eventual and resolute determination to embrace his new homeland that *Pioneers of the Modern Movement* (1936) was written in English. Swiftly recognised as a formidable – but accessible – work of brilliant scholarship, the book made Pevsner's reputation in England. British critics, gratified by the author's homage to their country's continuing influence on European designers, managed to overlook the fact that Pevsner, always true to his German roots, had chosen for his final architectural example a house that Walter Gropius had created in Germany before the First World War.

Pioneers marked the point at which its author – joined by his family in 1937 – was granted a unique position among England's academic elite. It's possible, had Pevsner not stubbornly continued to visit his beloved Germany right up to the outbreak of war, that he might even have escaped the humiliation of being interned as an alien. As it was, Pevsner spent three uncomfortable months in a camp near Liverpool. Released in 1940 and set to work on bomb clearance and road sweeping, he was appointed the first professor of art history at London's Birkbeck College in 1942.

The transformation of Nikolaus Pevsner into a cornerstone of Britain's cultural establishment continued, after the war, as steadily as the creation of one of those English churches with which his name remains most enduringly linked.[7] His classic work *An Outline of European Architecture* was published in 1942. Naturalised four years later as a British citizen, Pevsner became Slade professor at Cambridge for a record period of six years, and was subsequently – it was a remarkable honour to bestow upon a foreigner – appointed Slade professor at Oxford. Best known for his passionate, idiosyncratic – and, in their comprehensive nature, firmly Germanic – guides to the monuments of England, this most German of patriots also became a founding member (and later chairman) of that most English of organisations: the Victorian Society.

Such a magnificent contribution to England's awareness of her past might seem to be the noblest of the endeavours for which Nikolaus Pevsner was deservingly knighted in 1969. And yet, misguided though his commitment to Nazi Germany appears with hindsight to have been, perhaps it was still more valiant of Pevsner to continue, until the eve of war, to defend the very regime that had deprived him of his livelihood, his academic status and – greatly against his will – his homeland. With nothing to gain (Pevsner's dreams of being appointed as an artistic mediator in the Nazi state were, as he must always have known, hopelessly unrealistic), his fidelity to the Reich and to the leader he sincerely admired seems both foolish and heroic. Pevsner's perverse and wrong-headed loyalty does not disgrace him. He did love Germany. He did believe that Adolf Hitler, perceived by Pevsner as a last bulwark against chaos, was restoring Germany to greatness. He did, long after the time when self-interest could be produced as a justification for his behaviour or his defensive statements, continue to put the welfare of his own beloved homeland before himself.

23

THE YOUNG AMBASSADORS

(1930–39)

Hugh Greene, having spent five years speaking his mind about German politics in the *Daily Telegraph*, might have thought himself lucky to leave the country alive after announcing his intentions of coming back as a Gauleiter. But Greene, for all his forthright statements, never risked more than a brisk attack of local censorship. Antagonising the English did not form a part of the project of the man who had written in *Mein Kampf* that – of all Germany's neighbours – 'the last practicable tie remains with England'.[1] Far from it. Hitler, from his first months in power, had gone out of his way to win England's approval.

In May 1939, when Greene was asked to leave Berlin, the plans outlined so clearly in *Mein Kampf* were well under way; England, while unhappy about the invasion of Czechoslovakia that had taken place two months earlier, still wore a friendly face. Hitler's projections for the bloodless expansion of German territory had worked out as he had expected, and with – so far – remarkably little opposition from abroad or even from within Europe. In March 1936, a small contingent of troops had reclaimed the Rhineland for

Germany; in March 1938, the so-called Anschluss (Union) with
Austria had passed off without difficulty; six months later, England
had approved Germany's occupation of the mountainous north and
west borderlands of Czechoslovakia, known as the Sudetenland and
largely inhabited by ethnic Germans. The Jews, meanwhile, as
promised, had been deprived of citizenship and encouraged to
depart from an expanding Germany. The alternatives (the bloody
orgy of Kristallnacht, a series of linked attacks on Jewish property
and the rounding-up of Jews for brutal imprisonment that mas-
queraded, for the benefit of the press, as repatriation) had also
passed off without too much serious criticism. All, to date, had
gone smoothly, and Hitler could congratulate himself upon having
won as much approval from England as he required for his plans to
continue: Poland was already designated for attack at the end of the
summer.

Mein Kampf had clearly stated how important Hitler believed
it was to win England's trust. He had set about doing so, from
his first year in power, with a double-pronged charm offensive.
Putzi Hanfstaengl, coming from a high social class and speaking
English with only a faint American East Coast twang, was given
the task, as the Führer's liaison officer, of winning the trust of the
British aristocrats whose hands (in one of Hitler's few mistaken
assessments) clasped the reins of political power. Putzi's introduction to Lord Redesdale's beautiful daughter, Diana Guinness,
at a smart London party did not occur by chance; Hitler, a constant visitor to Wahnfried and an admirer of Houston Stewart
Chamberlain, had seen old Lord Redesdale's photograph promi-
nently displayed in Chamberlain's room and on Siegfried
Wagner's desk. He sought an introduction to Redesdale's descendants and – with a helping hand being given to Putzi by the
popular and socially grander Otto von Bismarck at the German
Embassy in London – it was achieved. Unity Mitford's whole-
hearted commitment to extreme politics came as an entirely
unlooked-for bonus.

The second line of attack was launched from the Ministry of Propaganda by Joseph Goebbels.

Today, it may seem perverse that so many British families were prepared to send their impressionable children out to complete their schooling in Germany, a country from which reports were steadily emerging of racial harassment, tyranny and torture. Should blame entirely attach to the well-meaning parents whose folly was primarily to read the wrong papers, and to place their faith in travel agencies as reputable as Thomas Cook's? How could they know that Goebbels was subsidising Cook's brochures, together with a series of advertisements for German tourism that England's most respected travel agency regularly placed in *The Times*? In 1934, at the time of the massacre in Munich, Cook's blandly assured nervous travellers that their own German tour guides to Germany had found 'everything absolutely normal ... great friendliness on all sides'.

Goebbels's team had done their research with care. Readers of Baedeker's 1936 guide to Germany might possibly have gleaned a hint that all was not quite normal in the Reich from the news that cameras were no longer permitted on planes and that travelling without an official escort was inadvisable. But the English middle and upper classes did not read Baedeker. They read *The Times,* and *The Times* was always eager to reassure its readers. In 1939, during a summer when even the least suspicious of English families became aware that something was amiss in the land of the Third Reich, the newspaper published a striking half-page advertisement from the German tourist board. 'Germany! Land of Hospitality!' it announced, before welcoming visitors to the spas of the Sudetenland.

Germany's propaganda programme was assisted by the absence of first-hand, uncensored information in a significant part of the mainline British press. The *Western Mail*, publishing the reports by Gareth Jones, was regional, not major; the *Manchester Guardian*, in which the half-German journalist Frederick Voigt had been speaking out against the Nazi Party since 1930, was perceived as the paper of the left, representing views that were frequently dismissed as Communist. Elsewhere, British journalists went out of their way to calm and reassure, with the press barons Rothermere and Beaverbrook sharing Geoffrey Dawson's eagerness for peace at any cost.

Among the largely rather innocent young people who travelled out to Germany during the rule of the Third Reich, a small number were making an honest endeavour to get behind the headlines and discover just what was going on. Christopher Sidgwick was an intelligent and open-minded teacher who, speaking German and wanting to see for himself what was taking place, set off on a four-month trip in 1934.

Sidgwick's tour of Germany included moments of unexpected comedy: he found it hard to keep a straight face when, having delivered a talk on British foreign policy to a school group of Hitler Youth, he was thanked by a heartfelt rendering of 'Pack up Your Troubles' and 'It's a Long Way to Tipperary'. He was mildly amused (while regretting the predictable absence of Mendelssohn) to find the Saxon King Alfred the Great gazing down at him from a plinth in the Valhalla, Nuremberg's new temple to Teutonism. But Sidgwick was troubled, in 1934, to observe a new autobahn that thrust straight towards the heart of Austria. It dismayed him to find that Bible exams had been banned and that – on the street corner nearest to each city school – only copies of the violently anti-Semitic *Der Stürmer* were on sale, from a newsstand that had often been decorated with the words 'The Jews are our Bad Luck.'

Sidgwick was given pause for thought again when, nearing Dachau, he found the road to the camp blatantly marked out for travellers by a stone post on which, in a circular frieze, uniformed men were depicted cheerily cudgelling Jews. Sidgwick (whose own robust view was that 'the sooner they [the Jews] have control of the world the better') photographed the monument and reproduced it in his book.

Admirably, Sidgwick set out to sound a warning. Having visited Dachau, he reported that the Jewish men to whom he spoke there were evidently 'terrified. They would not speak, they would not say anything . . .' One prisoner with a badly broken leg, when pressed by Sidgwick for an explanation, answered that he had tripped over in a grassy field. The guards' explanation for their detention of the Jews was that they were guilty of 'race defilement'. Quizzed, one of the guards acknowledged that at least four other such camps existed: 'Had they kept secret a lot more? I had no idea.'[2]

Sidgwick, who later married a German travel writer from Düsseldorf, wrote a brave book that went against the mood of the times in Britain. His *German Journey* was massively outsold by young Beverley Nichols's *Cry Havoc!*, a book that called for unilateral disarmament during the year in which Hitler came to power. It was the year during which – confirming the results of an armistice night debate held in 1932 – an Oxford Union audience memorably voted that England should never again go to war, neither for king, nor for country.

Sidgwick was an odd one out in a decade when it became conventional for young men and women to round off their education by spending a couple of months in Germany.

Germany's new category of visitors often arrived straight from home or school. Many of them were only sixteen; few knew or cared anything about politics. Welcomed by a country where the word had gone out that each and every German citizen should act as an ambassador for the Reich, the cheerful schoolgirls and their Etonian counterparts were given a splendid time. Ariel Tennant, whose gentle Uncle Ernest had not forgotten Germany's misery after the war, was among the tiny minority who caught a glimpse of what was happening and tried to speak out when they returned to England. 'It didn't do any good. If I tried to tell people what I'd seen, they just dismissed it. They always said the same thing: "You're too young to understand." They didn't want to hear.'[3]

Ernest Tennant was an enthusiastic supporter and facilitator of his niece's expressed desire, towards the end of 1933, to visit Berlin as an art student. As a bonus, he arranged for Ariel and his sister Nancy (acting as Ariel's chaperone) to dine there with his cherished friends, the Ribbentrops. Aunt Nancy, having been welcomed to Berlin by Putzi Hanfstaengl, explained her dilemma. She did not wish to dine with the Ribbentrops, of whom she had previously formed an unfavourable impression. She did, however, wish to have a few words with Adolf Hitler. Since Nancy spoke excellent German and Ernest Tennant was already doing everything he could for the cause of Anglo-German friendship, a meeting was arranged.

'Aunt Nancy did most of the talking. I was just looking around. The Chancellery was extraordinary. Such a place: you never saw anywhere so gloomy and enormous.' Hitler, having complimented the senior Miss Tennant on her command of his language, announced that he himself knew just four foreign words. In France, he had discovered the meaning of 'Vous êtes mon prisonnier'.

Possibly, the guests from England were being offered a rare example of the legendary humour for which Hitler was later so admired by those laughter-loving Mitford siblings Diana and Unity. More probably, the Führer was eager to spread the news that he had actually used those words in warfare: his prized Class One Iron Cross had been awarded for the single-handed arrest of a group of French soldiers whom he had discovered sheltering in a crater. Ariel was more interested in the expressive way that Hitler made use of his eyes; to her (as she later remembered it), the man she saw at the Chancellery seemed more like a charismatic actor than a leader to whom the German nation could safely entrust its future destiny.

Ariel's main companion during her first weeks in Munich was her younger cousin, Derek Hill; it was with mixed feelings that she learned that Derek's close friends, the Mitfords, were planning to pay a visit to Germany. Ariel Tennant had only met the Mitford family once, at their London home in Rutland Gate, and she was in no hurry to repeat the experience. 'Oh! That visit! It was awful!

The sisters all shouted at once and their mother looked desperate and went off into another room and played 'Tea for Two', but over and over again, on the piano. They weren't at all nice to me. I remember bursting into tears and wanting to go home. But Derek adored them.'[4]

Taken to the station in Munich to meet her cousin's friends as they got off the train, Ariel's first impression was of how heavily made-up Unity and Diana looked in comparison to all the fresh-faced German girls. 'Although Diana did look so beautiful. She was laughing and saying what bliss it was to be out of England with no nanny, no children and no husband in tow.' (In 1934, Diana was still married to Bryan Guinness, although entirely preoccupied by Oswald Mosley.) Unity, while startlingly tall and muscular in build, seemed the less formidable of the two sisters.

Ariel Tennant's account of the peculiar friendship that she formed with Unity in Munich is both touching and bizarre. Having already met Hitler herself, she found Unity's obsession with the man quite baffling.

> She really couldn't believe it when Derek told her that anyone could see Hitler and his bodyguards any time, just by dropping in at the Carlton Hotel on a Sunday afternoon. He put himself on show there, for the English. Our families all liked the Carlton. Unity was having tea there with Derek when she got the famous invitation to be introduced – and that was that. She rushed across the room and she never came back. Derek was quite upset at the time. But Unity was always a bit strange.

Unity's passion, from the point of that first encounter, became hard for her friends to handle. Strolling beside Ariel along the broad, sandy paths of Munich's English Garden, she would seize her slight companion by the arm ('and twist it, so it really hurt'), to make her say that she, too, was a worshipper. 'But it was much worse when we went to Austria.'

Unaffected, as foreigners, by the £40 surcharge imposed on Germans who needed to travel to that threatened country in the period when Austria's President Dollfuss (who would be assassinated in July) was resisting Nazification, the two English girls went off to visit a castle near Vienna.[5] Here, to Ariel's dismay, Unity announced (after they'd climbed onto the castle's roof) that she could hear the voices of imprisoned Nazis calling to them from deep within, far down below. 'So she lay flat down on the roof-leads and started singing the Horst Wessel Lied through a grating in the roof, but terribly loudly, and over and over. And she was so angry because I wouldn't believe in the prisoners. Everybody had to agree with Unity. It was terribly exhausting!'

While the bizarre figure of Unity Mitford overshadows Ariel Tennant's memories of Munich in 1934, she does offer two other striking recollections. One is of a woodland hike that she took with Derek Hill and of how they came, by chance, upon a secret army of young boys. 'All marching, and all with rifles on their shoulders. Some can't have been more than eleven. We felt sure that we'd stumbled on something we weren't meant to know about. And we were right!' Ariel also recalls the day in 1934 when she joined three young men who were making an investigative trip (one was a journalist) to Dachau. 'But they wouldn't let women go in. I sat in the entrance hall and waited, right under a sign saying that escapees would be shot on sight. I couldn't hear anything. I do remember that. There was a quiet that felt wrong.'

Later, on their way back to Munich, asking her companions for their impressions, Ariel found that while one was horrified, and another – the journalist – expressed his concern, the third of her companions took the line that whatever was happening at Dachau was nothing to do with them, and best forgotten at once.

'And that's how it was, when I came back to England,' Ariel reiterates, as if repetition could somehow alter the past. 'I did try to talk about the things I'd seen. But people simply didn't want to hear.'[6]

Today, at the age of ninety, my mother still possesses a clear memory of the dress she wore on her way out to Munich in August 1934. It was made of thin, cherry-coloured wool, with a white collar. 'And I had a beautiful new coat made of grey silk tussore.'

Rosemary Scott-Ellis, aged eleven, was on her way to attend the wedding of her brother, John, who was finally marrying, after a three-year engagement, Irene, the youngest of the five Harrach sisters. The Scott-Ellis family, with the exception of John's twin, who was nursing a baby, had all travelled out to Germany. My family still have photographs of the wedding group, gathered on the front steps of the Harrachs' long, low house on Biedersteiner Strasse; in the images that show them gathered around a big dining table in the hall, the absence of swastikas and peaked caps is instantly noticeable. 'Well, there was one. That man called Haupt Pappenheim who took John out driving. He turned up in a Nazi uniform. The Harrachs didn't seem very pleased.'[7]

Before my mother can deflect the conversation into telling me how hard it was for a small bridesmaid to carry a huge sheaf of gladioli in her arms, I ask if she has any historical recollections. This was, after all, Munich, just one month after the killing of Ernst Röhm and the Schleichers. Trying to help, she mentions visiting a museum.

> There was a tremendous din going on outside. When I looked out of a window, there were men in uniform marching everywhere. The din was the sound of their heels clacking across the cobbles. And there were big megaphones strapped to lamp-posts and the sides of buildings. They'd suddenly start up with that awful sound and everybody was supposed to stand and listen, whatever they were doing. I suppose it was Hitler giving one of his speeches.

Pressed to remember something – anything – more about a Munich that must still have been in the grip of terror after the June massacre, my mother looks confused. A massacre? There were the megaphones and the marching soldiers, but she heard no screams from cellars or shuttered rooms. She saw no bloodshed, witnessed no murders. All was in order. Nothing untoward was exposed to view. She wants to tell me, instead, about making friends with two of the little blond-haired page boys.

The Harrachs, like many of their friends, had discovered that escorting young English visitors around the city of Munich, while providing them with a home in which they could hone their language skills, was a useful way to raise funds in stringent times. In January 1934, the year of my Uncle John's wedding, Irene Harrach's sister 'Cucca' was acting as a hostess and cultural chaperone to two English girls, Rosaline James and Penelope Mills. Just down the road, Dorothy Gage was settling into a large, airy flat filled with Biedermeier furniture and owned by the Harrachs' artistic friend and neighbour in the Schwabing district of Munich, Anna Montgelas.[8]

A sociable young creature, Dorothy's diary for 1934 presents a teeming thicket of appointments to be kept with her new chums from England: two Yarde-Buller sisters; Ursula Strutt; Daphne Quilter, Henry Wyndham; David Russell* and – staying at the Montgelas flat – David's tweedily conventional but extremely beautiful younger sister, Barbara.

Dorothy was the kind of young ambassador that could only have been dreamed about by Hitler. She enjoyed everything in Germany and thought everybody there was wonderful. She went dancing at the Apache nightclub; she went skiing in the Alps; she

---

* David Russell, moving in a slightly older and more sophisticated group, later made his name as one of the audacious unit who broke into Tobruk by impersonating German guards.

even attended a tea at the Carlton that had been arranged by the staunchly pro-Nazi Countess Montgelas. ('We saw Hitler,' reported an excited Dorothy. 'Hurrah!')[8] Dorothy also – again thanks to the good connections of a hostess who made her girls curtsey to Hitler's portrait – attended one of the Führer's speeches ('Excellent seats'). Between studying German and watching several impressive ceremonies of Nazi oath-taking, Dorothy managed to work in the *Ring Cycle* ('too lovely') and Strauss's sophisticated domestic comedy *Intermezzo* ('very boring').

Away from the home indoctrination being practised by Anna Montgelas, Dorothy enjoyed vigorous sessions of 'ragging' with David Russell and Henry Wyndham ('Absolute gentlemen ... one can always trust them'). Sometimes, Cucca Harrach, who liked Anna better than her politics, sent her own young English charges along to join Dorothy for supper and the cinema. Watching the unblushingly propagandist film *Hans Westmar* (based upon the life of Horst Wessel, it opened with the emblem of a gigantic torch-flanked swastika), Dorothy got the point. The film about 'Hans Wessell [sic]' had been 'excellent'.

Dorothy Gage's diary is a guileless private document, a record of unblemished good cheer. 'This is a lovely way of living,' she wrote during her time in Munich, and, more joyfully still, during her skiing visit to Anna's second home in the Bavarian Alps: 'Perfectly glorious day and marvellous time. Oh what a good time I'm having.'

Living in Munich in 1934, a young English girl could remain untouched by trauma, unscathed by the evidence that anything might be amiss in this disciplined and glittering world. Elsewhere, the youthful visitors from England sensed that, while every endeavour was being made to offer them a pleasant experience, life in Nazi Germany was perhaps a little less straightforward than it initially appeared.

April Austen-Hall was the granddaughter of Edward Ritter, the

German director of Deutsche Bank's London branch during the First War. 'The English locked him *out* when the War started, because he was a German, and then, when he went to Holland to try to salvage some of his clients' funds, the Dutch locked him *in* as an intern and left my poor English grandmother stranded on her own in London. She was the one who brought me up. My mother died when I was only nine.'[9]

In 1933, when April was sixteen years old, her widowed father married again. His new wife was a Bavarian aristocrat whose family ran their castle-home, Marquartstein, as a private school.* 'My stepmother thought I was under-educated, so I was sent out to Marquartstein. You wouldn't believe how cold it was! The windows were always open and we had to run around the walls before breakfast every morning, even in the snow. The ink used to freeze up like a black worm inside my fountain pen.'

April ('Prilly') owns a Marquartstein album, filled with pictures of her former schoolfriends. Some wear the uniform of the Hitler Youth; Prilly herself wore the armband for the Bund Deutscher Mädel. It was, she says defensively, like being a Girl Guide. 'It made me feel that I could help people.'

Asked about signs of unrest, Prilly Crowther (née Austen-Hall) mentions the sound of shooting in the mountains at night, and the sudden disappearance of a cobbler from the local village. All newspapers were stopped during June 1934. No word reached the school about the massacre in Munich until Prilly's anxious father telephoned from London. He had read Hugh Greene's report of the killings in the *Daily Telegraph* and was understandably apprehensive about the safety of his daughter.

The names of two of Prilly's schoolmates suggest that they could have been Jewish. They were. The headmaster, officially a Nazi, made a point of taking the two girls with him to Stockholm when

---

* The school was founded by Hermann Harless, who had worked with A. S. Neill at Hellerau, at a precursor of Neill's English school, Summerhill.

they had to sit their exams. Both got high marks. In Germany, Prilly explains, that kind of marking would not have been possible for Jewish schoolgirls.

Asked what she thought about the Nazi regime under which she once received part of her education, Prilly is ambivalent. Grim stories were told by Ernst, one of her favourite schoolmates at Marquartstein, about the bleak years when his mother sent her small children out scavenging for discarded cabbage stalks under the market stalls. Some families seemed to think that Hitler was doing good for Germany. Ernst's mother did.

Asked if she kept up with Ernst and his friends after the war, April Crowther answers that they were all killed on the Russian front and that, because of the attitude of her own husband, an army doctor ('he was away in the war for four whole years, which was quite hard on us both'), all remaining contact with her German friends had to be severed. The friendships were lost. Only the album, showing page after page of laughing sixteen-year-olds, preserves them.

Photograph albums, letters and diaries offer a more honest picture of how the young visitors from England reacted to Germany at the time than the recollections they dutifully summon up in old age. Visiting friends in Rothberg during the summer of 1934, two stalwart country girls (photographs show them posing in baggy knickerbockers amid a waving sea of swastika-emblazoned pennants) wrote home to their family about the good that Hitler was doing for his German people. Whether saluting a parade of 20,000 flags at Nuremberg ('I can tell you my arm ached!') or admiring the handsome cavalry officer who arrived to tell the people of Rothberg to cast their 'free' vote for Hitler as president, Betsy and Dorothy Innes-Smith were enthralled. Bayreuth was disappointing, but Hitler never let a young fan from England down.

'There appear to be two Gods in Germany,' Dorothy wrote after her return to England. 'One is Hitler and the other is Work . . .

Germany has been very low and Hitler has been raised up and is preaching a New Germany: "Deutschland Erwacht" [Germany awakes] is on all their standards and this spirit is in almost every man, woman, and child.'[10]

Harold Atcherley was eighteen in 1935, the year he went out from England to stay with a family of Jewish academics, the Demuths, while he studied at Heidelberg. Jews were already being viciously targeted: the marriage of the Demuths' daughter to an Aryan had cost the university-educated young spouse his job and reduced him to stuffing sausage skins in a factory.[11]

Back for the following year of his studies, Atcherley discovered that the Demuths' pretty house had been boarded up. The whole family had disappeared; nobody could tell him what had happened. At the university, a new course was being taught: 'Die Judenfrage' (the Jewish Question). Attendance was required; heckling was strictly forbidden.

Atcherley describes the week in which the venerable university celebrated its 550th anniversary with glossy parades and various political grandees arriving to deliver speeches from a swastika-draped grandstand. One of Atcherley's friends, Bob Montgomery, decided to put on a show of British patriotism by hanging a Union Jack out of a window, floating high above a sea of Nazi pennants. 'Right opposite the grandstand! They couldn't have missed it, but nobody complained.' As Atcherley points out, a young student from England could be as bold as brass in his defiance and get away with it scot-free. No such freedom existed any longer for the youth of Germany. 'It was dreadfully unjust.'

In 1936, while Atcherley continued his studies at Heidelberg, sixteen-year-old Daphne Brock was living in Dresden with a discreetly anti-Nazi family called de Haucq. Each morning, Daphne studied German literature at the home of a Jewish professor ('small, frail, wonderfully dressed') until one day, when he disappeared.

Another teacher was found. Weeks later, an unsigned postcard from Switzerland discreetly allowed Daphne to know that her former tutor was safe.

Hitler was never mentioned in the de Haucqs' house. Daphne's knowledge of him was expanded when she allowed a handsome young admirer called Guscha von Wedel to take her along to one of the Nuremberg rallies. 'Guscha said it would be good for me to understand the effect that Hitler had. The crowds were enormous and Hitler was high up on a podium, shrieking gibberish.'[12] Daphne points out that her own German was already fluent, 'But I couldn't make out a word that Hitler said. The people around us all had their arms up and they were screaming and screaming. Guscha just watched me. I wondered, afterwards, what he thought of it all. He wouldn't say. It wasn't safe to say what you thought, not then.'

Later, shortly before the war, Guscha von Wedel visited Daphne's family in England. 'My parents liked Guscha a lot. He was highly intelligent, and very worried. He and my father spent a lot of time talking about Europe together. The Swiss Red Cross sent me a message after he was killed at Stalingrad. Poor Guscha.'

Persecution of the Jews had become more overt by the time that seventeen-year-old Elizabeth Lowry-Corry, a pretty girl with brown hair and light blue eyes, went out to study music at Dresden in 1938. Her hosts, the Riphahns, occupied a small flat near the Frauenkirche; in 1938, they were making plans to leave Germany. 'Having me to stay brought in a little extra money. They weren't at all well off. Frau Riphahn did all the cooking and cleaning herself.'[13]

Walking around Dresden, Elizabeth often saw and spoke to Jews with the yellow stars sewn on their clothes. 'I was English, so I could do as I liked. The Dresden people had to keep away from them. Somebody was always watching.'

Twice every week, Elizabeth would go on her own to attend the great Semper opera house, where Herr Riphahn ('a charming man in his forties with a little beard and such a kind laugh') was a member of the orchestra in which the first cellist was remarkable for the expressiveness of his playing. The Riphahns told her that the cellist had been ordered to divorce his Jewish wife or to stop playing in public. The cellist chose the orchestra. 'But then he fell in love with another Jewish girl, so he lost his contract anyway. The Riphahns had a lot of Jewish friends. It was so hard for them not to be able to do anything to help. At night, I'd hear Frau Riphahn crying and crying in her room.'

Elizabeth still owns the exquisite dancing figures and the lovely butterfly vase that Frau Riphahn encouraged her to buy during a visit to Meissen. 'Mostly, the factory was churning out busts of Hitler, but they still made the beautiful old things on the side.'

When Elizabeth left Dresden, the Riphahns were saving hard for their escape. They never succeeded. The whole family, the parents and their four children, died in the firestorm of bombs dropped by Britain. For herself, Elizabeth Lowry-Corry has no wish to return to the carefully restored post-war city. 'I loved my days in Dresden far too much,' she says. 'It was the happiest time I ever knew.'

Such an enduring and deep love for Dresden does not suggest that Elizabeth brought back hostile reports of her stay in Germany. Few did, even in 1938. Young Ronald Barker, transferred from his first Bavarian lodging to stay more happily with a headmaster, Herr Mayr, who disliked Jews and approved of Hitler, was more struck by the fact that the Mayr family took their baths in a tub in the cellar than by the regular visits to their home from two young nephews of Hermann Goering. Invited to produce drawings of Hitler for a local club, Barker readily complied with the request.

It's difficult to piece together what made Ronald Barker's initial experience in Germany so unhappy, but a story of going out alone – from his lodging – on a lake, heavily muffled in a coat, and then capsizing, has something about it that discourages further interrogation. He speaks with much more readiness about the

Mayr household, although not enough – for an inquisitive author's taste – about the visits of Goering's nephews.* Instead, Barker talks about the evenings when 'we boys' used to drive up into the mountains in an old T Ford and Herr Mayr's Mercedes. 'They showed me how to do mating calls to the stags on conch shells. After a bit, you'd hear the females roaring back. And, sometimes, we played a game with model soldiers, planting them out like an army on the mountainside in the snow.' It was, Barker says, a wonderful time in his life. 'I still go back whenever I can,' he declares. 'I loved Bavaria.'[14]

Young men and women like Prilly Crowther, Ariel Tennant and Ronald Barker came to Germany with an agenda that did not stretch far beyond having a good time. Robert Byron, a pug-faced young travel writer who had already established a brilliant reputation with *The Road to Oxiana*, came to Germany with a broken heart (the love of his life had died the previous year of Hodgkin's disease) and a stern desire 'to see the enemy for myself'.[15]

Opposed to dictatorships ever since he was sent down from Oxford and began a life of adventurous travel, Robert Byron had been disgusted by the tameness of England's response both to Hitler's invasion of the Rhineland and to the Austrian Anschluss. Arriving in Germany in early September 1938, Byron began his investigations by attending (on a pass that had been intended for his friend Tom Mitford) a Nuremberg rally, in the company of Unity and her parents. The enthusiasm of the Mitfords was heartfelt; to Byron, the occasion was redolent with evil.

Byron was still at Nuremberg when, writing in *The Times* of 7 September, the paper's deputy editor, Robert Barrington-Ward, published a leader article that warned Czechoslovakia not to oppose Hitler's planned invasion of the neighbouring Sudetenland. The

---

* Goering's nephews did not necessarily share their uncle's political beliefs. The Goerings, like the Schulenburgs, were a politically divided family.

Czechs were told – in the curt paraphrase Byron made in his diary the following day – to give up 'before it is too late'.[16]

It was articles of this appeasing nature that confirmed the impression in Germany that England would let her do as she pleased in Europe. At Nuremberg, the article was read aloud and praised. Speaking at an occasion where several journalists, including Byron, were present, Dr Karl Silex, the influential editor of the *Deutsche Allgemeine Zeitung*, cited the *Times* piece as evidence that Britain had adopted a sensible policy of non-intervention. For Byron, Silex had gone too far. 'I saw a red flush rising on Robert's neck,' wrote his fellow guest Virginia Cowles, an American journalist working for the *Sunday Times*.

> The next moment I heard him saying in a deadly voice: 'What happens on the continent is always England's concern. Every now and then we are unfortunate enough to be led by a Chamberlain – but that's only temporary. Don't be misguided. In the end we always rise up and oppose the tyrannies that threaten Europe. We have smashed them before, and I warn you we will smash them again.'[17]

Byron's defiance, while worthy of his namesake's reputation as a champion of liberty, was ineffectual. Three weeks later, Neville Chamberlain signed the Munich Agreement, approving Germany's invasion of the Sudetenland and obtaining, in return, the precious pledge by which Hitler solemnly agreed that their two nations had not the slightest reason ever to wish to go to war against each other again.

Peace pledges did not impress Byron. The dishonesty of the arrangements jarred with the sense of belonging to an England that had decided to celebrate Munich as the greatest achievement of Chamberlain's career.* On the day projected for Germany's taking

---

* The *Guardian*, however, followed the *New York Times* in criticising the pact and expressing considerable cynicism about Hitler's latest pledge of peace.

of the Sudetenland, a heated Byron rounded on a dinner party of friends and silenced their chatter with the demand: 'Are you proud to be English tonight?'[18]

Three months later, Byron returned to Germany, staying at the light-filled new Berlin home of his sister, Lucy Butler, whose husband was working as a foreign correspondent for *The Times*. A month after the November horrors of Kristallnacht, Byron went to an exhibition at the Reichstag. It was called 'The Wandering Jew'.

Already staged in Munich and on its way to Vienna, the exhibition was mandatory viewing for Berlin school children. Over the door, a gigantic poster showed a heavily built and straggling-bearded Orthodox Jew with one hand extended to beg and the other clenched into a fist that brandished a whip. Inside, in over twenty rooms, the walls offered crookedly hung images (accompanied by derisive descriptions) of such illustrious figures as Heinrich Heine, Felix Mendelssohn, Albert Einstein and the murdered Walter Rathenau.

The show sickened Byron. In Soviet Russia, he had been horrified by museums that were devoted to the mockery of religion, but this, as he pointed out to his sympathetic sister, was far worse: 'an anti-Jew exhibition is an attack on humanity itself . . . Has any people ever sunk so low?'[19]

Resistance was the only answer, in Byron's view. Back in London, however, he found himself dismissed as a warmonger and a troublemaker: a man out of tune with his peace-loving times.

Byron had signed up as a war correspondent when the boat on which he was travelling towards Alexandria was torpedoed on 24 February 1941. Robert Byron, when he drowned, was two days short of thirty-six, the age at which his famous namesake died at Missolonghi.

24

AND THEN, THERE WAS ROMANCE

(1930–39)

It was inevitable that love would play a role in the lives of some of Germany's impressionable young visitors – and that it would be tested when love could come to appear as an act of support to an abhorrent regime.

For the powerful and ambitious mother of Dick Seaman, one of Britain's finest young inter-war racing drivers, the news that her son intended to marry Erica Popp, the glamorous German daughter of the Nazi manager of BMW, came as a galling surprise.

Born into great wealth in the England of 1916, Seaman had been recruited to join the Mercedes team in 1936, following his outstanding victory that year on the celebrated course at Donington Park. (In the motor world, it was the big race at Donington the following year that would send out the signal, through the victory of Bernd Rosemeyer in an Auto-Union machine, of how thoroughly Germany was outstripping the technology of her European neighbours.)

Not everybody relished Seaman's defection to the German Mercedes team (his recently widowed mother had hidden their original telegram of invitation to her son) or the fact that, winning his first major victory for his adopted country in 1938, the British driver offered two Heil Hitler salutes from the podium. Lauded to the skies in Germany, where the girls from his local village garlanded the handsome young Englishman with wreaths of oak leaves and the German press paid tribute to his nerveless driving, Seaman's engagement to Erica Popp crowned his commitment to a nation to the regime of which his own mother remained fiercely opposed. When Seaman rashly wrote home to praise Hitler's efficiency in dealing with any form of opposition, Lillian Seaman responded with a withering tribute to the fine handling of the helpless and the weak by that same Führer whom he so admired.

Mrs Seaman relented enough to attend her son's marriage when it took place in December 1938, at Caxton Hall. Nevertheless, her disapproval had sown a seed of doubt. Five months later, Seaman asked his fellow racing driver Earl Howe about the possibility of coming home to England. Howe, responding on 5 May 1939, was against any such idea: 'stick with it . . . far better retain every individual contact with Germany in every shape and form'.[1]

The following month, while driving a Mercedes Silver Arrow at the Belgian Grand Prix in heavy rain, Dick Seaman crashed into a tree when he skidded on a sharp corner. Trapped in his blazing car, he was finally rescued and rushed to hospital, suffering from severe burns. Rather nobly, Seaman still managed to take full responsibility for the accident, apologising to his German manager for having let the team down. He died shortly afterwards. In Germany, Hitler sent a large personal wreath to the funeral. In England, the *Daily Telegraph* accorded just two short paragraphs to one of the finest British drivers of his era. Seaman was only 26. Mercedes still, to this day, take care of their English driver's grave in Putney Vale.

Delphine Reynolds was a characterful young woman (one portrait represents her grasping a whip) who had been given a part of

Croydon Airport in 1928, along with a Gypsy Moth biplane. Delphine, who took an airship tour over the site of the 1936 Olympic Games with the son of the celebrated Count Zeppelin, had been cutting her annual swathe through the susceptible schloss owners of Bavaria in the summer of 1939 when, back from frolicking around the glorious Czechoslovakian home of Count Kinsky, she was spotted by the British Ambassador tripping onto the floor at a ball in Berlin. The gala event was being held during the last torrid week of August; Nevile Henderson, taking the exuberant Delphine aside, brusquely ordered Miss Reynolds to pack her bags and take the next train back to England.[2]

Henderson's orders came just in time to prevent Delphine from joining the contingent of English women who, by virtue of their marriages to Germans, or ill-timed tourist visits, would find themselves living in a state of virtual imprisonment for the duration of the war.

Lady Camilla Acheson, the nineteen-year-old daughter of an Irish earl, had received a European education that culminated with six months at Neue Bern, a school run by a German aristocrat at her Bavarian family home. Staying at the schloss, and lending its owners a helping hand through the summer term of 1936, was a handsome former pupil, Christoph von Stauffenberg. Cast as Celia in a summer production of *As You Like It*, pretty Camilla found herself acting opposite Christoph's Oliver de Bois – and fell in love. Her mother, concerned by the fact that the dashing Stauffenberg was six years older than Camilla, a German and – graver still – a Catholic, promptly flew out to Munich and delighted Camilla's impoverished hostess by renting out half of the schloss while she took stock of the suitor. Apparently, Christoph passed muster. The couple were married, back in London, at Brompton Oratory, in 1937. By 1939, however, they had returned to Germany. Camilla, following the outbreak of war, found herself in the unhappy situation of Daisy Pless, back in 1914: a German's wife, she had become an enemy alien, trapped in a foreign land, and allowed no contact with her anxious British family.

Christoph von Stauffenberg, no fan of the Nazi regime, looked for work that would allow him to pass as a good German citizen without having to kill Camilla's countrymen. He signed up, but only as a reader of the English newspapers for the supposedly useful military information that – as Stauffenberg was cynically aware – would never appear in print.[3] Camilla, meanwhile, was able to learn of all the news at home, while escaping the very real risk of being treated as a spy. To read English newspapers in wartime Germany without specific permission was an act of treason, even for a foreign subject.

Margaret Geddes, a young Scotswoman who was known to one and all as 'Peg', travelled out to Germany towards the end of 1935 in order to join two beloved brothers at a pension in Bavaria. Unknown to Peg, a little advance plotting had been going on. Waiting to meet her at the local station in the place of her brothers and all ready to conduct her to Haus Hirth was a dark-haired and extremely good-looking young German. His name was Ludwig ('Lu') and he was the music-loving second son of Grand Duke Ernst of Hessen-Darmstadt.

The Grand Duke's connection to Haus Hirth went back a long way. Georg Hirth, whose widow, Johanna, now ran the pension adjacent to their family home at Grainau, was the publisher of *Jugend*, the influential magazine from which the Jugendstil movement took its name. Grand Duke Ernst had been *Jugend*'s chief sponsor and his family had remained close to Hirth's widow. (George Donatus, Lu's older brother, married to Princess Cecile of Greece, had just chosen the name Johanna for their newborn daughter.)

A cheerful, high-spirited and openhearted young woman, Margaret Geddes found herself instantly at home in the carefree atmosphere of a timber-framed house filled with art treasures and mementoes of earlier guests. Rex Whistler had stayed there with the Sitwells and William Walton; Johanna Hirth also spoke warmly of Helen Keller, whose discreet and sometimes lengthy visits to Haus Hirth were never mentioned in Keller's published work.

While Peg's younger brother, David, went off on cultural trips around the Bavarian towns with the prank-loving young Nazi owner of a beautiful nearby castle, Peg spent most of her time with Lu. The result, since Prince Ludwig came from a family who had always used English as their preferred language, was that Peg's German grammar progressed less well than did her romance with a kind, sensitive and humorous young man.[4]

Prince Ludwig had already spent a short time working as a junior official at the Büro Ribbentrop in Berlin. Seeking reasons to be near his beloved Peg, he arrived in London in October 1936 as one of the young attachés who were meant to help smooth the path of his former boss, a somewhat gauche new envoy to the Court of St James's. Lodged in an annex to the Embassy in Carlton House Terrace, Lu, Baron Dörnberg, Erich Kordt and Reinhard Spitzy were offered a first-hand view of a revamp to the old de Bunsen home that included marble cladding throughout, the installation of eighty-two telephones and the relegation of all domestic staff to the basement. The Ribbentrops, meanwhile, finding the noise of marble-cutting got on their nerves, decamped to a smart Eaton Square apartment that had been loaned to them by Neville Chamberlain.*

The stories of social ineptitude displayed during the brief sojourn in London of 'Herr Brickendrop' (Maurice Baring's nickname for the hapless Ambassador) are legion. Most focus upon Ribbentrop's compliance with Hitler's firm instructions to deliver

---

* Ribbentrop's Anglophile predecessor, Dr Leopold von Hoesch, had died in office, in sudden and faintly suspicious circumstances. His swastika-adorned coffin was paraded down the Mall and hailed from the Embassy's garden terrace with a fusillade of rifle-straight outstretched arms. A modest memorial tablet to Hoesch's dog ('Giro: A faithful companion') survives in a small fenced-off area beside the former Embassy.

the Nazi salute upon all occasions, whether standing in Durham Cathedral as the guest of the astonished Londonderrys, or while offering his formal respects to England's new king, George VI. Reinhard Spitzy's memoirs describe how the young German attachés collapsed in giggles during the heil that was delivered at Buckingham Palace; Ribbentrop, a man who craved social acceptance and now found himself mocked, grew ashamed and sullen. Taking refuge in prolonged baths and capricious departures to the cinema when he was meant to be attending semi-official dinners, he became – which was unfortunate in an ambassador – increasingly hostile to the English hosts whose occasional inquiries about his past life as a wine merchant (Ribbentrop had married a Champagne heiress in 1920 and worked for her family company while purchasing a 'von' title to improve his status) did nothing to improve relations.

Lavish financial support from Berlin provided a degree of compensation. Nobody in the German government had been especially pleased, in the bright summer of 1937, when George VI was crowned king, following the abdication of his older – and very proGerman – brother Edward. Reinhard Spitzy gazed down from the front windows of the Embassy upon the regal celebrations in the Mall: 'a sea of colours, gold, magnificence and splendour'. But only Ribbentrop could boast that he had managed to charter a private plane from Berlin to bring over a cargo consisting entirely of Champagne and caviare.[5]

Sir Auckland Geddes – belonging to the generation of those who lost close family in the war – had begun as a stern opponent of his only daughter's alliance to a Hun. Lu's considerable charm and Peg's evident happiness combined to prevail; in the summer of 1937, Geddes gave the alliance his grudging consent. Plans for an October wedding were deferred, but only out of respect for the death that month of Prince Lu's father, the old Grand Duke. (Buried out at Wolfsgarten beside the grave of his beloved first child, Elizabeth, Hessen-Darmstadt's gentle ruler would have been less happy with Hitler's command that his coffin should be carried through Darmstadt by a phalanx of steel-helmeted soldiers.) The London ceremony was hastily rescheduled for 20 November; Peg, still enchanted by her memories of Haus Hirth, made plans to wear a traditional wedding costume from Bavaria.

The Prince's forthcoming marriage to a woman of British birth was cause for rejoicing in a family that took pride in its close connection to Queen Victoria. Plans were made for Lu's widowed mother and his brother's whole family to come across to London four days before the ceremony. All was carefully arranged: Eleonore (the widowed Grand Duchess) was to stay with her late husband's sister, Victoria Milford Haven, while George Donatus and his family lodged with the Mountbattens on Park Lane. All promised to be both very grand and very cosy.

On 16 November, having been driven down to Croydon Airport by the chauffeur of a solicitous Lord Mountbatten, Lu and Peg started to scan grey skies for a Sabena, scheduled to be coming in soon from Belgium. Bad weather, apparently, had caused a delay. A few minutes later, the manager of Imperial Airways brought them devastating news. Attempting to make a stopover on the flight from Belgium, the royal pilot had struggled to land his craft in dense fog. A wingtip had nicked the edge of a tall factory chimney. Tipped, crashing against the structure, the plane went down in flames. Lu, transformed within a few stark seconds into the new Grand Duke of Hessen-Darmstadt, had lost his entire family, including the eight-month unborn baby of his beloved sister-in-law, Cecile. Only little Johanna had escaped, having been left behind with her nurse because she was considered too young to take along. Lu and Peg found one grain of comfort in taking an instantaneous decision to bring up Johanna as their own beloved daughter.

The wedding was immediately brought forward. Dressed in deep mourning, the desolate young couple were married at daybreak on the day after the crash, enabling them to fly straight out

Hardy Amies skiing with friends in Bavaria in 1929. A friend once said that Hardy was such a serious social climber that he took his alpenstock to parties.

Hardy and his friend Kenneth Partridge had a splendid time in Berlin in 1930. Partridge later recalled that their companions were 'not very hygienic.'

John Scott-Ellis marries Irene Harrach in Munich in the summer of 1934. The parents of the groom stand centre back left, beside the parents of the bride. The author's mother, John's sister, sits second right, bottom row.

When John Scott-Ellis travelled to Munich in 1931, he fell in love with Irene ('Nucci') Harrach, one of five sisters.

The pool in the Harrach garden where young John and his friend Oswald Mulgrave played a prank on the Harrachs. The statue was made by Count Harrach, a sculptor.

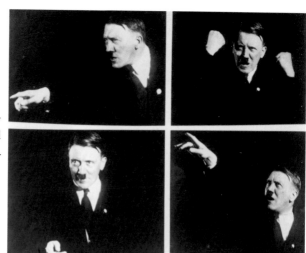

Images which indicate how meticulously Hitler rehearsed his performances.

The Grand Duke Ernest's son, Prince 'Lu' of Hesse, an ardent anglophile and music lover, at the time of his engagement to 'Peg' Geddes.

A happy Tisa Schulenburg at work in the garden at Warbleswick, Suffolk, where she and Fritz Hess lived in 1936.

An unhappy Theo Kordt looks on while Neville Chamberlain makes his celebrated announcement of 'peace for our time'.

A self-aware Philip Lothian poses with an open copy of *Mein Kampf*, which he read for the first time shortly before the war.

Lord Lothian's close friend – they were together in Paris during the Treaty of Versailles – Robert Brand. Praised as 'the wisest man in the Empire', Bob Brand married Nancy Astor's sister, Phyllis Langhorne.

An exhausted and grim-faced Adam von Trott on trial for his life after the 20 July plot in 1944.

Sir Robert Vansittart delivers his revised opinion of the German Resistance in a recording of *Black Record: Germans Past and Present* (1941).

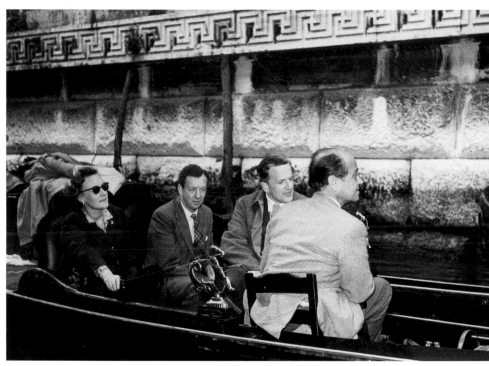

The Prince and Princess of Hesse in Venice with their close friends
Benjamin Britten and Peter Pears.

Hansel Pless and the beloved Green Steed on which he courted his second, british-born, wife Mary.

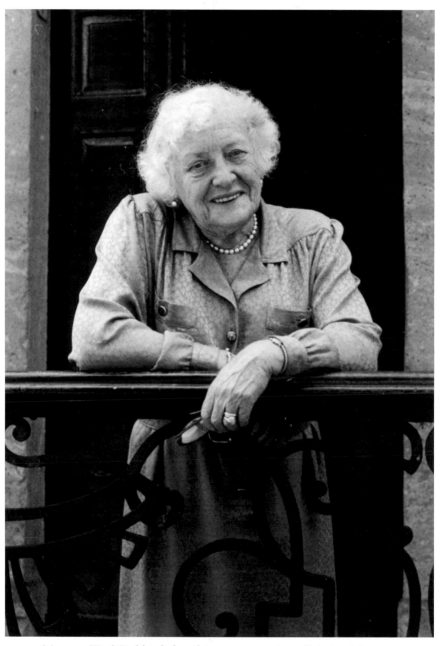

Margaret 'Peg' Geddes, beloved in two countries as Princess Margaret
of Hesse and the Rhine.

to Darmstadt for a mass funeral. Lu – thin, forlorn and white as a ghost in his new role as head of the family – led the sad procession through the streets. Following him (the only other male member of the family to wear a plain black coat instead of a Nazi uniform) was Cecile's young brother: Prince Philip of Greece, England's future Duke of Edinburgh.

Settling into their new life as the rulers of Hessen-Darmstadt, Lu and Peg suffered an additional blow in 1939, when Johanna, their adopted child, died after contracting meningitis. Although devoted to young people, the couple never had children of their own.

Shiela Grant Duff would end by marrying Michael Sokolov, one of Nikolaus Pevsner's fellow lodgers at Francesca Wilson's Birmingham refuge for exiles. But Shiela became far better known for an intense friendship – it began at Oxford in 1931 – that she formed with Adam von Trott.

Born in 1913, Shiela was only a year old when her father died leading his British regiment into battle in the war during which two of her uncles were also killed. Brought up, not surprisingly, to view war as the greatest of evils, Shiela reached Oxford at the time when the mood of the university favoured peace and reconciliation. The German Rhodes Scholarships, brought to a halt in 1914, had just been reinstated. Philip Lothian, as secretary of the Rhodes Committee since 1925, had pushed hard for their restoration; Albrecht von Bernstorff – enormous, jovial and well loved in both countries – acted as the principal advisor, having himself been a pre-war scholar.

Among the first candidates that Bernstorff picked out was a young aristocrat who had already experienced a little of Oxford life, having taken a term out from his studies at Göttingen in 1929 and fallen in love with England, the country of which he had been hearing all his life. His full name was Adam von Trott zu Solz and he came from a part of Germany so steeped in connections to his own family that the woods around the family home (Imshausen) where he had lived since 1919 – Adam was born in Potsdam – were known as the Trottenwald.

Reading between the lines of their published letters, and of Grant Duff's memoirs, it's fair to surmise that Shiela at some point did have a love affair with von Trott. Certainly, Adam proposed to her (she turned him down) during the mid-thirties. At the time when they met at Oxford, however, von Trott was involved in a relationship with Diana Hubback, one of Shiela's girlfriends from St Paul's, while Shiela herself had fallen for a brilliant young Marxist, Goronwy Rees. All of this youthful Oxford set, back in those ardent college years, were passionately idealistic and firmly committed to the left.*

Von Trott's astonishing good looks and romantic manner would become legendary among those who knew him during his Oxford days. Tall, lean and dark-haired, with a full mouth, high cheek-bones and deep-set violet eyes, he owed his near perfect English both to an English nurse and to an American grandmother proudly descended from John Jay, one of her nation's founding fathers. An almost mystical attachment to his German homeland – and especially to the countryside in which he grew up – added to the attraction of a young man who seemed both familiar and for-eign in his combination of blithe playfulness and grave intensity. At Balliol, he was instantly surrounded by a group of Oxford admir-ers. Leslie Rowse (a friend from Adam's first visit to England) was a clever young Cornish lecturer at Merton College who travelled with Adam to Berlin and was thrilled to be taken on a tour of the former Kaiser's home. Maurice Bowra, a discreet but regular vis-itor to Germany throughout the 1930s, shared Rowse's snobbish relish for Adam's illustrious ancestry. Closer by far was David Astor,

---

* Jonathan Steinberg has kindly drawn my attention to the fact that Adam was also romantically involved at Oxford with Ingrid Warburg, of the great banking dynasty. (Ingrid Warburg-Spinelli, *Erinnerungen: 1910–1989* (1990), pp. 109–123).

a shy and thoughtful student whose family home at Cliveden and friendship with Philip Lothian would later offer Adam an inside track for his urgent political mission. Astor's loyalty to his friend never faltered, even in the darkest of times.

Shiela's published account of the impact that Adam von Trott made upon her was written many years later. 'He was the first German I ever met,' she wrote in 1982, 'and for me he personified all the tragic implications of a "fratricidal war", which was how more and more people were describing the war of 1914–1918.'[6]

Close friends during their Oxford years, Shiela and Adam stayed in touch by letters during the period when Adam returned to – and rashly attempted to defend – the newly Nazified Germany that had emerged during his last year at Balliol. In February 1934, working in Breslau and stung by the British accusations of ethnic persecution that had been lodged against Germany (if only in a small section of the English press), von Trott went on the attack. In a letter addressed to the perceived culprit, the *Manchester Guardian*, he denied the mistreatment of Jews in his own part of Germany, while claiming that the only people to be held in camps were dangerous dissidents. Such misstatements, when combined with his truculent tone, did Adam great harm in English political circles and lost him many potential supporters. Shiela, while disconcerted by a public letter that sounded so unlike the friend she had known and loved, was nevertheless persuaded to put dismay aside and visit Adam during that summer, at his home in Hessen-Kassel.

That first visit to Imshausen, while it helped Shiela to understand how Adam could abhor the Nazis and yet love Germany, was not a total success. A fierce political quarrel that broke out between Shiela and Adam's strong-willed mother was patched up with difficulty. A pledge, however, was touchingly sworn between the two young people that their own Anglo-German friendship, their 'alliance', should continue to stand as a symbol for what might be achieved by their two countries.

Shiela returned to England filled with doubts. Adam, however, felt that he and his cherished English friend had been drawn closer by her evident delight in the landscape he adored. In correspondence with Shiela that autumn, he wrote like a lover about the strange, charmed feeling that had come over him as he recalled the scenes that he had shared with her. He wrote about the sound of village girls and boys singing their songs in the valley behind him as he strolled alone between wooded hills, 'a tinge of autumn over the crowns and a blue haze joining them to the pale night sky'. The meadows and hedges had turned silver in the pale moonlight, 'and it was so reassuring to walk quietly on the gravel of the white road with all the apple trees on either side . . .'[7] A little mischievously, in another letter, Adam mentioned that he had been reading *Lady Chatterley's Lover*, and had thought that he would not mind playing the lusty role of Mellors, identified as 'the forester'.

In her memoirs, Shiela insists upon the unfailing love she felt in 1934 for Goronwy Rees, a shocked witness of violent scenes taking place in Berlin during the June massacres in Munich. But it's hard to dismiss the glints of an emotional undercurrent swirling through the letters that passed between Shiela and Adam. An impressionable young woman may have loved more than a single, idealistic young man during those dramatic times.

In 1935, Shiela paid a second visit to Adam's home. By then, however, she had come under the influence of a fiercely anti-Nazi American journalist. Edgar Ansel Mowrer, having made a noble and unusual deal with the German authorities to quit his Berlin news post in exchange for their release of an imprisoned Jew, was continuing to savage the Third Reich from Paris, as bureau chief to the *Chicago Daily News*. (America's reports of events in Germany were less censored than those that – occasionally – made it into the British press.)

Working alongside Mowrer in 1934, Shiela was teased for acting (in her own phrase) like 'Hitler's girlfriend'. Slowly, she began to question the views not only of Adam, but of the whole crowd of her appeasement-minded friends at Oxford. At the beginning of 1935, she was despatched by the venerable editor of the *Sunday Observer*, J. L. Garvin, to report upon the real feelings of inhabitants of the coal-rich Saar about their chance to be governed by the Nazis. As with Wystan Auden's observations at the time of Hitler's election to the presidency, what Shiela observed was a coerced response to a supposedly free plebiscite, with a beaming pink-and-white Hitler prancing in on 1 March to claim his victorious role as the chosen one. The Saarlanders, in Shiela Grant Duff's indignant view, had been allowed no choice at all.* Was a country governed by such methods really worthy of Adam's passion?

In 1936, a far-sighted Garvin despatched his enthusiastic female reporter to Prague. Shiela, to her amazement, found herself to be the only British journalist in a captivating city that felt like the gentle hub of an earlier world: an un-Nazified, civilized Europe: '... no rioting, no vandalism, no terrorism, no pornography'.[8]

Travelling out to Czechoslovakia, Shiela had stopped, once again, to pay a visit to Adam von Trott. Their friendship, once so strong, had already begun to weaken. Adam had become closely attached to a fellow lawyer, Peter Bielenberg, and his Irish-born, English-educated wife, Christabel Burton, a niece of Lord Rothermere. But, while the Bielenbergs resolutely avoided joining the Nazis, Adam believed that opposition in Germany could only effectively be launched from a position within the Nazi party itself. Shiela,

---

* Many German-speaking Saarlanders resented an enforced integration that cut them off from Alsace-Lorraine, their main source for supplies, and introduced a regime of terror. One old lady who poked light-hearted fun at the Nazis to the shopkeeper in her local grocery store reached home to find that the Blockleiter had already issued a warning to her husband. Their house was kept, thereafter, under close surveillance: correspondence was censored, card games were forbidden, visitors were monitored. (Interview with Mary Ann Dickinson about the experiences of her Saarlander grandmother, Anna Schneider, 5 September 2010.)

unable to accept the idea of a Nazi resister, understood only that her friend planned to join an abhorrent regime. Adam defended his attitude. He tried, so Shiela later wrote, 'to make me understand the position of one who both loved and hated what he belonged to'. It was a contradiction that rang false with a woman of unsubtle beliefs. To Shiela, there was simply a right and a wrong. 'He had noble ambitions,' she conceded, 'but his roots were deep in the earth of Germany.'[9]

Shiela Grant Duff's first-hand observations in Prague of the increasingly tense situation in Czechoslovakia, as Germany turned its focus relentlessly towards the east, found powerful expression in her *Europe and the Czechs*. The book came out, with extraordinary timing, in 1938, published on the very day that Neville Chamberlain flew home from Munich, brandishing his proclamation of a purchased peace. At a time when almost nothing had been written about modern Czechoslovakia (the absence of any British journalists in Prague during Shiela's time there highlights England's utter indifference to Germany's eastern expansion plans), *Europe and the Czechs* became key reading in Britain: a best-seller, it made its young author's name.

Estranged though the former friends had become, Adam still craved Shiela's approval for his political views. To Adam, always trusting in England's underlying attachment to his beloved homeland, it seemed possible, even in the summer of 1939, that a deal might be done. The details of that plan belong to a later chapter (26); here, it is only necessary to point out that Adam, while visiting England, disclosed part of the strategy for avoiding war to Shiela Grant Duff and that she, under-informed and deeply alarmed, used her connections to help ensure that the proposals went no further.

On 25 August, one week before Germany's invasion of Poland, Adam wrote to Shiela for one last and bitter time, to lay responsibility for the destruction of his mission for peace upon her own 'complete incapacity to understand a natural ally'.[10] With that, their correspondence ended. A collaborative friendship between a principled English woman and an idealistic German man – an alliance that once blossomed into something close to love – had reached a point beyond which there was nothing left to say.

PART THREE

Moving Beyond Repair

25

EXODUS

(1933–8)

Back in 1928, at the height of Germany's revived economy, Philip Kerr and Albrecht Bernstorff, the Anglophile grandson of a diplomat, had overseen the rebirth of the Rhodes Scholarships, the educational exchange plan which would bring Adam von Trott to Balliol in 1931.

The opening speech at the resumption ceremony was given by Sir James Barrie, who – sounding a little like Cecil Rhodes himself – urged the first intake of German-born scholars to behave as if they meant 'to eat all the elephants in Hindustan and pick your teeth with the spire of Strasbourg Cathedral'.[1] Adam von Trott's willingness to act as a tour guide in Berlin (not forgetting to show off Wilhelm II's absurd imperial desk to new college friends like Leslie Rowse) was undertaken – if not with quite that gusto – in just the spirit of cultural exchange that had been envisaged by Bernstorff and Kerr.

Courage was a character trait that Sir James had stressed in his speech of welcome. Another early Rhodes scholar, Adolf Schleppegrell, might have won Barrie's heart by the brave passion with which he spoke out for the opposition on that famous night in 1933 when the Oxford Union voted never again to go to war for king and country. Schleppegrell – whose immediate appointment as the Union's first-ever foreign secretary suggests that the students had not felt entirely happy about their pacifist result – spoke out once again in 1934, when he insisted that the Oxford Union's invited speaker, Winston Churchill, should come clean about his views on the infamous war guilt clause of the Treaty of Versailles. When Churchill, at the third questioning, endorsed the clause, Schleppegrell left the room.[2]

The scholarships, initially intended to promote the cause of international friendship within an academic environment, had not been designed to act as an escape route from a tyrannous regime. Rules, as the situation in Nazi Germany deteriorated, were quietly bent to allow special assistance to be provided. Philip Lothian (Kerr had succeeded to his cousin's title of marquis of Lothian in 1930) used his influence at Rhodes House to facilitate Adam von Trott's return to Oxford and, later, to offer support for Adam's peace-seeking journey to America.

Other examples of how the scholarships were employed to assist the German students are less well known. Lord Lothian used the numerous American contacts available through his close friendship with the Astors to gain Fritz Schumacher (author, many years later, of the best-selling *Small is Beautiful*) an additional, post-scholarship year at Columbia University. In 1937, Philip Lothian stepped forward once again; Schumacher and his family had emigrated to England, but without meeting the requirement for guaranteed employment. Through Lothian's agency, Schumacher was housed on the farm of Robert Brand's country estate and provided with the wartime work that enabled him to escape internment in Britain.

In 1933 – the year in which a swashbuckling Hugh Greene followed a fellow Merton student, Robert Byron (vintage 1925), out of their cloistered quad life and into the world of journalism – it became apparent to the dons of Oxford that the modest bridge that the Rhodes Scholarship posts had offered to Germany needed to grow, and to evolve into a different form. William Beveridge, a former Balliol graduate who would become one of England's most admired social reformers, made use of all his Oxford connections to found the Academic Assistance Council as a means of providing support and work to the hundreds of professors who, having lost their jobs under the new Nazi embargoes, wanted to emigrate to England. Richard Haldane's equally pro-German brother, John, was placed on the AAC committee; at its first public meeting, Albert Einstein gave the keynote address. Speaking at the Albert Hall in October 1933 about the imperative need for AAC fundraising, Einstein was greeted by an unexpectedly large audience with enthusiasm and with commitment. England's gain – and Germany's considerable loss – would swiftly include the arrivals of Ernst Gombrich, Ernst Chain, Geoffrey Elton, Nikolaus Pevsner and (bringing with him the family's Bechstein piano) Claus Moser.

The AAC was not the only body to open its doors to Germany's newly dispossessed intellectual elite. In 1934, the Warburg, Hamburg's leading centre for the study of art, quietly re-emerged in London as part of the newly formed Courtauld Institute, where it extended a warm invitation to recent immigrants from the great art centres of Dresden, Munich, Hamburg and Berlin. Imperial Chemicals, combining philanthropy with pragmatism, waited until 1939 to despatch Churchill's advisor, Frederick Lindemann, out on a recruitment tour in a new Rolls Royce, from which the flamboyant Professor Lindemann offered both work and ICI's generous financial support to Germany's finest – and, by that time, fairly frantic – scientists.

Nikolaus Pevsner was one of the first recipients of help from the Academic Assistance Council, which presented him, in 1933, with a welcome grant of £250. But Pevsner, while glad of the financial aid, would always feel that he owed his greatest debt not to Beveridge's splendid organisation, but to the Quakers who came to his rescue at the moment he lost his Göttingen post. What Pevsner could not appreciate at the time was just how important the role of Quakers would become during those desperate pre-war years.

Vienna, the city that had helped to shape William Beveridge's ideas about social reform and stimulated him into creating the Academic Assistance Council, was also the seeding ground for the remarkable Quaker woman at whose home in Duchess Road, Birmingham, Pevsner spent his first lonely months of exile in Britain.

Born in Newcastle in 1888 and educated at Newnham, Francesca Wilson went out to Austria in 1919 to work with Quaker Relief, while writing home for the *Manchester Guardian* about Vienna's pioneering system of social aid: of its libraries, soup kitchens, hospitals and – above all – its programme of medical care for children. Vienna, as Wilson later declared, had offered the most inspiring experience of her life. From then on, she dedicated herself to philanthropy, settling in Birmingham to work as a teacher and – like her German neighbour, Johanna Selig Simmons – to provide housing for refugees.

Pevsner had not been the most grateful of Francesca's lodgers. Besides complaining about her cigarettes, her cats and her untidy habits, he grumbled about the ubiquitous scent of sweet chocolate (Duchess Road lay close to a Cadbury's factory); the poor condition of the city swimming-baths; the failure of the English to appreciate Hitler; and the way that the British deprived their poorer citizens of cultural experience. The German exile's sense of loneliness, while briefly defeated by a young student, Denis Mahon, who invited the music-loving Pevsner home to listen to his German record collection, was acute. Francesca – quietly feeding pennies into the gas meter that heated her unhappy lodger's chilly upstairs room, while striving to entertain a wistful expatriate with visits to the local cinema (where they enjoyed a Garbo film), to provide a steady supply of books (Pevsner fell in love with

Prince Albert in Lytton Strachey's *Queen Victoria*) and to find time between all this for reassuring chats – would finally receive her lodger's vote of thanks. Leaving the cosy squalor of Duchess Road for London in 1935, a grateful Pevsner told his hostess simply that 'I owe such a lot to you'. The fact that, four years later, this former supporter of Hitler went out of his way to urge a young Scottish friend to support the Barkas family's valiant work among the German Jews who were trying to escape from Göttingen spoke to Francesca Wilson more eloquently still.[3]

In Tisa Schulenburg's case, it was the gentle attitude and courage of a group of English Quakers that finally helped to ease the unsettled spirit of a German emigrant. 'Compared with these kind and friendly people, who was I?' she wrote. 'Despair left me, peace was given, hope returned . . .'[4]

Tisa's whole family – in which all the males espoused the new Nazi party from the very dawn of the Reich – had moved from Tressow to Berlin in 1932. Tisa, estranged from them by their politics and married to Fritz Hess, a Jew, had entered a different, threatened world. The first warning bell had sounded in February 1933, when the flight of their friend Emil Fuchs was swiftly followed by a visit from the Gestapo and a search of Tisa's studio. Plainly, they were under scrutiny. Hess emigrated to Britain in the early autumn of 1933; Tisa stayed on just long enough to see her stepson, Edmund, through his final exams at the newly Nazified Salem School.* In 1934, she joined her husband in exile.

There's something touchingly ironic about the fact that Tisa, while still brandishing her theoretical Marxism like a scarlet flag, had never experienced true poverty. Nor did she now. Fritz Hess

* Salem was founded (with the support of Prince Max von Baden) by the Jewish educator Kurt Hahn. Released from his German prison in 1933 through the intervention of Ramsay MacDonald, Hahn moved to Scotland, where he continued to teach Prince Philip (a former Salem pupil) at Gordonstoun.

had been forced to leave his splendid collection of paintings behind, but good banking contacts enabled him to transfer funds to England. Within two years, the couple had built themselves a cottage at what was fast becoming an exiles' stronghold at Walberswick, on the Suffolk coast. (They changed the name of their new home to Oak Barn when friends explained that 'the Refuge' sounded awkwardly close to 'refugee'.)

Tisa would never feel that she belonged among those forlorn newcomers to London who clustered around the German book-shops in Charlotte Street and wistfully queued up on Sunday afternoons to watch the latest German film on show at Elsie Cohen's Academy Cinema on Oxford Street. Tisa had arrived with a keen sense of relief and joy: she was at last connected to that beloved England in which her parents had spent their happiest years. As a good-looking, well-born and relatively well-off extro-vert (and one who spoke English with complete ease), she suffered from none of the feelings of isolation or despair that had so beset Nikolaus Pevsner. England was 'our home to be loved henceforth', she had told herself in advance. Happily, England provided a warm welcome. 'I don't know if there is in any other country such a capacity for friendship!' Tisa exclaimed, although she later quali-fied the remark, recognising that she had been fortunate to arrive 'in those early years after Hitler's rise to power [when] immigrants were received with remarkable kindness and helpfulness'.[5]

Kindness did not, however, mean contentment. By 1936, although still fond of her attractive and life-embracing husband, Tisa was living a separate life and filling its emptiness with love affairs. Searching for the sense of a purpose that seemed always to elude her, she rediscovered her talent as an artist. Working at one of the row of studios in Parkhill Road that were being used by Henry Moore and Barbara Hepworth's first husband, John Skeaping, she began to sculpt. It was Moore who suggested that Tisa should try her hand at carving in wood, a craft in which Germany has famously excelled. When a social services worker from the north of England suggested that the young Countess should give a talk on art to a group of unemployed Yorkshire miners, the impulsive Tisa accepted at once.

She was due for a brusque awakening.

In 1936, north-east England had gone on strike, with 200 unemployed workers marching 300 miles from the shipbuilding community of Jarrow to lobby Parliament for work. Given a pound each, to take them back home and out of sight, they did not give up the struggle. 'I had never really met a worker,' Tisa later confessed.[6] Confronted by the sight of a row of burly men queuing patiently in rainy, soot-grimed streets for their brief quota of sleep on a single all-purpose blanket, she was horrified.

Tisa's first venture north was not a success. She had arrived with a sheaf of drawings of emaciated working men and their desolate wives, gleaned from the same magazines in which Hubert Herkomer's first works had appeared as a revelation to the young van Gogh. An audience of thirty men, muffled in frayed scarves and threadbare coats against the freezing cold of their communal hut (grandly known as the Social Club), examined the drawings in silence, and then handed them back. Someone, finally, observed that nothing much had changed for the working poor. The silence was resumed. Tisa, mortified and upset, resolved to persist – and to do better.

In 1937, she was given a chance to try again. Her post, this time, was more secure, working as a tutor to the tiny community of Spennymoor, near Durham. Here, having learned from her previous mistakes, Tisa stopped showing grim prints and began, instead, to teach her newly acquired skill in carving wood. It was a breakthrough. Slowly, the Spennymoor men began to regard their German art teacher with cautious pride: they spoke of her as some sort of strange but exotic pet who appeared in pearls and furs to lecture them about the inalienable rights of the individual. Tisa's lessons in political theory bored them, however, and Tisa herself never understood why, when offered work in the south, the miners told her that they weren't taking it: 'they said they'd rather stay at home and bear poverty'.

By 1939, Tisa began to believe that she had found what she was meant to do in life. That summer, she was offered the task of supervising workers' art for the entire area around Durham. Was this – she wondered – where her future might lie?[7]

Tisa had arrived in England during the period in which Hitler began courting those members of the English press who seemed most likely to endorse Nazi Germany. In December 1934, Lord Rothermere, owner of the conservative *Daily Mail*, was welcomed to Hitler's first formal dinner party for eminent foreign guests. On 28 December, Rothermere's European correspondent, George Ward-Price, returned the favour with a glowing tribute to Hitler's success: 'What magic has restored hope to German hearts ... magnetised this mighty nation until one feels in its midst as if one were in a gigantic power-house? Hitler. That is the whole answer.' Referring to the accounts of Jewish persecution that kept appearing in the *Manchester Guardian*, the authoritative pages of the *Daily Mail* dismissed them as 'pure moonshine'.

Hitler had indicated in *Mein Kampf* that he would seek an alliance with England. Conversations with George Ward-Price – and with Wardie's friends, Unity and Diana Mitford – encouraged him to believe that his plans for getting rid of Germany's Jews would not impede progress towards the coalition with Britain that he desired. In May 1935, shortly after conscription had been introduced in Germany and – far more disturbingly to nervous foreign powers – soon after it had been announced that the German airforce had reached parity with that of Britain, Hitler issued the first of his overtures. A nine-page letter was despatched to Lord Rothermere, for circulation among British people of influence. Here, with flattering hints of his hopes for union between 'two great Germanic peoples', Hitler more directly demanded England's support for the creation in Europe of 'a force for peace and reason of 120 million people of the highest type'.[8]

In England, in 1935, there was a strong desire for peace; a desire which included regular proposals for disarmament or, at least, for a drastic cut in spending on defence. A few people, however, were growing uneasy about what was already happening to the Jews in Germany. Lady Londonderry, on 18 May 1935, alerted the out-going Prime Minister, Ramsay MacDonald, that Dr Melchior (that same Jewish banker who had so impressed Maynard Keynes during their negotiations over the Treaty of Versailles) had given her 'dreadful' news.* Robert Brand, among others, had been steadily reporting to his friends that terrible things were being done in Germany. In the event, Hitler's overture of 1935 was rejected, not because of the vicious policy at which that deadly phrase 'people of the highest type' so clearly pointed, but, rather, because England was worried by Germany's militarisation and afraid that her own connection to France would be undermined by any hint of a new alliance with their former common enemy.

Hitler's arrangements for the creation of a subject race of Jews came into force in Germany in September 1935 (just four months after his appeal for Britain's support), with the introduction of the Nuremberg Laws. But, with the eager assistance of England's ingen-uous and unofficial army of young ambassadors, the information that reached England remained unclear. Were families expected to disbelieve the fresh-faced and well-treated young people who assured them that – while having a lovely time, and with everybody being so friendly and kind – they had seen no sign of persecution? Were they to disbelieve the evidence of their own eyes, in 1936, when thousands of them visited Berlin (on free tickets) for the

---

* Lady Londonderry's warning was unluckily timed. MacDonald was about to be replaced by Stanley Baldwin, with whom she had no influence, and Baldwin was about to sack her husband as minister of air for defending bomber planes and a strong air force at a time when pacts for disarmament were being discussed. (Ian Kershaw, *Making Friends with Hitler: Lord Londonderry and Britain's Road to War* (2004), p. 122.)

Olympic Games and saw no ugly signs, no excluding boards, no corner kiosks selling *Der Stürmer*? What was all the fuss about? The Jews, it was clear, were in no danger from this splendid country. The country's ethnic minority had only to follow the legitimate orders of the Nazi authorities and all would be well.

In 1936, Wilfrid Israel paid a visit to the British Embassy in Berlin. Speaking in his role as an employer of some 600 Jews, Israel advised Nevile Henderson that the need of help for the country's Jewish population had reached a critical point: assistance must be provided in getting people out of Germany. Ambassador Henderson, rapturous in his admiration of all that Hitler was achieving, was both uninterested and unhelpful. Britain, deep in the throes of unemployment and unrest, felt no need to increase her personal burden of woe.

In May 1938, two months after the Anschluss, the Jewish journalist Bella Fromm noted that the 'Jew baiting' in Vienna had reached an intolerable level. Until 1938, Bella had considered herself invulnerable. Her life, so she was warned, was now at risk. On 9 September, outward-bound for a new life in New York, Bella gazed out from the upper deck of the *Normandie* for a last glimpse of St Nicholas's church and the (English-designed) tallest spire in Hamburg, before it sank from her view into the waves. That night, in her diary, Fromm chose one thankful word to describe her feelings: 'safe'.[9]

On 7 November 1938, three months after Bella Fromm left Germany in search of a new world, a young Jew whose entire family had been deported from Hanover to a camp in Poland walked into the German Embassy in Paris. In an act of premeditated protest, Herschel Grynszpan shot a junior official, Ernst vom Rath, twice in the stomach. The victim took two days to die. On the day of his death, as the culmination of a carefully laid and coolly orchestrated campaign by Joseph Goebbels, the Nazi regime responded.

Kristallnacht operated against the Jews with a ferocity and on a scale that nobody (except the Nazi leaders and the perpetrators, the SA and the SS) could have anticipated. Throughout Austria and Germany, beautiful old synagogues were set on fire, shop windows were smashed, homes were plundered and people were savagely attacked. The police, standing aside from the vandalism and offering no help to the victims, devoted their attentions solely to the protection of non-targeted buildings. The following day, it appeared that nobody had been responsible and that, therefore, nobody would be charged. When Jewish victims claimed insurance for their ruined homes and stores, the Reich stepped in with a counter-claim: for the damages caused by the riots, they demanded reparations of one billion marks.

Mercy had vanished and on the horizon loomed a future of absolute darkness for those who refused to leave the Germany that so many of them still loved. The most that a patriotic Jewish family could hope for now was to sell their home in foreign currency to a wealthy and well-disposed couple like the Bielenbergs. (Peter Bielenberg had been persuaded by his friend Adam von Trott to stay in Germany and to join the burgeoning German resistance; crucially, for the way that he himself would later be perceived, Bielenberg did not become a Nazi.)

Money comprised a large part of the problem for the Jewish families who now recognised the imperative of departure. The rich and influential could always bend the law, but the rule of the Third Reich – one that was intended to boost the Nazi economy – was that no private citizen could take more than ten marks out of the country. How, armed with such a pitiful sum, could any refugee expect to be welcomed into a country suffering from a decade of economic depression, and filled with people who were desperate for employment?

This was only one of the difficulties that the Quakers in England and in Germany – working hand in glove with an intrepid group of Jewish supporters – now set out to overcome.

In 1938, Wilfrid Israel's family department store was seized and put under Aryan ownership. Its 600 Jewish employees were deported to Sachsenhausen. Offered a plane flight to England, with a guarantee of his personal safety, Israel refused; instead, after rescuing his imprisoned former employees, he joined forces with Frank Foley, the British passport control officer in Berlin whose position had been assigned to mask his undercover work for MI6. Working together with Foley's colleague Hubert Pollack, the three men began to operate in league with a dedicated network of Quakers. Pollack identified families in need; Israel produced the necessary funding (and frequently much else); Foley stamped the visas (and often harboured the refugee families in his home).

The Quakers, meanwhile, operating out of a headquarters in the pretty old spa town of Bad Pyrmont, began working alongside Pollack at the painful task of identifying the most urgent cases for emigration. Using their English contacts, they were also attempting to enlarge a complicated network of British recipients willing to produce evidence of guaranteed employment and shelter. Both conditions remained necessary requirements for entry into England.*

Even before the horrors of Kristallnacht, a brutal truth had begun to emerge. A Jewish family could escape from Nazi Germany more effectively if it consented to divide itself up. Once children were removed from the equation, relatives stood a better chance of being hidden (if they fled), or of being employed (if they took the official route). And so, out of such despair, the idea of the Kindertransport was born. The childless Wilfrid Israel was one of its chief promoters and facilitators in Germany. In England, the heroes of the hour were a tiny and indomitable little group of Jews and Quakers.

---

* The employment pages of *The Lady* told their own sad story in the 1930s, as an increasing number of applicants repeatedly applied for any work whatsoever, in exchange for the required guarantee of a £50 sponsorship (roughly, £2,500 today) for a passage to England. 'Still in Germany' was a phrase that appeared with poignant frequency.

Time, after Kristallnacht had revealed what lay in store, could not be lost. On 15 November 1938, Britain's Home Secretary, Samuel Hoare (who was himself a Quaker), received an urgent appeal from Viscount Samuel for new legislation that would allow 10,000 Jewish children to be brought to England. Hoare turned the request down.

On 21 November, a second delegation arrived at Hoare's door. This time, Lord Samuel had brought along Hugh Greene's pacifist cousin, Ben, a young man who had worked with Quaker groups in Germany and who offered first-hand accounts of the fields of frozen and starving refugees whom he had found patiently waiting – for the transit permits that were not being given out – up on the borders of Holland. Standing beside Ben was Bertha Bracey, a forceful and articulate Birmingham-born Quaker who had worked alongside Francesca Wilson in Vienna before running, in 1933, the German Emergency Committee out of Berlin. More recently, Bracey had started to organise refugee aid from the crowded, jostling, kindly chaos of Friends' House in London. There, the target was to locate safe English homes for immigrants who were willing – whatever their qualifications – to work as farmhands, drivers, cooks, maids, stable workers, builders, or as any other kind of worker, in exchange for sponsorship and shelter. But now, standing in front of the Home Secretary, Bertha Bracey threw all of her considerable powers of persuasion into the cause of the children.

The children, Bracey pleaded, must be saved.

The cause was won. Already softened by the appeals of Philip Noel-Baker, his fellow Quaker politician, Hoare gave his word that action would be immediate. The Bill was heard – and was passed – on that very same night. By the following morning, word had reached the major cities of departure; preparations were hastily made for Quaker volunteers to travel out of Germany as escorts on the Kindertransport trains. The reason (protecting both the children and their modest possessions – one small suitcase apiece – from the ravages of Nazi guards) proved to have sound justification. It was one against which the gentle Quakers could not always prevail.

The arrival of the children began on 2 December. A few media-conscious society ladies were on hand to welcome the young refugees and to display their own pretty faces to the gentlemen of the press. It all made – if the children would only learn to smile more readily at the cameras – for a most attractive scene.

The children did their best to look appealing. Many had been coached in advance to say a few words of English. In the most frequently published photograph from that first week in December, they are seen waving to the camera from the deck of the boat as it chugs into Harwich. They look pinched, despite the warm wool coats intended to protect them from England's notorious lack of heated homes. Several of the children are holding a musical instrument; others clutch a book. All, on this occasion, wear bright smiles. None of them know what to expect, or when – if ever – they will see their parents again. For the present, however, they must remember to look cheerful.

Felix Gottlieb had just turned sixteen on 18 December 1938 when his parents – they had already despatched their daughter, Lilly, to British-mandated Palestine – put him on the midnight train at Vienna. At two in the morning, the train, crowded with silent children, finally creaked out and off on its journey towards the Hook of Holland. Here, the children were put onto the ferry for Harwich. The more fortunate ones would be greeted here by families who had consented to take them in.

Felix, a quiet, home-loving boy, came from a family who had no connections in England. The only contact provided to Felix was for a London hostel that had just been acquired by a west London synagogue. But events had moved with great rapidity in the autumn of 1938. The hostel was not yet ready. Felix was to spend the first two months of his life in England at a place called Dovercourt.

Built as a Warner's east-coast seaside summer camp for workers' families, Dovercourt had been caught unawares by the sudden need for refugee housing. The retired naval captain who ran the place had hastily recalled his summertime employees to act as hosts and cooks. Heaters had been placed in the dormitory huts and cork lining glued to the thin walls; nevertheless, the path to the communal showers was often deep in snow and no preparations had been made for what, exactly, the children should do. There were no teachers in those first months, and, since the camp had no library, the only reading materials were the books that the children had brought in with them from Germany. (Felix Gottlieb remains uncertain of the exact moment at which, reading *The Pickwick Papers*, he instinctively chose to make its world his model for the England he had not yet encountered.)

So what did they do, these children who had no homes to go to? They sang songs – community songs, led by their summer-camp hosts – and they played ball games. And they ate: strange dishes like tripe and onions and – until a rabbi issued a protest – bacon and eggs. Felix had enjoyed the bacon and eggs. Like everything else in England, it had the charm of novelty.

And if it was lonely, and if he missed his family (Felix's parents were sheltered by French farmers throughout the war, under the orders of a local priest), it mattered no more and no less than the knowledge that he had been welcomed in. It was comforting to know that he would not be travelling alone to the new hostel and that when he arrived at Ladbroke Grove, work was going to be found for him. (Felix, together with one of his Dovercourt friends, was offered work in a reputable jeweller's shop.)

Felix's England was a good place, filled with kind people who offered him safety when his life was at risk, and who enabled him to be reunited with his sister and parents after the war, when their family would all settle in England. Felix's sister married Jim Laker, an English cricketing hero, and went to live in view of Salisbury's great cathedral. Felix himself continued to look upon his adopted land as a beacon of decency, a bright light in that world over which Hitler had attempted to cast a mantle of darkness. Entering his nineties, Felix Gottlieb is – in everything but his scrupulous attention to detail, a lingering attachment to Bismarck herrings, and the strong trace of a Viennese accent – a very English man.[10]

Etta (born Etka) Weiner's family lived in Dresden. Her father owned two department stores and a house that he deliberately built in a part of Dresden where they would have no Jewish neighbours. The Weiners lived on the first floor; the tenant above them was a Catholic lady, not well off, who paid a reduced rent. Etta's father was well liked for the fact that, during hard times, he gave out free milk to all the local schools. It didn't feel comfortable for Etta when copies of *Der Stürmer* were sold on the corner of her street, but – even though she was the only schoolgirl who didn't wear the uniform of the Hitler Girls' Youth – nobody treated her in a different way. 'My friends came from families who didn't think about things like that.'[11]

Differences, however, would become increasingly apparent. When Etta took up singing, her teacher objected to having a Jewish girl in the choir. The lessons that she was given in private (her mother paid) confirmed that Etta had a voice worth training, 'but the teacher couldn't admit she was teaching me because I was Jewish. And every day, the Gestapo came and stood outside the doors of my father's shops, to keep people away.' The customers, as Etta explains, came in just the same – 'but through the tradesmen's door at the back'.

After the Nuremburg Laws of 1935, the Weiners were only allowed to keep one (Christian) servant, Emma. They were ordered to hand in their family treasures. Etta still displays her few precious relics of a Dresden childhood: a ruby and gold china dish; a white angel; two sets of dancing Meissen figures. These mementoes survived, she explains, because the Nazis had no use for them. 'They only wanted what could be melted down.'

And then came Kristallnacht. Etta remembers the shock she felt when she realised that nobody else in their street had been touched, while their windows, one after the other, were all smashed. 'We were the only Jews there, you see. But they knew. They knew which house it was safe to damage.'

Walking to school the following morning, Etta saw the smouldering remains of the old Italian synagogue. The women standing nearby screamed out when they saw Etta and her mother: 'Burn the Jews! Throw them in the fire!' The women, in Etta's opinion, were far more violent than the men. 'And then, after that day, we were all of us afraid. Even to hear a knock on the door ...' She shakes her head. 'We didn't know who would be there.'

Etta's parents told her she must give up her dream of a singing career. A rabbi in England had promised to take her in; she was to travel out on the next Kindertransport. The Catholic lady asked her forgiveness for all that was happening to the Jews. She gave Etta a card with an angel on it, and said that she must think of the angel, protecting her, always.

Etta doesn't remember much about the Kindertransport, except that a guard asked to look in her case and that some things had been taken out when he gave it back. The rabbi was kind. He helped her parents to escape, but they had to come with empty hands. Her mother cried when she realised that she couldn't even buy a cup of coffee on the journey to a foreign land. Etta found work. Her father was getting old to start again, but he bought cheap furniture and made it look nice. He rented rooms in a house and furnished them himself. He worked all the time and so did her mother. Etta sighs. 'I can only remember how they were always tired.'

Terrible stories reached them from Germany. It never made Etta hate the Germans. 'There were always good Germans,' she says. 'We knew so many. But they were hypnotised. I can't hate them for that.'

Etta describes how much she enjoyed going back to Dresden, long after the war, and resuming a few of her old friendships. She even met a niece of the singer who had once been going to help her make a career – so Etta had dreamed – on the concert platform.

And England?

Etta's answer is not so far from the one given by Felix Gottlieb. She thinks of England as if it were a cherished member of her family. 'If *I* speak against England, I speak as I would against my parents or my child. But if I hear somebody *else* speak badly of England – I won't allow it to happen! England saved us. And I never forget.'

Eva Steinicke grew up in Berlin in the thirties. Eva's mother was Jewish, her father was not. By 1936, when Eva was eight, Jews were forbidden to enter places of entertainment. 'But my father, Otto, could go where he liked, even though he was a communist. He took me to the circus and to Shirley Temple films. We went to the Olympics in 1936. My Jewish friends couldn't do any of those things.'[12]

Eva's happiest memories are of the flat in Berlin where her grandparents lived. Felix Opfer was a respected paediatrician with an excellent practice and a gently cultured home. There was a piano in the corner with an embroidered cloth cover; cupboards of neatly folded linen; a drawer of children's games; shelves of books. Eva was especially fond of *Dr Doolittle* and – she still has her copy, printed in the old gothic script – of *Alice in Wonderland*: '"*Ach wie langweilig*", *sagte Alice, die neben ihrer Schwester im Grase sass . . .*'

Eva's parents lived apart. In 1937, while Eva and her mother visited – such places were hard to find by then – a Thuringian pension that took Jewish clients, her father accepted a holiday for war veterans that was being offered at the beautifully old-fashioned spa town of Bad Pyrmont. While there, he made friends with the people at the Quaker centre. The couple who ran it, Leonard and Mary Friedrich, had strong connections to England. Mary had been born there; Leonard had married her after his internment (as a German in England) on the Isle of Man, in 1914. In 1933, worried about what was happening in Germany, the Friedrichs came to Bad Pyrmont to do everything they could to fight the persecution of the Jews.

'My father told them about us and they introduced him to a Quaker lady called Anne Lyall. She offered to provide the guarantees and housing if my mother and I needed to leave Germany. But of course, just then ...'

In 1937, the Steinecke family had no intention of leaving Berlin, a city they still loved. In January 1938, everything changed. Eva's grandparents were moved into a small flat in an area that was reserved for Jewish use only. They had to hand over all their possessions and keep just enough tableware for their daily meals. Felix Opfer was instructed henceforth to treat only Jewish patients.

'And then,' Eva says, 'came Kristallnacht.'

Otto Steinecke wrote to Anne Lyall. She told him that work as a housemaid had been found for his wife (a trained physiotherapist). Eva herself would be cared for by the Quakers. It would – so Eva's father promised her – only be for a short while, just until life returned to normal.

At school, meanwhile, Eva's fellow pupils were getting ready for more adventurous journeys. Her safe world was dissolving.

'But we're going to America!' someone shouted.

'Chile!'

'Shanghai!'

'Australia!'

And so the classrooms thinned out.[13]

Eva didn't come to England on the Kindertransport. Her grandfather had used the last of his savings to buy Eva and her mother their passages aboard the *Manhattan*, a splendid liner that was leaving Hamburg for New York, and stopping at Southampton along the way.

'They came with us to the station in Berlin. Everyone was doing their best not to cry. My grandfather took me aside. He bade God protect me and then suddenly said: "Dear child, we will not see each other again" and blew his nose.'[14]

Eva still owns a little raffia sweep, stiff-legged and stiff-armed, like a scarecrow. It was the last gift that her father pressed into her hand.

Placed in an English country house with three elderly Quaker ladies whom she learned to call her aunts, Eva went to the local school and worked hard to settle in, while her mother worked as a 'nippy', a Lyon's waitress, and (less happily, from a social view-point) as the hard-pressed housemaid to a family of Orthodox Jews in Stamford Hill.

Eva's mother took refuge in boyfriends, smart gifts and bold ventures towards a glamorous new life. Eva, longing for accept-ance, still remembers the guide book that was issued to all refugees: 'Don't dress conspicuously . . .' Collecting second-hand clothing from the refugee centre, she was dismayed to be buttoned into a heavily stained coat and to be told that it was good enough for an immigrant child. 'All I wanted was to look like English children, to be one of them.'[15]

In 1942, Eva and her mother heard that Doris and Felix Opfer had been sent away from Berlin. Doris's last letter was full of optimism. She was sure that Felix would be allowed to resume his practice when they reached their new and as yet unknown home.

Felix Opfer died of pneumonia at Theresienstadt, in November 1943. Doris Opfer died at Auschwitz in 1944. Otto Steinecke, Eva's English father, was killed during the last British bombing raid over Berlin.

The Quakers exerted an enduring influence on Eva's life. A Quaker convert, she ran an Interfaith Group in London for ten years. In 2006, she returned to Berlin, to speak at an event that honoured the city's Jewish doctors. Today, living in north London, Eva's faith in the goodness of the English remains invin-cible. Like Etta Weiner, and like Felix Gottlieb, she defends with quiet passion the country that, when Germany turned its back, offered her a second home.

Nicholas Winton's contribution to the Kindertransport effort remained unknown until 1988. An Englishman of exceptional modesty, he had hidden away all evidence of his work until his wife found a scrapbook in the attic of their Hampstead home and asked him about its significance.

Born in 1909 to German Jewish parents who changed their name from Wertheim to Winton when they reached England in 1907, Winton abandoned plans for a Swiss holiday in December 1938. Instead, he travelled to Prague to help a friend with getting children onto the Kindertransport trains. Setting up office in his hotel in Wenceslas Square, and aided by his mother at the English end of this independent operation, Winton, remarkably, succeeded in bringing 669 children to safety. The final group of 250 left Prague too late. Departing on 1 September 1939, they were unable to make the crossing as Poland had already been invaded.

Statues to Nicholas Winton have been erected both in England and the Czech Republic, where he was nominated for a Nobel Prize in 2010.

26

NOBLE ENDEAVOURS

(1933–40)

Elizabeth Fry, visiting Germany on a mission of prison reform in the 1840s, had included in her tour several of the places at which groups of Quaker Friends were eager to greet their English ally. The strong and long-established presence of Quaker families and communities in both England and Germany provided a solid foundation upon which political resisters to the Nazis were able to build during the thirties.

The long-standing and treasured Protestant connection between the two countries – reaching back over three centuries to the year when a Stuart princess from England married the young Protestant Elector Palatine – provided another area in which political and religious opposition could – and did – flourish.*

In December 1932, on the eve of Hitler's chancellorship, Gareth Jones had told an English radio audience a dark joke that was

---

* The widespread persecution of Roman Catholics in Nazi Germany seems never to have elicited a strong response in Britain, although Philip Lothian, himself brought up as a Catholic, organised a talk on precisely this subject for Lord's Astor's Chatham House forum.

already doing the rounds in Germany about how, when Jewish converts were ordered to leave the churches of Germany, Christ would be the first to step down from his place above the altar. The Nazi threat to the status quo of the Church was already apparent; all the Nazis lacked in 1932 was the authority that would soon enable them to outlaw any form of Christian worship that did not acknowledge the absolute authority of the state, while rejecting Christ's Jewish origins. Houston Stewart Chamberlain had proposed this route to a receptive emperor; Hitler would enshrine it in law.

It was against this background of a threatened faith that a friendship developed between two remarkable men: Dietrich Bonhoeffer, a young Lutheran pastor in Germany, and George Bell in England, the cultured and quietly outspoken Bishop of Chichester.

Bonhoeffer, the precociously intelligent son of an eminent Berlin psychiatrist, was still a schoolboy when, having announced his intention of reforming the Church, he set aside his piano studies (his aristocratic grandmother, Klara von Hase, had been taught by Liszt and Clara Schumann) to concentrate on theology. In 1930, having achieved brilliant results, and impeccably equipped for ordination in every qualification bar his extreme youth, Bonhoeffer went off for a year to study at a seminary in New York. Here, having made friends with a black seminarian (Frank Fisher), acquired an enduring enthusiasm for African spirituals and taught Sunday school at the Abyssinian Baptist Church in Harlem, he embarked on a tour of America and Mexico, while giving talks along the way on the value of a peaceful world. The prospect of staying in America did not tempt him; instead, Bonhoeffer returned home to embark on a more conventional life as a Lutheran pastor.

Sweet-natured, and deceptively boyish in appearance until the end of his short life, Bonhoeffer was uncompromising in his belief in religious freedom. The rise of National Socialism – a party to which his entire family were adamantly opposed – shocked him especially, because of its unconcealed hostility to all other forms of belief. On the eve of Hitler's appointment as chancellor, the young priest actually managed to obtain a personal interview with the octogenarian President Hindenburg.

Without success, he implored the bewildered but always courteous old gentleman to reconsider his decision to bestow the chancellorship of Germany on such a faithless demagogue as Adolf Hitler. Two days later, Bonhoeffer went on air to broadcast a warning of the terrible danger in which a comatose nation had placed itself: did the good people of Germany not understand that they were delivering themselves into the hands of a man who 'makes an idol of himself above God'?[1]

The speech was cut off, brusquely censored by the authorities before further offence could be caused to Germany's new leader. Bonhoeffer had been warned not to make trouble; it was advice that he would never be prepared to heed. In July 1933, Bonhoeffer protested against the rigged Church elections by which religious control was placed in the hands of the Nazi-supporting German Christians; in September, he spoke out again, to query the legislation that now permitted only Aryan-born priests to conduct services (for Aryan-born citizens) in the new Germany. This new Nazi decree, in a country where conversion to Lutheranism had been a widespread practice among Jews for over a hundred years, caused disruption in the Church, and widespread dismay in the country.

By the autumn of 1933, London's modest number of German pastors were overwhelmed by the task of dealing with a sudden influx of immigrants, both Christians and Jews, many of whom were little better equipped to deal with a new life than the stream of German exiles who had fled to England during the repressive aftermath of the 1848 uprisings. Utterly disheartened by what was happening to Germany, the 26-year-old Bonhoeffer decided that he could serve a better purpose in England. Established in London, he could comfort the German refugees of every faith: 'Only he who cries out for Jews has the right to sing Gregorian chants' was the way that Bonhoeffer would famously express his sympathy for people of all religions. But the young pastor also came to England to rally support against a regime that he believed it was his duty to oppose, both as a Christian and a patriot.

Bonhoeffer spent eighteen months in London. Officially, he was in charge of two German communities at Whitechapel and Sydenham; unofficially, he also helped out the hard-pressed pastor Julius Rieger at the splendid old Hanoverian church of St George's, Aldgate (where two great German boards of commandments still hang against the walls), in the heart of the area that was then still known as Little Germany. Bonhoeffer got on well with Rieger, but a more powerful ally, and an enduring friend, emerged in the agreeable form of George Bell, the Bishop of Chichester – a man whom many at that time assumed would one day become Archbishop of Canterbury.

In 1933, George Bell was fifty years old. The poetry-loving and artistic son of a Hampshire vicar, Bell had used his four years as Dean of Canterbury to give that city its first literary festival, one which offered a bold platform for new works of drama. As Bishop of Chichester, from 1929 on, Bell had maintained his close connection with the festival. *Murder in the Cathedral*, commissioned by the Bishop from T. S. Eliot and put on in Canterbury Cathedral in 1935, showed Britain – and the world – how a priest, Thomas à Becket, might be assassinated for daring to challenge the authority of the state. Such ritualised theatre, delivering its message through Eliot's veiled but powerful language, was one of the many routes through which Bell sought to wake England up to the truth about Nazi Germany.

Bell and Bonhoeffer met at a time when both men were searching for support in their crusade against a Nazified faith. Bell, too, had opposed the infamous 'Aryan paragraph' by which Germany's pastors were to be appointed on the strength not of their convictions, but of their racial history. Supplied with direct information about Germany by his new friend, the Bishop began addressing himself to the wider public through the only portion of *The Times* that could still occasionally avoid censorship: its letters column.

The friendship between Bell and Bonhoeffer, as both men swiftly recognised, came close to that of father and son. Bonhoeffer addressed the good-humoured and half-Irish Bishop as his 'Uncle George'; Bell, in turn, did his avuncular best to prevent Bonhoeffer from wearing himself out in an excess of zeal. (Might a hardworking young pastor be tempted to break away from duties in the East End for long enough to take breakfast at the Athenaeum, Bell teased his friend in February 1934 – or might such indulgence put his soul at risk: 'is that too dangerous?'[2])

Breakfasts at the Athenaeum were doubtless spent in discussing weightier matters than the excellence of marmalade on toast. Bonhoeffer was involved, from late in 1933, in discussions with Martin Niemöller, a fellow pastor, about setting up a form of resisters' faith, the Confessing Church, an underground organisation which would allow believers to avoid the repugnant order to hail Hitler – rather than Christ – as their supreme leader. Bell was all for it. On 1 June 1934, Bell signed his name to the Barmen Declaration, and thus to the formal birth of the Confessing Church.

Later in that same month of June, Bell once again proclaimed the need for support from England against the active force for evil that had taken hold of modern Germany. But England, in 1934, was not in the mood to consider such challenging questions. Bell's fellow churchman Dick Sheppard, the newly appointed Canon of St Paul's, attracted more interest that autumn with an appeal for the renunciation of warfare. The 30,000 male responses (women, as assumed pacifists, were asked not to reply) led to the founding, the following year, of Sheppard's well-intended Peace Pledge Union.

Back in Germany by April 1935, Dietrich Bonhoeffer was identified as an enemy of the state. The young pastor's unnameable crime was to have endorsed, in the form of the Confessing Church, an alternative to the worship of Hitler and the obliging 'Providence' that blessed an Aryanised country. Officially, at a time when virtually every spire in Germany was crowned by a swastika, Bonhoeffer's sin was to have failed to seek permission to take a group of young seminarists to liberal Sweden, where Lutheranism flourished with no state links (and with crosses firmly affixed to its church spires). A marked man from this point, Bonhoeffer's name attracted attention again the following year, when certain of his Confessing Church colleagues invited Hitler to respond to a list of queries about the current status of Christianity in Nazi Germany. Receiving no answer, and advised by a Jewish lawyer to act with courage, they leaked their loaded questions to the foreign press.

Their address to Hitler appeared in the newspapers in June 1936. Bishop Bell indicated his support for the protesters by circulating a very pointed prayer ('for all who suffer shame, on account of their race'), while despatching a valiant sister-in-law, Laura Livingstone, to help Bonhoeffer with his work among persecuted Jews and Christians in Berlin.

In the short term, the group of rebel clerics remained untouched, but only because their timing was singularly inconvenient. In June 1936, Germany was just two months away from hosting the Olympic Games in Berlin. Prodigious sums had been spent to ensure that the visitors would see a proud, successful Germany with which, in Neville Chamberlain's eloquent phrase, they could do business.

Writing with hindsight about the Games, it was easy for a spectator like Beverley Nichols to recall the scorn he had felt as 'the pudding-faced aristocracy of England' were chauffeured through the placard-free streets of Berlin, 'murmuring to each other that really the Hitler Jugend were rather wonderful'.[*3] At the time, the

* In 1933, Beverley Nichols had admired the Hitler Youth himself enough to welcome a group of them to the Garrick Club and take them to see an Ivor Novello play.

glamour of the massed parades and the affable prodigality of the Reich's grandees, when allied to the conspicuous absence of any signs of brutal oppression, proved marvellously effective. The world visited, allowed itself to be entertained and went away impressed. Shortly after its departure, the Jewish lawyer who had advised on the leaked memorandum was arrested and murdered; his colleagues were despatched to prison camps. Bonhoeffer, while disappearing from public view, continued to prepare young seminarians for work in the Confessing Church.

In 1937, conditions in Germany grew harsher for the dauntless members of the Confessing Church. In July, Martin Niemöller, one of its founder members, was arrested. Spared death, following a series of impassioned public letters from George Bell, Niemöller was imprisoned until the end of the war. A few weeks later, a flawed attempt was made to arrest Niemöller's successor, Franz Hildebrandt, while he was giving a sermon. Heckled and surrounded by the furious congregation after the breakdown of their getaway car, the kidnappers slunk away empty-handed. Hildebrandt left the country, surfacing only after he had joined forces with Julius Rieger in London.

The thwarted abduction of a priest from his church provided a rare moment of black comedy in a tragic year of religious repression; by the end of November 1937, more than 700 Lutheran pastors had been arrested and the secluded haven in which Bonhoeffer had been keeping hope alive was under threat.

From 1935 onwards, Bonhoeffer had been established at a seminary in Pomerania, far away from the centre of Nazi activity. Here, his patron and friend was an elderly widow, Countess Ruth von Kleist-Retzow, a woman of independent wealth who shared Bonhoeffer's passionate opposition to the Nazis.

Photographs of the Kleist estate at which Ruth spent part of her time, while also inhabiting a handsome town house in nearby Stettin, hint at a life of civility, culture and tolerance. One image shows Bonhoeffer and Ruth sitting out on a roughly cropped lawn: the smiling young man leans back in his chair beside a sturdy, white-haired, plainly dressed old lady whose face is alive with humorous intelligence. Probably, it was taken at around the time that Bonhoeffer had begun to take a romantic interest in one of the twenty grandchildren who were under Ruth Kleist's care. (In 1942, Maria von Wedemeyer and Dietrich became engaged.)

Accounts of life on the Kleist estate are scanty, but beguiling. Services at the seminary would usually be followed by games of garden ping-pong for the younger grandchildren, while Bonhoeffer, sitting in the shade of the massive chestnut trees for which the estate was famed, talked about religion and literature with the wise and profoundly religious old lady whom Dietrich, like her family, only ever addressed as 'Grandmother'. Later, after a frugal lunch with the novices and visiting pastors had been consumed around the seminary's horseshoe table, the entire cheerful group joined in reading or acting out a Shakespeare play. The comedies were especially loved. *As You Like It*, so ideally suited by theme and setting to such an environment, must have been a favourite.

Towards the end of 1937, the Gestapo closed down this gentle refuge for the Confessing Church. The following year, Hans Dohnanyi, Dietrich's brother-in-law, persuaded Bonhoeffer to join the secret German resistance (Widerstand) group that had formed in Germany's chief official intelligence organisation, the Abwehr, under the quietly subversive leadership of Admiral Wilhelm Canaris.

From 1939 on, with the exception of a last attempt to rally support in America for the German resistance (Bonhoeffer, rejecting the offer of a professorship, returned home on the eve of war), the young German worked covertly, out of the reach of suspicious eyes. He did not, however, abandon his contact with George Bell, with whom he riskily managed to meet up in Sweden in 1942 to discuss a plot – one of the many – for Hitler's assassination.

Arrested in 1943 and imprisoned, Bonhoeffer was subsequently sentenced to death for his connection to the 20 July plot and following the discovery of diaries that had been kept by his fellow prisoner Wilhelm Canaris. (The diaries shed an ungratifying light upon the ways of the Third Reich as viewed by a former intelligence chief.)

Implicated by association, Bonhoeffer was hanged at Flossenbürg on the same April morning as a pathetically frail Canaris: 9 April 1945, two weeks before Americans liberated the camp's final survivors. Stripped of his clothes before he mounted a primitive scaffold within a private cell, Bonhoeffer's serene farewell was recorded by the unhappy prison chaplain of one of Germany's most vicious camps: 'This is the end – for me the beginning of life.'

George Bell, meanwhile, continued to plead for compassion to an England that, in belligerent and desperate times, had no time for the Bishop. Dismissed by Anthony Eden (making a witty allusion to Thomas à Becket) as 'this pestilent priest', Bell made his boldest appeal on 9 February 1944. Addressing a profoundly sceptical House of Lords, he begged that the bombing campaigns being launched against Germany should try to spare both cultural institutions and civilian lives. His words won them no reprieve.

Bell died, still under a cloud, in 1958. Fifty years later, he was honoured by Bishop Huber in Berlin as 'an ecumenist, bridge-builder and reconciler': in England, during that same year, the Archbishop of Canterbury, Dr Rowan Williams, praised the former Bishop of Chichester as a man of valour, the prophetic founder of Anglo-German reconciliation.[4]

The Nazi leaders, with the exception of the English cleric's tiresome concern for the welfare of Martin Niemöller, took little interest in the endeavours of Bishop Bell. Searching for support in England, they turned instead to the press barons (Lord Rothermere proved especially obliging in this respect) and to the aristocracy in whose control Hitler continued to misplace his faith.

But how were the elusive nobility of England to be won? Putzi Hanfstaengl, a resourceful ex-officio ambassador into such circles, had fallen out of favour with Hitler by the mid-thirties. (Denounced

by Unity Mitford to Hitler for making what she considered trea-
sonable remarks, Hanfstaengl had wisely fled the country after being
subjected to the – supposedly playful – threat of being parachute-
dropped into Spain behind the loyalist lines.) Ribbentrop,
despatched as German Ambassador to England in the autumn of
1936, was urged to carry on the good work.

One of Ribbentrop's more intelligent ideas was to encourage
high-ranking Nazis (the Duke of Brunswick and the Duke of
Saxe-Coburg and Gotha were preferred for their English connections) to allow themselves to be entertained, as honoured
guests, by some of the elaborate cluster of Anglo-German societies
that had sprung up in Britain after the First War.

The Anglo-German Brotherhood; the Anglo-German
Fellowship; the Anglo-German Circle; the Link. All of these fraternal groups – and there were a shoal of others – shared a sturdy
core of aristocrats. Ribbentrop's personal favourite, the Anglo-
German Fellowship, had begun life as the Anglo-German
Association, an exclusive dining club for 900 of England's elite.
Founded in 1929 for the noble purpose of furthering international
understanding, the association had significantly lost its first chairman, the Jewish lawyer and peer Rufus Daniel Isaacs, 1st Marquess
of Reading, in 1933, the year of Hitler's ascent. Reborn as a fellowship in 1935, it was managed by Philip Conwell-Evans, an
academic who later became involved with the German resistance,
and Ernest Tennant, still grieving for the devastated Germany he
had visited after the war.

One thing had not changed since Lord Reading's pointed resignation in 1933: the reconstituted AGF remained sufficiently
anti-Semitic for a second disgusted chairman, Lord Mount
Temple, married to the Jewish daughter of Sir Ernest Cassel, to
resign from his position in 1938.

The AGF would serve Ribbentrop's interests well during his
brief appointment as an ambassador. Happily for him, an aristocrat
with political connections had already stepped forward to serve the

interests of the Reich. During the months when Ribbentrop was visiting England as an ambassador-in-waiting, Lord Londonderry stood ready to welcome him into that elusive world of the English nobility to which Hitler looked for authoritative support.

'I like to lead and control,' the Marquess of Londonderry wrote to his wife, Edith, on 30 March 1936.[5]

That bold assertion came after a first, triumphant expedition to Germany. It was a happy moment in the career of a man who had been unjustly dismissed from office the previous summer for supporting the building of bomber planes (at a moment when England was toying with disarmament) and – which seemed to reflect an entirely contradictory attitude – for failing to alert the British government to statistics that the luckless Minister for Air did not possess, relating to Germany's latest boasts about her massively increased air power.

The Londonderrys' links to Germany were still, in 1935, fairly slight. In 1934, however, Edith and Charlie's daughter, Maureen Stanley, had paid a visit to Berlin during which she proudly told Hermann Goering (a veteran pilot with a hero's record) that her father was head of the Air Ministry. News of Londonderry's subsequent demotion may have added to his attraction for the Nazis: a fallen minister in need of a morale boost could be worth cultivating.

In the closing months of a dispiriting year, Londonderry's own sudden interest in becoming a self-appointed ambassador to the Reich was fuelled by a lethal mixture of hubris and disappointment. He had always wanted (as he confessed in later, wiser days to his close friend, Lady Desborough) to 'dabble' in diplomacy. When news came that Goering was ready to provide a private plane to whisk Londonderry, Edith and Mairi, their youngest daughter, over to Bavaria for the Winter Olympics, and to arrange a follow-up programme of political meetings, the Marquess accepted with alacrity.

The visit went well. Travelling on from jollities at Garmisch-Partenkirchen (the Londonderrys had no idea that the hapless inhabitants of these two small rivalrous villages had just been ordered either to become a single unit for the convenience of the Games, or to face mass imprisonment), the visitors were conducted to Berlin. Hitler, holding a dinner in their honour, granted Londonderry the rare privilege of an extensive two-hour interview. The host performed his role with the same skill that he had displayed when entertaining Lord Lothian the previous year: Otto Schmidt, the Führer's sharp-eyed interpreter, was fascinated by the ease with which his master could don a tailcoat and play the role of a charming host, 'moving about amongst his guests as easily as if he had grown up in the atmosphere of a great house'.[6] But Schmidt, while conscious of Hitler's greater political skills, was also rather taken by the visitor, a tall, spare, ruddy-cheeked Englishman who reminded the interpreter of the likeable King Haakon of Norway as he awkwardly searched for the right words: 'one knew at once that this man sincerely desired an understanding with Germany'.[7]

Londonderry was both sincere and reassured. 'I feel we have never spent so full, interesting and delightful a time,' he told the British Ambassador, Eric Phipps.[8] Offering no criticism of Hitler's controversial march into the Rhineland that March, Londonderry listened to a suggestion from Ribbentrop that he might help to further good relations between their two countries by joining the elite company of the Anglo-German Fellowship in London. Already friendly with one of the original founders, Margrethe Gartner, Londonderry was happy to comply; he doubtless felt no qualms about reporting to Berlin on any interesting discussions that took place. It was pleasant, once again, to be of use.

In May, the Marquess went a step further.

Nothing has tainted Londonderry's name more than his decision to hold a three-day house party in May 1936 at Mount Stewart, his splendid Irish home, in honour of Germany's incoming ambassador. The event, from Ribbentrop's own point of view,

fell rather flat. He had expected to meet Britain's influential nobility. Instead, he found himself keeping company with Prince Viktor
zu Wied, an enthusiastic Nazi who had met the Londonderrys on
their recent visit to Germany, and the red-wigged, wealthy and
violently pro-Nazi Laura Corrigan, an American socialite so foolishly snobbish that she had once (so it was cattily whispered) shed
bitter tears at having missed an introduction to the Dardanelles.[9]

Secrecy formed no part of Londonderry's plan for the visit. RAF
planes ostentatiously circled the estate and the unctuous George
Ward Price was invited to stay and chronicle the occasion for the
Daily Mail. Uninvited members of the local press took revenge by
reporting, meanwhile, upon the descent of Ribbentrop's own
swastika-embellished plane, and the raising (although the family
later denied this) of the German flag over an Irish roof. Jokes about
'the Londonderry Herr' were swiftly circulated.

Further entertainment was provided for the gossips and the press
when Ribbentrop, visiting Wynyard Park (the Londonderrys'
equally enormous second home in the north of England) in the
autumn of 1936, had to be restrained from trying to perform a
Nazi salute during the church service at which Edith and Charlie
were being anointed as joint mayors of Durham. Londonderry,
according to the recollections of his daughter, Lady Mairi, was
mortified.[10]

Perceived by the Nazis in 1936 as a man with the influence to
bring a willing England to Germany's heel, the happy Marquess
was courted and flattered. There were visits to Karinhall, Goering's
splendid sporting estate, and only an occasional slap in the face for
Edith, the more outspoken of the two. ('Germany cannot forever
go on making offers to England,' Goering snapped when Edith
dared criticise his colleagues, before hinting that more obliging
allies might be found elsewhere.[11]) There were discussions with
Hitler, during one of which, in October 1936, the German leader
actually told Londonderry about his plans to invade Poland and
Czechoslovakia. Word, plainly, was intended to seep back to

England; on 24 December, Londonderry dutifully conveyed the startling news to Lord Halifax. (Two years later, a sadder and more enlightened Londonderry published that report as 'A Letter to a Friend' in *Ourselves and Germany*, wishing to demonstrate his own good faith.[12])

Possibly, Hitler had expected a warm response from the English government to his proposals; possibly, the Reich's leaders had become aware that, in this particular case, courting the aristocracy had led them to a dead end. Londonderry had a title, great wealth and many fine connections, but he was not, by 1936, a man of influence.

In 1937, it all unravelled. Londonderry's suggestion that Goering might stay at Londonderry House for the coronation of King George VI (leaked news of the invitation caused 3000 British protesters to express their outrage) was declined. Visiting Goering's estate once again that autumn, Londonderry found his host absent and his accommodation relocated. Shunted off to a hunting lodge near the Baltic – but still promised a splendid bison for his target – the Marquess was fobbed off with an old, enfeebled and hastily imported beast that died from the rigours of its train journey before Londonderry ever got near it. A stag was substituted, but the message was plain: the peer had lost his value to Germany. More sadly, he had lost his reputation back at home.

Lord Londonderry died, in 1949, a broken man. Too late, the Marquess had recanted his views and poignantly acknowledged the folly of his endeavours. The fact that he bothered to preserve and even display Ribbentrop's trashy house gift of a mass-produced white Meissen stormtrooper – it is still on show at Mount Stewart today – has been identified as proof of Londonderry's continuing enthusiasm for a regime that, by 1938, he had come to detest. It seems more likely that Ribbentrop's gift was his chosen scourge, a bitter reminder of his own repented stupidity.

'I have been a failure,' Londonderry wrote to Lady Desborough during his last years.[13] What was in his mind was not an ill-judged attempt to make peace with Germany, a country for which he had lost all tenderness, but that he had fallen short of the standard to which he had always aspired. It had been Londonderry's dream to prove that he, too, like the great mastermind of the Congress of Vienna who looked down from his walls in daily and silent reproof, could be a master of diplomacy.

Speaking to students at Nottingham University on Armistice Day 1931 about the possibility of a Nazi leadership in Germany, Lord Lothian, a gangling, friendly figure in a crumpled suit and with a ruffled mop of grey hair, cautioned them not to worry too much. The stories from Berlin were, just then, disturbing (Lothian had heard a few of them himself from Bob Brand); nevertheless, he remained optimistic that, once the German nation received what he vaguely termed 'effective equality', reforms and improvements would quickly follow on behind.

The inheritance of a title and five splendid houses in 1930 had done nothing to diminish the guilt that the former Philip Kerr felt about his contribution to the harsh conditions imposed on Germany in 1919, when he wrote (and then re-wrote) the war guilt clause by which the weight of responsibility had been laid upon the defeated nation. In 1937, Lothian gave away one of his family's two principal seats, Newbattle Abbey in Scotland, to serve as a university summer school. The other, Blickling Hall, one of England's loveliest Jacobean houses, was already, by the mid-thirties, playing a role in which its new owner sincerely believed. A great house, in Lothian's view, was built for the use of society, not a single family. In time, this would encourage him to turn Blickling over to the National Trust, to draw upon as a model; in the interim, Blickling became a discreet and valued meeting place for politicians, newspaper magnates, industrialists and international leaders. When the doors to the great South Drawing Room – still furnished today as it was then by Philip's sister, Minna – were closed, all disturbance was forbidden. Here, rather than the more celebrated Cliveden, was Britain's chief seat of private discussion. Much of it revolved around Germany's position in Europe.*[14]

Hitler's decision, in January 1935, to grant a two-hour interview to Lothian (a man he had never met before and whose few brief visits to Berlin had been strictly connected to Rhodes Scholarships issues) indicates how highly the English peer was regarded by the German Foreign Office. Ribbentrop, describing him to Hitler, identified Lothian as 'the most powerful man in England outside government'.[15] Often wildly inaccurate in his estimations, Ribbentrop, on this occasion, came close to the truth.

Hitler managed the 1935 interview with his usual skill. Readers of Lothian's glowing accounts in *The Times* learned with joy that the German leader had no appetite for war (which was true, if Hitler could get the territories he wanted without bloodshed). Robert Brand, raising a cynical eyebrow, reported to his wife that Philip had returned praising Hitler (who had preached at him without pause for an entire hour) as 'a naïve little carpenter prophet'.[16] Lord Lothian, familiar with Nancy Astor's fierce ways, seemed to think the Führer was rather sweet. Brand's own, more abrasive, view was brushed aside.

Having taken up his stance, Lothian was like a knight locked to his lance. Nothing fazed him. When Hitler advanced upon the Rhineland in March 1936 (challenging the boundary lines ordained by the Treaties of Versailles and Locarno), Lothian sprang

---

* Blickling continued the process of international lectures (under Lothian's direction, and with many contributions from him) held at the Astor-owned Chatham House in St James's Square. But Blickling was far less formal. Glints of Blickling life come through the memories of John Pert, a footman, of a kind employer, a teetotaller, who always had wines for his guests ('decent, damn nice people') and who was himself 'a very quiet man'. Lady Astor was a different matter: 'every time she came down the whole house had to be absolutely, as you might say, bunged up with cut flowers'. Lady Astor, plainly, got her way and – to a degree – ran the show. Tales of her sharing the Chinese Room with Philip and of their being found coming out of it together in night attire, in response to a fire alarm call, were provided by a spicy-minded later tenant and are unverified. (Jan Brookes, Transcripts of Life at Blickling Hall; Merlin Waterson, *A Noble Thing: The National Trust and Its Benefactors* (2011), p. 48.)

to the Führer's defence. Geoffrey Dawson, editor of *The Times*, admiringly passed Lothian's attitude on to a younger Oxford friend: 'It's their own back garden they [the Germans] are walking into.'[17] Thomas Jones, the influential deputy secretary to the Cabinet, was enjoying the comforts of the South Drawing Room at Blickling during the Rhine invasion. Following his host's lead, Jones informed a less honoured friend that a fortunate Europe had just bought herself twenty-five years of peace.

The Rhineland was never going to satisfy Hitler's needs and Lothian was perfectly aware of that fact; eyeing Soviet Russia, Hitler opened a new argument in favour of allowing Germany to enlarge herself as a powerful bulwark against Communism. In 1936, while staying at Rest Harrow (the Astors' fifteen-bedroom beach cottage near Sandwich), Lothian presented an attentive – and rather charmed – Ribbentrop with his thoughts about how German boundary lines could best be revised. In February 1937, a full seventeen months before the British public knew of Hitler's plans to invade Czechoslovakia, Lothian once again spoke to Ribbentrop, reassuring him that there would be no intervention in Germany's plans for expansion. He even added that some Cameroon colonies might be returned to her empire 'if he [Hitler] did not go throwing his weight about'. That June, addressing a Chatham House audience upon 'Germany and the Peace of Europe', Lothian advocated a receptive attitude to Germany's need for '*Lebensraum*' or living-space growth.[18]

Nancy Astor, while devoted to Philip Lothian, disliked orders. Even Philip (whose restraining influence over a strong-willed and contrary character was much missed by her family in later years) could not get Parliament's first elected female representative to pay a visit to Hitler in Berlin. She did, unwillingly, consent to give a lunch for Ribbentrop in London. The occasion was not a success. Jokes about Hitler's moustache and his resemblance to Charlie Chaplin were ill-received; Nancy's name went on the Nazi black-list, together with that of her husband. Waldorf Astor, according to his son, David, was the only man who ever dared to suggest to Hitler, in front of several nervous aides, that the Führer ought to change his policy towards the Jews: 'And Hitler got a spasm, an actual spasm.'[19]

The Astors' friendship with Lord Lothian caused them considerable damage. It was he, above all, who earned them their unlucky and undeserved reputation for seeking friendship with Germany.

In the autumn of 1937, Lothian, acting as a close friend of the tall and ardently religious Edward Halifax, was drawn into plans to bring this future foreign secretary together with Hitler. Goering, mastermind of the scheme, had insisted upon absolute discretion. All went smoothly forward, with the sports-loving aristocrat paying his visit to Berchtesgaden in November under the guise – which deceived nobody – of attending a hunting exhibition. The lunchtime meeting (with Schmidt in attendance as interpreter, together with Dr von Neurath, Germany's foreign secretary, and Ivone Kirkpatrick from the British Embassy) was judged to be a success. Halifax, while determined not to perform the required Salaam to his brown-uniformed host (the visitor raised his hat to the heiling crowds instead), found Hitler pleasant to deal with, although sorrowful that the British newspapers were so unkind to him. Good news came home. Philip Lothian was absolutely right, Halifax declared; Britain, so long as she stayed out of Germany's projects in the east, need fear no war. King George VI was delighted. The more appeasement-minded newspapers hastened – once again – to tone down all critical references to the Reich.

A plan that had been hatched in the British Foreign Office, meanwhile, had gone awry. Robert Vansittart, permanent under-secretary of the Foreign Office, a position that put him supremely in charge at Gilbert Scott's opulent palace for civil servants, loathed appeasement. He intensely resented Lord Halifax and Lord Lothian for arranging visits to further that suspect policy, and for doing so without his permission. Knowing that Goering had insisted upon discretion, Vansittart had waited until just before Halifax left England to leak news of the mission to London's most gossipy left-wing journalist: Claud Cockburn, editor of a Soviet-funded news-sheet called *The Week*.

On 17 November, in a damaging article that entirely failed to derail Halifax's visit, *The Week* identified 'that little knot of expatriate Americans and "super-nationally-minded" Englishmen' who were said to move in the Astors' circle. It went on to accuse them of conspiring with Halifax to fix the English peer's mission to Berchtesgaden in order to offer Hitler a 'deal'. Accuracy was not *The Week*'s strong point; Halifax was not even at Cliveden on the weekend that Cockburn had pinpointed for the crafting of this insidious plot. It hardly mattered: the purpose, for a mischievous editor with a clear agenda, was to raise trouble for the wealthy Astors and their friends. Eleven days later, another small paper, *Reynold's News*, repeated the allegation and added a catch-all name for the Astor circle. That phrase, 'the Cliveden Set', became part of the language after the brilliantly topical cartoonist David Low mocked the perceived group as 'the Shiver Sisters', skipping to the beat of Dr Goebbels's baton. Taking their place in Low's high-kicking chorus line of appeasers alongside Lord Lothian, Waldorf Astor and Nancy were the two newspaper editors with whom the Astors were most closely linked: Geoffrey Dawson of *The Times* and James Garvin of the *Observer*. (Shiela Grant Duff had left Garvin's newpaper in 1937 because of his pro-appeasement policy.)

Low's image, although swiftly taken for the truth, was not quite fair. Cliveden had never been just a haven for appeasers. Bob Brand, to offer one exception, was among the Astors' most regular visitors; he was also fiercely anti-appeasement. Robert Barrington-Ward, the deputy editor of *The Times* and an ardent appeaser, never went to Cliveden at all.[20]

Robert Vansittart paid heavily for his tricksy intervention in government plans. In January 1938, he was given a fine new job title and a powerless role; Anthony Eden, his boss as foreign secretary,

was replaced by Lothian's friend and fellow appeaser Edward
Halifax.* Nancy Astor consoled herself, when she finally encountered Claud Cockburn, by threatening to spit at him. Cockburn,
unperturbed, remarked that he admired Lady Astor's spirit.

Lothian's intentions had been all for the best; recognition that
he had dangerously misjudged the intentions of the Reich came
slowly to a brilliant and opinionated man. Following the invasion
of Czechoslovakia in the spring of 1939, Lothian recorded his new
view of Hitler as 'a fanatical gangster who will stop at nothing to
beat down all possibility of resistance anywhere to his will . . .'[21] But
this was a private confession in a letter to a friend. It would take
another three months before Lord Lothian was ready to announce
his conversion in the House of Lords. In September, as evidence
of his complete change of heart, Lothian took up Edward Halifax's
offer and went to Washington as ambassador to the United States.

Philip Lothian was arguably at his best in the final year of his life.
Lord Halifax had given him the post of ambassador because of his
extensive contacts both on Capitol Hill and within the American
press. (It was Lothian who had helped the *Washington Post* get its
world scoop on Wallis Simpson's relationship with Edward VIII.)
His mission, a delicate one, was to secure aid for England from an
America that did not, in the autumn of 1940, relish the prospect
of involvement in another war with Europe.

Lothian's first step gave the advantage to a mistrustful America,
offering her – the act of barter was diplomatically crucial – strategic landing spots in the Caribbean in exchange for a transatlantic
gift of fifty thoroughly obsolete warships. A gesture had been made;
America had ceased to be neutral. That symbolic act was all that the
Ambassador required. Returning to England in November, Lothian

* Eden resigned in February 1938 over issues regarding the process of agreements with
Mussolini that were being sought by Chamberlain. Eden did not, however, share the hostility to appeasement that was felt at that time by Vansittart. He had, in 1934, expressed
a high opinion of Hitler, and was not, at the time of his resignation, opposed to the
policy of negotiating with the fascist powers in Europe.

pushed swiftly forward with the more complex task of persuading America to provide Britain with arms and financial aid. President Roosevelt, while privately supportive, needed to justify the proposal to Congress; Lothian, by persuading Churchill to spell out in a letter the imperative need for assistance, created the conditions that were required. The result was the Lend-Lease Act. Passed in 1941, it marked the introduction of a massive programme for arms production that would ensure, when America herself entered the war, that she was already well prepared.

Philip Lothian died of uremia on 11 December 1940, having refused – in accordance with the strict principles of his Christian Science beliefs – to be treated by the methods of conventional medicine. Speaking in the House of Commons, Churchill paid glowing tribute to a brilliant, conscientious and beguilingly charming man who had died – as Churchill carefully stressed – with honour.

Declassified documents and a fascinating documentary film, *The Restless Conscience*, have recently helped to highlight a connection between Lord Lothian and a fellow Christian Scientist. Helmuth von Moltke, half-English, toweringly tall and very handsome (an awed Leslie Rowse recalled Moltke as slender, grave, dark and glittering like a sword), came to Oxford in 1934 with the ostensible purpose of furthering his legal studies. But Moltke had also come to explore the mood in England about a possible change of government in Germany. Introduced by Lothian to a group of his fellow Round Table members in 1935, von Moltke spoke to them of his desire to bring Hitler to trial – murder was against every principle of his Christian Science conscience – before establishing a new democracy in Germany. Since Moltke made no further visits to England, it would seem that his proposals received a disappointing response.*

---

* Arrested at the beginning of 1944, Moltke was himself granted only the most tawdry of Nazi puppet trials before being murdered as a result of the 20 July plot, in which he had (for purely ethical reasons) refused to play an active part. Hava Kohav Beller's *The Restless Conscience* was released in 2005.

Lord Lothian is better known for his connection to another German student at Oxford, a latecomer to the resistance group whose larger meetings were held at Kreisau, the cultured, sleepily old-fashioned country home that had once belonged to von Moltke's illustrious great-uncle, the celebrated Prussian general.

Adam von Trott was staying at Cliveden in 1931, as a guest of his Oxford friend, the liberal-minded and intensely shy David Astor, third son of Waldorf and Nancy, when he held his first political conversations with Philip Lothian. Philip, from this point on, would use his position as secretary to the Rhodes Scholarships to simplify Adam's travels in and out of a Germany that had become, for anybody who did not retain the luxury of Wilfrid Israel's dual nationality, a form of prison. Between February 1937 and November 1938, the young German – Adam was still under thirty – was free to live outside the country about which he remained so painfully torn, loving his Fatherland, hating its Nazi regime. Exile was not a luxury. Like Nikolaus Pevsner, Adam felt constantly homesick; unlike Pevsner, Adam von Trott, a young lawyer of impeccable Aryan background, always had the option to return and find employment.

Back in Berlin in the spring of 1939, and working in a branch of the German Foreign Office, Adam agreed to return to England as the unofficial representative for a plan that might, so the opposition hoped, fend off the growing threat of war, if only England's approval could be gained. In June, Adam paid a return visit to Oxford where, or so they later recalled, old friends like Leslie Rowse and Maurice Bowra received his plans with horror and disgust. (Bowra, concerned for his new image as warden of Wadham College, actually claimed to have slammed his door shut in Adam's face.)

Cliveden had proved more welcoming. On 3 June, Adam arrived there to address an assembly of influential politicians and journalists.

Handsome, assured, intelligent and forceful, Adam spoke,

according to the eyewitness account given by David Astor in *The Restless Conscience*, about Germany's unwillingness for a war and the German Army's need for support in the undercover plottings of its resistance group. A good impression was made. The proposals – Germany's right to retain the occupied Sudetenland, and, far more disturbingly, a promise from Britain and France to stand aside if Poland was annexed – were not dismissed. Plans were made for Adam to visit an unresponsive Chamberlain on 7 June, and then talk to Churchill. A carefully phrased document (it was drawn up by Adam and his friend Peter Bielenberg for the eyes of Hitler) informed the Führer that peace might yet be possible, and on acceptable terms.

Adam's ambitious project was less warmly received by Shiela Grant Duff and her (horrified) Czech house-guest, Hubert Ripka. A warning letter was sent to Churchill, whose predictable disapproval of the scheme was swiftly conveyed to Cliveden. Waldorf Astor was not pleased. When David Astor travelled out to see Adam in Berlin later that summer, he went against the orders of his father.

In 1940, Adam von Trott married Clarita von Tiefenbacher. Three years later, he joined the intrigue against Hitler's life that would lead, in 1944, to his show trial, to be followed by a slow, cruel death at the hands of the Gestapo, at the Plötzensee jail in Berlin.

Between 1969 and 1971, when the German Rhodes Scholarships were once again in the process of being revived, the author James Fox conducted a series of detailed interviews with the German survivors among von Trott's colleagues at Oxford, and with Charles Collins, one of his closest English friends at Balliol. An eminent group who were, by 1969, dispersed across Germany, Britain and America, the former scholars still spoke with fondness about their days at Oxford. Karl Gunther Merz, who had rowed Oriel to victory in 1936, confessed that he still treasured the cut-down blades and carried them on his travels as a treasured mascot. Fritz Caspari recalled his pleasant surprise, on returning to St John's in 1946, to be presented with a half-drunk bottle of Moselle. The bottle, carefully preserved in the college cellars, was still marked with his name, and with the date of his last drink: May 1936.

The scholars had not, contrary to James Fox's expectations, formed a close community during their time at Oxford; it appeared, nevertheless, that they all held strong and individual views about Adam von Trott.

Dietrich von Bothmer, who went on to become an eminent museum curator, expressed disapproval of what he perceived as von Trott's aristocratic approach to diplomacy. ('I did not run around the country getting myself invited to country houses.') Adolf Schleppegrell, the University College fellow who had attended the celebrated 1933 Oxford Union debate on king or country, proved equally dismissive. The idea of conducting undercover negotiations with England had been, he thought, 'a pipe dream ... unthinkable. I never understood it.'[22] Fritz Schumacher of New College was uncomfortable about Adam's decision to work from within the Nazi machine. To take employment from the Nazis, in Schumacher's crisply expressed view, was equivalent to endorsing their regime. The only options for an opponent were either to go undercover (as Bonhoeffer had done) or to leave the country (as Schumacher himself had elected to do).[23]

But Adam von Trott – conceded by all the former scholars to have possessed exceptional charisma, charm and integrity – also won support from some of them for the heroism of his lonely endeavours to negotiate a peace. Charles Collins, his contemporary at Balliol, admired Adam's persevering determination to convince the appeasers that their cause was worthwhile. It was tragic, he believed, that 'a remarkable and a noble young man' was never allowed to put his views to Churchill: 'the consequences could have been significant'.[24] Fritz Caspari agreed with Collins that Adam's mission had deserved more support from England;

Alexander Boker, from Corpus Christi, spoke more strongly still. He had himself provided Adam with some valuable contacts, including an introduction in America to Germany's former Chancellor, Heinrich Brüning (enabled by the Academic Assistance Council to become an Oxford academic, before he took up a post at Harvard). Boker, writing to James Fox in 1969, expressed the view that Britain's reluctance to commit to the German resistance had been a grave mistake. 'I do indeed feel that Adam von Trott and other German anti-Nazis deserved more trust and encouragement and support abroad and especially in Britain than they received. If they had been able to give more encouraging reports to their fellow conspirators at home things may have taken a better turn for all of us . . .'[25]

27

RESISTERS AND INFORMERS

(1933–40)

In January 1938, Robert Vansittart's important role as permanent under-secretary to the British Foreign Office was taken over by the uncle of Lady Camilla Stauffenberg (the pretty young Englishwoman who fell in love with – and later married – the young man she met while acting in *As You Like It* at a Bavarian schloss). Small, brisk and ruddy-cheeked, Alexander Cadogan was perched in the seat of authority throughout the month that Hitler coolly annexed the land of his birth to Germany, in the Anschluss. Vansittart might have considered issuing some form of protest; Cadogan saw no point in getting mixed up in foreign affairs. 'After all, it wasn't our business,' he wrote to Nevile Henderson, Britain's pro-Nazi ambassador in Berlin on 22 April: 'we had no particular feelings for the Austrians'.[1]

Cadogan, having made his opinion clear, saw no reason to consult Henderson about a report relating to further expansion plans that had reached him a month earlier. The informant was Captain Malcolm Christie, a former pilot who had become, since 1932, one of Robert Vansittart's most trusted agents in Berlin. Christie sent word that Hitler's next targeted victim was to be Czechoslovakia; he added that 'cooler heads' in Germany (by which he meant Hitler's opponents) were hoping that France and England would condemn this venture. He anticipated that an attack on the Czech borderlands would be launched within two to three months.[2]

With retrospect, it is easy enough to see how, from the Anschluss onwards, Hitler's designs to seize Germany's neighbouring lands followed a six-monthly pattern: Austria in the spring; the Sudetenland in the autumn; Czechoslovakia in the spring; Poland in the autumn. At the time, although Czechoslovakia's future was giving cause for anxiety in England ('The German Minority in Czechoslovakia' had been chosen for discussion at Chatham House as early as 1 November 1937), such a programme was not apparent. The warning from Christie was passed to Neville Chamberlain – and was set aside.

In Germany, Hitler proceeded as he had planned. Czechoslovakia, in the summer of 1938, was ordered to prepare to yield its western borders (the Sudetenland) to Germany, or to face armed invasion. England, so Hitler's envoys had led him to believe, would not object. Ribbentrop had brought back scornful accounts of an enfeebled island nation, run by elderly, peace-loving aristocrats who dreaded nothing more than confrontation. A recent interview with Lord Halifax by Hitler's tigerishly handsome adjutant, Captain Fritz Wiedemann, had produced further reassurance. Halifax, according to Wiedemann and his enterprising Jewish mistress, Princess Stephanie Hohenlohe, was longing for that happy moment when England's friend, the Führer, would ride forth along the Mall at the side of George VI.*

---

* This remarkable image owed less to the cautiously spoken Lord Halifax than to the fantasies of Princess Stephanie's British paymaster, Lord Rothermere. Rothermere was later obliged to admit that the voluptuous Princess received $20,000 a year for her services as a press informant and go-between. Rothermere himself went so far as to suggest that Hitler should add Romania to his land-grab list.

A different view of Britain was held by a group of high-ranking dissidents who controlled the only military intelligence unit in Germany that could rival the powers of the SS: the Abwehr. Informed of Hitler's plans for expansion as early as the beginning of November 1937, these sober Prussian generals had been appalled by his ambitions. By the summer of 1938, Admiral Wilhelm Canaris and Colonel Ludwig Beck had prepared a scheme of action of their own. Confident that Britain and France would oppose any further acts of annexation, they proposed to use that moment of attack on the Sudetenland to stage a coup, arrest Hitler and establish a new government in Germany. On 19 August, a lone envoy was despatched to secure the backing of the British. War was never on the agenda. What was required from England by the Abwehr generals was a simple show of moral resolve and diplomatic support: at the moment that Hitler moved, Britain must speak up for the menaced territory. They asked, in short, not for war, but for the threat of war.

Born in 1881, the envoy was an old-fashioned aristocrat who belonged to the same religious, monarchist and resolutely anti-Nazi family as Dietrich Bonhoeffer's hostess in Pomerania. Dressed in civilian clothes, Ewald von Kleist passed unobtrusively through Tempelhof Airport and was flown to Croydon. Arriving at the Foreign Office, he was interviewed by Robert Vansittart, the embittered man who now bore the impressive title of chief diplomatic advisor. Kleist presented the bare bones of the plan; Vansittart, impressed, did the best he could. He put Kleist in touch with Winston Churchill. (Later, when Sir Robert turned against the resistance, he claimed that Kleist had made unacceptable demands for 'a deal' over the ever-contentious Polish corridor. That was an embellishment; the corridor had formed no part of the discussion.)

Churchill, during the mid-thirties, had been one among the many politicians in foreign governments who admired Hitler's achievements. Writing for the *Strand Magazine* in November 1935, he declared that England, if placed under the moral and economic strains that had been imposed on Germany after the war, would consider herself fortunate indeed to find such a powerful leader as Adolf Hitler, a man 'to restore our courage and lead us back to our place among the nations'.[3] By 1938, however, Churchill had reached the unfashionable viewpoint that today seems admirably prescient. Hostile to Hitler and profoundly uneasy about the Führer's future intentions, the 64-year-old statesman embraced the idea of any activity that would cut the German despot down.

The meeting took place at Chartwell. Kleist, once again, explained the need not for action, but for a display of strength. Churchill, acting with the approval of Lord Halifax, the Foreign Secretary, and breaking all the rules of diplomatic protocol, offered to provide Kleist with a letter of written assurance. If Hitler proceeded with his threatened attack upon the Sudetenland (envisaged by Churchill as an act of military aggression), Britain would not stand peacefully aside. Indeed, he wrote to Kleist: 'The spectacle of an armed attack by Germany upon a small neighbour and the bloody fighting that will follow will rouse the whole British Empire and compel the gravest decisions. Do not, I pray you, be misled upon this point.'[4]

Churchill's letter – it was incriminating enough to seal the recipient's fate when it was later discovered among his papers – was joyfully shared with Kleist's fellow conspirators in the Abwehr.* What these principled men failed to understand was that, however fine such assurances sounded, they were worthless. Robert Vansittart, by the summer of 1938, commmanded a degree of influence but very little authority; Winston Churchill, not the Foreign Secretary,

---

* Kleist, implicated in the Stauffenberg Plot of 20 July 1944, was hanged at Plötzensee Prison in April 1945. He was 64 years old. His son and namesake, whom the elder Kleist had encouraged to undertake a suicide attack on Hitler in January 1940 (it failed because the Führer suddenly decided not to show up for his appointment) survived the war.

had signed the letter. Fretfully established on the fringes of power, Churchill was helpless to influence events if his less warlike Prime Minister disagreed.

The Abwehr plan for a coup d'état against Hitler remained on course, despite the resignation of Colonel Beck, throughout the anxious final days of August 1938. Hitler, once challenged by Britain, was to be arrested and certified by Dietrich Bonhoeffer's father, Karl, one of Germany's most eminent psychiatrists. Fritz Schulenburg, the only one of Tisa's brothers who had turned entirely against the Nazi regime (a change of heart which had been prudently hidden from his family, including Tisa), was to secure the administrative sector of Berlin, pending the establishment of a new government in Germany.

On 5 September 1938, news of the imminent coup was conveyed to Lord Halifax by Theo Kordt, a resistance worker who was operating from within the German Embassy in London. On 12–13 September, a German envoy flew into England with a further message for Vansittart. Hitler was preparing to march east towards Czechoslovakia on 25 September. The moment had come for England to stand by her promise.

And – notoriously – the moment passed. Apprised of the need for urgent action, the Prime Minister flew out to meet Hitler – it was only the second time in his life that Neville Chamberlain had ever left England – on 15 September 1938. Having assured the Führer that Britain would neither threaten Germany, nor oppose in any way Hitler's current plans, Chamberlain held a further discussion with President Daladier of France about what – without risk – might be done to demonstrate good faith. The Czechs were advised that England and France would defend their country's own continued state of independence, but only if they conceded to Germany the mountainous Sudetenland in which lay all their defences. France, at this moment, exhibited more courage than England. When Czechoslovakia responded, on 23 September, by mobilising her troops against attack, the French followed suit.

Daladier had acted as the Abwehr generals still hoped that their friends in England would. Chamberlain pursued an entirely different course. The humiliation of the Czechs and the loss of the Sudetenland seemed to him a small price to pay for the future security of England. To the anger of Daladier and the dismay of the Czechs (who were excluded from all negotiations), the Munich Pact was signed by an exhausted but triumphant Chamberlain at 1.30 a.m. on 30 September 1938. Hitler had been confronted with no challenge. Instead, he had acquired, without bloodshed, the right to enter and possess himself of the Sudetenland and – implicitly – to exercise control over an unprotected Czechoslovakia.

Alighting at Croydon a few hours later, Neville Chamberlain delivered a proclamation that was, for a habitually sober speaker, almost ecstatic. Behind him, in several of the news photographs, it is possible to see the wan figure of Theo Kordt staring straight ahead, expressionless, as the Prime Minister flourishes the document on which Hitler had, without a moment's hesitation, scribbled his signature. Chamberlain himself had chosen the wording. Hitler, having seen how easy it was to gain Britain's acquiescence, was delighted to endorse every word. Certainly, he shared in the 'desire of our two peoples never to go to war against each other again'. How could he ever wish to go to war against such an obliging ally?

Back in England, where almost nothing was known, in the years before the war, about the existence of an opposition movement within Germany itself, Chamberlain's announcement was received with relief, but not with universal rejoicing. Duff Cooper, addressing an almost silent House of Commons in his speech of resignation on 3 October, pointed out that Chamberlain, referring in Parliament six days earlier to the Czechs who inhabited the Sudetenland as these 'people of whom we know nothing', could just as well have been talking about the people of Serbia in 1914.[5]

At the Oxford Union, two weeks after Duff Cooper's resignation, a young Edward Heath defended (and won by 320 to 266 votes) a proposal startlingly different to that of 1933: 'That This House deplores the Government's Policy of Peace without Honour'. In Charlie Chaplin's American studios, the English-born director prepared his own response: *The Great Dictator* set out to make Hitler look both menacing and absurd. Warnings were instantly issued from Chaplin's anxious homeland that any film making fun of the Führer would be banned from view in Britain.*

Walking through London a day or so after Chamberlain's announcement, the novelist Morgan Forster mused on the hollowness of the applause with which the Prime Minister's words had been greeted: 'I knew at once that the news was only good in patches. Peace flapped from the posters, and not upon the wings of angels.'[6]

Peace, nevertheless, remained welcome to England in the autumn of 1938; not least because its politicians, dismayed by Hitler's claims of Germany's military strength, believed their country was – as yet – entirely unequipped to win a war against such a formidable power. Behind the scenes, with ever-increasing urgency, strategies were being frantically sought for the preservation of peace.

The group of men who had assembled around Wilhelm Canaris at the Abwehr were only a few among a considerable number of German subjects who were desperately searching, between 1937 and December 1940, for the framework of a negotiated peace that might save the world from a second devastating war. In Britain, one of the most tireless groups of peace-seekers convened regular meetings at an unobtrusive flat in Cornwall Gardens. This 'safe house' for agents and visiting diplomats, tucked away in the streets behind the Albert Hall, belonged to Philip Conwell-Evans, a

---

* War changed everything. Released in England in 1940, *The Great Dictator* became one of Chaplin's greatest successes.

Welsh-born academic who had translated Georges Duhamel's *Civilization* (a disturbing collection of wartime stories) and written on international affairs in collaboration with the Labour politician Lord Noel-Buxton, before accepting a chair in international diplomacy at the University of Königsberg.*

Conwell-Evans's distressing experience of working at a German university in 1933, during the period when professors were being brusquely dismissed, was offset by his sense that Hitler was bringing confidence and strength back into a broken land. Returning to England in 1934, Conwell-Evans's German connections led him to join the new Anglo-German Fellowship, the body that he would faithfully serve as secretary, alongside Ernest Tennant. Introduced to Philip Lothian, Conwell-Evans found himself in sympathy with Lothian's views about the injustices that had been inflicted upon Germany at Versailles. He became a regular visitor to Blickling, participating in the conferences held there during the mid-thirties, but always taking the view that a victimised Germany was entitled to increase her boundaries and to conduct her internal policies, however disagreeable, without interference from Britain. It was a view which Lord Lothian, back in the mid-thirties, promoted and endorsed, both at Blickling and through the series of international talks that he was tirelessly organising at Chatham House in London.

Enlightenment came to Conwell-Evans in 1937, when he was introduced to two remarkable German brothers. Erich Kordt was a pre-war Rhodes scholar who had access to privileged information through his position in Ribbentrop's Berlin-based Ministry of Foreign Affairs. Theo, his older brother, had taken over Erich's previous position as an attaché at the German Embassy in London. Both brothers were profoundly concerned by what was happening in Germany, as was their lively and attractive young cousin, Suzanne Simonis, a girl whose formidable memory added to her

* Lord Noel-Buxton's interests included the Balkan States and the League of Nations.

value as a willing go-between and message courier. The Kordts, once their new associate had expressed a wish to assist their clandestine activities, introduced him to a man for whom Philip Conwell-Evans would conceive an enduring admiration. His name was Malcolm Christie.

Born (like Conwell-Evans himself) in 1881 and trained as an engineer, Malcolm Christie had been educated in Germany before he joined the Royal Air Force in 1914. Following four years as an air attaché in America, and a further three-year stint at a similar post with the British in Berlin, Christie's circle of contacts was both wide and impressive. In 1926, aged 45, he was officially retired on grounds of ill-health; unofficially, as a fluent linguist with a coolly rational mind, a formidable memory and a gift for inspiring loyalty, Christie became an invaluable undercover agent for MI6.

Respected in London for his friendly connections with various German industrialists (he was especially close to Gustav Krupp von Bohlen, an anti-Nazi in a family whose armaments business bound them to Hitler), Christie's especial value lay in the close links that he had formed, in part through his experience as a pilot and a skilled engineer, with Hermann Goering. The friendship, dating back to the years before the Reich, was intimate enough for the loquacious and boastful Goering to act, unwittingly, as one of Christie's most cherished sources of information.

Quiet, intelligent, resourceful and courteous, Christie was both liked and trusted by Robert Vansittart, with whom – in the years when 'Van' was a force to be reckoned with and one of the German resistance's most powerful allies – he shared the conviction that England's salvation lay in arming herself to the teeth.

Much of the information that Christie supplied to Vansittart was kept by him in copy and forms part of a collection now held at Churchill College in Cambridge. The detail of the espionage, some of which was supplied by the Kordts, but much of which came from a range of sub-agents who worked for Christie, is remarkable for its specific nature. Reports included a minutely factual analysis of Hitler's takeover of the Saar region in 1935, and the ensuing plebiscite; conversations with Goering, and quantified disclosures, regularly submitted between 1933 and 1939, on the current strength of the Luftwaffe. Christie's contacts were located in Switzerland, Holland, Czechoslovakia and inside Germany itself, where an intriguing figure called Gerhard Ritter, signing himself most frequently as Kn, acted as Christie's most regular source of information. The material that Malcolm Christie meticulously passed along to Robert Vansittart from this richly diverse group of informants indicates that the Foreign Office was made aware, at all stages before the war, of what was being planned in Germany.

For Christie and his associates, the knowledge that so much was being supplied, while nothing was being done, must have been both frustrating and painful. In March 1936, Christie warned Vansittart of the Rhineland invasion a day ahead of that event. On 6 July 1937, he alerted Vansittart to a state of dissension both in the German government and on the General Staff. (Vansittart himself made a note that this report had been personally 'suppressed by Eden', the foreign secretary.)

Christie's information was already being consistently blocked, buried or ignored at the Foreign Office before the abrupt removal, in January 1938, of Robert Vansittart from his position of power. Vansittart himself was reluctantly acknowledged to have acquired a level of expertise that proved hard to dispense with. Still called in for advice, he could, on occasion, control events as if nothing had changed. It was not to be expected that Christie, as his most valued agent, would receive similar respect from the new regime of Cadogan and Halifax. Nor did he. Among several disconcerting examples, one glares out.

In the spring of 1939, Ivone Kirkpatrick, recently transferred from the British Embassy in Berlin to advise on German affairs at the Foreign Office in London, read a note from Christie to

Vansittart dated 18 May. It warned the Foreign Office of plans for a Nazi Soviet alliance. Having read it, Kirkpatrick marked the document 'Unreliable' and stowed it away. Three months later, the Nazis and Soviets shocked the world with their Russo-German pact. Questions were asked at the British Foreign Office about what, precisely, their intelligence operatives had been doing? No answer was forthcoming from a department that was already doing everything it could to cover its tracks.[7]

Christie did not give up. On 27 June 1939, he advised the Foreign Office of a September invasion of Poland; on 26 August, more precise details were given of where, and with what level of strength, the attack would take place.[8] No response to this information was received or ever recorded. Doubtless, Christie's letter went the way of its predecessor: slipped into a drawer and marked as unworthy of attention.

The attempt to influence larger events had failed. On a smaller, human scale, the intelligence agents and resistance fighters saluted each other for a valiant mutual effort that, as Germany prepared to invade Poland in September 1939, seemed doomed to failure. Malcolm Christie wrote to Theo Kordt, his tubby, tenacious and gallant ally at the German Embassy, as Kordt prepared to depart:

Dear Friend,

I hope you do not mind my addressing you thus, for friend you have been and are to your own great people, to us Britons, and to all who are struggling to restore the conceptions of honour and integrity amongst nations.

I am writing you these few lines to wish you a deeply felt 'Auf Wiedersehn'. If you must leave us soon, ours is the loss: if a miracle should keep you here, ours to rejoice. Thank you a thousand times for all your noble work: come what may, we shall regard you always as a great gentleman and a great Christian.

Believe me, yours ever, M. Graham Christie.[9]

Peace, in the fear-filled autumn of 1939, was still being eagerly sought by both Britain and Germany. The first of many compromises proposed to England by Hitler, on 6 October 1939, aroused a frenzy of excitement and hope. Andrew Roberts, in his fine biography of Lord Halifax, *The Holy Fox*, has noted that 2450 letters reached Chamberlain's office over the next three days and that 75 per cent of them begged Britain to accept Hitler's proposals. In November, when the Kings of Holland and Belgium presented another peace overture, the renowned pacifist and former Labour leader George Lansbury received a postbag from 14,000 eager advocates. Halifax, writing to his friend Philip Lothian in his new post as ambassador to the United States during that same month, passed along the news that the Foreign Office was now in 'almost daily' receipt of peace feelers from the German resistance.[10] His groan is almost audible.

By November 1939, Lothian had ceased to see any merit in a negotiated peace and Halifax himself had become sceptical. In March 1940, the Foreign Secretary was handed a remarkable peace proposal originating from one of the most eminent German resistance figures, Ulrich von Hassell, a former German ambassador to Italy. Written on 28 February, Hassell's document ranged far beyond the usual compromises. Poland and Czechoslovakia were to be restored and allowed to become free democracies; Germany was to become a democratic republic, adhering to Christian ethics and restored to unfettered intellectual activity. It was not, however, explained just how this utopian world would be achieved, and Hassell's proposals had initially reached a very doubtful Alexander Cadogan through a man called J. J. Lonsdale Bryans for whom Cadogan felt an instinctive mistrust.

Perhaps Cadogan's instincts were right. Bryans reported back to von Hassell on 14 April that the letter had won over Halifax and gone straight to the Prime Minister. That was untrue. The letter reached Halifax – and stopped. Halifax went to Washington in December 1940, to serve as British ambassador to the US in the place of his late and dear friend Philip Lothian. Before leaving, he annotated the letter: 'Mr Hassell. Note on principles considered essential for the re-establishment of permanent peace.' In 1992, that proposal was still tucked away in a collection titled, with almost wilful drabness, 'Private Office Papers from 1940'.[11]

By the close of 1940, Churchill had been prime minister for half a savage year. France was an occupied country; Britain, having survived a terrifying summer of aerial warfare, still lacked the substantial backing from America of which she increasingly stood in desperate need. Power and experience had hardened Churchill. Some 60,000 Germans living in England had been interned or deported within the first months of his leadership. In December 1940, a new order went out: all future appeals for peace or collaboration from Germany must be categorically rejected. Any members of the German resistance who attempted to negotiate a deal would henceforth be met (so Churchill instructed Anthony Eden, his secretary of state for war) with 'absolute silence'.[12]

Robert Vansittart retired at the beginning of the war to live near the Denham film studio for which he had helped his friend Alexander Korda to secure government funding. Between diverting himself by writing poems, the newly ennobled Vansittart wrote a book. He broadcast it as his personal pep talk to the nation.

Published in 1941, *Black Record: Germans Past and Present* launched a savage attack on Germany and on the German people. While discreet about his own previous connection to the German resistance, the author was not afraid to dismiss his former friends and allies as feeble, unconvincing and dishonest.

Having repudiated the resistance in print, Lord Vansittart went on to marry his actions to his words. After the war, he was asked for a letter of support by gentle, reticent Theo Kordt, who was struggling to return with his wife to their home in the British-occupied Rhineland. Vansittart responded by posting off a public declaration that condemned Theo Kordt as a man whose policy had always been to give Hitler 'a free hand in expansion to the limit'.[13]

Vansittart did worse. Approached by both of the Kordt brothers to help defend the name of Baron Ernst Weizsäcker (the widely respected former secretary of state) during the time when their heroic undercover colleague was put on trial as a war criminal by the United States, the former Foreign Office supremo fired off another public salvo. On this occasion, Vansittart proposed that neither Weizsäcker nor the Kordts themselves merited clemency of any kind, since none of them had done anything 'in particular' to help the British.[14]

Vansittart's behaviour was shameful, but he was not alone in letting his former contacts down. Alexander Cadogan, to whom his niece, Camilla Stauffenberg, sent frantic pleas for support to be provided to Baron Weizsäcker's case, found himself suddenly too busy to check his files for evidence of any link between Weizsäcker, the Kordts and the Foreign Office. (A strong connection had existed, however, and Cadogan assuredly knew it.) Lord Halifax, a deeply religious man, showed more of a conscience. Having despatched a sworn affidavit that declared, with untypical bluntness, that Lord Vansittart was lying through his teeth about the Kordts, Halifax sent a private letter of protest to President Truman about Ernst Weizsäcker's entirely unjustifiable seven-year sentence to the Landsberg Fortress (a prison in which Hitler himself, back in 1924–5, had spent a mere eleven months for trying to overthrow the government). Halifax's plea, combined with appeals for mercy that arrived from Bertrand Russell, Gilbert Murray, George Bell and even, eventually, the Pope, resulted in a qualified success. Imprisoned for a year – one month longer than Hitler, and without the degree of luxury that had been conferred upon a leader-in-waiting – the emaciated, stooping and prematurely aged Baron Weizsäcker died shortly after his release in 1950. Half a century later, his legally trained younger son, Richard, who had helped to defend his father at the trial, was appointed as president of the Federal Republic of Germany.

Erich Kordt's *Nicht aus den Akten* was published in Germany in 1948, in direct response to the arraignment and trial of Ernst Weizsäcker, Kordt's friend. The fact that it contained detailed information about the reports that were passed by the Kordts and their allies to the Foreign Office caused a degree of concern in Whitehall. A refutation was mooted and, after a period of consideration, was abandoned. The book remains, to this day, without an English publisher.

Conwell-Evans wrote *None So Blind: A Study of the Crisis Years 1930–1939* in 1941, basing it upon the voluminous bundles of papers that he had prevented Malcolm Christie from destroying in 1939, following the declaration of war. Meticulously, Conwell-Evans chronicled and cited the reports that Christie had passed, over the years, to Robert Vansittart. Christie himself contributed a final chapter to a remarkable account of the life of a secret agent.

Conwell-Evans hesitated to publish the book in wartime. In 1947, however, a hundred copies were privately printed for distribution to a carefully selected group of readers. The book never reached them. Instead, for reasons that remain undisclosed, the hundred copies were embargoed and placed in a bank vault, from which they were only (and most unwillingly) released to an executor after the death of Conwell-Evans in 1958. Since the book remains almost impossible to find (Amazon unfailingly lists it as 'currently unavailable' and no copy is held at the British Library), chances are that an embarrassing publication was then destroyed.

Conwell-Evans severed his connection with the Kordts after the war. The reason that their names do not appear in the pages of *None So Blind*, a book written during the war, is most likely to have been protective: identification would have endangered their lives in Germany. Even Malcolm Christie, paying tribute to their courage in his final chapter of Conwell-Evans' *None So Blind*, described Theo and Erich only as 'my German friends who worked during the years 1933–1939 to defeat Hitler's war plans'. These brave men had, he wrote, taken great risks and shown uncommon courage in all their endeavours. 'They were inspired by one purpose – to liberate their own country from the blight of Nazi rule and to help to save Europe from the devastation of another war. They were Europeans in the best sense of that term . . .'[15]

In 1971, the ninety-year-old Christie died after mysteriously falling from his bedroom window. In 1972, the former agent's devoted housekeeper donated all of his surviving papers to Churchill College, Cambridge. Separately, and prudently, she lodged with the London Library Christie's single precious copy of the elusive *None So Blind*. It is there still. The flyleaf label of a book that is not often read carries a simple inscription, written by an unknown hand: 'In Memory of Malcolm Christie'.

28

FATE AND CIRCUMSTANCE

(1939–45)

War, in retrospect, seems to have loomed bleak as a certainty beyond the cheating brightness of the summer of 1939. Richard Haldane's great project, the Territorial Army, had been instructed to double its intake that March. On 27 April, six months of military training became compulsory for all males aged twenty or twenty-one. By July, plans were being laid for the swift future evacuation of children from cities in Britain. By August, sandbags had become a familiar eyesore to Londoners, while gasmasks were being distributed, together with instruction handbooks. On 24 August, Neville Chamberlain requested – and received – Parliament's approval for a new Emergency Powers Act. A hundred measures were set in place, during the next five anxious days, for the improved defence of Britain.

With hindsight, the warning signs were large and glaringly apparent. And yet, in England, the approach of war brought no grave alterations to the pace and form of daily life. A few privileged souls threw their money about with singular ostentation that summer, but it would be unrealistic to suppose that the owners of

Blenheim Palace and Osterley Park (to name but two grand houses in which magnificent balls were held on successive weeks) were acting in a spirit of magnificent defiance. To attendants of the parties presided over by Lady Jersey (Osterley) and the Duchess of Marlborough (Blenheim), the most thrilling news of the night might be that light-fingered thieves had pilfered a couple of treasured trinkets from their hostess.

Retrospect robes everything in significance. A couple of weeks before the outbreak of war, Count Clement ('Cle') Franckenstein, an admired Munich music director who had lost his job under the Nazis, visited his beloved brother in London. Hitler's stringent currency laws had made it almost impossible to travel outside Germany by 1939. Did Georg Franckenstein, the Austrian ambassador to the Court of St James's, suspect what was coming when he arranged for his brother Cle to be paid to conduct a concert in London during that final August of possibility? Did Churchill, too, intuit that this would be a last encounter when he went out of his way to wish Franckenstein a friendly farewell, and to urge him to return to Britain? When, two years later, Cle died of cancer in Germany, a loving friend noted that the gentle Count's final, unhappy cries of appeal had been only for a last brief glimpse of Georg: 'the brother in England [whom] he loved most dearly'.[1]

Churchill, while he had almost no personal experience of Germany, was wise enough, as war became inevitable, to pick the brains of his more knowledgeable friends. On 4 September 1939, the night after Germany's brutal attack upon Poland's borders and airfields had led England – at last – to declare war, Churchill invited Hansel Pless, a Polish citizen since 1924, to come and dine. Hansel was not the only guest, but Churchill was keen to gather information about Germany's Polish borders from a man who was well-equipped to advise him, having struggled for over ten years to run Pless in tandem with administrators from Poland.

Prince Hansel, by 1939, was estranged from Countess Maria ('Sissy') Schönborn-Wiesentheid, the beautiful young German wife who, forced to choose between a high life among the Nazis (whom Hansel loathed) and a quiet life in the land that her husband adored, preferred the Reich. Hansel's recollections, although always courteous, do not suggest that Sissy was much missed.

'England shall have my bones!' Hansel had once exultantly confided to his diary. By 1938, settled into a flat on his uncle's London estate and taking long, happy excursions through the English landscape that he had loved since boyhood, the Prince had taken a formal pledge to serve his mother's birthland. With touching pride, he even copied the wording into his diary. 'I swear by Almighty God that I will be faithful and bear true allegiance to his Majesty King George, his heirs and successors.'[2]

Hansel, dining with Churchill and his own uncle, the Duke of Westminster, on that momentous evening, did his best to be reassuring as he expressed, once again, the passionate devotion to their country that he felt. He had already found himself work as a stretcher-bearer at St George's Hospital. He hoped to do more. Armed with excellent Polish contacts, and with the evident good will of such a powerful man as Churchill, there was every prospect that an able-bodied and well-connected man of just under forty might do as much for England in this war as he had done, with equal commitment, in a previous one, for Germany.[3]

In April 1939, while staying with Quaker friends in Cornwall, Tisa Schulenburg had experienced a hopeful moment of epiphany that, disappointingly, led to no new sense of resolve about her life. In May, while still awaiting the finalising of an amicable divorce from Fritz Hess and pondering whether she wanted to take up full-time work among the Durham miners, Tisa received news from Germany that her mother was seriously ill and that her father was dying. Naturally, the elderly Schulenburgs wanted their only daughter to come home. Conscious of her family's commitment to the Nazi regime, Tisa deferred the visit. Her mother's letters grew more plaintive. *When* was she coming to Germany? *Why* did she not come? Still, Tisa hesitated. 'All my friends were in England ... yet I longed to see my parents.'[4]

Family feeling won out. Tisa returned to Germany in time to be reconciled with her father before his death. General Schulenburg had become – despite strenuous attempts to step aside in 1934 – a prominent figure in Nazi Germany. A state funeral held in Potsdam at the end of May was even attended by Hitler. Tisa and her mother stayed away. 'If one could not kill him' (Hitler), Tisa fiercely wrote, 'why go?'[5]

It seemed that one funeral, for the Nazis, was not enough. When Heinrich Himmler attempted to stage a second ceremony at Tressow, the General's family home, Fritz Schulenburg quietly indicated that the idea was unwelcome. And, to Tisa's surprise, Himmler backed off. How had her sharp-witted favourite sibling achieved such influence in the Reich? Dressed in his new uniform as deputy chief of the Berlin police, Fritzi looked formidable; so why had he opposed the second Nazi ceremony with such vehemence?

Fritzi waited until the day before his sister returned to England, just a week after their father's funeral, to reveal the truth. Back in 1938, he had secretly committed himself to the Abwehr plot for the overthrow of Hitler. That mission had never been abandoned. With Hitler gone, so Fritz Schulenburg and his friends believed, peace could be swiftly restored and the rule of law regained. Fritz had shared his hopes only with Charlotte, his wife. His brothers – Johannes Albrecht, Wolfgang and Heini – knew nothing, and (as ardent Nazis) must know nothing. Their secret, as Fritzi warned his loquacious sister to remember, must never be betrayed, if Tisa valued her brother's life.

Tisa, while thrilled by Fritz's revelations, had no desire to linger longer in a marching, militaristic Germany that perpetually reminded her of all the friends who had lost their jobs, their homes, even their lives. Flying thankfully back to England on 2 June, and armed with a talismanic copy of her favourite poet, John Keats, she was called over by the single iron-faced officer who was running the immigration sevices at Croydon Airport. Asked, on that stifling summer afternoon, to produce her papers of identity, Tisa foolishly displayed the cuttings that showed her to be the daughter of a prominent Nazi general whose funeral had recently been attended by Hitler. She even made a weak joke about her shaky qualifications for re-entry. The officer grew more thoughtful.

Later, Tisa persuaded herself that her undoing had begun before she ever left England, when a Secret Service investigator of Hampstead's alien residents had paid her a visit, and had bafflingly demanded to marry her. Naturally, she turned down the absurd proposal: 'he drank and he wore creaking stays'.

The story is an odd one: what could have made the inspector imagine that Tisa would welcome such an offer? It seems more likely that the photographs of a Nazi funeral, combined with a flippant manner that bordered on arrogance, had been enough to seal her fate. Still stranded at Croydon, Tisa made some frantic calls. Fritz Hess arrived, followed by representatives from the Quakers, and finally, by members of the Artists' International Association, led by Misha Black and Julian Trevelyan. The officer's answer remained the same: as a German national, the Countess was obliged to return home to Germany.

'And if I refuse to do so?'

His answer was clear: 'Then we will use force.'

Back again in Germany and disconsolately lodged at the Cologne flat of one of her Nazi brothers, Tisa pulled every string within her vigorous reach. But the British Foreign Office, by July 1939, had larger matters on its mind than the fate of the daughter of a German general. Nothing could or would be done. The door to England was shut, and Tisa, to her utter dismay, had reached 'the dreaded dead end'.[6]

Nobody had ever accused Tisa Schulenburg of being unre-
sourceful. Realising that she faced being trapped in Mecklenburg
for the duration of the war, she hastily took up with a former
lover, Carl Ulrich von Barner. In September, Tisa married him,
and while the likeable von Barner (always known as C. U.) went
glumly off to fight for Germany, his new wife settled into running
Trebbow, the beautiful old Barner estate that lay, like her own
former family home, close to the Baltic Sea.

From 1942, Tisa shared Trebbow with Fritzi Schulenburg's
wife, along with Charlotte's attractive brood of children. Together,
the sisters-in-law turned Barner's pretty old house into a kind of
bohemian transit hotel for anybody who was on the run or had
lost their home, while trying not to attract the suspicion of the
Barner estate's most dangerous employee.

'Ha' was a quiet and violet-eyed woodsman who had been
appointed by the Nazis as the area's *Ortsgruppenleiter*. He terrified
Tisa. ('During all those years he was the main opponent I had to
deal with . . . The forester watched me as the huntsman watches
his prey.') She dreaded that Ha would discover the truth about her
brother Fritzi ('a born leader of men'), whose secret life she could
discuss only with Charlotte, his valiant wife. The Schulenburg
children, for their own safety, were kept in complete ignorance of
the plot; the mother and aunt, bound together in anxious admiration for Fritz's courage, fastened their hopes upon his ability to
win support. Fritzi, so Tisa wrote, was '"the drummer" . . . the one
employed to win others to the cause'. Her brother was good at it.
In 1943, Fritz told her that the net of resistance against Hitler was
spreading, and that it had become a great underground organisation, drawn from people of every rank and creed throughout
Germany.

'"And if you don't succeed in killing Hitler?" I asked my
brother.

"We must succeed," was his answer.'

Easter 1944 marked a high spot at Trebbow in a life of daily dread and increasing privation. Fritz Schulenburg arrived unexpectedly one evening; accompanying him was the charismatic Claus von Stauffenberg, destined to become the most famous of all the July conspirators who plotted to assassinate Hitler.

Stauffenberg, evidently, was a captivating guest. Short of elegant attire, Tisa and Charlotte decked themselves out for their romantic visitor in the finest brocade curtains they could find. When the guest asked for a 'White Lady', they rushed to drain the household's last measure of gin into his glass. Fascinated, they watched the resistance hero, a black ribbon masking his lost eye, as he sipped his cocktail and delicately manoeuvred a matchbox against the stump of his missing arm to light a cigarette. Rapt, they listened as he talked, between gales of merriment and infectious jokes, about nothing and everything: about 'Shakespeare and England and Catholicism and Stephan George' (the poet revered almost as a patron saint by the Stauffenberg family). It was the gaiety that Tisa remembered best: 'Roars of laughter. I have never known anyone with such a capacity for laughter. It was a glorious evening.'[7]

The July plot failed. Saved by the mere width of a sturdy table leg, Hitler escaped with a few burn marks and a ruined pair of trousers from the briefcase bomb that should have ended his life. The plotters, together with such courageous associates as Wilhelm Canaris, Dietrich Bonhoeffer, Carl Langbehn and Helmuth von Moltke, were arrested.

The plotters themselves had been scrupulous about the form of trial that Hitler, if they could only capture him, was to be granted. No such mercy was meted out to them. Arriving in Berlin on 10 August – the day of Fritz's trial – his wife and sister found the city's centre in ruins and the so-called People's Court closed to all those who failed to produce special Nazi permits. They never saw him again. Fritz Dietlof Schulenburg was hanged, together with Stauffenberg's brother, Berthold, at four o'clock that same afternoon. Official confirmation reached his widow in mid-September, when Charlotte was requested to reimburse the Nazis for the cost of killing her husband, together with the additional expense of preparing, and posting, an invoice.

Sippenhaft, the act of collective punishment for a crime, was not applied to all the families of the plotters. Charlotte, accompanied by her young children, escaped to safety during the last and most terrifying stages of the war, when the penalty for flight was death. Tisa, staying on in Germany, was briefly reunited with her agreeable second husband, following von Barner's release from an Italian POW camp in the autumn of 1945. Fidelity had never been Tisa's strongest suit; in 1946, Barner, like Hess, divorced his wife for her faithlessness. Deprived of her home, family and husband, Tisa found herself suddenly alone.

It would be easy to predict that Tisa Schulenburg, after the war, would return to England, where she retained enduring connections with her friends in the mining communities of Jarrow and Durham. Instead, in 1948, she moved to the harsh landscape of the Ruhr, converted to Catholicism, joined an Ursuline convent and settled, as Schwester Paula, at bomb-shattered Dorsten, a former mining town. Here, committing herself with equal fervour to her art and her faith, she produced a remarkable series of drawings and a sculpture (one among many works of arresting beauty and strength) inspired by the horrors of the Holocaust.

Tisa's decision to become a nun is less surprising than the choice, by such a life-affirming woman, of such a barren environment in which to end her life.

'I chose the Ruhr', Schwester Paula explained to her friend Christabel Bielenberg (who had settled with her husband in Ireland, as the couple had planned to do before the war), 'wanting to live where others *had* to live. No more roar of the sea, nor the smell of bracken and gorse. I have delighted in it [that] to the full.'[8]

Mechtilde Lichnowsky, following the death of her husband, and the taking over of Kuchelna by her eldest son, Wilhelm, had chosen to stay away from a country that had become alien to her nature. Letters and notebooks suggest that she remained in close contact with her sister, Helene Harrach, who shared Mechtilde's hatred of the Nazi dictatorship. But while Helene and her husband retreated into the home of their eldest daughter at Niederarnbach (a moated Bavarian schloss that offered an escape from prying eyes and enforced behaviour), Mechtilde was given a chance introduction that led to a second, and exceptionally happy, marriage.[9]

Mechtilde had been only twenty-three when she first met the tall, fair-haired and quietly humorous Ralph Peto at the British Legation in Munich. There was a romance. Marriage was discussed, but was not considered suitable by Mechtilde's ardently Catholic family. Instead, two years later, the young Countess married the eminently eligible Karl Max Lichnowsky.

Major Peto, who had married and divorced during those interim thirty years, shared Mechtilde's fondness for music. The two friends rediscovered each other in the 1930s, while independently attending a concert at London's Queen's Hall. They soon became inseparable. Major Peto, although less bookish and knowledgeable about modern art than Mechtilde, shared her sense of humour, her energy and her intense love of the English landscape. Not a writer himself, Ralph Peto was filled with admiration by the nonchalant cleverness and originality of the Princess's books and delighted by the adroit and topical drawings with which she punctured many an inflated reputation.

In 1937, Mechtilde Lichnowsky married her dashing major and took British citizenship. Settled in the London of rose-brick terraces and wide green parks about which she wrote with such tenderness in her memoirs, she clung to the memory of her German family. Wilhelm, her son, sent letters from Kuchelna. News of her sister was regularly conveyed by Helene Harrach's pretty daughter, Irene, who continued to pay visits from England to her parents at Niederarnbach until the eve of war.

By August 1939, the news from home had grown sufficiently

alarming for Mechtilde to decide that she must, however briefly, go back to Germany. Over four years had passed since her last visit. Despite the warnings of an anxious husband, she seized what felt like a last opportunity to see her family.

Major Peto's unease was well founded. When war was declared, Mechtilde, like Tisa, found that her return to England had been blocked. In 1939, she became the prisoner, in her own land, of a political regime that she abhorred. Cut off from her husband (no correspondence was permitted between Britain and Germany during the first three years of the war), Mechtilde was tarnished in Germany by her previous marriage to Lichnowsky, a man still hated by the Nazis for his public acceptance of Germany's culpable role in 1914. Classified as a '*feindlichen Ausländer*', Mechtilde was kept under close observation and required to report every week for interrogation by the Gestapo. The discovery that her brother-in-law, Rudolf Marogna-Redwitz, had been closely linked to the 20 July plotters increased suspicions of a woman whose own writings were among the first to be purged by fire from the Nazi canon.

Little survives to indicate how Mechtilde received the news – if it reached her – that Ralph Peto, who had been tirelessly struggling to find a way to bring his wife home to England, had, by 1944, fallen seriously ill. What could she do? Mechtilde did what she had always done in times of despair. She wrote two books. For a woman whose last memoir would declare that 'Der Schreibtisch ist mein Hafen' ('My desk is my harbour'), work was the only conceivable solace.[10] Her wartime writings were not, however, intended for publication. One manuscript, an attack on Hitler, *Der Werdegang eines Wirrkopf* (The Making of a Fool), was so incendiary that she hid it in a casket and buried it deep underground.

In September 1945, following the confiscation of both Kuchelna and Graz, together with their contents, and the news that her eldest son Wilhelm was in flight, hoping to join his younger brothers in Brazil, Mechtilde received, at last, a letter from England. It brought bleak news: her beloved husband, Ralph, was dead.

Mechtilde did not, as might perhaps have been expected, choose either to stay in Germany with her sister's family or to join her children in South America. Instead, she returned to England. Living in London among a circle of literary exiles who included Elias Canetti and a beautiful Czech baroness (Sidonie Borutin, a patroness of Rilke) whom she had known since childhood, Mechtilde continued to write, to sketch, to go to concerts and to remain joyously unconventional until her death in 1958.

In the spring of 1940, Hansel Pless took a couple of weeks off from his light duties as a stretcher-bearer to pay a visit to his mother's old friends, the Londonderrys, at a time when their son, Lord Castlereagh, was also present. The principal subject of conversation, in alarming times, was Hansel's mother, Daisy Pless.

Short of money (the Pless estate had ceased to provide an allowance), and almost immobilised by multiple sclerosis, Daisy was still living in the gatehouse at Fürstenstein, where she continued to be cared for by Dolly Crowther. During the early months of the war, she had managed to get word out to her sister, Shelagh, that all was well. ('Don't worry about me, everything is warm and comfy.'[11]) More recently, Hansel had received ominous news. Photographs of himself taking part in an air-raid exercise in the mandatory gas mask and steel helmet had been published in Germany, offering conclusive proof that the Prince had become an enemy of the people; it followed that the traitor's immense estates were now open to confiscation. Pless had already been taken; Hansel's younger brother, Lexel (a former Nazi supporter whose handsome car was used to transport the 1923 'blood banner' to meetings), had fled, together with Daisy's cousin Ena Fitzpatrick, first to Poland and then to France. Fürstenstein was now under threat of confiscation and Hansel was desperately seeking ways to get funds out of England to enable his mother to be moved to the nearby village of Waldenburg. Such currency exchanges, during wartime restrictions, were not easy to transact. Possibly, Hansel

thought that Lady Londonderry, possessed of good banking connections in Germany through her friendship with Dr Melchior,
might help him to transfer the necessary sum.

Listening to these conversations, the Londonderrys' son formed
the view that his parents were being asked to implicate themselves
in unpatriotic activities. He did not, however, choose to speak out
until later.

On 10 May 1940, following the news that Germany had
invaded Belgium, Holland and Luxemburg, Neville Chamberlain
resigned and was replaced by Winston Churchill. Three days later,
the new Prime Minister vowed his absolute commitment to winning the war by whatever means it took for England to prevail and
triumph. One of the first steps taken in that direction was to guarantee, by securing the immediate arrest of all German males living
in England, that no enemy treachery could be harboured at home.

Hansel, as a Pole who had given his allegiance to England,
remained untouched during the early summer. Ben Greene's good
works for the Kindertransport, on the other hand, counted for less
by the summer of 1940 than the fact that he had a German mother
and a sister, Barbara, who was living with a German in Berlin. Far
more seriously, Ben had drifted away from his Quaker friends to
become a central figure in Lord Tavistock's BCCSE. The innocu-
ously named British Council for a Christian Settlement in Europe
had been attracting attention from MI5 since January 1940 for its
unpatriotic activities. Reports that Ben, the Council's treasurer,
kept a Nazi eagle on his desk (the eagle was a family heirloom) did
not sound reassuring. On 23 May, Ben was arrested and taken to
Brixton. This particular swoop took a further 700 suspects into
custody.

The internment programme, resulting in the arbitrary rounding
up of 27,000 men and 4,000 women with German connections,
was not well planned and England had not been well prepared for
such mass arrests. Chaos ensued. Fritz Schumacher found himself
briefly confined at Paignton among a group of starving internees

who had not been fed for nine days. Michael Kerr, the teenage son of Germany's most eminent theatre critic, was carried off in his tennis clothes from Cambridge to be lodged at a disused ice-cream factory and, later, in an underground car park until, still bewildered by his fate, he was deported to join, on the Isle of Man, a German prince, a Cockney stable boy and a certain Pastor Hildebrandt, freshly arrived from his work with Julius Rieger at the Church of St George's in Aldgate.

Hansel Pless, throughout May and June 1940, remained at liberty and impatient to do more than stretcher-bearing to demonstrate his commitment to the England that he loved with such passion. Thinking, perhaps, that his Uncle George's twelve-year marriage to Churchill's mother might work in his favour, he decided, on 15 July, to ask the Prime Minister's secretary if more active work could be found for 'a healthy and fit man [able] to serve the national cause'. Hansel hoped for an appointment to the Scots Guards.[12] Instead, reported by the Londonderrys' son to have displayed Nazi sympathies, the forty-year-old Prince was arrested and taken to Brixton jail, where, according to his own unselfpitying recollections, he was provided with the bare minimum of subsistence: a cell, a mattress and a slop pail. Initially, Hansel was baffled as to what his crime could have been; at some point, however, he recollected something about the manner of the Londonderrys' son that had seemed unfriendly. Could such a man – the son of his trusted friends – have set out to do him harm?

One MP, Victor Cazalet, spoke up in the House of Commons that summer about the injustices that were taking place in Britain due to the new German internment policy. On 22 August 1940, Major Cazalet declared that tragedies 'unnecessary and undeserved' were taking place and that he was not prepared to rest 'until this bespattered page of our history has been cleaned up and rewritten'.[13] It was a splendid speech. No changes took place.

A year later, on 25 September 1941, conscious of Cazalet's humane attitude and of his particular sympathy to Poland's cause

(Cazalet was closely involved, from the summer of 1940, with President Sikorski's London-based government in exile), Hansel wrote – during a brief spell of imprisonment on the Isle of Man – to ask for his help. Typically, however, the Prince expressed far less concern about the release of his person than the rescue of his reputation. He had, he wanted Cazalet to understand, been the victim of 'a wicked calumny' [in] . . . a trumped-up case'. Without quite pointing a finger at Castlereagh, his nemesis, Hansel asked that Lord Londonderry should be informed that 'beyond doubt there is no reason for my detention'. Characteristically, Hansel went on to congratulate Cazalet on behalf of the 3000 men who had – unlike himself – already been released: 'Thank God,' he wrote, with no conscious irony, 'this still is England.'[14] It is not known whether Major Cazalet found time to enter a plea on Hansel's behalf. If so, it went unheeded.

Michael Kerr, following an appeal by his distinguished father, was released from his internment in November 1940, and – following service as a bomber pilot – was naturalised as English. He later became Britain's first foreign-born judge. Kerr had, so he wrote in his memoirs half a century later, felt no bitterness about being interned. The greater cause was all that mattered: 'In fact, throughout my internment, I never met anyone who felt bitter against the British government.'[15] Ben Greene, who felt very bitter indeed about the fact that his arrest had been set up by MI5, responded to his release in 1942 by unsuccessfully suing the Home Secretary for libel and false imprisonment. Haunted to the end by his sense of unjust persecution, Greene died in 1978 and was buried in Suffolk, following a Quaker service attended by his German mother, then in her mid-nineties.

Hansel remained in Brixton. Eventually – typed out on one of the small cards through which the Red Cross were permitted to transmit international post after March 1942 – he received the contents of a letter that his mother had written from her new home in Germany. The news was reassuring. Hansel's funds had come through and Daisy liked her new Waldenburg home ('such beautiful big sunny rooms and a lovely view'.) The fact that she and the ever-loyal Dolly dwelt in almost total solitude troubled the gallant Princess less than putting her son's mind at ease: 'Hansel darling, don't let anything worry you, everything is in perfect order, just as you would wish it to be ... I am so proud of you.'[16]

Daisy Pless died, in Dolly Crowther's arms, in June 1943. In Germany, Daisy's status as an enemy alien guaranteed her little more than cursory death notices. In *The Times*, two weeks later, tributes to Daisy were overshadowed by the obituaries of Victor Cazalet and President Sikorski of Poland, killed in a suspicious plane accident shortly after Sikorski's request for an inquiry into the massacre of Polish officers at Katyn.* Nevertheless, Hansel (if allowed to read *The Times* in Brixton) would have been proud to see how warmly his seventy-year-old mother was praised in the newspaper's densely printed pages for her work as a reformer on the Pless estates, for her courageous help to British POWs and for unceasing attempts 'to help Anglo-German relations remain on an amiable footing'.[17] No mention was made, however, of the fact that Daisy's son, godson to both Edward VII and the German Emperor, was presently serving time in a London prison.

It's unlikely that either Daisy's death or George Cornwallis-West's well-intended endeavours to bribe the Prime Minister with a freshly caught salmon and an assurance that Hansel was 'entirely guiltless of subversive activity towards this country' affected the status of the unfortunate Prince.[18] Nevertheless, towards the end of 1943, Hansel was finally released and informed by the Governor

---

* Wilfrid Israel, seeking homes in Palestine for emigrating Jews, died in that same month, shot down by German fire in the civilian plane that was carrying the Hungarian-English actor – and sometime British agent – Leslie Howard back to England from Lisbon. Of the responses to these tragic deaths, the newspaper homages to General Sikorski were the most prominent. Churchill read the funeral address for his Polish friend at Newark-on-Trent.

alsoof Brixton that 'a terrible mistake had been made'. The courteous Prince, having stayed on for lunch in order to wish all his Brixton friends farewell (Hansel was popular with his fellow inmates), soon afterwards achieved his cherished wish to contribute to the war effort.

As a trained lawyer, he was put in charge of investigating the cases of Irish soldiers who were accused of desertion after joining the British Army. To judge from the vivacity with which he discussed his work on the tapes that recorded his memories, the Prince found the task both sad and satisfying.[19]

After the war, Hansel lost all his estates to Poland ('they even took my clothes and my boots') together with his only source of income. Naturalised as an English citizen in 1947, he became a keen cyclist and a less keen businessman, whose venture into lumber-drying failed to prosper. It was characteristic of Hansel that, following the register office ceremony of a happy second marriage, he unselfconsciously carried his Irish bride off on honeymoon in a tiny bubble car into which his tall frame could scarcely bend itself to fit. The delight of skimming past larger and grander cars on narrow alpine passes apparently compensated for cramped space to a man who, modestly renaming himself Mr Henry Pless, would become a much-loved member of that English world to which he had always given his heart.[20]

Dolly Crowther was less fortunate. Having cared for her beloved princess until the end of Daisy's life, Dolly was forced to flee when the Soviet troops approached Waldenburg. While making her way, on foot, to the US safety zone, Dolly was murdered and left in a roadside ditch. Daisy's own grave, although swiftly dug up by the incoming Soviet troops, was almost as swiftly put to rights.

Back in 1914, when Queen Victoria was still a remembered presence, royal connections, or noble birth, still carried a mystique that allowed soldiers, swapping photographs on Christmas Eve, to exclaim over the beauty ('*Schöne Prinzessin!*') of some member of the enthroned family that still, confusingly, seemed to belong to both camps. All that, as Hitler faced Churchill across the lines of war, had disappeared. Nothing – or nothing that was linked to great culture or to noble families – remained sacred. Charlie Coburg, the unhappy schoolboy appointed to rule over Prince Albert's own duchy by a loving grandmother, had grown into a man who wore Nazi uniform, supported the Nazi party and who understandably gained little in the way of post-war clemency. (The by then very frail Duke, following a period of imprisonment in the American zone, died in a German estate cottage in 1954, still sleeping in his cherished bed from Claremont, the English mansion that had been his childhood home.)

A contributing factor to the approval that was granted for the launching of attacks on civilian towns and on Britain and Germany's most treasured monuments (among them, St Paul's in London and the great cathedral of Cologne) was the fact that neither Churchill nor Hitler knew much about the other's country. Churchill had paid one visit to Berlin 1932; Hitler, even though a possible future home had been picked out for his victorious later years, had never once set foot in England.

The use of Darmstadt, home to the part of Victoria's family that had always remained most faithful to England, as a practice ground for carpet-bombing by the Allies, demonstrates how much the mood had changed in thirty years. Neither the British Princess Margaret ('Peg') nor Prince Ludwig, her intensely musical German husband, had ever approved of the Nazis. Expelled from the army in 1943 (as were all the German princes) and briefly imprisoned in his own small city (where the relaxed conditions of imprisonment allowed the Princess to feed daily cigarette rations into her husband's upheld fingers through a road grating), Prince Lu had born his fate with equanimity. Placed under house arrest for the rest of the war, he and his wife turned their secluded home, Wolfsgarten, into an oasis for refugees (among them, in due course, the motherless children of Lu's cousin, Prince Philipp of

Hessen-Kassel, while their father served time from 1946–8 in the local camp).

Lu, like Peg, was always sympathetic to the British cause. But how can the couple have felt on the night of 11 September 1944 when pretty little Darmstadt was singled out for one of the heaviest air raids of the war? Out of 110,000 citizens, 66,000 lost their homes and 12,300 died in an attack for which the target was the medieval town's wooden centre, ideal for the creation of a firestorm.

It's harder to guess how Prince Ludwig, whose grandmother, Princess Alice, had done so much to support the German Hospital in London, felt when he heard about the sad ending of one of the most esteemed connections between the old England and the old Germany, created back in the days when the two countries had shared a vision for social reform.

The hospital's troubles had begun when Ribbentrop, acting in his role as ambassador to the Court of St James's, attempted to have its patient list Aryanised. His only supporter, the hospital chaplain, left London for Germany in August 1939. But Pastor Schönberger had failed to convert the nurses, over whom a more powerful influence was exerted by the memory of the hospital's splendid role in the previous war. A handful returned home to Germany. Confident of the protection that was traditionally extended to a religious nursing order, the majority of the nun-sisters (most of whom came from Darmstadt) remained in London under the inspiring leadership of Sister Anna Jochmann. At Hitchin, the hospital's convalescent branch, none of the German nurses dreamed of quitting their posts because of the war. There was not one among them, according to the hospital secretary, Herr Loeffler, who concerned themselves with politics: 'their lives were consecrated to the care of the sick'.[21]

On 28 May 1940, the hospital was subjected to a surprise visit from Scotland Yard. Crying and carrying bundles of clothes in their arms – Sister Anna had a coat draped over her long night-gown – the sisters were forced down the front steps and into the vans that took them to Holloway Prison. Three months later, on 18 August, the entire group was deported to Port Erin on the Isle of Man.

The arrests had taken place during the first hysterical period of internment, at a time when even old gentlemen in Hampstead's public libraries were hustled from their seats by zealous officials and ordered to produce their papers. But the decree that had gone out from Whitehall was for the arrest of all German males below the age of sixty. The arrested persons, on this occasion, were middle-aged nurses and elderly nuns.*

Even before their menacing prisoners had reached Port Erin, the authorities had begun to acknowledge the possibility of error. It now embarrassingly emerged that a medical chest in which munitions were alleged to be stored at the hospital held nothing more dangerous than the supplies of plaster used for making leg casts. That revelation did not prevent the hospital's last remaining German resident, Sister Gertrud, aged sixty-eight, from being immediately gathered up and despatched to Port Erin. Sister Sophie, aged sixty-seven, a widely loved local figure who had run the Hitchin convalescent hospital on the Schröder family's behalf for over twenty years, was also arrested and deported.

Throughout the rest of the war, the hospital struggled to retain a minimal service with a skeletal staff, but the powerful bridge linking it to Germany was broken beyond repair. Appeals for funding after the war received no response from a ruined country. In

---

* A group of German Benedictine nuns migrated to Minster, on the Isle of Thanet (with which there was an ancient German connection through Saint Walburga), in March 1937, with help from the dashing and good-hearted Delphine Reynolds. In wartime, the abbey was requisitioned for use as an army mess. But, rather than being deported, these Bavarian-based Benedictines were permitted to take refuge at a sister convent in Devon. The German connection has been upheld at Minster (despite the abbey's near-destruction through lightning in 1987) to this day.

1948, after over a hundred years of charitable service, the hospital renounced its voluntary status. Today, while still fondly referred to by locals as 'the German', one of the great monuments to Anglo-German philanthropy has been converted into flats.[22]

The hospital, had it been allowed to serve the role that it performed so ably during the First War, might have helped to heal more than wounded bodies. Wounds of a different nature were incurred by acts of such splendid, quixotic loyalty as the determination of the middle-aged Prince Charles de Rohan to serve two and a half years of hard labour in Germany rather than renounce his British nationality.[23]

Rohan's story is an extraordinary one, of supreme pettiness (he was arrested for having failed to stop a hotel clerk from mentioning a British news item) and of uncommon powers of survival. While one of his many torments had included being forced to balance on a narrow ledge within the dark neck of a chimney, while a fire was lit beneath him, such experiences paled beside the Prince's stories of the sufferings of his comrades. At Theresienstadt, where he worked as a stone-breaker for the railroad, he saw elderly Jews being pushed off a high wall to be torn to pieces beneath by the ravenous Great Danes owned by the notorious 'Pindja', the camp commandant. Together with his fellow prisoner Count Czernin, the deeply religious Rohan was forced to witness the slow boiling alive of a Catholic priest.

Admirably, Rohan continued to reject the bait that was always extended: to be freed, he had only to become a citizen of Nazi Germany. A proud English subject to the end of his days (he died in Croydon in 1965), Rohan not only rejected the offer, but – encased in a subterranean cell below the centre of that very city – actively cheered on the pilots he proudly called 'our boys' as they strafed Hamburg.

Rohan's defiance of the Nazis was admirable, and even heroic, but it did not open the way for more than the salvation of his own fierce integrity. Elsewhere, the scaffolding was being erected (and in a most improbable venue) for a bridge towards the first faint glimmer of post-war reconciliation.

Germany, up until 1933, honoured Shakespeare as a compatriot. Hamlet, melancholy, tortured and profound, was – and still is – identified as the mirror of the country's darkest self. Shakespeare's plays, as English travellers were always charmed to discover on their visits to Germany, were performed almost every week in, as it sometimes seemed, every tiny town throughout the nation.

In 1927, Saladin Schmitt lifted the idolatry to a new level by devoting an entire week at Bochum – from 3 p.m. to 2 a.m. each day – to nothing but the performance of all ten of Shakespeare's histories. Ten years later, the Nazis repeated the Bochum Festival. On 23 April 1940, Shakespeare's wartime birthday was celebrated in Germany with only a little less enthusiasm than Hitler's (conveniently occurring during the same week). In Berlin, throughout the 1930s, the Shakespeare plays that were mounted by Gustaf Gründgens and sponsored by Goering at Berlin's Prussian State Theatre had competed against those being put on with equal splendour at the Deutsches Theater by Goebbels's man, Heinz Hilpert.

The Nazi interpretation of Shakespeare's works was, inevitably, tainted by their creed. *Richard II* lent itself to jeers at the corrupt Anglo-Saxon nobility; *Hamlet*, however, began to give cause for concern. (Could a true hero be allowed to vacillate?) *Troilus and Cressida*, with a message that spoke unquestionably against the glory of war, was banned. *The Merchant of Venice* continued to play, but with a caricatured, posturing Shylock being presented as the improbable foster-father to a Christian girl. (A non-Jewish Jessica could thus marry Lorenzo and enjoy a happy ending without contravening the Reich's inflexible new laws about inter-racial alliances.)

The texts were perverted to suit the Nazi ethos; the passion for Shakespeare, however, remained unquenched.

It was within this context of a shared – and profound – cultural

devotion that some of the strangest and most significant productions of Shakespeare that may ever have been performed in Europe
took place, in wartime Germany, with British actors.

Michael Goodliffe was an English vicar's son who, after gradu-
ating from Oxford, had joined the Royal Shakespeare Company.
Wounded at Dunkirk in 1940, Goodliffe was reported to have
been killed and was duly accorded a brief obituary in *The Times*.
In fact, the 26-year-old actor's capture had led to his being imprisoned in a Bavarian hilltop castle and then, after a variety of camps,
at Eichstätt, a secluded valley famous for the splendour of its
Benedictine monastery.

The experience of the prisoners who shared Goodliffe's captivity was not pleasant (shaven heads in icy conditions and without
the provision of caps; a diet of mint tea and old potatoes), but
monotony was the principal enemy.* Escape, both at Tittmoning
and Eichstätt, remained the prime objective.

Possibly, the Nazi guards took the view that a bit of diversion
would keep the prisoners' minds off digging tunnels. Possibly, they
themselves shared their boredom and welcomed the prospect of
some culture in the camps. For whatever reason, Michael Goodliffe
was encouraged to put his stage experience to use, with his
admirable British superior officer, General Victor Fortune, urging
him forward: 'Put on some shows as soon as you can.'[24]

Slowly, the performances staged by Goodliffe (who fashioned
the scenery from Red Cross crates and the reflector lights from
dried milk tins) created a new dynamic between the captors and
their prisoners. Both sides had discovered an outlet, far removed
from the sphere of politics and war, in which some semblance of
humanity could be restored.

---

* Such calculated discomfort is reminiscent of the experiences of Leonard Friedrich, the
Quaker who had been removed from the centre at Bad Pyrmont well before the outset
of war. Friedrich recalled how, in midwinter, large holes were cut in the centre of the
back of the coats of those prisoners who worked outside.

Simple enjoyment, without doubt, played a dominant role. A repertoire that ranged from Shakespeare and Oscar Wilde to Gilbert and Sullivan was designed to please – and did so. ('Three Little Maids from School Are We' received ten encore requests at Hohenfels, another POW camp.) But Goodliffe's fellow prisoners were also professional soldiers, keen to bring the same high level of competence to their productions as they would to any other mission. The camp commandants, too, became increasingly enthusiastic. They started importing costumes from the Munich Opera House; they asked for boxes of Leichner's theatrical make-up to be requisitioned from Berlin. Music was composed by the prisoners; instruments, often borrowed from local orchestras in return for free attendance at performances, were fetched in by their play-addicted guards. Clear evidence of the goodwill that began to develop appears in the fact that, after the Nazi audience had left the room, the actors – British captives in a German prison camp – were given permission to belt out, as loudly and often as they pleased, their own national anthem.

One potential difficulty for theatre productions in a single-sex camp lay in an absence of female performers. Greatly to Goodliffe's surprise, this presented no obstacle to an attentive and eager audience who knew their Shakespeare plays. They accepted the males in girlish attire, he wrote, 'exactly as the Elizabethans accepted their boy-actors'.[25]

It's a startling thought. Here, in a hilltop medieval castle in Bavaria, assembled for a performance – it was a favourite – of *The Winter's Tale*, the guards and prisoners were unconsciously reliving the experience of a young English princess and her German groom, celebrating a marriage that was being called 'the union of Thames and Rhine' as they watched that same play being performed by male actors, at the Palace of Whitehall, in 1613. Arriving at the hilltop medieval castle of Heidelberg that summer, Elizabeth Stuart (the future Winter Queen of her own Bohemian tale) seemed almost to have pointed the way forward when she initiated the creation of a new Shakespeare theatre – for Germany.

Hamlet – performed at Eichstätt – was looked upon by Michael Goodliffe as his greatest triumph. Attracting an audience of 200 for its opening performance, the production was extended for a further ten days by popular demand. But it was in Stalag 383, at Hohenfels in Bavaria, that the bravest wartime Shakespearean tragedy was mounted: a completely uncensored presentation of *The Merchant of Venice*. Ian McKibbin, one of the actors, remembered that the Germans were shamelessly enthusiastic about the idea: costumes were even brought in from the Goering-approved State Theatre of Berlin for a play that had become, in Nazi times, a popular farce.

Shylock, in Nazi productions, was always played for laughs: a comic villain of the lowest kind, ridiculed and ridiculous. His greatest speech ('Hath not a Jew eyes ...') was invariably omitted, doubtless from a fear that it might elicit sympathy. That caricature was not how Shylock was presented at Hohenfels. McKibbin, writing after his release, described how the Australian professional actor who took the part had gone to particular trouble to represent a heroic Shylock, a presented of 'fine dignity'. The performance had, McKibbin added (perhaps a touch complacently), been 'rather disturbing to the Germans in the stalls'. And yet, after the initial pause, and an anxious moment of uncertainty, the Germans had applauded with whole-hearted approval. 'A grand production was most enthusiastically received.'[26]

Michael Goodliffe's son suggests that his father and his fellow POWs were simply doing what professional soldiers learn to do: they were 'building bridges'. These bridges, nevertheless, were of a special kind. However tentatively, the extraordinary stagings of works by the most humane of playwrights – presented by British prisoners to complicit Nazi guards – reached towards the faint possibility, following all the bitterness and the horrors that would still arise in the future, for the performance, in a post-war world, of a dramatic experiment.

29

ONLY CONNECT

In 1943, the year in which Churchill finally granted Hansel Pless his release from Brixton, the Prime Minister still felt – understandably – savage enough to demand, at a private party, three encores of Noël Coward's musical indictment of appeasement: 'Don't Let's Be Beastly to the Germans'. Nevertheless, Churchill was beginning to look ahead, and to display prudent concern that the mistakes of Versailles should not be repeated. In 1943, he asked his ministries to supply ideas about how (after a war that he betrayed little public fear of losing) co-operation with Germany could best be achieved.

The answer, put forward by Churchill's deputy PM, Clement Attlee, and subsequently endorsed both by the War Cabinet and by the Foreign Office, was that the job had already begun. The process of the re-education of German POWs was being actively pursued, although on an informal basis, in various prison camps. What was required, in Attlee's strongly expressed view, was to put this admirable but disorganised project onto a systematic basis, give it a home, and provide it with funding.

The British government had, in fact, by the end of 1943, already anticipated the conclusion that Herbert Sulzbach would summarise on the BBC in 1948, following his own unique contribution towards the task of reconciliation. 'The German POWs going home to Germany now', Sulzbach told his audience, 'will become the best envoys for peace and understanding between our two countries.'

Attlee was right. Herbert Sulzbach, working first at Comrie in Scotland, and then at Featherstone in Northumbria, between 1945–8, had achieved extraordinary results, among hardened men, through his quiet commitment to the cause of reconciliation, and through the force of his unique personality. But if steps were to be taken towards leading Germany back to democracy, and towards a return to her place in Europe, then a formal, government-backed programme was required.

On 18 September 1943, Churchill's government approved plans for the Foreign Office to employ the German branch of its political intelligence unit (led by Richard Crossman, an ardent Germanophile) to ensure that financial support was found for the re-education of German POWs. On 12 January 1946, the Foreign Secretary, Ernest Bevin, approved Ivone Kirkpatrick's choice of the man – and the place – for an adventurous new step towards the maintaining of peace. A new attitude for a new era was best summed up by a young Dutch resistance fighter. 'The last war', this unidentified young woman had stated to Sir Robert Birley, one of the scheme's supporters, 'was the kind of war that one can only win after one has won it.'[1]

The man that Kirkpatrick, with Crossman's approval, had picked to head a complex and diplomatically delicate mission was a naturalised German Jew. His name was Heinz Koeppler.

Educated at Magdalen College, Oxford, after a family friend gave him a free ticket out of Germany in 1933, Heinz Koeppler fell in love with the university, its social life, its architecture and – as a man who was a scholar to his energetic fingertips – its sense of intellectual vitality. Subsequently appointed to Magdalen as a lecturer in history, Koeppler had settled in well enough by 1938 to make sure, when he brought his sister Hanni across from Germany to join him, that she was given house-room at the home of his friend Richard Crossman (away writing a book in Greece) and that Hanni met up with Gilbert Murray, one of his warmest allies.

Koeppler, implausibly disguised as 'Professor King', had already started giving well-received pep talks to POWs when Bevin approved the choice of location in which to formalise the process known – Koeppler hated the term – as 're-education'. The place was Wilton Park, a handsome country house that had been most recently used as an MI19 interrogation centre. Although hardly welcoming (the rooms were bugged; the gardens were filled with Nissen huts; plumbing and lighting were in the raw), Wilton Park was offered to Koeppler as the working centre for a scheme that, so Crossman and Kirkpatrick believed, only a man as remarkable as their protégé could induce to work.

It's not hard to see why. Koeppler, in contrast to the tiny, delicate-boned Herbert Sulzbach, was a massive figure, with a personality to match it. Towering, intelligent, assertive and furiously energetic, the cigar-loving Koeppler shared with Sulzbach only a fondness for being well dressed (he always wore a rose in his buttonhole) and a determination to do his utmost for the two countries to which he belonged.

Oxford was Koeppler's chosen model and Wilton Park, from its beginnings in January 1946, might just as well have been called Koeppler College. Lectures were thrust aside in favour of chaired debates; participants were instructed to be 'brief, trenchant and, if possible, witty'. There were just over 200,000 German POWs in the UK in 1946; 300 of them, initially taken from local POW camps, were recruited for courses lasting six weeks. Students were given civilian clothes and a ration of fifteen cigarettes a week. Access was guaranteed to a broad range of newspapers, radio in several languages and a library – a characteristic Koeppler touch – that placed Churchill's works alongside *Mein Kampf*. Food was adequate and plentiful, a bonus in ration-ruled times. The provision of actual beds was looked upon as an unexpected luxury.

As fiercely opposed as Herbert Sulzbach to any form of censorship, Koeppler gave his students the greatest surprise when he told them that agreement with his views was not required. Students on a spring course in 1947 took their course leader at his word when, invited to accept that the Third Reich merited a degree of blame, they left the room. Normally, Koeppler relied upon his good humour and relish for intellectual combat to win through. 'He was astonishingly adept with words, and ideas,' Heinz Koeppler's family doctor told Richard Mayne, the historian of Wilton Park. 'That was one of the things that made him very formidable . . . I don't think he was in awe of anyone.'

Six courses were held each year, with daily lectures and debates. Women students were introduced in 1947; as speakers, women were there from the start. Nancy Astor, haranguing the POWs in 1947 upon the subject of dictatorships, drew the awed comment from Max Dalhaus, editor of a Communist newspaper, *Die Freiheit,* that 'such a person would be unthinkable in Germany'.

Bertrand Russell, Jennie Lee, Lord Longford, Tony Benn, Harold Nicolson, Victor Gollancz: the list of those who came, unpaid, to speak at Wilton Park testifies to the widespread faith in the value of Koeppler's project during the early post-war years. Returning to their camps, the POWs became enthused ambassadors for the idea that Germany and England could work together. 'These are certainly the spearhead, who are ahead of public opinion,' Alfred Klug (a POW recruit) wrote on 29 March 1946 to friends in Germany. 'It is to be hoped that the German people realise this, and that they do not push aside these helping hands . . . We must first of all give proof of our sincerity, and only then can the German nation be admitted into the community of peace-loving nations.'

Scepticism was not, however, tossed overboard. Was Lothar Hegewisch angling for an early release when he announced on 17 September 1946 that a mere six weeks at Wilton Park had transformed the resident POWs into 'full citizens of a democracy such as many of them had not experienced even in the Weimar period'? Did Engelbert Brandt hope to improve his prospects when he assured his tutors on 25 September, in that same year, that 'today I see politics in quite a different light, and above all far more clearly'?[2]

A measure of cynicism was necessary; the evidence of an enduring influence was, however, clear. Herbert Sulzbach, following his departure from the Featherstone Camp in 1948, received over 3000 letters of thanks from ex-prisoners who, having already been released, had nothing to gain from their gratitude. It is worthy of note that the Featherstone Park Association, set up after the war in Düsseldorf with the support of former POWs, was still actively involved in the task of furthering Anglo-German reconciliation when Sulzbach himself was eighty years old.

Sulzbach never ceased to strive for the time when a united Britain and Germany might put an end to what he still sorrowfully perceived, in 1984, as the 'old distrust'.[3] He died the following year. Neal Ascherson, writing in the *Observer* on 7 July 1985, stated that Herbert von Sulzbach 'did more than any other human being to bridge the gulf of bitterness which the last war left between the British and the Germans'.

Sulzbach had always preferred to work independently, trusting to his own faith in humanity to bring about the desired results. Heinz Koeppler, by 1950, had become used to running what was effectively a private university. Aghast when the Foreign Office, doubtless planning to close the organisation down, announced that they wished to reclaim Wilton Park, the dauntless Koeppler set out to find his college a new home.*

He found it in a building that would have pleased both Mary Portman and Philip Lothian, whose heir would speak there at the Jubilee Conference of 1971. Wiston House was an Elizabethan

---

* Wilton Park, once reclaimed, was demolished and replaced by a modern building.

family home, complete with gables, mullioned windows and a medieval chapel, set at the top of a sweeping drive and standing under the soft bulk of the Sussex Downs. It was ravishingly symbolic of a time that was vanishing from view. Koeppler fell instantly in love with it. From 1950 on, Wilton Park (the name was preserved) resettled itself at Wiston House.

Not everybody approved. A concept that had seemed magnificent to Mary Portman in 1914, and to Philip Lothian in 1930, felt uncomfortably elitist during the pinched climate of the fifties. America, however, provided welcome additional funding and, by broadening the scope of Wilton Park's ambitions, Koeppler steered his way through perilous times. Wilton Park, as he defiantly announced in 1971, was indeed elitist; its elite was comprised of the brightest and the best of those young men and women of all societies who believed that free discussion, in any true democracy, lay at the heart of every governmental decision.

Koeppler was knighted in 1978 and died the following year. Wilton Park, however, remained faithful to his ideal. Willi Brundert, a POW who arrived at Wilton Park from Sulzbach's Featherstone Camp and later became mayor of Frankfurt) summed that ideal up. Wilton Park, so Brundert declared, had given its German students the opportunity denied them in their pre-war life both 'to think for ourselves ... and to understand the other fellow's point of view'.[4]

Known today as the Executive Agency of the Foreign and Commonwealth Office, Wilton Park has maintained its close links with Germany, while providing a discreet forum for international conferences. In the 1980s, when black majority rule in South Africa was under discussion, black African leaders used Wilton Park to meet and debate with members of the ruling National Party. During that same decade, it was recorded that a Soviet interpreter had burst out of his booth to join a passionate Wilton Park debate about Russia's political future; in 1988, a Roumanian speaker predicted the collapse of Communism, a full two years before Germany's re-unification. Throughout its life, Wilton Park has never (in the words of its historian, Richard Mayne) lost sight of Koeppler's enlightened purpose: 'to turn ignorance into understanding, prejudice into appreciation, suspicion and hatred into respect and trust'.[5]

It was no coincidence that Yehudi Menuhin and Benjamin Britten were both public supporters of the Featherstone Camp mission of reconciliation between England and Germany presided over by Herbert Sulzbach. Britten, an ardent pacifist and lifelong admirer of the Quakers, had voluntarily accompanied Menuhin to give a series of concerts, directly after the war, to the survivors of Belsen.[6] It was an experience, according to his biographer, Paul Kildea, that marked all of Britten's subsequent work and confirmed the Suffolk-born composer's deeply felt belief that all war (as he and Peter Pears proclaimed in a 1949 programme note) was 'immoral'.[7]

In 1952, when a performance of *Billy Budd* was being given at Wiesbaden in Germany, Britten's close friends, the Earl and Countess of Harewood, asked two of their own friends, the Prince and Princess of Hessen-Darmstadt, whether (in return for taking them to the opera) they could bring the British composer along on a visit to Wolfsgarten.

The Wiesbaden *Billy Budd* performance was a disaster. Redemption came back at Wolfsgarten, where Britten unforgettably imitated the attempt of an intoxicated pianist to play Tchaikovsky's Piano Concerto No. 1. Visiting Aldeburgh later that year, Prince Lu and his wife confirmed a friendship that would form an important part of their personal and gallant endeavour, after the war, to use their German home as a place for cultural bridge-building between two devastated nations. For Britten, as for Peter Pears, Wolfsgarten would become both a precious refuge and a source of inspiration.

On the evening of 11 September 1944, Prince Lu had been standing in the wooded park of Wolfsgarten, the secluded college-like building (it is built around the equivalent of a small quad) standing about ten miles outside the medieval city of Darmstadt, when he heard the low roar of bombers. Helpless, the prince watched the sky over Darmstadt turn from red to the glaring yellow of a burning city, targeted by 222 Lancaster Bombers and 14 Mosquitos on a night raid.

The Hessen–Darmstadt family's city palace, along with all its treasures, was obliterated in an attack that left more than half the little city homeless. No convincing justification was forthcoming. This had been a practice run, a try-out before striking a bigger target.

Hospitable, Anglophile and ardently musical, Lu and Peg displayed no rancour and did all they could to help with the reconstruction of Darmstadt. At Wolfsgarten, they quietly set out to transform their surviving home, with its great golden concert room (the *Saal*) extending along the whole of one wing of the house, into a source for peaceful reconciliation.

And they succeeded, to a remarkable degree. Wolfsgarten, according to the German composer Hans Werner Henze, swiftly became the kind of haven to which Mary Portman had long ago aspired: a house where musicians, writers, painters, historians, composers and philosophers were welcome. There were frequent concerts, played by the best instrumentalists of the time, and friends of the house were often invited to stay with Lu and Peg.[8]

Benjamin Britten had been charmed in 1952 to be shown Marie Antoinette's portrait of one of Lu's ancestors, furniture left behind by Napoleon, photographs of royal holidays in the Crimea and the signature, cut into a window pane, of the murdered Tsar Nicholas. Returning the following Christmas, he couldn't hide the glee behind his groan that the Hesses had compelled him to sit through a dinner with no less than seven European princes seated around him at the table.

Wolfsgarten, throughout the years, became a second home in Germany to both Britten and Peter Pears. (Their names joined that of Tsar Nicholas on a window pane, keeping company with Elizabeth and Philip, Edward Heath and Golo Mann.) Holidays were taken with Lu and Peg to Greece, to India and – in Peg's widowhood – to Australia; visits were paid to Schloss Tarasp, the couple's hilltop castle in Switzerland. But it was in the dusty golden serenity of the *Saal* at Wolfsgarten that this Anglo–German friendship had set down its roots. At Wolfsgarten, the sometimes tormented spirit of Britten seems always to have found peace. His sense of ease is reflected in the fact that he chose the Hesses' home, during a month's visit in 1974, as the scene in which to create one of his most candidly English works: *Suite on English Folk Tunes*. Six years earlier, in the same rooms, he composed a more Germanic tribute for Prince Lu's sixtieth birthday: *Sechs Hölderlin Fragmente*.

For Prince Lu, so German in his habits, so English in his loyalties, it was difficult to find a way to offer, beyond the gift of his surviving home, some token of reparation for what England had suffered. A starting point was found during one of the first visits that he and Peg paid to Aldeburgh. Back in those early years of the festival, recitals and concerts were presented either in unheated local churches or in the cramped darkness of Aldeburgh's Jubilee Hall. To Lu and Peg, Britten's wheezing audiences appeared to suit their surroundings far too well. Everybody, so the cheerful Princess remarked, seemed so ancient, while Britten's music – surely? – spoke to youth.

A solution was found. The founding of the Hesse Fellowships ensured that musically talented young people could attend all the concerts free of charge and, better still, organise a concert as a way of displaying their own virtuosity.

Arrangements were set up, in 1959, to sponsor a dozen promising students over a two-week summer period; within three years, that number had tripled. Prince Lu (his artistic father's son) proudly designed them an insignia, a Hesse Student Badge; Peg, following her husband's death in 1968, created a lecture series in the Prince's honour. As a president after the festival moved to Snape, Peg Hesse was praised both for the loyalty of her support and for the unstinting nature of her encouragement. Thirteen years after her death, the Hesse Student Scheme is still going strong. Its successes have included Jane Glover, Steven Isserlis, Michael Chance and Iain Burnside.[9]

Earlier, during the thirties, George Christie had found it easy to welcome the German refugee trio of Busch, Bing and Ebert to his new home for opera at Glyndebourne. A spirit of reconciliation and mutual understanding did not need to be sought, back before the war. The achievement being wrought at Aldeburgh and at Wolfsgarten was of a different and more fragile kind. It was threatened, at all times, by the simmering bitterness of the recent past.

Reconciliation, during the harsh post-war years when Britten first visited Wolfsgarten, in 1952, still felt remote. Britten's own greatest gift towards the hope of its eventual achievement would come ten years later, in a period still spiritually poised between the devastated, churchless cities of Coventry and Dresden.

Officially, *War Requiem* paid homage to Sir Basil Spence's new Coventry Cathedral, built beside the dark ruins of its predecessor. Unofficially, Britten drew inspiration from Wilfred Owen's poetry to make an appeal, through the meeting of two ghostly soldiers and the call that arises from the music, following their needless deaths, for peace.

Speaking to his sister, Barbara, after *War Requiem* received its premiere in 1962, Britten praised not his music, but Owen's poetry. Of his own creation, he used the only words that, repeated here, can hope to count, in a history of noble endeavour and bitter loss; in the story of two countries that once thought of themselves as united by bonds – not only of blood – but of goodness, commitment and faith.

'I hope', Britten said to his sister, 'that it will make people think a bit.'[10]

AFTERWORD

Growing up in an isolated house in the Midlands in the late fifties and early sixties, I didn't give much thought to Germany. My father had never seen action in the war; my mother didn't talk about the experiences of a seventeen-year-old private working in Plymouth and Bath, both of which cities were heavily bombed, the latter on what were called the Baedeker Raids. (Historic cities targeted in reprisal for the 1942 bombing of Lubeck were York, Bath, Norwich and Exeter; Canterbury was later bombed in reprisal for Cologne.)

I don't recall when I first learned that my German aunt, Irene Harrach, had spent the first few years of the war living at my grandfather's Welsh home, Chirk Castle, and working with evacuees, before she moved closer to London, renting a house near Godalming. There's a family story that Irene, who was both engaging and extremely pretty, was given a hotline on which to call Winston Churchill if she ever ran into difficulties. I sometimes wonder if my mother left Chirk to sign up at such an early age (she turned eighteen in 1940) because she found it difficult to live alongside a German sister-in-law. If she did, she'd never say.

Last summer, we found, immaculately preserved, the gramophone records that my Aunt Irene (Nucci to everybody who knew her) had brought over from Munich when she married John. We listened to her favourite German group, the Comedian Harmonists, as they sang, in sweet but melancholy harmony, 'Tea for Two' and 'Night and Day': perfect for a thirties' foxtrot at the elegant Vier Jahreszeiten Hotel in Munich, back in 1934. But in 1939, Nucci stacked her record collection of 78s away in an attic. Her daughters don't remember hearing them played. They did, however, hear Nucci talk about growing up in Florence and how much she loved her later life, when her parents settled in Munich. Aged twenty in 1955, Irene's eldest daughter went out to Munich to study photography – and discovered a city in which she, like her mother and father before her, felt instantly at ease.

Aged eight, exploring the Victorian books ranged along the nursery bookshelves, I found a thin red copy of *Max und Moritz* by Wilhelm Busch and took cold pleasure in frightening myself. I couldn't decipher or understand the clotted gothic script; the pictures of the imaginative punishments meted out to two fat little boys with leering faces told a story that needed no words. In the downstairs library, where my father used to read to my brother and me from *The Pickwick Papers* after tea, I pulled down, one evening, another German book. An oddly combined nineteenth-century guide to knitting and childrens' games, it had been dedicated to England's Dowager Queen Adelaide (the German wife of King William IV) by the admiring German-born author, Madame Apolline Flohr. When I turned the dusty pages, two fragile cobwebs of yellow wool dropped out. Somebody in our home, long ago, had taken the trouble to follow this guide to the art of German (also known as continental) knitting – and had given up in despair.

In Germany, Max Sebald, born into a devout family of Bavarian Catholics, was shown newsreel images of Belsen while still at school. No explanations were offered for what was being shown. Studying German literature at Freiburg while the Auschwitz Trials were being held at Frankfurt, Sebald encountered among his tutors a quiet but unified resistance to the history of the recent past. Befriended by a visiting professor from Britain, Ronald Peacock, Sebald followed him back to Manchester. Engels's city, transformed from an industrial powerhouse to a desolate waste-land by the 1960s, became the setting for Sebald's evocation of Max Ferber, in one of the four poignant stories of German alien-ation and displacement that he obliquely unfolded in *The Emigrants*. The book, as with all Sebald's works, was first written in the German language.

'Horror must be absolved by the quality of the prose,' Sebald told his students at the University of East Anglia, three days before his death, aged fifty-seven, at the wheel of his family car. Can it be? Can any writing aspire to do so much?

In 2003, the first of Sebald's non-fiction books was translated into English by Anthea Bell. A collection of essays, its title was taken from the first. *On the Natural History of Destruction* examined a subject upon which German writers had remained strangely silent: the Allies' bombing, during the last years of the war, of 131 German cities, killing 600,000 civilians and destroying three and a half million homes. (Hitler, as Sebald points out, had presided over the bombing of Guernica, Warsaw, Belgrade and Rotterdam; in 1940, Hitler spoke with enthusiasm of Goering's plans to destroy London in a single blaze of flame.) The morality and the effect of the bombings continue to be explored in Germany, but slowly. In 2007, Jörg Friedrich's *The Fire: The Bombing of Germany* was translated into English. In 2012, Karl Heinz Bohrer's memoir, *Granatsplitter*, recalled his experiences of growing up in Cologne, and the pleasure that besieged city children like himself took in gathering bright shards of shrapnel (*Granatsplitter*) from the street after an air raid. 'The shrapnel', the author wrote, 'was the most beautiful thing you could think of.'

Granatsplitter tells another story, of how the author, in the last pre-war days of the summer of 1939, was taken on a beach hol-iday by his parents, up in the far north of Germany. Two small boys – one English, one German – made friends while building, side by side, their moated castles in the sand. One day, the English boy stopped building his castle to point a finger out across the sea.

'That's England!'

In the summer of 1958, when I was ten years old and staying with relatives in Norfolk, I met my first German. Aged about sixteen, Franzi seemed like a god in his remoteness. Standing outside the wire cage that enclosed their family tennis court, Jane and I watched Franzi as he raised his golden arm to serve, or ran, light as an antelope, across the court. At breakfast, when Franzi thanked me with a shy nod for passing a jug of milk across the table, I burned with pride. Jane did better. When her family drove Franzi back to Germany – the visit was an exchange – my cousin was allowed to sit beside their guest in the back of the Rover. Her arm, apparently, had brushed against his and Franzi had not moved away. Fifty years later, the memory remained vivid enough to make her smile at me before, quite briefly, she glanced away.

Leaving a home where the war was rarely, if ever, discussed, to experience a new life in London, I saw Germany through the eyes of the film-makers. Erich von Stroheim's melancholy portrait of von Rauffenstein in Renoir's old classic, *La Grande Illusion*, caused a pause for thought about the possibility of good Germans, long ago. But the Germans who most regularly crossed the screen of my local movie-house, the Chelsea Coronet, were sinister men in uniform who strutted and spoke in a harsh spitting accent – Nazi-speak – that made it hard to distinguish one fictitious villain from another. My brother, younger and more adventurous than I in his travels, went off to see their country for himself. He came back aglow, bringing stories of our German cousins, Nucci's family, and the warm welcome that he had received.

Meanwhile, sitting down to weekend breakfasts in our family's country home under a looming portrait of Prince Albert – nobody

ever explained quite why we came to possess it – I thought, occasionally, about the fact that it had taken just twelve years of
monstrous, meditated evil to eradicate a history of mutual affection. Relations, however grimly overshadowed by the attribution
of war guilt (*Schuld*) to a country that must pay its debts (*Schulden*)
in reparation, had been restored after the First War. Following the
exposed horrors of the Holocaust, it had come to seem that
Germany never could – never should – escape from the guilt she
communally bears for the activities of the Third Reich. What was
done to Germany herself cannot eradicate what she set out, with
cold deliberation, to do to others.

Herbert Sulzbach had called, in 1984, for an end to the old mistrust. It seems, in the current economic climate, that this ending
is unlikely to be achieved at any time in the near future. The
wounds are real and deep, and they continue to cause torment. But
our two countries do also share a long history of mutual admiration and commitment; this, too, should be remembered.

When I set out to research this book, five years ago, I planned
to write about the years between the two world wars. Increasingly,
however, I found myself drawn back into the stories of what it was
that had once bound England and Germany together, the history
that led back to the joining of two Protestant powers in that celebrated 'marriage of Thames and Rhine' on Valentine's Day, 400
years ago. I began to wish that I had known about this longer history when I was a schoolgirl and that I could have placed the
history of recent, unabsolvable horror – seventy years on, it still
feels like yesterday – within the context of that long connection.

Nothing can alter what took place between 1933 and 1945. But
another history lies behind it. Here lay the story that I would write
to please not others, but myself. It would be my education.

The stories that emerged, some familiar, some unknown, were
of the men and women who, in some action or attitude, strove to
bring together the best and finest aspect of two great nations.
Some, like the valiant Elizabeth Fry, well primed with porter and

a high sense of her duty as she sailed out to reform the German prisons, would evidently qualify as noble in their endeavours. Others, like the capricious and often quite unbearable Emperor Wilhelm II (Willy), were undoubtedly misguided both in their vision and in their actions. But all had a part to play. All – none more than the German Prince, Ludwig von Battenberg, who resigned as Britain's first sea lord before changing his name to Lord Louis Mountbatten – had genuinely believed that they were acting for the good of both countries. In a story made up of many lives, all would speak for themselves.

The biographer Richard Holmes once aptly described the sensation of writing about the dead as being like a handshake across the past. I feel sad at having to say goodbye to the extraordinary cast of characters with whom I have been lucky enough to shake hands during the last few years. I think of dashing Prince Pückler-Muskau and his loyal Lucie, and wistful, shrewd Theodor Fontane. I think of poor Sir Edward Goschen, pacing the platform of a London station under the watchful eyes of the press as he waits for his dear son, Bunt, to come home; of Prince Lichnowsky and his spirited young wife, and impulsive Margot Asquith rushing into the German Embassy to say a last farewell. I think of Daisy Pless and her son, Hansel; of the unquenchable Tisa Schulenburg venturing off in her pearls and furs to talk to the miners at Durham; of Hubert Herkomer setting out to build his great German house in an English village; of Coleridge laughing with delight at the greeting he first received in a little German town; of young James Boswell, trying so hard to capture the attention of his German hero, and being identified only by the quaintness of his blue bonnet.

And I really don't want to say goodbye. I certainly will never forget them. They've been my friends and my educators. I honour them all.

NOTES

CHAPTER 1

1 Herbert Sulzbach, *With the German Guns: Four Years on the Western Front* (London, 1973; 2003).
2 Ibid. Small wonder that Nazi reviewers, unaware of the author's Jewish background, praised Sulzbach's diary when it was first published as *Zwei lebende Mauern* in 1935.
3 Hubert Pollack, *Captain Foley, der Mensch und anderen Berichte*, Yad Vashem Holocaust Museum, YVS 01/17.
4 Benno Cohn, testimony from the transcript of Adolf Eichmann's trial, session 14, 25.4.1961. Cited by Michael Smith, *Foley: The Spy Who Saved 10,000 Jews* (1999) p. 273.
5 Quoted from Sulzbach's speech at Comrie by Terence Prittie, a former POW in Germany, Sulzbach, op. cit., p. 13.
6 Ibid.
7 Herbert Sulzbach, speaking on 'Comment', produced by Fiona Maddocks, Channel 4, 1984.

CHAPTER 2

1 Lady Mary Wortley Montagu to Lady Bristol, 25.11.1716, *The Complete Letters of Lady Mary Wortley Montagu*, Vol. 1, ed. Robert Halsband (1965).
2 James Boswell, *The Journal of His German and Swiss Travels, 1764*, ed. Marlies K. Danziger (Edinburgh University Press, 2008).
3 Goethe, 'Rede zum Shakespeares-Tag' (1771).
4 Carl Philipp Moritz, *Journeys of a German in England, 1782* (2011), ch. 12.

CHAPTER 3

1 Samuel Taylor Coleridge, *Biographia Literaria* (1817), ch. ix.
2 Henry Crabb Robinson, *Diary, Reminiscences and Correspondence*, ed. Thomas Sadler (1869), p. 178.
3 William Beckford, 13.7.1780, *Dreams, Waking Thoughts and Incidents* (1783).
4 Sherer of Claverton, *Notes and Reflections During a Ramble in Germany* (1826), pp. 364–5.
5 *The Life and Correspondence of Thomas Arnold*, ed. Arthur Penrhyn Stanley (1901, reprint 2012). Thomas Arnold's innocent observation would be meticulously recycled in Sir Arnold Wilson's homage to Hitler's Germany: *Walks and Talks Abroad* (1936), p. 65.
6 Goethe, 19.10.1823, *Conversations with Eckermann* (1836).

CHAPTER 4

1 Peter Bowman, *The Fortune Hunter: A German Prince in Regency England* (2010), p. 162.
2 *Westminster Review*, January 1832, reviewing Vol. 1 of Pückler's *Tour of a German Prince*.
3 Lotte and Joseph Hamburger, *Contemplating Adultery: The Secret Life of a Victorian Woman* (New York, 1991) p. 147.
4 Sarah Austin, *Germany from 1760–1814, or Sketches of German Life* (1854), p. 99.

CHAPTER 5

1 G. H. Lewes, 27.9.1854, quoted in Rosemary Ashton, *George Eliot: A Life* (1996), p. 113.
2 George Eliot, 'Three Months in Weimar', *Fraser's Magazine,* L1 (June 1855), pp. 699–706.
3 W. M. Thackeray to G. H. Lewes, 28.5.1855, printed in Lewes's *Life of Goethe* (1855), Book vii.
4 George Eliot to Charles Bray, 12.11.1854, *Letters of George Eliot,* ed. Gordon S. Haight, Vol. 2; and Eliot, 27.3.1855, *Journals of George Eliot,* ed. Margaret Harris (CUP, 2005).
5 *Blackwood's Magazine*, October 1841, p. 456.
6 Privately published family leaflet on Charles de Bunsen in the Broughton Archive, p. 7, citing Leopold von Ranke's introduction to the letters between Alexander von Humboldt and de Bunsen.
7 Augustus Hare, *The Life and Letters of Baroness Bunsen,* Vol. 1 (of two),

p. 490, citing Fanny's letter to their Prussian friend and colleague Heinrich Abeken (18.12.1838). All quotations in this chapter that relate to the de Bunsens' domestic and diplomatic life are taken from these two volumes and from Fanny's life of her husband, *A Memoir of Baron Bunsen* (1868).

CHAPTER 6

1 De Bunsen's involvement with the hospital is described in a privately published work by Maureen Specht, whose own family, of German origin, lived next to – and were closely involved with – the German Hospital. *The German Hospital in London and the Community It Served, 1845–1948* (1989), p. 9 and onwards.
2 Elizabeth Gurney's unpublished diary is in the Broughton Archive.
3 Cecil Woodham Smith, *Florence Nightingale* (1950), p. 63.

CHAPTER 7

1 Princess Victoria to Leopold I, King of the Belgians, 17.5.1836, quoted by Stanley Weintraub, *Albert: Uncrowned King* (1997), p. 49.
2 *Blackwood's Magazine*, April 1838, p. 514.
3 Victoria to King Leopold I, quoted by Lytton Strachey, *Queen Victoria* (1921), pp. 128–9.
4 Victoria to the Crown Princess of Prussia, quoted in 'Marriage, Family and Nationality' by Monika Wienfort in *Royal Kinship: Anglo-German Family Networks 1815–1918*, ed. Karina Urbach (KG Saur, Munich, 2008), p. 127.
5 De Bunsen to Baron Stockmar, New Year, 1852, *The Life and Letters of Baroness Bunsen,* op. cit., Vol. 2, p. 275.
6 Max Müller, *Chips from a German Workshop* (1871), Vol. 3, p. 2.
7 Rosemary Ashton, *Little Germany: Exile and Asylum in Victorian England* (1986), p. 21.
8 Ian Buruma, from his fine essay in *Voltaire's Coconuts* (2000 reprint edition), p. 186.
9 Richard Monckton Milnes, 'Reflections on the Political State of Germany', *Edinburgh Review* (April 1849), pp. 537–8.

CHAPTER 8

1 Mary Shelley's observations are taken from *Rambles in Germany and Italy, in 1840, 1842 and 1843* (1844).

2 Mary Wescomb went to Germany from Thrumpton Hall, where her unpublished diary survives in the library.
3 Theodor Fontane, *Ein Sommer in London* (1854). This delightful book is one of many by Fontane that remains without an English translation. Translations here are the author's own.
4 *Murrays Handbook to Northern Germany* (1849), p. 215.
5 All Duthie's quotations are taken from William Duthie, *A Tramp's Wallet* (1858).

CHAPTER 9

1 Richard Monckton Milnes (later Lord Houghton), 'The Political State of Prussia', *Edinburgh Review*, 83 (1846), p. 224.
2 The account of Fritz's visit to Balmoral in 1855 is based on that given by Hannah Pakula, *An Uncommon Woman: The Empress Frederick* (1996), ch. 6.
3 Bismarck to General Leopold von Gerlach, Egon Caesar Conte Corti, *Alexander von Battenberg* (1954), pp. 26–7.
4 Walburga Paget, *Embassies of Other Days* (1923). All of Wally von Hohenthal's observations are taken from her volumes of memoirs.
5 Alice to Queen Victoria, 21.8.1866, *Alice, Grand-Duchess of Hesse: Letters to Queen Victoria* (1884).
6 Ibid.
7 Fanny de Bunsen to Hilda de Bunsen, 22.2.1873, Baroness Deichmann, *Impressions and Memories* (1926), pp. 57–8.
8 Lady William Russell to Sir Austen Henry Layard, 18.10.1870, Layard Papers, BL, 38.998 f.303.
9 Karina Urbach, *Bismarck's Favourite Englishman: Lord Odo Russell's Mission to Berlin* (1999), p. 97.
10 Poultney Bigelow, *Prussian Memories: 1864–1914* (1916), pp. 40-41.
11 Vicky to Queen Victoria, 25.3.1890 (RA: Z 48/6).
12 Wilhelm II to Queen Victoria, 27.3.1890 (RA: 58/32).

CHAPTER 10

1 Sir Hubert van Herkomer to his students, 10.3.1900 (from Berlin), Bushey Museum Archive.
2 'Working for Morris, Burne-Jones and Ruskin: The Memories of Thomas Rooke (1842–1942)' by Simon Fenwick, photocopy from an unsourced and undated article held at Bushey Museum.
3 J. Saxon-Mills, *The Life and Letters of Hubert Herkomer* (1923), p. 177.

4 Vincent van Gogh to Theo van Gogh, 19.8.1883. From the superb online source for the collected letters of Vincent van Gogh: www.vangoghletters.org.

5 Hubert Herkomer, *The Herkomers* (1910), Vol. 1, p. 165.

6 Herkomer, a student lecture, 29.10.1884, quoted by Rosemary Treble, *A Passion for Work: Sir Hubert von Herkomer 1849–1914* (Watford Borough Council 1983), p. 27.

7 Herkomer, 'The Pictorial Music Play: An Idyl', *The Magazine of Art* (1889), pp. 316–22.

8 J. Saxon Mills, op. cit., p.189.

9 Cited, without further details, in a photocopied article by Grant Longman for the *Watford and Herts Review* (Bushey Museum, n.d.), p. 14.

10 Hermann Muthesius, *Das englische Haus*, first published in Germany in 1904; UK abridged reissue (1987), ed. Dennis Sharp, p. 52.

11 Ibid., Book 3, p. 216.

12 Ibid., Book 1, p. 9.

13 Ethel Smyth, *Impressions that Remained* (1919), Vol. 2., p. 169.

14 Ethel Smyth, *Memoirs* (abridged), p. 242; variant version: *What Happened Next* (1940), p. 191.

15 Ethel Smyth, *Streaks of Life* (1921), p. 162.

16 Ethel Smyth to Alice Davidson, her sister, 11.3.1902. Ibid., p. 183.

17 Ibid., p. 205.

CHAPTER 11

1 Daisy Pless, *Daisy Princess of Pless by Herself* (1928), p. 51.

2 Hansel Pless. All quotations from Prince Hansel are taken from the recorded interviews he made, aged seventy-five, owned by his former wife, Lady Ashtown.

3 Lady Susan Townley, *Indiscretions* (1922), p. 57–8.

4 Lamar Cecil, *Wilhelm II*, Vol. 2 (US, 1996), p. 79.

5 Daisy Pless, op. cit., p. 96.

7 Baron von Eckardstein, *Ten Years at the Court of St James, 1895–1905* (1921), pp. 83–5. Eckardstein was told by Lord Salisbury (when Salisbury was prime minister) that de Soveral's action had prevented the outbreak of war between England and Germany. Reference to the incident also crops up in the memoirs of Friedrich von Holstein, political head of the German FO in 1896: *The Holstein Papers*, eds. Norman Rich and M. H. Fisher (1954), Vol. 1, ch. 10.

8 Vicky to Queen Victoria, 11.1.1896, *Beloved and Darling Child: Last Letters between Queen Victoria and her Eldest Daughter*, ed. Agatha Ramm (1990) and quoted from throughout this chapter.

9 Ibid., 3.10.1896.

10 Cecil Spring-Rice to Stephen Gwynn, 2.11.1895: *The Letters and Friendships of Cecil Spring-Rice: A Record*, ed. Stephen Gwynn (1929), from which Spring-Rice's further observations are taken in this chapter.

11 Richard Seymour, *The Last Quarter 1875–1900* (unpublished family memoir).

12 Ibid.

13 Edward to Wilhelm, 7.3.1900, quoted by John C. Rohls, 'Anglo-German Family Networks before 1914', in *Royal Kinship: Anglo-German Family Networks 1815–1918,* ed. Karina Urbach (Munich, 2008), p. 142.

14 *The Times*, 6.2.1901; but see also an excellent summary of the post-funeral press by Miranda Carter, *The Three Emperors* (US ed. 2010), pp. 230–31.

15 The phrase 'the exalted gentleman' appears as a description of Edward VII in Wilhelm's unpleasantly self-serving *Memoirs* (1922), p. 127.

CHAPTER 12

1 Wolf-Dieter Dube, *The Expressionists* (1972), p. 158.

2 Cecily Sidgwick, *Home Life in Germany* (1908), p. 1.

3 Robert Graves, *Goodbye to All That* (1929), ch. 1.

4 Ibid., ch. 10.

5 Max Saunders, *Ford Madox Ford*, Vol. I (1996), p. 176.

6 Karen Usborne, *Elizabeth* (1986), p. 111, quoting Forster's 'Recollections of Nassenheide', *The Listener* (1959), from which the description of his arrival also comes.

7 E. M. Forster, *Howards End* (1910), p. 5.

8 Ibid., p. 73.

9 Ibid., p. 102.

10 Ibid., p. 184.

11 Ibid., p. 167.

12 Usborne, op. cit., p. 135; Elizabeth von Arnim, *The Caravaners*, p. 8.

13 Constance Smedley, *Crusaders* (1929), pp. 126–9.

14 Daisy Pless, *From My Private Diary* (1931), p. 162.

15 Cecil Spring-Rice to Mrs Roosevelt, 5.10.1905, *The Letters and Friendships of Cecil Spring-Rice: A Record*, ed. Stephen Gwynn (1929).

16 Anne Topham, *Chronicles of the Prussian Court* (1926), pp. 187–8.

17 Ibid., pp. 206–7.

18 Daisy Pless, quoting from her diary 10.2.1909, op. cit.

CHAPTER 13

1 Evelyn Wrench, *Uphill: The First Stage in a Strenuous Life* (1934), p. 33.
2 Ibid., pp. 73–5.
3 Ibid., p. 246.
4 Ibid., p. 241.
5 D. George Boyce, *The Crisis of British Power: The Imperial and Naval Papers of the Second Earl of Selborne, 1895–1910* (1990), p. 113.
6 Matthew S. Seligmann, 'Prince Louis of Battenberg', from *Royal Kinship: Anglo-German Family Networks 1815–1918*, ed. Karina Urbach (KG Saur Munich), p. 166; John B. Hattendorff, 'Admiral Prince Louis of Battenberg (1912–1914) in *The First Sea Lords From Fisher to Mountbatten*, ed. Malcolm H. Murfett (Westport, Connecticut, 1995), p. 76.
7 Louis of Battenberg to George V, 5.12.1912, RA: PS/GV/M 520A/1.
8 Daisy Pless, *From My Private Diary* (1931), p. 239.
9 Robert Graves, *Goodbye to All That* (op.cit.), ch. 1.
10 J. A. Cramb, *Reflections on the Origins and Destiny of Imperial Britain* (1900), pp. 113–116.
11 Houston Stewart Chamberlain to Baron Brockdorff-Rantzau, 23.9.1914, *Briefe und Briefwechsel mit Kaiser Wilhelm II* (Munich, 1925).
12 I. R. Wylie, *A Year in Germany* (1910), p. 1.
13 Ibid., p. 271.
14 Ibid., p. 282.
15 Schücking was reviewing a new book on Shakespeare by Swinburne. *The English Review*, Vol. 1 (1908), pp. 188–192.
16 Daisy Pless, *Daisy Princess of Pless by Herself* (op. cit), p. 229.
17 Information from Richard Bowden, archivist to the Portman estate. Information has also been taken from Das Kranzbach, the spa hotel of which Mary's original house provides the striking central feature.

CHAPTER 14

1 All observations by Sir Edward Goschen are taken from *The Diary of Edward Goschen: 1910–1914* (1980).
2 Transcript of 'Zweite Heimat London über Mechtilde Lichnowsky', produced by Bedrich Rohan for *Südwestfunk Literatur* 25.9.1988.
3 Goschen, op. cit.
4 Mechtilde Lichnowsky transcript, op. cit., quoting from ML's novel, *An der Leine* (Munich, 1930).
5 Harry F. Young, *Prince Lichnowsky and the Great War* (1977), p. 90; *Berliner Tageblatt*, 4 June 1914.

6 Georg von Hase, *Kiel and Jutland* (c.1920).
7 Ibid., p. 28.
8 Ibid., p. 62.
9 Horace Rumbold to Ethel Rumbold, 30.7.1914, quoted by Martin Gilbert, *Sir Horace Rumbold: Portrait of a Diplomat: 1869–1941* (1973), p. 114.
10 Berta (Lowry-Corry) de Bunsen's diary is among the de Bunsen papers at Broughton Castle. (A small section has been published in *Historical Research* (51) 1978, ed. Christopher Howard, pp. 209–225.)
11 Maurice de Bunsen to Baronness Deichmann, 29.6.1914; Berta de Bunsen to Marie de Bunsen, 2.7.1914, Edgar Trevelyan Stratford Dugdale, *Maurice de Bunsen, Diplomat and Friend* (1934).
12 Maurice de Bunsen to Edward Grey, 1.8.14, discussing a message from a worried Count Benckendorff at the Russian Embassy in London, Dugdale, ibid.
13 Diary of Berta de Bunsen.
14 Dugdale, op. cit., pp. 304–5; Benjamin Bruce, *Silken Dalliance*, (1947) p. 123.
15 Harold Nicolson, *King George V* (1952), pp. 245–6. Nicolson's informant on these exchanges is likely to have been his father, Sir Arthur, who, as permanent under-secretary at the Foreign Office, was a party to the discussions.
16 Young, op. cit., p. 124.
17 Daisy Pless to HRH George V (Royal Archives), John W. Koch, *Daisy Princess of Pless: A Discovery* (2004), p. 21.
18 Nicolson, op. cit., p. 247.
19 Koch, op. cit., p. 208. The account of George V's message is correct, but Daisy Pless was a great romancer. Her diary suggests that she left London for Berlin on 31 July, before the declaration of war.
20 Lichnowsky, *My Mission to London*, 1912–1914 (1916), p. 89.
21 Ibid., p. 88.
22 Young, op. cit., p. 127.
23 Goschen, op. cit., 15.12.1914; 30.12.1914.

CHAPTER 15

1 All Sorley quotations are from *The Collected Letters of Charles Hamilton Sorley*, ed. Jean Moorcroft Wilson (1990).
2 Ibid. Both letters, to Sorley's parents and to the headmaster of Marlborough, were written from Schwerin on 20.2.1914.
3 Reports in the *Daily Mail* and the *Daily Telegraph*, 27.11.1915, kindly supplied by George Goschen's daughter, Tana Fletcher. Additional information provided by the Revd Sir Timothy Forbes Adam, 20 April 2013.

4 Philip Heseltine, 'Some Notes on Delius and his Music', *Musical Times* (1915), pp. 137–42.
5 Sefton Delmer, *Trail Sinister: An Autobiography* (1941), p. 40.
6 Robert Graves, *Goodbye to All That* (op. cit), ch. 16.
7 Daisy Pless, *Daisy Princess of Pless by Herself* (op. cit), p. 312.
8 Melvyn Higginbottom, *Intellectuals and British Fascism: A Study of Henry Williamson* (1992), p. 23.
9 Captain Edward Hulse to his mother, 28.12.1914, *War Letters of Fallen Englishmen*, ed. Laurence Housman (1930).
10 Daisy Pless, *What I Left Unsaid* (1936), p. 124.
11 Daisy Pless, *Daisy Princess of Pless by Herself* (op. cit), pp. 375 and 459.
12 Tisa Schulenburg, unpublished English variant memoir of *Ich hab's gewagt* (Header, 1981).
13 Ibid.
14 Evelyn Blücher, *An English Wife in Berlin* (1920), p. 38.
15 Friedrich Hochberg to Daisy Pless, 29.5.1917, Daisy Pless, *What I left Unsaid* (op. cit), pp. 91–2.
16 Ibid., 17.6.1917.
17 Ibid.
18 Hansel Pless, Interviews, see ch. 11, n. 2.
19 Ibid.
20 Ibid.
21 Ibid.
22 Baroness Deichmann, *Impressions and Memories* (1926), pp. 222–6; additional oral information from the de Bunsen family.

CHAPTER 16

1 Daisy Pless, *Daisy Princess of Pless by Herself* (op. cit), p. 326.
2 Robert Graves, *Goodbye to All That*, op. cit, ch. 17.
3 Siegfried Sassoon, *Memoirs of a Fox-Hunting Man* (1929), pp. 293–4.
4 *Daily Herald*, 15.5.1915.
5 Hansard 7, 13.5.1915.
6 Arnold White to Leo Maxse, 4 February 1915. Stephan Koss, *Lord Haldane: Scapegoat for Liberalism*, p. 136.
7 Mark Kerr, *Prince Louis of Battenberg* (1934), p. 289.
8 Baroness Deichmann, *Impressions and Memories* (op. cit), p. 278.
9 Ibid., p. 279.
10 Hansard 16.11.1916, vol. 87, cc. 965–7.
11 Timothy Schröder, *Renaissance Silver from the Schröder Collection* (2007), p. 16.

12 Maureen Specht: *The German Hospital and the Community It Served:1845-1948* (op. cit), ch. 13.

CHAPTER 17

1 Prince Heinrich of Pless to Daisy Pless, 4.6.1918, Daisy Pless, *Daisy Princess of Pless by Herself* (op. cit), pp. 470–1.
2 Friedrich Hochberg to Daisy Pless, 17.6.1918, ibid.
3 Hansel Pless, Interviews, see ch. 11, n. 2.
4 Ebert's speech was made on 3 December 1918. John W. Wheeler-Bennett, *The Nemesis of Power: The German Army in Politics*, 1918–1945 (1953), p. 31.
5 Hansel Pless, op. cit.
6 Count Harry Kessler, *The Diaries of a Cosmopolitan 1918–1937*, 9.11.1918 and 18–28.12.1918.
7 See ch. 15, n. 12.
8 Ernest Tennant, *True Account* (1957), pp. 85–98.
9 Baroness Deichmann, *Impressions and Memories* (op. cit), pp. 282–5.
10 Philip Kerr to Violet Markham, 10.6.1920, in J. R. M. Butler, *Lord Lothian, Philip Kerr, 1882–1940* (1960), p. 77.
11 John Maynard Keynes, 'Dr Melchior: A Defeated Enemy' (1949), quoted by Robert Skidelsky, *John Maynard Keynes, 1883–1946: Economist, Philosopher, Statesman* (2004 edition), p. 221. Skidelsky views this remarkable essay as the finest piece of writing Keynes ever produced.
12 John Maynard Keynes, *The Economic Consequences of the Peace* (1919), p. 251.

CHAPTER 18

1 Hansel Pless, from the recorded interviews he made, aged seventy-five, owned by his former wife, Lady Ashtown.
2 Lord D'Abernon, *An Ambassador of Peace: Pages from the Diary of Viscount D'Abernon* (1929–30), 8.10.1926 and 24.8.1926.
3 Jonathan Petropolous in *Royals and the Reich: The Princes von Hessen in Nazi Germany* (OUP, 2006) draws both on the Sassoon correspondence lodged at Cambridge University Library (ULC) and on the Hessen Archives at Darmstadt.
4 Interview with Julie Wheelwright, 20.9.2010.
5 Count Harry Kessler, *The Diaries of a Cosmopolitan 1918–1937*, (op. cit) 3.3.1923.
6 Joseph Goebbels, *Die Tagebücher von Joseph Goebbels*, ed. Anne Munding (2005), December 1929–May 1931.

7 Norman Rose, *The Cliveden Set: Portrait of an Exclusive Fraternity* (2000), p. 127.

8 Baroness Deichmann, *Impressions and Memories* (op. cit), p. 285.

9 Tisa Schulenburg's unpublished memoir, see ch. 15, n. 12.

10 Ibid.

11 Ibid.

12 Houston Stewart Chamberlain to Adolf Hitler, 7.10.1923, *Briefe und Briefwechsel mit Kaiser Wilhelm II* (Munich, 1925). The letter was written shortly after their first, momentous encounter at Bayreuth and on the eve of the planned putsch, about which Chamberlain would seem to have been informed.

13 Adolf Hitler, *Mein Kampf* (1925), pp. 128 and 564.

CHAPTER 19

1 Cicely Hamilton, *Modern Germanies as Seen by an Englishwoman* (1931), p. 246, citing James W. Angell, *The Recovery of Germany* (1929).

2 Lord D'Abernon, *An Ambassador of Peace* op. cit, quoting Dr Schacht's words on 23.1.1926.

3 Ibid., 25.10.1925.

4 *The Early Goebbels Diaries: The Diary of Joseph Goebbels 1925–1926* (1962).

5 Ibid.

6 Count Harry Kessler, *The Diaries of a Cosmopolitan* ,op. cit, 28.2.1925.

7 Tisa Schulenburg's unpublished memoir. See ch. 15, n. 12

8 Hansel Pless, Interviews, see ch. 11, n. 12..

9 *Universal Filmlexikon* (1932), ed. Frank Arnau, published simultaneously in London and Berlin; Kevin Brownlow, Interviews, 19.6.2012 and 21.6.2012; James Whale, 'Our Life at Holzminden', *Wide World Magazine* 43 (July, 1919), pp. 314–19.

10 Julia Wolff, interviewed for *Cinema Europe: The Other Hollywood: Germany*, written and directed by Kevin Brownlow and David Gill, *Photoplay*, BBC and ZDF.

11 John Heygate, *These Germans: An Estimate of their Character seen in Flashes from the Drama* (1940), pp. 14–15.

12 Ibid., p. 59.

13 Diana Mosley, *A Life of Contrasts* (1977), p. 73.

14 Ibid.

CHAPTER 20

1 Barty Redesdale to Houston Stewart Chamberlain, 25.1.1912, Geoffrey C. Field, *Evangelist of Race: The Germanic Vision of Houston Stewart Chamberlain* (1918), pp. 462–4.

2 Randolph Churchill, *The Young Unpretender: Essays by His Friends*, ed. Kay Halle (1971).

3 Interview and correspondence with Lord Moyne (October 2009), Jonathan and Catherine Guinness, *The House of Mitford* (1984), pp. 280–81.

4 Tom Mitford to his parents, February 1927 and 9.3.1927. Ibid., p. 282.

5 Diana Mosley, *A Life of Contrasts* (op. cit), p. 59.

6 Interview with the Duchess of Devonshire and Charlotte Mosley, 6.8.2009.

7 Tom Mitford to Unity Mitford April/May 1935, Guinness, op. cit., p. 375.

8 Unity Mitford to Diana Mosley, 8.6.1935, *The Mitfords: Letters Between Six Sisters*, ed. Charlotte Mosley (2007).

9 James Lees-Milne, *Diaries, Prophesying Peace* (1977), 27.8.1944.

10 Diana Mosley, *Loved Ones: Pen Portraits* (1985), p. 187.

11 Nancy Mitford to Jessica Treuhaft, 15.11.1968, *The Letters of Nancy Mitford*, ed. Charlotte Mosley (1993).

CHAPTER 21

1 Harold Nicolson, 4.8.1928, *Diaries 1907–1963*, ed. Nigel Nicolson (2003).

2 Bella Fromm, 1.2.1930, *Blood and Banquets: A Berlin Social Diary* (1943).

3 Robert Bruce Lockhart, 13.2.1929, *The Diaries of Sir Robert Bruce Lockhart, 1915–38* (1973); Gareth Jones, 'Poland's Foreign Relations', *The Contemporary Review* (July 1931).

4 Ethel Rumbold to her mother, 31.7.1933, Martin Gilbert, *Sir Horace Rumbold, Portrait of a Diplomat* (1973), p. 387.

5 Fromm, op. cit., 14.10.1930.

6 Gareth Jones, 29.11.1931, *The New York American*.

7 John Howard de Walden, *Earls Have Peacocks* (1992), p. 14, and to the author, in conversation. The anecdote opens Craig Brown's collection of random connections in history: *One on One* (2011).

8 Rumbold's observations are taken from Martin Gilbert, op. cit., p. 373.

9 Tisa Schulenburg's unpublished memoir. See ch. 15, n. 12.

10 Gilbert, op. cit., pp. 377–9.

11 Ibid., p. 386.

12 Fritz Stern, *Five Germanys I Have Known* (2006), p. 95.

13 Katherine Bucknell and Nicholas Jenkins, 'W. H. Auden: The Language of

Learning and the Language of Love', *Uncollected Writings: New Interpretations* (OUP 1994), pp. 21–2.

14 John Heygate, *Talking Picture* (1934), pp. 198–9.

15 John Heygate, *Those Germans: An Estimate of their Character Seen in Flashes from the Drama*, (op. cit) pp. 195–6.

16 Details about Gareth Jones's life and work are taken from Margaret Colley, *More Than a Grain of Truth: The Biography of Gareth Jones* (2005), from the articles published in the *Western Mail*, and from the *Berliner Tageblatt*, 17.8.1935.

17 All quotations from Jones's published writings are taken from the *Western Mail*.

18 Ibid.

19 Unity Mitford to Diana Mosley, 1.7.1934, *The Mitfords: Letters Between Six Sisters*, ed. Charlotte Mosley (2007).

20 The *Daily Telegraph*, 4.7.1934.

21 The *Daily Telegraph*, 8.8.1934

22 Michael Tracey, *A Variety of Lives: A Biography of Sir Hugh Greene* (1983), p. 52.

23 Ibid. An excellent account of Hugh Greene's German adventures is given by Jeremy Lewis in *Shades of Greene: One Generation of an English Family* (2010).

CHAPTER 22

1 Stephen Games, *Pevsner: The Early Life: Germany and Art* (2010), p. 155.

2 John Ratcliff to his mother, 17 April 1932, quoted by Games, ibid., p. 146.

3 Nikolaus Pevsner in private interview with Frank Hermann (24 June 1976), cited by Games, ibid.

4 Ibid., p. 159.

5 Rosalind Priestman, daughter of Pallister Barkas, in conversation with Stephen Games, 6 March 1984, ibid., p. 180.

6 Francesca Wilson, *Birmingham Post*, 5 April 1933.

7 Pevsner's career is meticulously charted by Susie Harries, *Pevsner* (2010); Stephen Games, *Pevsner*, op. cit., deals only – so far – with his life until 1934. This chapter is largely based upon these two authoritative books.

CHAPTER 23

1 Adolf Hitler, *Mein Kampf* (1925), p. 564.

2 Christopher Sidgwick, *German Journey* (1936), p. 175–7.

3 Interview with Ariel Tennant Crittall, 12 April 2011.

4 Ibid.

5 The detail about surcharges comes from Berta de Bunsen's unpublished reports on her visit with Sir Maurice to Germany in 1933–4 (Broughton Archives).
6 Ibid.
7 Rosemary Seymour to the author, 10 August 2012.
8 Dorothy Gage's observations come from a private diary in the possession of her children.
9 Interview with April Crowther, 5 August 2010.
10 Dorothy Innes-Smith, unpublished letters from July and August 1934, owned by Robert Innes-Smith.
11 Interview with Sir Harold Atcherley, 1 December 2010.
12 Interview with Daphne Davie, 7 July 2010.
13 Interview with Elizabeth Lowry-Corry, 2 July 2010.
14 Interview with Ronald Barker, 8 November 2010.
15 Robert Byron to Christopher Sykes, 1938, quoted by Christopher Sykes, *Four Studies in Loyalty* (1946), p. 166.
16 Robert Byron, Nuremberg Diary, 8 September 1938, from James Knox, *Robert Byron* (2003), p. 398.
17 Virginia Cowles, *Looking for Trouble* (1941), p. 16.
18 Percy Muir, *Minding My Own Business* (1956), p. 215.
19 Knox, op. cit., p. 408.

CHAPTER 24

1 Earl Howe to Richard Seaman, 5 May 1939, quoted in *The Seaman-Monkhouse Letters: 1936–1939* (2002).
2 Interview with Simon Reynolds, 8 December 2010.
3 Interview with Patrick von Stauffenberg, 5 May 2012.
4 Interviews with Hugh Geddes, Ariane Bankes, Jane Geddes, Euan Geddes, 2010 and 2011. I am also indebted to Jonathan Petropoulos, *Royals and the Reich: The Princes von Hessen in Nazi Germany* (op. cit), David Duff, *Hessian Tapestry: The Hessian Family and British Royalty* (Friederick Muller, Fleet Street, 1967) and, for Hesse background details, to Landgraf Moritz of Hesse and his very helpful archival team.
5 Reinhard Spitzy, *How We Squandered the Reich* (1986), pp. 68–9, 106, 109-110.
6 Shiela Grant Duff, *The Parting of Ways: A Personal Account of the Thirties* (1982), p. 36.
7 Adam von Trott to Shiela Grant Duff, 2.9.1934, *A Noble Combat: The Letters of Shiela Grant Duff and Adam von Trott zu Solz, 1932–1939* (1988), ed. Klemens von Klemperer.
8 Grant Duff, op. cit., p. 125.
9 Ibid., p. 121.

10 Adam von Trott to Shiela Grant Duff, 25 August 1939, Grant Duff, op. cit., p. 211.

CHAPTER 25

1 Sir James Barrie, 'Barrie and Brown', *The Literary Digest*, 14.7.1928.
2 James Fox, between 1969–70, interviewing former Rhodes scholars (Rhodes House), with grateful thanks to Rhodes House and to James Fox for his generous information and assistance.
3 Susie Harries, *Pevsner* (2010), pp. 171, 200, and for details of life at Duchess Road.
4 Tisa Schulenburg's unpublished memoir. See ch. 15, n. 12.
5 Ibid.
6 Ibid.
7 Ibid.
8 Viscount Rothermere, *My Fight to Rearm Britain* (1939), pp. 80–82. Original German document in PRO, FO 800/290, fols 241–8 (3 May 1935).
9 Bella Fromm, 9.11.1938, *Blood and Banquets: A Berlin Social Diary*, op. cit.
10 Interview's with Felix Gottlieb (January, June 2010; August 2012).
11 Interview's with Etka Green (11 December 2009; 3 December 2012).
12 Interview's with Eva Tucker (8 July 2009; 2 October 2012).
13 Eva Tucker, *Berlin Mosaic* (2005), p. 136; I have also drawn upon the sequel, *Becoming English* (2009).
14 Eva Tucker, Memorial Day Address for Berlin's Jewish Doctors, 5 November 2006.
15 See above.

CHAPTER 26

1 Eberhard Bethge, *Dietrich Bonhoeffer* (Augsburg Fortress Publishing, 2000), pp. 259–260.
2 George Bell to Dietrich Bonhoeffer, 24.2.1934, Bell Papers, vol. 42. 368 volumes of Bell papers are kept at Lambeth Palace Library, ref GB.109 BELL. Also accessible at www.lambethpalacelibrary.org.
3 Beverley Nichols, *All I Could Never Be* (1940), p. 276.
4 Bishop Dr Wolfgang Huber, Berlin, 2.10.2008; the Archbishop of Canterbury, Dr Rowan Williams, *The Times*, 24.12.2008.
5 Lord Londonderry to his wife, Edith, 30.3.1936, Ian Kershaw, *Making*

Friends with Hitler: Lord Londonderry, the Nazis and the Road to World War II (2005), p. 128.

6 Otto Schmidt, *Hitler's Interpreter* (1951), p. 25.

7 Ibid., p. 54.

8 Lord Londonderry to Sir Eric Phipps, 21.2.1936, Phipps Papers, Churchill Archives, Churchill College, Cambridge.

9 Loelia Westminster, *Grace and Favour: The Memoirs of Loelia, Duchess of Westminster* (1961), p. 114.

10 Interview with Lady Mairi Bury, 7.4.2009.

11 Diane Urquhart, *The Ladies of Londonderry: Women and Political Patronage* (2007), p. 199.

12 N. C. Fleming, *The Marquess of Londonderry: Aristocracy, Power and Politics in Britain and Ireland* (2005), p. 189; Lord Londonderry, *Ourselves and Germany* (1938) pp. 130–34.

13 Lord Londonderry to Lady Desborough, n.d. but seemingly 1943, quoted by Kershaw, op. cit., p. 337 and H. Montgomery-Hyde, *The Londonderrys, a Family Portrait* (1979), p. 259.

14 Interview with Lord Lothian, December 2012, and with grateful thanks for information, transcripts and names from the Visitors' Book, to Jan Brookes at Blickling Hall.

15 James Fox, 'Cockburn's Cliveden Set', in *The Langhorne Sisters* (1999), p. 500.

16 Ibid., p. 492.

17 A. L. Rowse, *Appeasement and All Souls: A Contribution to Contemporary History* (1961), p. 40.

18 Fox, *The Langhorne Sisters*, op. cit., p. 497, quoting a private family letter from Nancy Astor to Bob Brand, February 1937, in which – with characteristic insouciance – she passed on the latest news from their mutual friend.

19 Ibid., quoting from an interview with David Astor, p.485.

20 Norman Rose, *The Cliveden Set* (2000), p. 174 and p. 152.

21 Lothian to T. W. Lamont, 29.3.1939, J. R. M. Butler, *Lothian* (1960), p. 226.

22 James Fox, unpublished interviews with Carl Gunther Merz, Fritz Caspari, Dietrich von Bothmer, Adolf Schleppegrell, 1969–70, by permission of James Fox and Rhodes House.

23 Ibid., interview with Fritz Schumacher, 1969.

24 Ibid., interview with C. E. Collins, 8 August 1969.

25 Ibid., interview with Alexander Boker, 1969.

CHAPTER 27

1 Alexander Cadogan to Nevile Henderson, 22.4.1938, Sir Alexander Cadogan, *Diaries, 1938–1945*, ed. David Dicks (1971).
2 Malcolm Christie – www.spartacusschoolnet.co.uk, which indicates its source for this information as FWWM6.htm. Malcolm Christie is identified at this site by his second name, Hugh.
3 Winston Churchill, the *Strand Magazine*, November 1935.
4 Churchill Archives, CHAR 2/340B, 152–7.
5 Hansard: Duff Cooper to the House of Commons, 3.10.1938; Chamberlain to the House of Commons, 27.9.1938.
6 E .M. Forster, 'Post-Munich' (1939) in *Two Cheers for Democracy* (1940).
7 Patricia Meehan, *The Unnecessary War: Whitehall and the German Resistance to Hitler* (1992), pp. 223–35. The account given here of Christie, Conwell-Evans, the Kordts and their dealings with the Foreign Office is based on the Malcolm Christie Archive at Churchill College, and on Patricia Meehan's invaluable account.
8 Philip Conwell-Evans, *None So Blind* (1947), privately printed, pp. 195–8.
9 Malcolm Christie to Theo Kordt (n.d, but probably at the beginning of September 1939). Cited by Meehan, op. cit., p. 246. Also in Case XI Doc Bk 9 No. 931, Kordt Papers, in the case of US v Baron Ernst von Weizsäcker (US Printing Office, Washington).
10 Halifax to Lothian, 21.11.1939, Patricia Meehan, *The Unnecessary War*, op. cit.
11 Ibid, pp. 272–4.
12 Giles MacDonogh, *A Good German: Adam von Trott zu Solz* (1989), p. 331.
13 Meehan, op. cit., citing Foreign Office document FO 371/46852, p. 343.
14 Meehan, op. cit., citing Weizsäcker, Case XI, Prosecution Document Nos. NG-5186 and 86A, p. 371.
15 See 8 above, p. 211.

CHAPTER 28

1 Friedrich Reck-Malleczewen, 30.10.1942, *Diary of a Man in Despair* (2000).
2 Hansel Pless, from his papers (Ashtown).
3 Interview with Lady Ashtown, 12 September 2011.
4 Tisa Schulenburg's unpublished memoir. See ch. 15, n. 12.
5 Ibid.
6 Ibid.
7 Ibid.

8   Tisa Schulenburg to Christabel Bielenburg, n.d. unpublished (Schulenburg family).

9   Interviews and letters from Mechtilde Lichnowsky Peto's great-grandson, Eduardo Graf Lichnowsky (in Brazil), and from her great-nephew, Cajetan Pfetten, in Salzburg (2011 and 2012).

10 Mechtilde Lichnowsky, *Heute und Vorgestern* (1958).

11 Daisy Pless to her divorced sister Shelagh, 7.11.1939 (Ashtown).

12 Hansel Pless, see n.2 above.

13 Hansard, 22.8.1940.

14 Hansel Pless to Victor Cazalet, 25.9.1941, enclosing his original detention order and responses received. See n. 2 above.

15 Michael Kerr, *As Far As I Remember* (2002), p. 133. Kerr's sister, Judith, is the celebrated children's author and illustrator.

16 Daisy Pless to Hansel Pless, 3.4.1942, John W. Koch, *Daisy Princess of Pless: A Discovery* (2004), ch. 11, and Koch in conversation with the author, February 2012.

17 *The Times*, 13.7.1943.

18 George Cornwallis-West to Winston Churchill, 29.3.1943 CHAR/1/374/32–3 (Churchill College).

19 Hansel Pless, interviews, see ch. 11, n. 2.

20 Interview with Lady Ashtown, 12 September 2011.

21 The *Hackney Gazette*, 3.6.1940.

22 Maureen Specht: *The German Hospital*, op. cit, and *Hackney Gazette* (June, July, August 1940).

23 Unpublished memoir of World War II, by Charles Victor de Rohan, with thanks to the Prince's granddaughter, Ann Buchanan.

24 Information about Goodliffe's activities can be found in Midge Gillies, *Barbed-Wire University: The Real Life of Prisoners of War in the Second World War* (2010), and Terence Prittie and Wearle Richards, *South to Freedom* (1946), and at the website www.mgoodliffe.co.uk, compiled by the actor's son, Jonathan Goodliffe.

25 Ibid.

26 M. N. McKibbin, *Barbed Wire* (1947), p. 85.

CHAPTER 29

1   Material regarding Koeppler and Wilton Park is taken from conversations with the team at Wiston House (Wilton Park), and from Richard Mayne's indispensable book on the subject: *In Victory, Magnanimity, In Peace, Goodwill: A History of Wilton Park* (2003), pp. 5–6. The details concerning letters to Koeppler are also taken from Mayne.

2 Ibid., pp. 57–8.

3 Herbert Sulzbach, Channel 4 (1984), with thanks to Fiona Maddocks (interview, 7.6.2012); with reference to Terence Prittie's foreword to the 1998 UK edition of *Zwei lebende Mauern* (1935).

4 Mayne, op. cit., p. 92.

5 Ibid., p. 416.

6 Murray Schafer, *British Composers in Interview* (1963), p. 231.

7 Paul Kildea, *Benjamin Britten: A Life in the Twentieth Century* (2013). I am also indebted to Ariane Bankes and to George St. Andrews for details about Wolfsgarten, and Britten's visits, described here on pp. 445–447.

8 Hans Werner Henze, Programme Book for the Aldeburgh Festival of Music and Arts (1997), p. 23.

9 With grateful thanks to Dr Nicholas Clark for supplying material and information relating to the Hesse Student Fellowships.

10 Kildea, op. cit., p. 454.

SELECT BIBLIOGRAPHY

Many of the books used are mentioned in the reference notes. Readers will not need their attention drawn to the works of Sir Martin Gilbert, Professor John Röhl (whose own English and German background and work exemplifies the subject of this book), the late Lord Bulloch and Sir Ian Kershaw. Their works have been of inestimable value when writing this book, as have those of the matchless Barbara Tuchmann.

Those listed here have each contributed something, and not always because I agreed with their author, to this book. This list makes no attempt to be comprehensive, only to act as a signboard.

Walter Abish, *Wie Deutsch ist Es* (1979)

Benedict Anderson, *Imagined Communities* (1991)

Eric Ashby and Mary Anderson, *Portrait of R. B. S. Haldane at Work on Education* (1974)

Nicholson Baker, *Human Smoke* (2008)

William Beckford, *Dreams, Waking Thoughts and Incidents* (1783)

James Boswell, *The Journal of his German and Swiss Travels* (1764), ed. Marlies K. Danziger (Yale, 2008)

Nicholas Boyle, *German Literature: A Very Short Introduction* (OUP, 2008) and the first two volumes of *Goethe, The Poet and the Age*, extending, so far, until 1803 (OUP, 1991 and 2000)

Walter Benjamin, *Berlin Childhood Around 1900* (2006)

Inka Bertz, *Familienbilder* (2004)

Tim Blanning, *The Romantic Age* (2010)

A. S. Byatt, *The Children's Book* (2009)

Miranda Carter, *The Three Emperors* (2009)

Justin Cartwright, *The Song Before It Is Sung* (2005)

John Charmley, *Chamberlain and the Lost Peace* (1989)

Rupert Christiansen, *The Visitors: Culture Shock in Nineteenth-Century Britain* (2001)

Christopher Clark, *The Sleepwalkers* (2010)

Peter Conradi, *Ernst Hanfstaengl: Hitler's Piano Player* (2006)

Gordon Craig, *The Germans* (1991)

Otto Dietrich, *The Hitler I Knew* (1957)

Johann Peter Eckermann, *Conversations of Goethe* (1829; 1970)

Hermann Eich, *The Unloved Germans* (1963, translated 1965)

Joachim Fest, *Hitler* (1974)

Erica Fischer and Simone Ladwig-Winters, *Die Wertheims: Geschichte einer Familie* (2008)

David Fromkin, *Europe's Last Summer: Who Started the Great War in 1914?* (2005)

Peter Gay, *Weimar Culture: The Outsider as Insider* (1998)

Ronald Harwood, *An English Tragedy* (script, 2008)

Deborah Hertz, *Jewish High Society in Old Regime Berlin* (Yale, 1988)

John Heygate, *Talking Picture* (1934)

Oliver Hilmes, *Cosima Wagner, the Lady of Bayreuth* (2010)

Richard Davenport-Hines, *Auden* (1995)

Michael Holroyd, *A Strange Eventful History: The Dramatic Lives of Ellen Terry, Henry Irving and Their Remarkable Families* (2008)

Paul Kennedy, *The Rise of the Anglo-German Antagonism 1860–1914* (2nd ed., 1988)

Harry Kessler, *The Diaries of a Cosmopolitan, 1918–1937*, ed. Charles Kessler (1971). This is still handy, despite a more extensive publication of the diaries still in the making.

Ivone Kirkpatrick, *The Inner Circle* (1959)

Emil Ludwig, *The Germans: Double Portrait of a Nation* (1940)

Giles McDonagh, *Adam von Trott: The Good German* (1995)

Margaret Macmillan, *Peacemakers: Six Months that Changed the World* (2001)

Peter Mandler, *The English National Character: The History of an Idea from Edmund Burke to Tony Blair* (2006)

Robert K. Massie, *Dreadnought: Britain, Germany and the Coming of the Great War* (1991)

Mark Mazower, *Hitler's Empire: Nazi Rule in Occupied Europe* (2008)

Peter Parker, *Isherwood: A Life Revealed* (2004)

Roy Pascal, *Shakespeare in Germany, 1740–1815* (1976)

Jonathan Petropoulos, *Royals and the Reich: The Princes von Hessen in Nazi Germany* (2006)

Gitta Sereny, *The German Trauma: Experiences and Reflections* (2000)

Anne Dzamba Sessa, *Richard Wagner and the English* (1979)

George Bernard Shaw, *How to Become a Musical Critic*, ed. Dan H. Laurence (1960)

Ethel Smyth, *Abridged Memoirs* (1987)

The Collected Letters of Charles Sorley, ed. Jean Moorcroft Wilson (1990)

Reinhard Spitzy, *How We Squandered the Reich* (1986)

Jonathan Steinberg, *Bismarck* (2011)

Zara Steiner, *The Foreign Office and Foreign Office Policy 1898–1914* (US edition, 1986)

Gerwin Strobl, *The Germanic Isle: Nazi Perceptions of Britain* (2000)

John Sutherland, *Stephen Spender* (2004)

Rodney Symington, *The Nazi Appropriation of Shakespeare: Cultural Politics in the Third Reich* (Edwin Mellen Press, 2005)

Eva Tucker, *Berlin Mosaic* (2005); *Becoming English* (2009)

Petra Utta-Rau, *English Modernism, National Identity and the Germans, 1890–1950* (Aldershot: Ashgate, 2009)

Peter Watson, *The German Genius* (2010)

Harry F. Young, *Prince Lichnowsky and the Great War* (University of Georgia Press, 1977)

ACKNOWLEDGEMENTS

I wish to thank Her Majesty the Queen for graciously permitting me to quote from letters in the Royal Archives.

My thanks are deeply felt. So many friends and strangers and colleagues have given me thoughts, ideas, papers, photographs, access to private collections. I have listed everybody I can find in my records of letters, texts, emails and conversations, but I fear I will have omitted many who were just as kind, patient and encouraging as those listed below. I could not have written this book without you all. Your support, suggestions and contributions have been constructive, cheering and immensely helpful.

Here is a list, then, that doesn't begin to be comprehensive, and isn't even alphabetically in order – how could I put such a heartening enthusiast as Benjamin Zander at the end of a list?

I would, however, like to say special thanks to two neighbours: Kevin Brownlow, across the street, was marvellously generous in sharing some of the treasures of his collection, and in giving me ideas. Alice Sommer Herz, who knew Kafka when she was young, and who is still, aged 108, playing the piano, was inspiring not only because I could hear her piano every time I walked out along the street and round the corner, but because of the magnificent optimism that she has displayed throughout her life, and in circumstances that few could have endured with such courage.

Among the many who loaned papers, diaries and memoirs, the first and perhaps the most welcoming of them all was Mariette Saye at Broughton Castle, whose portrait of her splendid forebear, Sir Maurice de Bunsen, looked down on me as I read – among other absorbing diaries and letters from a remarkable family – his wife's account of the last days in Vienna, before the war. Margreta di Grazia's thoughts on Shakespeare and Germany proved of inestimable value; I wish that the lovely woman for whom both she and I feel such admiration, Inga-Stina Ewbank, were still alive to offer her comments on this book. Inga-Stina was my tutor at Bedford College. She taught me how to study and also how to write. I owe her so much.

My gratitude to my family is profound. Above all, thank you to my mother, my brother, and my beloved husband, Ted Lynch, whose steadfast encouragement, close reading and wise advice have meant so much.

At Simon and Schuster, I am grateful to a magnificent team. Mike Jones, Briony Gowlett, Hannah Corbett, Karl French, Juliana Foster, Clare Hubbard and Marie Lorimar have looked after me – and the book – with an enthusiasm and care that was so much appreciated. My agents, Anthony Goff and George Lucas, have been wonderful, as have the matchless and patient staff at the London Library.

Thanks are also due to Peter de Bunsen; Piers Brendon; Nicholas Clark (Britten-Pears Foundation); Laura Bell; John Searby; Peter Münder; Bruce Arnold; Kate Crowe at the Foreign Office (for an unforgettably thrilling tour of the Locarno Rooms); Mary Ashtown; Harold and Sally Atcherley; Heather Dean at the Beinecke Library, Yale; Rufus Albemarle; M. A. B. Mallender; Frank Akers-Douglas; Michael Bloch; Susie Buchan; Ronald Barker; Ariane Bankes; the late Mrs George Budd; Robert Beavers; Dr Matthias von Bismarck-Osten; Friedrich-Karl von Bismarck-Osten; Frederick Stüdemann; Ann and Hugh Buchanan; the archivist at St Bart's Hospital; Angela (Schulenburg) Bohrer and Karl Heinz Bohrer; Frank Barratt and Wendy Driver at the *Mail on Sunday* travel pages; George St Andrews; Sylvana Tomaselli; Rupert Christiansen; Pat Barker; Tim Schroder; Roy Foster; Donald and Diana Franklin; Sarah Ducas; Victoria von Preussen; Pam Sebag-Montefiore; Hugh Geddes; The Rt Hon Ken Clarke; The Rt Hon William Hague; Christopher Bielenberg; Nicholas Bielenberg; His Excellency, the German Ambassador, Georg Boomgarden; Paul Smith at the Thomas Cook archive; April Crowther; Griselda Cuthbert; Ariel Crittall; The Dowager Duchess of Devonshire; Warner and Fiona Dailey; Athena Dormer; Dorothea Depner; Richard Davenport Hines; Susan Elliott (at the family archives of Philip Lothian); James Fox; Helen Bailey and Jan Brookes at Blickling Hall; Jamie and Maggie Fergusson; Astrid Forbes; Tana Fletcher and also Sir Edward Goschen; Edgar Feuchtwanger; Fred Smoler; Adelheid (Schulenburg) Gowrie and Grey Gowrie; Miko and Dorothee Giedroyc; Euan Geddes; Etka Green; Julian and Dagmar (Langbehn) Grenfell; Lady Garvey; Flip Gibbons for translating help; Hazel Howard de Walden and Joseph Czernin; Stewart Howson; Victoria and Miles Huntington-Whiteley; Roland Hill; Gary Haines at Tower Hamlets Archives; Richard Heygate; Caterina (Hoyos) Schneemann, Jonathan Steinberg; Selina Hastings; Dr Ernst and Baroness Brigitte Jung; Rachel Johnson; 'Jess' at the German Hospital; Sir Ian Kershaw; Griselda Kerr; Judith Kerr; Dorna Khazeni; John Koch; Lady Rose Lauritzen; Jeremy Lewis; Benedict Flynn; Elizabeth Lowry-Corry; Michael Lothian; Eduardo Graf Lichnowsky; Lord Moyne; Benjamin Zander; Nicholas Mosley; Charlotte Mosley; Jeffrey Manton; Albrecht von Moltke; Helmut von Moltke; Duncan Maclaren; Father Heinz Medoch; Professor Stefan Muthesius; Edward Maze; Penelope Sitwell; HRH Landgraf Moritz and also Professor Eckhart G. Franz at the archives of the House of Hesse; Fiona Maddocks; Professor Onora O'Neill; the late Dowager Duchess of Northumberland; David Pryce Jones; Angelika Patel; Cajetan

Pfetten; Panikos Panayi; Peter Parker; Simon and Beate Reynolds; Dr Petra-Utta Rau; Frances Russell; Adam Ridley; Elizabeth Ruger; James Sempill; Chris Schuler; Adam Ridley; Barbara von Freitag; Raymond Salisbury Jones; Mrs Berkeley Stafford; the staff of the Bushey Museum; Andrew Sinclair; Noel Toone and Robert Tickle at Pitsford (Northamptonshire Grammar School); Patrick Stauffenberg; Kirsty Hardie; Graeme Segal; Alexander Waugh; Daniel Snowman; Canon Stephen Trott; the late Daphne Tennant; Karina Urbach; David Irvine; Caroline Gathorne-Hardy; James Stourton; Eva (Steinecke) Tucker, Felix Gottlieb; Meike Ziervogel of the splendid Peirene Press, specialising in translations of German masterpieces to English readers.

A special thank you goes to Hilary Spurling for the confidence she expressed in this large project at a time – the many times – when my heart was in my boots. Those encouraging words kept despair away on many occasions.

The help I have received, on every level, (including that of Friederike Powles, my patient German teacher), has been prodigious and heart-warming. I am particularly grateful to all the delightful guides in Germany who showed me the towns, villages and landscapes that they know so well.

All mistakes are, of course, my own.

PICTURE ACKNOWLEDGEMENTS

The author and publishers would like to thank the following copyright-holders for permission to reproduce images in this book:

HRH The Prince Philip, Duke of Edinburgh; Royal Collection Trust / © Her Majesty Queen Elizabeth II 2013; The Bushey Museum, Hertfordshire; The Hulton Archive; National Portrait Gallery, London; © Getty Images; Eduardo Graf Lichnowsky; Sir George Goschen and family; The Lady Howard de Walden; Austin Mutti Mewse and the Hardy Amies archive; Angela (Schulenburg) Bohrer and family; Lady Ashtown; the Marquis of Lothian; James Fox; Ariane Bankes; the Britten Archive, Suffolk; the late Clarita von Trott zu Solz.

All other images are care of the author.

The author and publishers have made all reasonable efforts to contact copyright-holders for permission, and apologise for any omissions or errors in the form of credits given. Corrections may be made for future printings.

INDEX

German Legion 19, 168
German Navy 130, 136, 140, 164–5
  mutiny 229
  scuttling of 237
  see also naval power, German
German POWs, re-education project
  6–7, 439–43
Germanophobia 84–5, 90, 152–3,
  154–5, 169, 199, 215–18, 222, 250,
  275
Germany
  civilian starvation 232–3, 234, 239,
    243, 252
  Communist Party 229, 260
  Depression 287
  fear of encirclement 149, 180
  Franco-Prussian War 59, 95–6, 98, 99,
    236
  hyperinflation 243, 247, 251–2
  industrial growth 140
  Lebensraum 390
  rearmament 295
  superpower 140–1
  unification 46, 48, 49, 68–9, 91, 94,
    95, 104
  uprisings of 1848 69, 143
  war reparations 227–8, 236, 237, 239,
    251, 258
  Weimar Republic 243–4, 251, 286
  see also First World War; Nazism;
    Second World War
Gessner, Salomon 15
Gladstone, William Ewart 46
Globe Theatre, London 11
Glover, Jane 448
Glyndebourne 448
Goebbels, Joseph 250, 260–1, 302, 305,
  306, 307, 319, 362
Goering, Hermann 254, 303, 332, 333,
  384, 386, 387, 391–2, 407, 408,
  435, 451
Goethe, Johann Wolfgang von 14, 15,
  20, 23, 24, 26–8, 32, 33, 34, 39,
  40, 56–7, 67
Gogh, Vincent van 110, 141
Goldschmidt, Otto 70

Goldsmith, Oliver 15
Gollancz, Victor 442
Gombrich, Ernst 355
Goodliffe, Michael 436, 437, 438
Gordonstoun 357n
Goschen, George ('Bunt') 193–4, 198–9
Goschen, Sir Edward 180, 181, 182,
  183, 184, 188, 189, 193–4, 198,
  285, 454
Gosse, Edmund 274
Göttingen 16, 18
Gottlieb, Felix 366–8
Gounod, Charles 128, 142
Grant Duff, Shiela 343–4, 345–9, 392,
  396
  Europe and the Czechs 348
Grant, Duncan 240, 309
Graves, Robert 143–4, 169, 200, 212,
  214, 218, 246, 247
  Goodbye to All That 144
Great Depression 287
The Great Dictator (film) 405
Great Exhibition 67–8
Great Ormond Street Hospital 143
Green, John 74
Greene, Ben 304, 365, 426, 428
Greene, Graham 304
Greene, Sir Hugh Carleton 304–5,
  306–7, 317, 328, 354
Grey, Sir Edward 163, 190–1, 192
Grillparzer, Franz 24
Gropius, Walter 311, 315
Grosz, George 272
Gründgens, Gustaf 435
Grynszpan, Herschel 362
Guardian see Manchester Guardian
guild hostels (*Herbergen*) 81, 82–3
Guinness, Bryan 273, 278, 323
Guinness, Diana *see* Mitford, Diana
Gurney, Elizabeth *see* Bunsen, Elizabeth
  de
Gurney, Samuel 54

Haeckel, Ernst 155
Hahn, Kurt 357n
Haig, Field Marshal Alexander 217